FULCRUM

FULCRUM

A Top Gun Pilot's Escape from the Soviet Empire

ALEXANDER ZUYEV
WITH MALCOLM McCONNELL

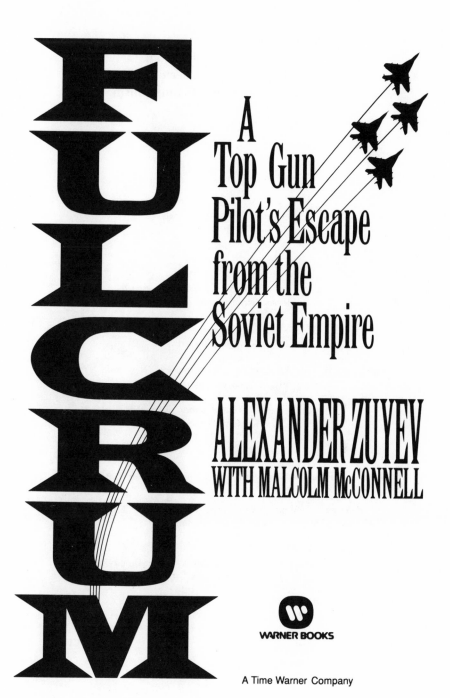

WARNER BOOKS

A Time Warner Company

For all those who have lost their lives
in the fight for freedom.
And for those who have died
fleeing the tyranny of communism.

Warner Books, Inc., 1271 Avenue of the Americas, New York, NY 10020
W A Time Warner Company

Printed in the United States of America
First printing: October 1992
10 9 8 7 6 5 4 3 2 1

Library of Congress Cataloging-in-Publication Data

Zuyev, Alexander.
   Fulcrum : a top gun pilot's escape from the Soviet Empire /
Alexander Zuyev with Malcolm McConnell.
      p.   cm.
   ISBN 0-446-51648-1 :
   1. Zuyev, Alexander. 2. Fighter pilots—Soviet Union—Biography.
3. Defectors—Soviet Union—Biography. 4. MIG–28 (Jet fighter
plane) I. McConnell, Malcolm. II. Title.
UG626.2.Z89A3   1992
358.4'14'092—dc20
[B]   91–51175
                                                           CIP

L. McRee

Acknowledgments

I am pleased to acknowledge with gratitude the many people who have supported me in this project. This book would not have been possible without the help, friendship, and support of the following people:

Larry Bond, Sergei Sikorsky, Steve Collins, Bill Reesman, Wayne Handley, Vice Admiral Richard M. Dunleavy, Bill Chana, Don Duncan, Mike Warren, Chuck Brady, John Hansen, Dwight Murray, David North, Sandy Sanders, Barbara Woodbury, David Maybury, Pat Moneymaker, Ken Watters, Brant James, and all the others who assisted me.

My special thanks and appreciation goes to:

Victor Belenko, for surviving his own escape flight, and for giving me advice (even when I didn't want it!).

Tom Clancy, for all his insight and know-how.

Robert Gottlieb and Mel Parker, for taking a chance.

Malcolm McConnell, for his patience and understanding, even though he didn't speak Russian.

Tom Boyd, for teaching me invaluable aviation terms like "sheet hot."

Tim, Harry, Ken, and Jan, for their trust and support working with me.

And, most of all, I am grateful to my mother and brother for their love and support.

Alexander Zuyev

Contents

Author's Note

Several of my friends and former colleagues described in this book are patriotic officers currently serving in the armed forces of the Commonwealth of Independent States. In order not to jeopardize their careers, I have disguised some of their actual identities.

Measurements of weight, distance, and altitude have been converted from metric units to the British/American system. Airspeed is expressed in knots.

Prologue

I pulled the Makarov pistol from the left breast pocket of my leather flight jacket, cocked the action, but did not set the safety as I normally did. There was now a 9mm round in the chamber and seven more in the magazine. The serrated plastic grip felt comfortably familiar. Almost every day of my seven years as a pilot in Frontal Aviation regiments, I had handled the weapon. And I had carefully cleaned it only the day before. I knew I could trust the small automatic to shoot straight, but hoped I would not need to fire it. Slipping the gun into my right front jacket pocket, I strode through the cool dawn toward the duty-alert apron. As I walked, I checked the maintenance buildings and the line of the squadron ready rooms to the left. There was no one in sight.

I had to hurry. The rising sun was already above the snowy wall of the Caucasus to the east. Ahead, the familiar outline of a soldier wearing a black quilted jacket and floppy southern field hat, an AKM assault rifle slung on his right shoulder, was silhouetted against the flank of the first aircraft. The four MiG-29s in the alert section were parked in two pairs, sharing the two squat generator trucks between their wings. Even trailing engine-start umbilical cables, their canopies, missiles, and instrument

1

probes sheaved in canvas ground covers, the lean, shark-gray aircraft evoked power and speed. Drawing near the planes, I felt the same old excited anticipation that had always gripped me before an important wrestling match. But that emotion was shattered by the bizarre reality of my situation. It was just after dawn on a clear spring morning in the Soviet Socialist Republic of Georgia. In half an hour I would be in Turkey, having escaped from the Soviet Union aboard one of my country's most advanced fighters.

But now I had to concentrate on the task at hand: disarming and binding Corporal Chomayev, the alert apron guard standing ahead in the shadows. It would have been simpler to slip up behind him and slit his throat with my thick-bladed Gypsy knife. But I had vowed to complete this escape with no bloodshed. I looked back one last time to the duty-alert building 350 yards behind me. It was still possible that someone there might wake up and sound the alarm, despite the elaborate precautions I had taken. Even with the telephone lines cut, they could use the emergency radio in the control tower. And there was certainly enough time for a resourceful officer in regimental headquarters on the far side of the base to order the runway blocked with fuel trucks or maintenance vans, even though I had already disabled the vehicles down here.

But I was a fighter pilot trained for combat. I had carefully considered my decision. The time for doubts had passed. It was too late to hide what I had done. Conceivably I could blame food poisoning for the effects of the drug-laced cake I had fed the men of the alert section and the guardhouse. I had chosen that method to incapacitate them because I did not want any of my friends charged with aiding my escape.

But there would be no way to explain the phone lines I had cut or the armory padlock I had jammed. These were acts of treason. And further undeniable proof of that treason was here in my blue flannel helmet bag that held my handwritten diagrams and specifications of weapons systems and air-combat maneuver tactics. If I were captured before escape, the security investigators of the Osobii Otdel would have ample evidence that my action was a meticulously planned hijacking of an advanced multi-role combat aircraft. Stealing a MiG-29 armed with the

newest missiles and electronics and flying it to the West was high
treason to the Socialist Motherland.

There was no way back for me. I stepped around the number
four plane and onto the apron. Chomayev stood near the nose of
the number three aircraft. I knew he would be worried, prepared
for a reprimand from the justifiably angry duty-alert officer.
Arriving twenty minutes late to his guard post on the apron could
cost a soldier a severe reprimand and an extra detail cleaning the
latrine.

"Chomayev," I snarled in my best parade-ground voice, "tell
me why you were late."

The burly Tatar soldier braced his shoulders, but did not
come to rigid attention as I had hoped. "Comrade Captain," he
stammered, "it wasn't my fault. They didn't wake me up in time."

We were only three feet apart now, and he still gripped the
stock of his Kalashnikov. I could no longer posture. I swung the
pistol up and leveled it at Chomayev's chin.

"Hands up!" I hissed.

For a shocked moment, Chomayev glared at me with flat
Asian eyes. Then stunned recognition flashed. He knew why I
was here. The guard bellowed hoarsely and lunged at me, seizing
my right hand and forcing the pistol away from his face.

It would have been easy to jam the muzzle into the folds of
his quilted collar and pull the trigger. But that was murder. No
matter how difficult, I intended to complete my escape with a
minimum of violence. There had already been too much blood
shed in seven decades of Soviet history.

Chomayev dragged my pistol hand down and to the left, and
was savagely twisting back my thumb. I heard the bone crack and
saw my thumb jutting at a bad angle. So I dropped the pistol
before he managed to injure my wrist. All those years on the
wrestling teams at school and the Armavir Academy had tuned
my reflexes. I was confident that I could quickly knock Chomayev
out and bind him. As the gun fell to the concrete apron, I
clubbed Chomayev with my left fist, putting all my force into the
blows to strike his bent neck. The AKM rifle slung on his right
shoulder was swinging clumsily, blocking his attempt to fend off
the blows.

He loosened his grip on my arm. I grabbed the front of his
jacket with both hands and tried to drag him down so I could

kneel on his chest and subdue him. His assault rifle clattered away to the left, and I pinned the weapon with my boot, then kicked it under the nose of the aircraft. Chomayev's wide-brimmed hat went flying as he struggled against me.

He was too strong for me to drag down by brute force, so I slipped sideways, jamming my right shoulder against his chest while shifting my grip to his right sleeve and collar to flip him. This was one of the most basic and effective maneuvers in mat wrestling. But there was no mat here to protect my opponent from injury.

He flipped perfectly and came down hard, flat on his back. I heard the breath whistle from his open mouth. He should have been knocked out, but his thick, padded coat protected him.

I was on top of Chomayev now, about to club him senseless. But he was too fast. He rolled away and was suddenly on top of me, his fists pounding. I now realized that Chomayev knew something about self-defense. He was a good barracks-room amateur, not highly skilled. That made him dangerously unpredictable.

I flailed my legs and twisted away. Struggling to my feet, I dragged him up from the concrete. It was better to fight him upright. He had me by the front of my jacket now, and we grappled like two drunks in a street fight. But I controlled the situation, forcing him four or five yards in front of the aircraft, away from the rifle.

Chomayev had the front of my jacket twisted stubbornly in both his hands. No matter how I jerked and pushed him, he would not let go. I tried to trip him, but he dodged away. I had to drag him down again to break that grip. This was an awkward way to drop an opponent, but he gave me no other opening.

Too late, I saw the maneuver was not going to work. As I bent, putting my strength into dragging him down, Chomayev reared back. And when he finally fell off balance, his weight crashed onto my shoulders. My forehead smashed into the cold concrete. For a moment I saw a pinwheeling explosion of neon-yellow stars before my eyes. I had almost been knocked unconscious.

Fighting the dizziness, I pushed Chomayev underneath me and pounded his face with three hammerblows. But my right was not working well. The thumb would not close into a proper fist. I knew that I was weakened by the blow to my head and that I had to finish this fight quickly, before Chomayev got lucky and did some real damage.

I dragged him back to his feet, hoping to body-throw him again so that his head would smash into the apron even harder than mine had.

Chomayev responded by grabbing my jacket again with both hands. I held his collar as best I could with my right hand and slammed at his face with my left fist. The shoddy material of the coat collar tore away, and Chomayev could dodge some of my blows.

"Litovkin!" Chomayev screamed, calling for his friend in the guardroom of the maintenance control tower one hundred yards to the left. But I had checked the guard post and knew it was empty. "Litovkin . . . help me!" Chomayev yelled again. Each time I struck him, Chomayev yelled for his friend.

This young Tatar soldier would simply not go down. I tried to strike him with a karate punch in a vulnerable spot, the sternum, throat, or the notch where the bridge of his nose joined his skull. But my left hand was clumsy, and when I tried to strike with my right, my damaged thumb would not move into a proper fist. Despite the blows, Chomayev clung tightly to my leather jacket.

I kicked his knees viciously several times to weaken him. Still, he would not back off so that I could hit him a crippling blow. This fight was not going to end without bloodshed. I dug my left hand into the front pocket of my jacket and managed to flip open the blade of my Gypsy knife. But I had to pull the knife free in order to lock the blade.

Chomayev saw the blade flash and again bellowed hoarsely like a startled animal. He broke free and dove backward for his rifle. I dropped the knife and scrambled to the right to retrieve my pistol. As I bent to snatch up the Makarov, I heard Chomayev cocking the bolt of his AKM.

I rose and spun in one motion, bringing up my pistol in a two-handed combat grasp to sight on his chest. He was only three yards from me, crouching beneath the nose of the number three fighter, raising his rifle toward me. I saw the muzzle swing to level at my chest. But Chomayev was not braced well to fire, and the AKM always pulled hard right. In survival school we had been taught to sway like a serpent to confuse an enemy firing at close range. I swayed to my right just as Chomayev fired. The muzzle flashed with a short tongue of red flame. The burst cut through the air to my left, the bullets rasping loudly as they passed over my shoulder.

I aimed at his torso and fired deliberately, cupping my right hand with my left to steady the gun. He was so close that I kept both eyes open as I fired. This was not a pistol range. I swayed to the left now as Chomayev swung his rifle muzzle back, correcting his fire.

Then Chomayev screamed as one of my bullets hit. He rolled over under the number three plane, but managed to fire a second, shorter burst. The bolt slide of my pistol sprang open. I had fired eight rounds and the magazine was empty. This was no place to reload.

I dashed around the nose of the airplane and sprinted toward the tail of the number two aircraft. Chomayev pivoted under the nose of the third plane and fired another burst. His aim was off. The bullets howled all around me, several whipping between my legs as I ran. Then my upper right biceps was seared by a hot knife of pain. A bullet had clipped me.

The plane to my left was hit several times in the nose and left wingroot. Jet fuel leaked to the concrete. But I kknew there was no danger of explosion because the tanks had been purged with inert gas. Reaching the tail of the second lane, I was past Chomayev's field of fire. I stopped and reloaded my pistol with the spare magazine.

Chomayev was out of sight. I knew he was wounded, maybe fatally. But I had no time to waste. He had fired a full thirty-round magazine. And the alert staff in the operations control tower behind me must have heard the noise, as had those men still awake in the duty-alert building next door to the tower.

I would fly the number one plane, the aircraft furthest from the ramp guard, four hundred yards to my left. Dashing behind the fighter's tail, I turned and ducked under the right wing. I had to work fast but carefully to prepare the plane for takeoff. One mistake now could mean the end. I bent at the right main landing gear and dragged the heavy red steel wheel chock away from the tire. Despite the blow to my head, I was thinking clearly. If I left the chock here on the ground, Chomayev might manage to sneak back and replace it on the wheel while I was up in the cockpit. The wheel chock had tempered steel claws that would dig into the pitted concrete of the apron, anchoring me in place. So I tossed the chock up onto the right wing, too high for Chomayev to recover.

I scurried forward to the big rectangular inlet of the right engine, which was protected by a tan nylon ground cover. I jerked the pins from the restraining cord and stripped away the cover, then ducked under the nose to pull off the cover on the left engine inlet. After dragging the wheel chock from the left main gear, I found my right arm was going numb and I didn't have enough strength to lift the heavy steel chock to the wing. Instead I tossed it backward, clanking on the concrete apron, toward the tail.

As I bent, I saw the long centerline belly tank that held a ton of fuel. Every jet fighter pilot valued fuel. But I knew I would have to drop the tank soon after takeoff. The 30mm cannon in the left wingroot could not be fired while the fighter carried the external tank.

And I certainly intended to fire the cannon. This escape was much more than one man's personal liberation. I planned to avenge the innocent Georgians killed and maimed in the brutal Tbilisi massacre forty days before. After takeoff I would loop back on a cannon run and destroy twelve of the regiment's MiG-29s parked in a neat line on the ramp to my left.

As I ducked back under the nose, I saw the R-73 and R-27 missiles slung on the pylons beneath the wings. The missiles' radar-homing and heat-seeking sensors were capped with canvas ground caps, and the pylon release points were locked with pins. I had no time to prepare the missiles. If any aircraft from this base managed to take off in pursuit, or if another regiment launched interceptors after me, I would have to depend on the plane's 30mm cannon for self-defense.

The main avionics Pitot tube thrusting from the nose radar dome like a medieval lance was still shrouded with its ground cover, which was linked with an elastic cord to the red aluminum cap of the infrared search and track sensor dome forward of the canopy. I tugged hard on the Pitot tube cover, but it would not rip free.

"*Huy's ney,*" I swore. "Fuck it."

There was no time to drag over a mechanic's work stand and climb up to strip off this web of canvas and elastic cords. I would have to fly without the major instruments or target acquisition systems. At least I had the angle of attack tube. That instrument, the radar altimeter, and the standby magnetic compass would have to see me through.

I was back on the left side of the nose, scrambling up the orange steel ladder to the canopy. Pausing at the top, I scanned the nearby ramps, the duty-alert building, and operations control tower. To my amazement, I saw no one. They had slept through the noise of the firing. Then I spotted Chomayev, peeking from behind the tail of the number four plane. My vision was still slightly blurred from the blow to my forehead, but I raised my pistol, sighted carefully, and fired. He disappeared. All this firing *had* to wake someone. I had four minutes at the most before they showed up here on the apron. There was no more time to waste.

The canopy was ajar, still sheathed in the dew-damp ground cover. I couldn't reach the cover-release points on the other side, so I just shoved the canvas back. It would blow off when I closed the canopy and taxied. I reached inside awkwardly with my left hand, then twisted the canopy opening lever.

I jumped into the cockpit, slid into the ejection seat, and wedged the pistol between my thighs, so that it would be there if I needed it. The unbuckled straps of the ejection-seat harness were stiff against my back. But I had no time to pull the safety pins from the system and strap into the harness. The cockpit felt familiar, even though I hadn't flown for two months. Then I recalled the generator truck cable still plugged into the left wingroot. Never mind that. The plane's big engines would blast out enough thrust to pop the cable the moment I advanced the throttles.

Now I had to work fast but well. I breathed in deeply and exhaled to clear my head. My left hand jumped across the main electrical integration panel beneath the right cockpit sill. I used the panel's quick-start frame to snap on all the circuit breakers with one movement, then flipped off the unneeded switches. The cockpit hummed with power from the onboard battery, and the main caution and warning panel's red lights blinked on.

I had to ignore the urge to start both engines manually, blast free of the generator umbilical, and taxi out for takeoff. On this advanced aircraft the automatic engine-start sequence I had selected was actually faster than attempting a manual start.

I reached across with my left hand to hit the button for the number two engine auto start. Nothing. Just the dry clicking of the igniter.

My eye shot forward to the voltmeter. The battery was at full charge, twenty-four volts. I hit the starter again. Nothing. I turned and craned my neck out of the cockpit, but saw no one near the apron or alert building. I engaged the starter a third time. Nothing, just that bone-dry click.

I knew I was dead. The Osobists must have installed some secret new coded lock on the starting system of the alert planes. They had locked the throttles of the nonalert aircraft after an intelligence report that Western espionage agents planned to infiltrate the base and steal one of our MiGs. But I never thought they would go so far as to disable the alert planes.

I sagged in the ejection seat. The duty dispatcher was probably already on the emergency radio in the tower. The guard van from regimental headquarters could arrive in less than a minute. I suddenly recalled the last time I had flown, a clear, bright February day. On that final training sortie, I had been alone over the Black Sea, only twenty-five miles from Turkey. As I maneuvered in the mock dogfight, I had dropped below the ground controllers' radar. How easy it would have been to escape. I had been a fool not to do it then. Now I was finished.

But my years of training would not permit surrender. When a system failed, there was a reason. A good pilot does not panic.

PART
ONE

— 1 —

Mikha Tskhakaya "Ruslan" Air Base
February 13, 1989

It was a perfect afternoon to fly. The Georgian winter sunshine poured through the canopy, warming the cockpit as I taxied the MiG-29 slowly down the ramp from the 1st Squadron apron to the end of Runway 09. The sky above was a deep, aching blue: ceiling and visibility unlimited. In my curved center mirror, I saw my wingman, Captain Nikolai Starikov, trundling along behind. As always, Nikolai maintained the correct interval between the two fighters.

Steering with the nosewheel control button on my number two throttle, I quickly scanned my engine instruments. Oil pressure and RPM were identical for both of the big Leningrad Klimov RD-33 turbofans rumbling behind me. Their tail pipe temperatures were normal.

I slid the throttles back to idle and braked to a stop at the maintenance checkpoint. While the enlisted mechanic on the ramp checked for leaks and verified that my control surfaces were unblocked, I completed my preflight cockpit check. The canopy was closed and locked. The navigation systems display in the lower left instrument panel was properly aligned and the heading matched the small standby magnetic compass mounted between my center and right cockpit mirrors. I made sure there were no red lights on the caution and warning panel. The fuel gauge read 7,056 pounds, the proper amount for an air-combat training

13

sortie. Now I pulled the lever at my left hip to tighten the harness of the ejection seat.

Below the canopy the young conscript mechanic stared up, then saluted, the signal that he had completed his checks. This was my third and last scheduled training sortie of the day, and, as always, the airplane was behaving well.

That was good. I certainly did not want a maintenance scrub. Although none of my friends back in the ready room or the regimental officers observing the takeoffs and landings from the control tower could possibly have guessed, I had secretly planned that this training sortie would be my last flight as a Soviet Air Force pilot.

I was glad a dogfight scenario was scheduled. Once Nikolai and I took off and headed west for the air-combat zone over the Black Sea, our flight would be immediately followed by the two MiG-29s flown by our opponents, a pair of regimental staff officers. The opponent lead was Lieutenant Colonel Dmitri Shatravka, the newly appointed deputy regimental commander for operations. His wingman was Major Valera Chayka, the regimental intelligence officer. In theory they were more experienced fighter pilots than Nikolai and me. But we had chalked up much more air-combat training in the MiG-29 than either of these two staff officers, and I planned to kick them both squarely in the ass on this flight. An indisputable dogfight victory over senior officers would be a fitting end to my Air Force flying career.

I advanced the throttles and steered carefully down the center of the ramp, keeping well clear of the soft grassy margins. Ruslan had been built after the Great Patriotic War on spongy, reclaimed swampland, and was ringed by reedy drainage canals. The long, single east-west runway was made of huge precast-concrete blocks laid side by side with tar-line joints. In effect, the blocks floated on a wet layer of crushed stone and gravel. Rumor had it that there were at least two sunken runway layers beneath this one. And in wet weather when planes exited the eastern end of the runway, blocks would shift and swamp water would squish through the joint lines.

With my left hand I slid back the throttles to idle and simultaneously squeezed the beavertail brake handle on the forward edge of the control stick with my right hand. The aircraft slowed at the end of the ramp. Working the nosewheel button, I allowed the residual momentum to swing the plane left onto the runway. The MiG-29 taxied as smoothly as it flew. It was a true pilot's airplane, and I was going to miss it. I stopped exactly midway between the white stripes marking the two-plane takeoff lane on the left side of Runway 09. In my right cockpit mirror, I saw Nikolai turn into the correct takeoff position behind me. His nose was forty-five feet right and seventy-five feet behind my right wingtip, close enough to follow my visual signals, but clear of my turbulent engine exhaust and wing vortices.

Here at Ruslan we kept radio communications to a minimum between planes in a formation and between aircraft and ground controllers. There were American electronic ferret satellites overhead constantly, sweeping the air for our radio transmissions. And this near the frontier with Turkey, the problem was even more acute. That mountain frontier only fifty miles to the south bristled with NATO electronic eavesdropping posts.

After the MiG-29 from the 2nd Squadron that had just landed cleared the runway, I swung my head in a wide arc, double-checking that the runway and landing approach were free of other aircraft. The takeoff light at the side of the runway flashed from red to green. The tower had cleared my flight for immediate departure. I knew everyone in the tower was watching us closely. Nikolai and I were in the 176th Frontal Aviation Regiment's "Dogfight Masters" 1st Squadron. People expected to see a perfectly coordinated takeoff when we flew. And I certainly did not want to disappoint them today.

My left index finger went to the cockpit console beneath the throttles to set the flap button in the correct takeoff position. I waggled the control stick to move the horizontal stabilizers to get Nikolai's attention. Then I pulled the stick back which tilted the leading edge down, the signal to Nikolai to advance throttles to 100 percent: full military power. I slid my own throttles open and waited the mandatory ten seconds for the whining turbofans to stabilize with equal RPM. Then I saw movement in my right cockpit mirror. Nikolai's plane was beginning to slide forward, even though he had not released his brakes. I realized one of his wheels must have been on a slippery tar line between the concrete runway slabs, and the brakes could not hold. There was no way he could back up now, and we risked a sloppy, unprofessional takeoff.

This would not do on my last flight, not with all those people watching in the control tower. As I centered the stick to the neutral position, my right fingers popped the brakes, and I clamped my left hand on the spring-loaded throttle release and jammed the two throttle knobs full forward to afterburner. I was thrust back hard in my seat by an invisible piston of acceleration. Cones of flame now pulsed from the twin tail pipes, producing over 36,600 pounds of thrust. With my fuel load today, the aircraft had a positive thrust-to-weight ratio. The rear of my helmet sagged into the hard padding at the top of the ejection seat.

The triple row of broken, white runway lane stripes flew by in a blur. By going to afterburner, I had kept ahead of Nikolai. In my mirror his plane was pegged in the correct position behind me on the runway. My helmet thrust harder into the seat cushion, and I felt myself grinning inside my oxygen mask. By a lucky quirk, this last takeoff was going to be on afterburner, one of the most powerful experiences a fighter pilot enjoyed. As always on afterburner takeoffs, rock music seemed to echo in my head. Today it was the crashing rhythms of the Rolling Stones.

My airspeed hit 100 knots and I pulled the stick back gently to rotate the nose. One second later we were at 135 knots, and the main gear lifted clear of the runway. This was a critical moment on an afterburner takeoff. The hinged, perforated screens protecting the engine air inlets had been in the down, closed position. During taxi and takeoff, engine air was fed through inlets on the leading-edge wing extensions below the cockpit. These louvered ducts in the gray tapered skin of the fighter always reminded me of the gills behind the streamlined head of a deep-ocean shark. At rotation speed the engine airflow was transferred from these upper inlets back to the main lower intakes as the protective screens automatically retracted. The sudden aerodynamic shift always caused a nose-down swing, which I had to parry with the trim button on the stick.

I retracted gear and pitched the nose up sharply to a fifty-degree climb. As the altitude and airspeed increased, I raised the flaps and glanced back in the mirror to find Nikolai's aircraft. He had lifted off in perfect position behind me. I could see his left hand raised thumbs-up to show his appreciation at my quick response in going to afterburner.

Still on the burners, I banked left and leveled off at precisely 13,500 feet and a heading of 270 degrees, due west toward our training zone, thirty miles away over the Black Sea. Now I throttled back and trimmed for an airspeed of 350 knots. Although this altitude was reserved for westbound traffic, it was always smart to keep your eyes open around a military airfield. The MiG-29's cockpit, perched high and well forward on the nose, provided great visibility. And today the view was spectacular.

The layout of the Ruslan Air Base below was typical of Soviet fighter regiments. Hangar and maintenance facilities and the pilots' ready room were strung out along the parking apron that ran on an oblique angle to the runway. I could see the regiment's aircraft parked in pairs along that apron. Regimental headquarters was near the far eastern end of the runway, a good twenty-minute walk from the squadron areas. There were two control towers near the western end of the runway, one to handle air traffic, the other for the engineering and maintenance section.

The duty-alert building, which had its own small dormitory and dining room, stood close to the air traffic control tower. There were four fully fueled and armed duty-alert aircraft parked separately just inside the taxi ramp. Normally the alert planes were parked on their own apron right beside the duty-alert building. But that apron had been ripped up for repaving, a repair that could take months, using lazy, inefficient Stroybat construction troops.

In principle, the alert section could be airborne within five minutes of an order to scramble, in half that time if the pilots had been pre-alerted and were ready in the cockpit waiting to start engines.

The explosive ordnance and missile maintenance shops were also near that end of the runway. Both the PPR missile shop and the RTB nuclear weapons storage and assembly sites stood within their own guarded compounds. The RTB facility was surrounded by a high wall capped with barbed wire and guarded by a separate contingent of troops who reported directly to the Strategic Forces Command in Moscow.

I gazed down at the familiar scene I would probably never see again. The base arrangement was designed to efficiently facilitate flight operations. Given this widely dispersed layout, however, nonflight operations—the mundane bureaucratic housekeeping chores of military life—were often inconvenient. From this altitude I could still make out the clunking old bus on its infrequent circuit of the base. It was turning onto the main road to the officers' housing complex a mile and a half away. Usually the rickety bus was out of service because of a lack of spare parts or the terrible maintenance habits of the conscript soldiers responsible for it.

Division regulations prevented officers with their own cars from driving on the base because some might steal fuel. Fat chance. No one wanted the base gas. One of our staff officers was a true Socialist "entrepreneur." He stole so much gasoline and watered it down with TS-1 jet fuel kerosene that the stuff couldn't be safely used in a car. So we often had to ride bicycles or waste time walking when we were summoned from the ready room to regimental headquarters or took our turn in the simulators.

The base slid past below. Closer, the city of Mikha Tskhakaya was a jumble of orange tile roofs surrounded by citrus groves. To the north, the towering wall of the Great Caucasus range stood, icy white and silent, marking the boundary between the Republic of Georgia and the Russian Federation. The Caucasus were splendid mountains, higher and more rugged than the Alps of Europe or North America's Rockies. Some Swiss fellows I'd met skiing up there told me the Caucasus had more spectacular and dangerous runs than the Alps. I could believe that.

I shifted in my seat to stare south over the left wing. The Maliy Kavkaz mountains of the Turkish frontier were only half as tall as the Caucasus, but their summits were still crusted with winter snow. Below, the wide Rioni River glinted in the sun, meandering through the green coastal marshland toward the Black Sea ahead.

Enough nostalgic sight-seeing. It was time to verify that my cockpit was ready for a simulated dogfight with Lieutenant Colonel Shatravka. The training scenario called for us to use all three of our air-combat weapons systems: the long-range R-27 Alamo radar-controlled missile, the shorter range R-73 Archer infrared-homing missile, and the inboard GSh-301 30mm cannon mounted in the left fuselage below the cockpit. These weapons would rely on all three of the MiG-29's modern sensor systems: the pulse-Doppler radar, the infrared search and track system

(IRST), and the laser ranger finder. On training sorties the radar missiles were simulated by a small electronic pod mounted on the inboard pylon of my left wing. The sensor head simulating the infrared seeker of the Archer missile was in the inner pylon beside it.

We always flew with a full load of 30mm cannon ammunition—150 shells—even on training flights. So it was important that the master arm switch on the weapons sensor control panel remain in the off position. Once, a *zampolit* political officer had become confused on a bomber-intercept sortie and had turned on the master switch, thinking he needed that circuit to activate his gun camera. Apparently he had been too busy studying Marx and Lenin to read his aircraft manuals and hadn't realized the cannon was loaded, even on training flights. The cannon had chattered off fifty rounds before the zampolit realized his mistake. Luckily, like most of his kind, the political officer was a shitty pilot. So he hadn't shot down the Tu-16 bomber.

I checked out my aircraft for mock combat in the recommended manner, working from left to right, starting with the missile-select button on the number two throttle, then moving to the systems on the left, lower left cockpit console.

The MiG-29 was a "fourth generation" fighter that could engage or evade the best NATO aircraft at extreme or short ranges, throughout a wide flight envelope. Its powerful and complex weapons were linked to equally sophisticated sensors. Now I had to verify that I had chosen the correct weapons systems, and that the sensors, both the radar and the infrared search and track system, were ready for combat.

As the IRST would probably be used second, in the close-combat phase of the engagement, I began with the long-range radar missile control. The armament control panel was at the forward head of the left cockpit console. I flipped the lock-on switch to "friend," which meant the radar could track and lock onto another Soviet aircraft, hopefully in this case, either Lieutenant Colonel Shatravka's or Major Chayka's MiG-29. If I had left the switch in the "enemy" position, the radar would have recognized their coded SRZO aircraft identification signals and not operated during the mock dogfight. I now verified that the munitions fusing system was set in the *vozdukh* "air" position, before moving on to the radar modes panel on the left forward instrument board.

In air combat today, combined aircraft closing speeds can total Mach 4 and the engagement can slash through 45,000 feet of vertical airspace in less than a minute. So human senses and reflexes can be inadequate to detect and defeat the enemy. Modern air-combat tactics, both Soviet and Western, call for a fighter pilot to destroy the enemy at extreme distances—"beyond visual range"—*before* that enemy's stand-off missiles could be launched on friendly targets. A powerful and versatile radar is absolutely essential.

And the MiG-29's improved NO-193 pulse-Doppler radar was a versatile and sensitive sensor and tracking system. But there was a lot of controversy about this radar in the Soviet Air Force. In intelligence briefings, I had learned that the radar was code-named "Slot Back" by NATO, which believed Soviet spies had stolen the basic technology from America's Hughes Corporation. As they did about so much else in the modern arsenal of the Soviet Union, the Americans apparently chose to believe we had just slavishly copied their innovations. This was only partly true. Soviet scientists usually let their Western counterparts invest years and billions of dollars in basic research, which the Americans then dutifully published in their open aviation magazines. What detail was not available in the press, the Soviets then obtained through spies. Only then did Soviet designers set to work to modify and improve on the basic Western technology.

But the NO-193 radar was an interesting variation on this theme. The Soviet design bureau did, indeed, benefit from espionage. But after the equipment was perfected, the KGB discovered that a Soviet electronics expert who helped design this radar was actually working for Western intelligence. Not only had he fed our design details to the West, he had actually sabotaged the initial capabilities of this important system. The original NO-193 was very sensitive and could detect fast-moving targets at extreme range, but the set's computer was incapable of holding the lock-on needed for missile launch. When we first tested this radar during the combat evaluation of the MiG-29 in 1985, my colleagues and I had been deeply disappointed in the capabilities of the "advanced" look-down, shoot-down pulse-Doppler radar.

A year later, after this Soviet traitor had been caught and executed, electronics technicians descended on our base to quietly install modifications to the radar, which allowed it to retain lock-on much more efficiently. Our Intelligence Directorate hoped that their NATO counterparts still believed the MiG-29's radar was crippled by the sabotage of the Western mole.

I now quickly configured the radar modes panel. I planned to attack my opponents from below, so I turned the Delta-H switch to the number two position, which would set the antenna scan for anticipated targets about 6,000 feet above my flight level. Then I turned the radar modes switch to auto and the hemisphere switch to forward hemisphere. The radar's computer would automatically take over the search and tracking of up to ten targets. This computer measured their relative speeds and ranges by Doppler effect, analyzed their closing angles, and presented the target in threat-priority order on the clear rectangular Plexiglas head-up display (HUD) above my main instrument panel. On a modern fighter the HUD was the pilot's closest friend, the simplified window into the dense network of sensors and computers jammed into the nose of his aircraft. I left the radar in the *nakal* standby position, warmed up and ready, but not actively scanning the airspace ahead, so as not to be detected on an opponent's radar-warning receiver.

The coast was coming up fast, and I would soon have to contact Brigadier, the Ground Control Intercept center in the bunker beside the regimental headquarters back at Ruslan. A battle-control officer at the Brigadier GCI center would be working with Nikolai and me today, feeding us data on the "enemy" formation we would engage. Lieutenant Colonel Shatravka's flight would be directed by another controller sitting at a radar console in the same room as mine, but using a different radio channel. Today I had Senior Lieutenant Vitaly Shevchenko as my battle-control officer. I could picture those fellows down in "the pit," craning forward in their chairs, glued to their radar screens. These engagements were not simply fought in the cockpits, the battle-control officers always reminded us. They got just as excited as we did.

At the upper right-hand corner of the main instrument panel, I deliberately pointed my finger to verify that the master arm switch was definitely off. But I did switch the weapons control system modes switch to radar, thus completing the linkage of the entire Alamo missile circuit.

Another setting for that switch was *shlem*, "helmet," which I would not be using today, but Shatravka would. This was the helmet-mounted sight (HMS), a Soviet innovation that used a pair of infrared sensors mounted on the pilot's helmet to track and lock onto targets for the Archer missile. You could achieve this lock-on simply by turning your head, not the entire aircraft. Intelligence officers had briefed us that the Americans had either been unable to perfect such a system or considered it superfluous. This was nonsense. There were many occasions in a close-in dogfight where the IRST sensor mounted in the clear Plexiglas dome forward of the canopy lost lock-on while the pilot could still see his target above or below. The helmet-mounted sight gave the Soviet pilot an extra set of sensors that could save his life one day. And the HMS was easy to use because the weapons computer linked the helmet sensor data directly to the swiveling IR seekers in the Archer missile nose.

In a close-in dogfight we had learned to fly with the missile trigger on the control stick depressed. If either the HMS or main IRST sensor in the nose dome locked on a fast-closing target, the computer would automatically fire the missile. These computer-aided sensors were much faster than human reactions. So there was no danger of missing a shot on an enemy slashing past your nose at supersonic speed because your reactions were too slow to pull the trigger. The beauty of the helmet sight was that you could kill the enemy, even if you did not have time to swing the nose of your plane to bear on him. The system was a quantum improvement over the traditional IRST sights I had trained with on the old MiG-23.

Having prepared the radar-homing and infrared missiles, it was time to set up the gun. After adjusting the cannon rate-of-fire control and gunsight for the thirty-five-foot wingspan of the opponents' MiG-29, I squeezed the gun trigger to verify the system on the HUD. A funnel-shaped column of broken white lines appeared, wide end highest, with the small "11" symbol above it. The afternoon sun glare was bad, bleaching out the data on the clear panel of the HUD, so I pulled up the thick, smoked-glass sunshield plate to shade it. Now the electronic compass rose, indicating 27, due west, and the altitude and airspeed data showed in crisp computer-white digits. I was exactly at 13,500 feet and my airspeed was pegged on 350 knots. The large "27" in the lower right center of the HUD indicated I had two armed Alamo radar-homing missiles.

My final stop on the instrument panel was in the right corner, the SPO-15 radar-warning receiver. When I activated the receiver's control panel on the right front cockpit console, the rings of green, yellow, and red threat lights surrounding the stylized aircraft symbol on the display flashed like the lights on a New Year's tree and the beeping warning tone sounded in the cockpit. The SPO-15 was now active. Any opponent's radar, or missile-guidance radar on the ground, sweeping my aircraft would appear on the display and a warning beep would sound in my earphones. The instrument was quite sensitive and would give me the bearing, relative power, and type of radar that was scanning me. If more than one enemy radar was active, the receiver would display the most dangerous threat by priority.

I had completed my cockpit air-combat setup just as we crossed the marshy coastline. I was now thirty miles from Ruslan and switched radio channels from 7 to 6.

"Brigadier," I called my GCI controller. "Three five zero with 351 on channel 6."

My call sign for this three-month period was 350, and Nikolai's was 351. Actually our official five-digit call sign was prefixed with 48, but few Soviet military pilots used all five numbers.

"*Ponyal*," Vitaly's crisp professional voice replied. "Roger, 350, altitude 13,500 feet."

Now we popped up to 15,000 feet to intersect the oval air-combat range fifteen miles offshore. I banked left and headed south toward the far end of the circuit where Nikolai and I would hold orbit in the combat air patrol (CAP) sector just north of the Turkish frontier buffer zone. At this speed we covered the twenty miles in less than two minutes. Just as my distance measuring equipment and radio compass indicated I was in the CAP zone, Vitaly's voice sounded again in my headset.

"Three five zero, you are in the holding zone."

"*Ponyal*."

I was never much of a talker on the tactical radio net. Some fellows, especially zampolits, were real chatterboxes. They were so nervous in the cockpit and so uncertain about controlling these powerful airplanes that they called out every bank and turn, every new heading and altitude change, as if they were air-control cadets in a classroom simulator, not Soviet combat pilots. The radio range of the electromagnetic spectrum might be invisible to human eyes, but certainly wasn't to modern electronic scanners. Overly talkative pilots tended to forget that NATO ferret satellites and even the American AWACS radar planes could track you by your voice transmission. This might have been my last fight, but I still intended to maintain my own high professional standards.

I turned again onto a westward heading and checked my mirrors to make sure Nikolai was tucked up nice and close. There he was, in perfect position, less than 150 feet from my right wingtip. We both had on our navigation strobe lights at 100 percent power. This was a little trick we used to distinguish our flight from the "enemy" on a training sortie. One of the weakest points in Soviet training was that we did not often fly against different types of aircraft representing Western fighters, as did our American counterparts.

For a moment I stared at his plane, absorbing the rakish beauty of the powerful fighter. They say that function dictates form in both natural and human design. And just as Nature had evolved the predatory shark with smooth, hydrodynamic curves, the designers at the Mikoyan-Guryevich OKB had produced an aerial predator with a long, sharp nose, knife-edge wings, and the powerfully tapered fins of its vertical and horizontal tail surfaces. I loved this airplane and it would be hard to leave it behind and find another life.

But my decision to leave the Air Force was final. As much as I loved flying, I could no longer serve the Soviet government and the system where everything was based on lies, deceit, and personal and institutional corruption.

"Three five zero," Vitaly called.

He wanted an indication of the tactics I planned for the air-combat engagement so the ground controllers could be certain there was no gross violation of safety standards. His request meant that Shatravka and his wingman had already crossed the coast and turned north for their own holding zone, about forty miles from ours. The safety regulations called for our flight to maneuver at odd-number altitudes—3,000, 9,000, or 15,000 feet—while Shatravka's flight used the even numbers.

"Plan Number Four."

"Roger."

I was about to begin my last dogfight as a Soviet fighter pilot.

On this leg of the holding orbit, I was flying parallel to the Turkish coast. The narrow band of green, backed by winter-brown foothills below snowy summit ridges, was the frontier of imperialist NATO, the sworn enemy of the Socialist Motherland. But to me, those mountains represented freedom. This CAP zone was only twenty-five miles from the frontier. It would have been so easy to tell Nikolai to take the lead because I had "problems with my radar." Then, as he pulled ahead, I could have chopped my throttles, slid off on my left wing, and dove for the sea. Once below the GCI radar horizon, I could have applied full military power and dashed into Turkish airspace undetected. Certainly Vitaly in the GCI bunker would not have been unduly alarmed. He knew my dogfight Plan Four called for me and my wingman to separate, with Nikolai staying high while I dropped below Vitaly's rival battle-control officer's radar sweep.

I actually felt my left fist close on the throttle knobs and my right index finger slide onto the radio call button on the control stick. It *would* be so easy. For a moment I hung there in the clear winter sunlight, balanced as if on a pivot. Then I recalled the NATO code name for the MiG-29, "Fulcrum," *tochka opori*. How appropriate. At this instant my life and this top-secret Soviet aircraft were indeed balanced on a fulcrum.

Then, from nowhere, I heard the words of the Military Oath of Loyalty I had taken as a brand-new cadet on Armavir's sunny Lenin Square eleven years before. After swearing to defend the Union of Soviet Socialist Republics with courage and discipline, "until my last breath," I had chanted the final phrase of the oath, my unwavering voice joining those of the three hundred young men around me.

"And if I should break this solemn oath, then let me suffer the severe penalties of Soviet law and the universal hatred and contempt of the Soviet people."

As a *kursant* of seventeen, those words had stirred a deep emotion. My loyalty to the Soviet State had been unshakable. I had firmly believed that the Soviet Union, led by its Communist Party, was the most progressive and humane nation in history. And if young men like me defended that State and its Party, the Soviet Union would lead the suffering peoples of the world to a new dawn of harmonious prosperity. I had loved my country and my people. And I had been absolutely certain that nothing could ever make me betray them.

Now, as a First Class pilot captain in the Soviet Air Force, I was a different person. I now understood that the Soviet State, manipulated by a tiny clique of corrupt Party criminals and their accomplices in the military and "Organs of State Security," maintained the cruelest and most repressive system in human history. But my loyalty to my people had not changed. The final phrase of the oath still bound me.

Suddenly my radar-warning receiver beeped and the forward right quadrant flashed with green and yellow. Shatravka's search radar had just swept us. From the band of intensity lights, I knew he was still at extreme search range, too far for a lock-on. But our two flights were closing fast. With Nikolai tucked up so close, we were presenting only a single target echo on both airborne and GCI radar. And I hated to relinquish this advantage too soon. But in a closing engagement with radar-homing missiles as the initial weapon, a pilot who stubbornly tried to retain a minor perceived advantage would not survive very long. The Alamo accelerated to Mach 5 and was damned hard to shake.

Suddenly Nikolai's voice sounded in my earphones. "*Na mnye*. He's got me." Shatravka's radar now had a solid lock on Nikolai's aircraft. It was time to split our flight.

"*Nachalie*," I ordered Nikolai. "Let's go."

I chopped the throttles back to idle, pulled the stick hard left, and hit the air brakes. The fighter rolled onto its left wing and dropped toward the sea. As I fell, I looked quickly back over my right shoulder to see Nikolai banking hard right in a fast, high-G break at our original altitude of 15,000 feet.

By turning perpendicular to the threatening Doppler radar, Nikolai and I hoped to break Shatravka's lock-on before his computer authorized missile launch. Doppler radar depended on differential speed to generate a target. We had abolished that speed by turning hard right and left, perpendicular to the enemy radar. If Nikolai could keep this angle for twelve seconds, the logic memory of Shatravka's radar computer would be overpowered and the lock-on broken.

My own gambit was a variation of this tactic. As I dove west, I would be invisible to Shatravka's Doppler radar. And I knew that the GCI radar used by his battle-control officer had a seven-second scan sweep, and that two complete scans were required to register a solid target blip at this range. So, if I could be down below the GCI radar horizon within fourteen seconds and maintain my own perpendicular aspect to the enemy flight, they would have lost me. And when they picked up Nikolai again, they would naturally assume *that* blip represented both of us, still flying tucked-up tight. Air combat was not a gentleman's sport. You had to be deceptive to survive.

Ten seconds later I slid my throttles forward to eighty percent and pitched up to slow my rate of descent at the official minimum maneuver altitude of 1,800 feet. I sagged in my seat. The rubber bladders of my G-suit inflated, squeezing my belly and thighs to keep the blood from rushing away to my legs and causing gray-out. But today I planned to go much lower to avoid radar detection.

I pushed the throttles to ninety percent and eased the nose over. In a moment I was down on the deck, only 600 feet above the softly rolling blue swell of the sea. Now I was invisible to both Vitaly and his rival controller's radars. And Shatravka was too preoccupied searching for Nikolai up at 15,000 feet to sweep for me down here. That was my game plan, which also included using the sun to mask my position. Because on these clear winter afternoons, anyone flying low to the west was difficult to see against the glinting surface of the water.

My airspeed had now hit five hundred knots and I swung onto a northeast heading of 050 degrees. After forty seconds I pushed the throttles to full military power and pitched back to a steep *gorka* climb. I turned my oxygen control to full pressure, 100 percent, pure oxygen. In the high-G dogfight I expected, I would need all the oxygen the system could deliver to prevent diminished vision. Again, my G-suit hissed as the bladders inflated hard against my midsection. Now I turned my radar modes switch from "standby" to "illuminate." My HUD lit up with a swarm of parallel white lines, electronic glowworms marching to the commands of my radar computer. These were target blips, most of them false returns. The radar quickly sorted through the clutter to reveal an authentic target block on a bearing of 010 degrees, ten miles ahead, at least 6,000 feet above me.

That was either Shatravka or his wingman, or both. I hoped they were still searching for Nikolai's bait.

The rectangular radar cursor jumped from one group of glowworms to another, and finally settled on a fast-moving blip crossing from left to right. I was climbing a bit too steeply for easy visual acquisition, so I had to strain forward against the Gs to peer around the HUD. There he was, a gray dart, sweeping straight and level to the south at 12,000 feet altitude. I saw no flashing navigation strobe and knew the target was not Nikolai.

On the inner throttle knob, I clicked the white button to activate the radar lock-on system. Once the radar computer calculated the target's course and speed, the data would be fed to the Alamo missile's radar-seeking nose sensor. The computer would interrogate the entire system for verification, and the friendly, synthesized female voice of "Rita" would sound in my earphones announcing, "*Pusk razrayshon.* Launch is approved."

When we had received our new aircraft, four years before, Rita's voice had been a scratchy monotone, hardly the sexy companion most pilots wanted. So we had asked Natasha, one of the maintenance dispatchers, to rerecord all the announcements of the female voice warning system. She had the sweet voice of a television star.

Now as I topped 9,000 feet, I heard Natasha's recorded voice announce, "Launch is approved."

I flipped over the missile trigger to arm it and squeezed off two simulated Alamos. I wasn't squandering weapons. If you launched only one of the big missiles, the unbalanced load on your wing pylons limited your dogfight maneuverability to a maximum angle of attack (AOA) of only fifteen degrees. I wanted a full twenty-four-degree AOA when I mixed it up at close range.

Now that I had acquired Shatravka visually, I switched to his radio channel as a safety precaution. I also intended to probe him psychologically. Even as my simulated missiles were electronically converging on Shatravka to "destroy" his aircraft, I unveiled my next deceptive gambit.

"*Rubege odin,*" I called, a message I knew both Shatravka and the opponent battle controller would also receive. "Radar lock-on."

I wanted them to think I was still at maximum lock-on range even though I had already launched.

Then, as my simulated missiles closed on Shatravka, I called, "Range Two" and "Range Three," as if I had just launched my missiles.

"Enemy on the right," I heard his controller warn.

He banked into a diving roll toward me in a vain effort to break my lock-on. But it was too late. He was already dead. As I had hoped, Shatravka was blinded by the afternoon sun and unable to achieve "tallyho," visual contact.

Now I planned to kill him again, first with my infrared missiles and then with the gun.

I switched the sensor control knob from "radar" to "close combat infrared" and my HUD lit up with IRST target imagery. Shatravka was still banking into me, and I hoped that we were closing too fast for him to use his helmet-mounted sight. But my standard IRST sensor in the dome on my nose was tracking him. The two narrow vertical range lines of the IRST lock-on zone hung in the center of the HUD. My finger was poised on the missile trigger as I banked hard right into his approach. As soon as the gray blur of his aircraft entered the "ladder" of the lock-on zone, my headset buzzed with launch approval and I squeezed the trigger. A simulated Archer was on its way.

"*Pusk*," I called, announcing a lock-on launch of an Archer. Shatravka was "dead" again. Actually, had I fired a real missile, he might have survived, but his plane would have been destroyed. The R-73, which NATO called the Archer, was almost impossible to evade in these close, highly dynamic encounters. The heat seeking sensor head was linked to its own logic memory system that resisted IR decoy flares. And because the missile employed a thrust vector system, it could turn inside any known fighter, no matter how skilled the pilot. An Archer literally followed its nose straight up the tail pipe of the enemy to explode inside his engine. But the missile's warhead was relatively small. We called it our "humane" weapon; it killed the enemy's engine, but not the pilot, who would hopefully be able to eject even after a solid hit.

Shatravka was still closing, and I rolled harder with him to keep his aircraft locked on. The beauty of the new Archer was you could engage these rapidly converging targets head-on. I still had a good tone, and another simulated missile automatically launched.

"*Pusk*," I called again.

Shatravka slashed past me in a transonic blur. I retarded my throttles to idle and pulled back hard on the stick. Once more I was pressed into my seat, and I saw the G-indicator on my HUD increase from 6 to 7.5. I was using this high-G energy to reduce speed and minimize my turning radius. Shatravka was out there somewhere below to my right, in his own high-G "arcing turn," trying to maneuver for missile lock-on.

I kept the stick full back against my left thigh, and the aircraft pitched up toward a low-energy turn with the nose reaching the maximum maneuverable angle of attack, twenty-four degrees. The stall limiter immediately engaged, knocking the stick forward in my hand and reducing my AOA. I had achieved my goal of bleeding off energy and reversing course well inside Shatravka's wider turn radius.

Just before a full stall, I jammed the throttles to afterburner and kept the stick in my lap. The Fulcrum accelerated, thrusting me against my ejection seat. I managed the best turn this Fulcrum had to offer and arrived at his six o'clock.

He had made the common mistake of relatively inexperienced MiG-29 pilots. By keeping his power settings too high, Shatravka flew wide-radius arcing turns, allowing me to get inside of him. I had been flying this powerful Fulcrum as long as any regimental line pilot in the Soviet Air Force. I had learned how to manage my energy and not to arc. It was not how fast you flew through the sky but *where* you placed your aircraft relative to your opponent in order to achieve a quick kill.

Shatravka now banked into a tight diving barrel roll and I rolled with him. It was time to kill him with the gun. The horizon spun crazily past my canopy, and I was aware of the altitude digits winding down on the upper right corner of my HUD while my airspeed increased dramatically on the opposite corner. But, like a hound, I had a taste of blood in my mouth. Reaching instinctively with my left hand, I flipped my weapons sensor zone switch to "narrow field of view" so that the IRST scanner would lock on quicker. The gunsight aiming circle wavered across Shatravka's aircraft, and I eased my nose up and right to move the fixed cross hairs on the HUD to overlap the circle and the opponent fighter. I had set the fire-rate switch to "burst," which meant twenty-five 30mm rounds would fire for each second my finger was on the trigger. The GSh-301 was a very accurate cannon. When the enemy was within that aiming circle, locked in the cross hairs, he was dead. This cannon simply did not miss.

I saw a bold "A" appear on the left margin of the HUD and knew my laser range finder was probing him with an invisible finger, feeding the firing solution into my weapons computer. At this close range I hoped that Shatravka did not look back over his shoulder and catch the laser full in the face. He was an arrogant bastard and a Communist true believer, but I certainly didn't want to blind him with my laser.

Still he rolled, and still I kept behind him. Almost, but not quite. Shatravka's gray fuselage slid into the aiming circle. The cross hairs straddled his cockpit and wings. I heard the steady tone of laser/IRST lock-on. Now.

I squeezed the gun trigger on the stick. "*Ogon*," I called. "Firing."

Just as I killed my opponent for the third time, I heard Nikolai call, "*Pusk*." He had killed Major Chayka with a missile.

Too late, Shatravka finally did something intelligent. He chopped power and dropped off in a leaf spiral toward the sea, hoping I would dive past him into his own IRST kill zone. If I hadn't been anticipating his maneuver, I would have lost him. But I had already cut my own throttles and used the air brakes to stay behind him.

"*Ogon*," I called for good measure.

My flight was victorious. I heard Shatravka's gruff, sullen voice announce he was separating. The dogfight was over, and he and his wingman headed north to complete their own individual training maneuvers. Nikolai was scheduled for cannon runs on the Kulevi coastal *poligon* rectangular weapons range. He checked in with GCI and received an altitude and vector back to the coast.

I was alone over the Black Sea, still only minutes away from Turkey. But I shook my head, rejecting that final temptation. I knew the Ruslan GCI was watching me on radar, so I leveled off and proceeded with the remainder of my scheduled sortie maneuvers.

I completed one fast, tight climbing combat turn and rolled into a hard right bank on the second. As the G-indicator on my HUD blinked to 8, I dragged the throttles back and centered the stick, letting the airplane mush into level flight without completing the turn.

I breathed deeply and licked my dry lips. It was time to begin the deception.

"Brigadier... 350." I made my voice hoarse and hesitant, then groaned and spoke through clenched teeth, as if in severe pain. "Finished... finished mission. I have a sharp pain in the back."

I groaned again and let my breath hiss audibly in my mask.

Vitaly replied immediately. "*Shto? Povtari*. What? Repeat."

"Pain... in the back." Again I groaned, more softly now.

"Can you control the airplane?" Vitaly's voice was on the edge of panic.

"I can."

"You are cleared for a straight-in approach. Switch to tower frequency, channel 7."

I turned due east and aligned my radio compass needle on the Ruslan beacon. With the throttles set at eighty-five percent, I maintained an airspeed of 350 knots. I would be back in less than five minutes. As I crossed the coast, I opened my oxygen mask and jammed three fingers far back into my throat. I wanted to vomit to make the show even more convincing. But I could not. This was more than ironic. As a young cadet flying L-29 trainers, I had almost been grounded for airsickness and had to conceal my nausea by puking into a plastic bag and hiding it. Now when I needed a convincing display of vomit on my flight suit, I could not produce, even though I was gagging hard.

The city of Mikha Tskhakaya appeared in the green citrus groves and marshes ahead. I saw the long Ruslan runway. The straight-in approach was easy. And I decided not to overdo the deception by wobbling on final.

After I touched down and popped my tan, clover-shaped drag chute, the tower called, asking if I wanted to park on the emergency ramp.

"Negative," I replied. "I can taxi to the squadron apron."

As I turned left onto the taxi ramp, I saw the flashing orange lights of the ambulance and the white jackets of the emergency medical crew. I also saw the faces of the squadron and regimental officers. They looked grave. Obviously Vitaly had announced I was in bad shape.

I let my shoulders sag in the ejection harness and tried to assume a suitable expression of pain and disorientation. My whole future now depended on my ability to convince the medical staff I had received a serious injury in this last, violent dogfight.

— 2 —

Central Aviation Hospital, Moscow
March 21, 1989

T he early spring sun felt good as I stood at the window, waiting for the nurse who would escort me down the corridor and up to the second floor for my ten o'clock appointment with the psychologist. The hospital was a quiet oasis of luxury surrounded by the melting snow of Sokolniki Park.

Beyond the park's budding maple and birch trees, several million of my fellow citizens were struggling through another dreary morning of perestroika. Some stood in endless lines, waiting to buy a kilo of rationed sugar, or for a State shoe store to finally open. There might be imitation-leather sandals for the children to wear this summer. More likely, the shelves would be empty. Others waited in the lines for the promise of a shriveled Cuban grapefruit or a bag of Moroccan oranges. Many crowded the sidewalks like cattle, clutching their *avos'ka* net bags, simply hoping to find the last of the winter's bruised cabbage or maybe even laundry soap. Young people were wandering among the stalls of the Riga Bazaar, searching for an authentic pair of Levi's or Reebok sneakers. This was the fifth year of glasnost, the fourth of perestroika. By all accounts, conditions were still deteriorating, even here in the capital.

The food shortages were nothing new, but now people lined up to feed a type of hunger many never knew existed before glasnost. They stood patiently beside news kiosks from early

33

morning, waiting for the bundles of *Ogonyok,* Moscow News, or *Argumenti i Facti* to arrive. These new, independent publications contained an intangible commodity sweeter than sugar, more stimulating than vodka or coffee. They published the truth.

For months the men and women who stood in ranks along the sidewalks, clutching their string bags of cabbage, no longer gazed back impassively at the Zil limousines and Volga sedans as the bosses sped from their luxury apartments on Leninsky Prospekt to the Party and government buildings across the river. Now the people had learned the truth about the Party's "eternal concern" for the welfare of the masses. Now working people, not just intellectuals, recognized the term *gulag,* and knew the bloody history of the Party's Organs of State Security.

The only thing perestroika promised was more degrading shortages and hardship. But glasnost had begun to open the door of a cage that had been barred for over seventy years. People were no longer afraid. The Russian bear had been in hibernation all those decades. Now he was stirring. Soon, like me, he would be fully awake. And, like me, he would be angry.

There were already clear signs that the anger was about to erupt. For the first time in decades, there had been street demonstrations in Moscow. Several times in recent weeks, crowds had gathered in Pushkin Square, demonstrating for independence of the Baltic Republics or demanding the speedy establishment of a true parliamentary democracy. Some were mothers of young men who had been killed in Afghanistan. The demonstrators had been harshly suppressed by the militia and by the newly formed special OMON paramilitary units of the Interior Ministry. Hundreds of people had been beaten or arrested. But they mastered their fear and returned to the square.

The simmering anger of the people on the street, however, was not the concern of the men who ran this modern, four-hundred bed medical complex. The hospital was reserved for the elite of the Soviet Union: About half the patients were retired senior military and KGB officers or their families; the other half were Air Force pilots. Some came from strategic bomber and helicopter regiments.

Many were helicopter pilots wounded in Afghanistan. It always made me sad to see these young men, limping on artificial legs or waiting for plastic surgery to repair their rippled burn scars. A few helicopter pilots here were victims of another man-made disaster: the catastrophe at Chernobyl. I'd seen them wheeled down the third-floor halls to the intensive-care ward, prematurely decrepit, shrunken and bald, wasting away from the fatal radiation doses they had received flying above the Chernobyl plant to drop sand and boron into the caldron of the burning reactor.

But most of the younger pilots here were perfectly healthy. Like me, they flew high-performance MiG-23s or the new "super-maneuverable" fighters—the MiG-29 and Su-27—in elite Frontal Aviation regiments. This hospital was a good example of the primacy of the Air Force, the Voyenno-Vozdushniye Sily (VVS). Supposedly our sister service, the Air Defense Force, Voiska Protivovozdushnoy Oboroni (PVO), had equally modern facilities outside Moscow.

This was a polite fiction. Everybody knew our hospital was the best in the military. Air Force pilots were brought here from all over the vast country. The pilots of the VVS who flew several of the world's most advanced high-performance fighters were recognized as the State's elite warriors. Each of us represented an investment of several million rubles. Like champion race horses, we required specialized care to maintain our competitive edge. So the State invested millions more in scarce hard currency for the West German X-ray machines, the Japanese CAT scanners, and the computerized Westinghouse blood-chemistry apparatus that stood like polished icons in the treatment rooms I passed along the main corridor of the diagnostic wing.

Moscow's Central Aviation Hospital specialized in urology, ophthalmology, and neurology. These departments, I'd been told, were staffed and equipped almost as well as their counterparts in the West. Obviously they were far superior to the State hospitals open to the "workers," who lacked Party or military connections. In those squalid wards, patients' families had to bring their food, and you had to bribe the nurse just to empty a bedpan. But you couldn't even bribe the doctor to provide medication. There was none. For decent treatment, people had to spend their life savings in the new cooperative, private clinics that were springing up like mushrooms in all our cities.

So the Party elite and the military and KGB *nomenklatura* who were treated here well understood how privileged they were. Not only was the treatment superior to that of any other hospital; it was free.

But high-performance fighter pilots were not so pleased to be here, where the medical and personnel bureaucrats of the Air Force, not operational officers, ran the show. All aviation academy cadets had to obtain a Category 1 health certificate, the same as the rigorous standards required of the cosmonauts. So we had all started our careers in absolutely perfect condition. And, by directive of the Ministry of Defense, a pilot qualifying for the MiG-29 or Su-27 also had to be certified Category 1. In reality, however, most line pilots in MiG-29 or Su-27 regiments maintained a Category 2 certificate, which was only slightly less rigorous than the highest standard. And we each had to preserve our perfect "one-by-one" vision if we wanted to keep flying. No one with eyeglasses flew a Soviet fighter. But if any of these pilots developed a medical problem or ejected from a crippled aircraft, he was brought to Moscow for a complete reevaluation. And here in the Kingdom of the Bureaucrats, that damned ministry directive was enforced: A pilot had to be recertified to a full Category 1 before he could fly super-maneuverable fighters again.

On previous visits to the hospital, I'd learned from other officers that perfectly qualified MiG-29 and Su-27 pilots were being grounded because they could no longer meet the impossibly high standards of the Category 1 health certificate. The slightest irregularity in heartbeat, reflex, or motor response might mean a man's flying career would end in a medical discharge.

It certainly was ironic that the generally soft and overweight medical staff of this hospital controlled the destinies of the country's most vigorously fit pilots and cosmonauts. In the past, I understood, a politically well connected pilot—or certainly an experienced cosmonaut—could bypass these doctors' authority. A few years before, a playboy cosmonaut had even begun an extended mission to the Mir space station while suffering from gonorrhea. It was a pretty bad bout of clap, however, and the cosmonaut had to cut the mission short and descend in a *Soyuz* spacecraft for emergency treatment. There had been similar excesses by senior Air Force pilots who had managed to circumvent medical authority. But now the medics reigned supreme, and we were controlled by harsh regulations like the chief of staff's directive.

In December 1988, two months before my last flight, an event occurred that made clear to me the logic behind this directive, and also presented me with an opportunity to honorably stop serving the system that I had come to hate. Soviet President Mikhail Gorbachev had dramatically announced to the United Nations General Assembly in New York that the Soviet Union would "unilaterally" reduce its armed forces by 500,000 men and 10,000 tanks, in order to ease military tension in the world. Both *Pravda* and *Izvestia* had praised Gorbachev for this unprecedented gesture, and had gone on to explain that the reduction of Soviet armed forces graphically demonstrated the peace-loving nature of our government. We were told that the reduction in force of 500,000 men would be shared by all branches of the military, including the Air Force.

Four days after my February 13 flight, when my air division's medical staff formally requested that I be sent to Moscow for a complete medical evaluation, I presented a formal request of my own to Lieutenant Colonel Anatoli Antonovich, my regimental commander:

To: Commander, 176th Frontal Aviation Regiment

I hereby request a discharge from the ranks of the VVS due to my physical condition, and to the fact that I am not willing to continue service on the ground.

Signed: Zuyev, Alexander M., Captain

Now I was in Moscow, completing three weeks of intensive medical examinations. The Air Force hoped that I could soon be returned to flight status. But I had other plans: to secure a medical discharge from the Armed Forces of the Soviet Union. Once out of the service, I planned to emigrate to the West and a life of freedom. I was confident that I would find a way out of the Soviet Union without an exit visa. Most Soviet citizens believed the frontiers were impassable, tightly sealed by KGB border guards. But people had simply built these prison walls in their minds after decades of repression. I had traveled the southern republics, and I knew there were plenty of smugglers' trails connecting Georgia, Armenia, and Azerbaijan with Turkey and Iran.

*   *   *

I nodded to a pair of Su-27 pilots on their way to the gym in the hospital's administrative wing next door. In their blue warm-up suits, they looked like young Olympic athletes. All of us who flew the "fourth generation" aircraft were fine specimens, representing the top one percent of our peer group in terms of physical condition, mental ability, and psychological balance. And Air Force propaganda made the most of our physical perfection and skill. In the crowds at airport terminals and railroad stations, and on the Metro among sophisticated Muscovites, the uniform and wings of an Air Force pilot still drew expressions of respect.

Even those who bitterly opposed the Afghan war recognized our skill and dedication. This was noteworthy because popular support for that war had been almost completely eroded by shocking revelations made possible by glasnost. Independent Soviet journalists now brought the country the truth about the performance of our "internationalist duty" in Afghanistan. The Muslim Mujahedin were now called guerrillas, not dismissed as *dushmani*, "bandits." And we now had to accept the grim reality that these guerrillas controlled most of the country. The Soviet Army had been driven back into a few fortified enclaves that the Mujahedin raided and shelled at will.

Finally, one month earlier, the last Soviet troops had been withdrawn, a defeated army.

However, the average citizen on the street did not blame Soviet soldiers and airmen for this disaster. They knew we had been trained and equipped at great expense to defend the Motherland, the Rodina. This trust, of course, grew as much from fear as from sincere patriotism. Fear of invasion ran deep in our history. The Motherland had been overrun and pillaged so many times—by Mongols, Swedes, French, and Germans—that most people believed it was only a matter of time before the tanks of the NATO imperialists or the renegade Socialist Chinese hordes spilled across our borders. Naturally the Party did much to keep this fear alive.

But the people's respect for the military did not depend on artificial stimulation. They sincerely admired us, which was remarkable, considering that there had always been so much official *pokazuka*—the all-pervasive and transparent official sham—in everyday Soviet life. Despite glasnost and perestroika, slogans were still plastered across building façades on banners half as wide as a soccer field, proclaiming the Party's eternal concern for the welfare of the toiling masses, the profound wisdom of Marxist-Leninist dogma, the steady progress of Soviet agriculture and industry... and all the rest of the empty claptrap. Few people out in those food lines believed that shit anymore.

Fundamental doubts about the Soviet system were even splitting the ranks of the military, basically along the lines of the generations. I shared my ten-bed dormitory here at the hospital with four other pilots, two of them young officers like myself, and the two others elderly retired veterans who had seen combat in the Great Patriotic War and had served out their careers in the preglasnost totalitarian decades. Every time a new issue of *Argumenti i Facti* or *Ogonyok* was published, the young pilots found some hot issue to debate late into the night with the veterans. Usually they argued the validity of the shocking revelations of past repression, Stalin's purges of the 1930s, the gulags of the postwar years, or the cruel treatment of dissidents in the State psychiatric hospitals.

The old veterans simply could not admit that they had spent their lives serving a corrupt and evil system. The stories in the new publications, they said with bitter scorn, were just lies spread by Jews and imperialist agents. But the younger pilots, who, like me, slipped away from the hospital to walk the streets of Moscow, recognized the truth. And they also recognized the swelling impatience and frustrated anger that were gripping their fellow citizens.

No matter how persuasive the evidence in the published exposés of mass deportations and the genocidal deaths of millions—sealed in boxcars during the cruel *étape* and worked to death on starvation diets in the countless gulag camps—the elderly veterans could never admit they had protected a system as cruel as the Nazi regime against which they had fought so bravely. My younger colleagues dismissed these bitter retired officers as "skiers," an allusion to their shuffling gait. But I knew that there was a more robust generation of senior officers still on active duty who were every bit as adamant in their defense of the rotten system. It was those marshals and generals who held my fate in their hands.

Coming toward me down the corridor, I spotted the ambling figure of a tall, young pilot. Only one fellow I knew had those long, heavy legs, stooped shoulders, and huge feet: Igor "Karpich"

Karpov, whom I had first met as a cadet at the Armavir Academy eleven years before.

"Karpuha," I called, using our old nickname for him, "since when do they admit the slackers of the PVO to this fine Air Force institution?"

He turned to face me. It was Karpich, all right. Nobody else had that eagle's beak of a nose.

"Shurka," he said, grabbing my hand and smiling. "What are *you* doing here? I thought you'd be Air Force chief of staff by now."

We grinned at each other. Karpich hadn't changed much in those years. He looked like the same rumpled, good-natured braggart I'd always known. The last I'd seen him was two years before on a visit to his MiG-23 PVO regiment near Smolensk, west of Moscow.

"So," I asked, "what's up with you?"

Karpich moaned and flashed me his old cocky smile, then glanced quickly up and down the corridor. "Never trust a zampolit with a combat airplane." He laughed out loud now. "I got shot down by my deputy regimental commander for political administration."

"You *what?*" This seemed to be the lead-in to a standard pilot's joke, but Karpich was serious.

"We were out on the missile poligon, firing R-23s at LA-17 target drones," he said quietly. "GCI was vectoring a pair of aircraft on the target because the drone was almost out of fuel."

The LA-17 drone was a fast, very maneuverable target drone powered by a solid-fuel rocket engine. Firing R-23 radar-guided missiles at these drones was realistic combat training. You had to fly well and act with quick decisiveness. Unfortunately for Karpich, one of the other two-plane flights operating that day was led by his zampolit. These officers were always much better chatterboxes than pilots. I thought of the political officer in my own regiment who had almost blasted the Tu-16 with a burst of cannon fire. The VVS recognized the zampolits' shortcomings. A directive from the chief of staff of the Air Force limited our zampolits to a maximum of four training sorties a day and prevented them from flying late in any given training day's schedule because "fatigue" might jeopardize safety.

Karpich checked the corridor to make sure we weren't within

earshot of strangers, a reflexive gesture we all repeated many times a day. "The zampolit was so excited to actually get a solid lock on the LA-17 that he fired his missile without interrogating the target with the SRZO."

"That really doesn't surprise me, Karpich," I said. The Soviet SRZO was similar to the coded Information Friend or Foe system employed in the West. Any pilot using live weapons with friendly aircraft nearby *had* to electronically interrogate the intended target to verify it was an enemy before firing.

"The next thing I heard," Karpich continued, "was the colonel screaming on the radio, 'Karpov, eject! *Now!*' I ejected just before the missile hit."

I couldn't help grinning, despite Karpich's pained expression. During our preliminary flight training with the L-29 trainer at the Pirsagat Air Base in Azerbaijan, he had revealed that he was terrified of ejecting from a crippled aircraft. Despite all our efforts to hammer into his thick head the simple truth that a pilot's life was worth more than an airplane, Karpich had stubbornly refused to even consider using his ejection seat.

"How was it?" I asked. "Did you hurt your back?" The MiG-23 ejection seat was notorious for compressing your vertebrae.

Karpich scowled and nodded. "My back is fucked. I probably won't be flying jets anymore."

Thanks to the rotten zampolit system, here he was undergoing the rigorous standard postejection medical exam. That had been bad luck for him, but a pleasant surprise for me. I was happy to have found an old friend in the hospital.

"So, why are you here?" Karpich asked. "Are you about to become the first cosmonaut in our illustrious class?"

"No," I said, "hardly that. It's a long story, Karpuha."

I began to tell Karpich a version of that story, being careful not to reveal any information that might implicate him in my deception.

But I was interrupted by the arrival of my nurse escort, a good-looking brunette named Nina. She wore her starched white uniform so tight that her nipples—"circuit breakers" to the young pilots—showed clearly through the fabric. Here patients had to be escorted to their appointments by nurses who carried the patients' medical records. Most pilots objected to the degrading hospital regulation. But, unlike the others, I certainly did not mind walking a few paces behind Nina's seductively swaying hips. Normally I would have made a pass at her. Nina, however, had made it clear that she was "engaged" to a snot-nosed kid just finishing secondary school. It turned out the boy had relatives in West Germany, and Nina was trading on her good looks for the chance to emigrate to the West. Her story was indicative of the desperation people felt.

I wanted freedom, too. But I had chosen another means to obtain it.

Walking down this corridor, we passed the outpatient reception area, where the hospital's unofficial clientele arrived each morning. They stood out in dramatic contrast to the young pilots. The paunchy old men with faces as red and mottled as a plate of borscht were the elite of the military *nomenklatura*, active duty and retired. Their black GAZ-31 sedans crowded the parking lot. You knew they were the big shots by the number of zeros on their license plates. The sleek men in their thirties dressed in well-tailored American suits were the rising stars of the KGB. Their equally stylish wives and well-groomed children were always led to the head of the line at each diagnostic or treatment department. These people had never stood in line for cabbage or laundry detergent. Their chins were not nicked by dull, rusty razor blades that had to last through fifty shaves. They took what they wanted. They did not wait to be thrown scraps like those angry millions in the endless lines.

This was still the way the world worked, despite the "reforms" of glasnost and perestroika. My fellow pilots and I were the official reason the State had invested so generously in this hospital and its expert staff. But the *nomenklatura* were here, as always, to skim the cream off the State's generosity.

Passing the library, I glanced at the inevitable bust of Lenin. Here he was portrayed in a meditative pose. My entire life I had been watched by Lenin: "Dedushka," "Grandfather" Lenin smiling down on my kindergarten class, Lenin the Military Expert gracing the walls of the Armavir Academy, Lenin the Friend of Humanity, Lenin the Universal Genius. I was sick of looking at him.

When I was sixteen, my mother and I visited Moscow. She assumed that, like every other normal young Soviet citizen, I wanted to visit Lenin's mausoleum on Red Square. But when she explained we would have to get up at five-thirty to begin standing in line at six, a full three hours before the Tomb opened, I told her I could wait until I visited the capital in the summer. It was February and I certainly had no intention of risking frostbite simply to pass before the glass coffin of a waxy corpse. Maybe that was the unrecognized first tentative step down the path that led me to this hospital. Maybe not. More probably I was just a typical lazy adolescent who preferred a warm hotel bed to the icy cobblestones of that windswept square. Twelve years had passed and I had not yet made the pilgrimage.

In any event, Lenin's body, as rosy and firm as New Year's marzipan, still lay in that mausoleum. And people from all over the Soviet Union still lined up in the winter frost and summer sun to pay their homage. To me, their devotion to Lenin was a touchstone of our nation's progress toward freedom. As long as simple people on the street believed in the Great Leader's Universal Wisdom, the Party would retain control of their minds.

We turned left from the medical diagnosis wing and climbed the stairs to a quieter, more softly lit department on the second floor. This was the realm of the psychologists. Here the decor was less clinical. Rich wood trim and bookcases replaced the spotless tile and electronic apparatus, giving the department an academic atmosphere. Nina led me to the office of Lieutenant Colonel Sergei Frolov, the clinical psychologist assigned to my case.

Lieutenant Colonel Frolov rose from his desk, took my records from the nurse, then greeted me. He was a lean, vigorous man in his late thirties, with dark hair and intelligent hazel eyes. His white medical coat was starched and spotless.

"Alexander Mikhailovich," he said, addressing me formally, a gesture of respect from a senior officer to a pilot captain. His handshake was firm. "Please sit down."

His office was large and handsomely furnished. The hard-wood parquet floor glowed from recent polishing, matching the shoulder-high maple wall paneling. The desk was wide and well varnished. There were two telephones on the right corner.

Frolov's office reflected his status as the hospital's chief clinical psychologist. His diagnoses and recommendations were taken seriously by Air Force personnel. I had to accept that the specialists in the internal medicine, neurology, and orthopedic departments had found nothing physically wrong with me during their exhaustive examinations. So Frolov represented my last real hope of obtaining a medical discharge.

He offered me a comfortable armchair, then sat at the desk and opened the thick pasteboard dossier containing my medical records. He withdrew a neatly penned chart covered with a sharply spiked graph. I saw my name and service number on the corner of the chart. Apparently this was the plotted result of the intensive psychological tests I had taken three days before.

Frolov frowned as he reviewed the graph. There were preplotted parallel lines running horizontally across the graph, which no doubt measured the "norms" so valued in all official Soviet life. The peaks and valleys circled in red of my plotted test results fell far above and far below these accepted norms.

Ever since I'd been a *kursant* at the Armavir Higher Aviation Academy, I had shared a basic tenet of survival with my fellow cadets and later with the pilots in my regiment: "Never tell the truth to a psychologist." Even as boys fresh out of school, we had understood that there were "safe," officially acceptable answers to the long psychological profile tests we were obliged to take. And I had followed that policy through four years at the academy and seven years as a fighter pilot. During those eleven years, I must have taken different versions of this test at least ten times, always trying to shield my true feelings. I always got a headache trying to thread my way through the minefield of questions.

But I had answered with brutal honesty the six-hundred-question psychological test that Frolov's staff had administered in the quiet room down the corridor on Monday. The test had been one of a battery of examinations designed to evaluate my manual dexterity and coordination, professional judgment, and personality in the wake of my aborted February flight. Only two hundred of the questions, the test staff had assured me, actually dealt with "personality traits." And these questions were often linked to control questions salted throughout the exam to expose any attempt at deception.

I had no problem with that. Rather than attempt to deceive the authorities by espousing reverence for the ideals of Marxism-Leninism, I had proceeded to vent my disgust for the system. And I also honestly revealed the bitter depression I first felt when I'd learned about my country's history of bloody repression.

Each question had three possible answers: Yes, No, or Uncertain.

To such questions as "Do you believe in God?" and "Are people conspiring against you?" I had answered Yes.

There had been the usual collection of questions to test my loyalty and faith in the wisdom of the Party's leadership. "Do you read foreign magazines?" "Do you like foreign clothes?" to these I had answered Yes.

My answers to the questions that were obviously testing my attitude toward "collective decision-making" made clear my individualist nature.

One section of the test concerned personal and family relations. "Do you look forward to coming home after duty?" The questions were subtle, but clear in their intent. My answers made it obvious that I was not happy in my marriage.

To make certain my answers would be taken seriously, I searched for the control questions. "Do you like to watch fire?" Yes, I had answered. Any Russian who had camped and fished in the Volga heartland liked his campfire. "Have you ever been attracted to fire?" Yes again. And I had been careful to answer "Uncertain" several times.

In the two hours allotted, I had diligently answered all six hundred questions, then carefully reviewed my answers.

Now Lieutenant Colonel Frolov sat across his tasteful hardwood desk, his lips pursed as he tapped the graphed test results and precisely verified my answers to certain key questions. From his calm, exact manner, I assumed he was a man accustomed to reaching important decisions after some deliberation.

While Frolov reviewed my file, I gazed past the inevitable framed portraits of Gorbachev and Lenin and out the office window at the park. Warm, weak sunshine lit the trees. Pilots in red-trimmed, blue warm-up suits were out on the exercise paths, the younger men jogging, the older officers walking at a steady pace.

I focused on the short figure of a lieutenant colonel who had commanded a fighter regiment in Germany. His name was Peotr Petrov and I had been shocked to learn when I'd met him in my ward that he was only forty-two years old. He looked like a man in his sixties.

A doctor at the centrifuge G-stress unit in the Aerospace

Medical Center near Dynamo Stadium had frankly revealed to me the disastrous cumulative effects of flying high-performance fighters. During Lieutenant Colonel Petrov's twenty years of service, he had chalked up thousands of hours of high-G flight in MiG-21s and MiG-23s. The human body could only take so much of that punishment. When you combined almost daily high-G maneuvers with the adverse effects of breathing pure oxygen, and the hazard of ionizing radiation from supposedly well shielded aircraft radars, the result was a pilot like Petrov, a man we younger pilots called a "squeezed lemon."

This brave and loyal officer had flown several combat tours in Afghanistan. For years, he and his family had endured the harsh existence of primitive, isolated bases in the Far East and Central Asia. All those years he had flown, in good weather and bad, in blizzards, dust storms, and frozen fog. And the cruel physics of high-performance flight had inevitably taken a toll. The connective tissue of his abdomen was so distended that he had to cinch up his G-suit as tightly as a weight-lifter's belt during his entire last year on flight status.

He was now receiving his final medical examinations before retirement. The standard pension for this officer's long service to the Socialist Motherland would be 250 rubles a month. Today, in Moscow, a dinner in a cooperative restaurant costs 100, a decent overcoat, over 1,000. If he was very lucky, he would be retired with a "generous" disability bonus: an additional 50 rubles per month. In either case, the reward for his long and courageous service was poverty. Depending on his connections, he might also be fortunate enough to be granted a lease on a one-room apartment in a shoddy high-rise block of a *microrayon* near some reasonably prosperous city. But a lieutenant colonel Sniper pilot with a good combat record was probably not so politically astute as to have secured such luxurious retirement housing.

One of Lieutenant Colonel Frolov's telephones rang, the muted double ring of the hospital's internal switchboard. "Yes, good morning," he said cheerfully, reaching for a small notepad. The person at the other end spoke for almost a minute, and I watch Frolov writing a neat, two-column list on the pad. The caller was from the Voyentorg, the military supply exchange that served all branches of the Soviet armed services.

But the Voyentorg in Moscow's Central Aviation Hospital was clearly different from that in a motor rifle regiment in some forlorn garrison on the Mongolian border. Out there the troops might be lucky to find rusty razor blades one month and tins of bitter peach jam another. Supplies at the military exchange at my own base in Georgia had become increasingly scarce in recent months. Now officers' wives had to wait in line for hours each week to buy their subsidized sugar and obtain the milk ration for their children. And when they did receive their supplies, their cabbage was often rotten and the milk sour.

But Frolov was not writing a list of sour milk. The column on the right side of his pad was headed, "Package with Salmon," the other, "Package with Caviar," the Voyentorg's weekly offering to the hospital's *nomenklatura*. From what I could read on his lists, both packages included East German salami, Hungarian frozen chicken and fruit compote, coffee from Africa, Darjeeling tea, chocolate candy, and sweet biscuits. The main difference was in the "luxury" item, smoked salmon from the Siberian Pacific or two hundred grams of Caspian sevruga caviar. In reality, of course, every item on both lists was a luxury far beyond attainment by all but a few of the privileged.

Frolov's careful deliberation showed me he was human, after all. Maybe I had a potential ally in him. And I certainly was going to need all the influential allies I could find to win my discharge.

Only the day before here at the hospital, I had seen how an officer who did not have connections was treated. Major Beryozovoy was a middle-aged MiG-23 pilot, whom I had first met at Gudauta on the Black Sea. This poor old fellow was a "squeezed lemon" if ever there was one. He had given his all to the State. Now he had only two years remaining before retirement and wanted desperately to stay on the Black Sea. His fourteen-year-old son, Misha, was asthmatic and could not tolerate the long northern winters. The boy had almost died the year before on a visit to the Ukraine. Now the Air Force intended to transfer the major to the Transbaikal Military District deep in Siberia. So far he had been able to obtain a medical waiver. The major was a brave and honest Soviet soldier. Not a politician.

I had recently learned just how powerful the politically well connected rear-echelon bureaucrats were. My friend Valery, a decorated veteran of almost four years in Afghanistan, where he had served as a forward air-ground controller in the combat zone, confronted a typical staff-rat personnel officer. This arrogant idiot told Valery, "You may well be a hero of Afghanistan, but I have more power." He held up a pencil in one hand, an eraser in the other. "Today," he continued, pointing to a pilots' personnel roster, "Ivanov is in Moscow and Siderov is in Siberia." He erased the two names and reversed their assignments. "Tomorrow, things are different. *That* is my power."

"Then it will be the Package with Caviar," Lieutenant Colonel Frolov finally said. "Of course, I would like to exchange the salami for a double portion of coffee."

I couldn't hear the other side of the conversation, but I saw Frolov neatly cross out the salami and write "2" beside coffee on the caviar list. Frolov was proving himself astute. Caviar was doubly valuable, not only as a luxury item for barter here in Moscow but also as one of the few available Soviet commodities that could be sold for hard currency, *valuta*. Most caviar was exported, of course, but enough was doled out to the *nomenklatura* to help meet their hard-currency needs. Such transactions kept their children in Western clothes and their wives in French silk scarves and designer sunglasses.

At a higher level, the unofficial benefits of office increased with rank, as did ostentation. Raisa Gorbachev's escapades with her American Express credit card were well known, thanks to glasnost. But another scandal was emerging about the Gorbachevs' new luxury holiday villa in the Crimea. Apparently Raisa—herself a professor of Marxism-Leninism—had not been pleased with the dark marble entrance staircase. She had ordered it demolished and replaced with snow-white marble.

Frolov politely thanked the Voyentorg and replaced the telephone receiver. "Excuse me, Alexander Mikhailovich," he said with an almost conspiratorial smile. "My son is due to take his eight-form foreign language examinations soon. We are planning a small party for him."

More likely the "small party" would be a small *prezant* of Caspian caviar to the chairman of the examination board. Or perhaps Frolov could arrange a prescription for a hard-to-find medication needed by that chairman's ailing mother. The possibilities were limitless within the network of influence and privilege bounded by Moscow's Ring Highway. For men like Frolov, many doors were open. It was well known among my fellow pilots that doctors in this hospital would barter treatment with the German ultrasonic kidney-stone machine in the basement for access to good restaurants or entry to Beryozka hard-currency stores. Smaller favors were arranged with the discreet presentation of an appropriate *prezant*. Among the elite of Moscow, Kiev, Gorkiy, or a dozen other Soviet cities, influence and wealth were interchangeable.

There was an expression known to every Soviet citizen above the age of ten: *Rukha ruku moyet*, "One hand washes the other." The opulence of this hospital's Voyentorg was clear proof that this system was flourishing, despite all the sanctimonious nonsense about glasnost and perestroika.

Frolov was now neatly sorting the test pages and graph. He folded his fine, white hands precisely on the desk and smiled.

"Well, Comrade Lieutenant Colonel," I said, as sincerely as I could, "how are my test results?"

Frolov shook his head. "We have some problems here, Captain Zuyev." In his precise manner, Frolov lifted the chart with the plotted test results. "I am convinced these results are not valid." He tapped the red peaks on the graph paper with the tip of an expensive imported pen. "These answers go far beyond the norms. Are you absolutely certain you read the questions carefully?"

"Absolutely, Comrade Lieutenant Colonel."

Again, Frolov shook his head. Then he smiled reassuringly. "No, Alexander Mikhailovich, I think you were feeling some temporary confusion during this examination."

"I answered each question as honestly as I could," I said with open-faced sincerity.

Frolov nodded and held up another document. I could see it was a printed extract of my service record. Again he slipped on his reading glasses. And again, he used his slim gold pen to emphasize the points of his argument. "Captain Zuyev, there is clearly nothing in your personnel file to indicate the type of unstable personality or antisocial attitudes evidenced by this test." He seemed honestly confused, eager to find a logical explanation for this strange dichotomy.

I nodded without speaking, then turned away to glance out the window toward Sokolniki Park once more. Poor old Colonel Petrov had tried jogging behind a group of younger officers, but now he was walking stiffly along the path, taking a shortcut to the hospital.

Frolov was reading from my service record. His accent and diction were pure Moscow staff officer, not the rough edge of a Soviet Army field commander berating an insubordinate junior officer. "Comrade Captain," he said, smiling again to show his concern, "I have reviewed the records of hundreds of pilots during my career. As you know, the Army's selection process is rigorous, designed to identify the best-qualified young men for flight training." He looked down again at my service record and frowned with concentration. "Everything in your background is absolutely normal . . . your school records, the entrance test scores at the Armavir Academy. Your flight training and academic records there demonstrate the highest possible aptitude . . ." He shook his head and smiled again. "Alexander Mikhailovich, I simply cannot believe that you possess an undetected personality flaw that would account for the answers on this test." For emphasis, he placed his open hand on the test booklet and the plotted answer graph.

I was carefully weighing Frolov's sincerity. He might be the critical factor in my campaign for a discharge from the Air Force. If I could convince him I actually was psychologically unstable, he might facilitate the discharge with a minimum of notoriety. On the other hand, Frolov had the power to brand me as a shirker, and incorrigible egoist, which was anathema in the collectivist dogma, of Marxism-Leninism. "Comrade Lieutenant Colonel," I finally said, "I answered those questions honestly."

Frolov cleared his throat and frowned more deeply. "Let me quickly review your record." His voice was cooler now. "Born Kuybyshev, 1961." He smiled. "Only twenty-seven years old, Alexander Mikhailovich, and you have been a First Class pilot for four years, a captain for two. You are a flight leader and a respected tactics instructor in one of the Air Force's leading combat fighter regiments." He hefted the service record for emphasis, then continued. "Last year you qualified for the military test pilot school at Akhtubinsk. You've been a full member of the Party for four years." He flipped over the carbon copy of an official form. "And I see you have recently received the Defense of the Motherland Medal."

I nodded. These medals were a joke to good pilots in line

regiments. We called this particular citation "the medal for sand from your ass." It had nothing to do with professional skill, but the staff rats in Moscow put a lot of stock in medals. In fact, you could usually spot a true rear-echelon hero by the number of medals on his chest.

Frolov was staring at me now with a fatherly expression of concern. "Your wife is the daughter of a distinguished Air Force officer. Comrade Captain, your career to date has been nothing short of exceptional. You have an extremely promising future in the Air Force. Yet you seem determined to make us believe that you are some kind of mental defective. Honestly, Alexander Mikhailovich, what are we to make of this?"

Suddenly I knew that it was time, finally and irrevocably, to state my case. I had to accept the fact that all medical tests would be inconclusive, at best, and that this officer was too skilled and politically astute to accept the results of my psychological test as valid grounds to grant me a discharge. "Comrade Colonel, I no longer wish to serve."

Frolov sighed audibly and closed the dossier. Clearly he was frustrated. He impatiently flipped open my dossier again. "In September 1978, when you entered the Higher Aviation Academy at Armavir, you took an oath, a solemn oath to serve the Soviet Union." He fixed me with his intelligent eyes. "You told all your superiors that your sole ambition in life was to become a fighter pilot." He sighed again. "Now you sit there and tell me you no longer wish to serve. Comrade Captain, what has happened? Tell me more about yourself. Help me understand."

I understood his frustration. The man was a Communist in a privileged position. He had no reason to doubt the system that treated him so well. Until recently, I had been like him, a believer, one of the Communist elite. How could I explain my transformation?

"Well," I finally asked, "where can I begin?"

Frolov smiled warmly now. "Why not begin at the beginning?"

PART TWO

3

Samara
1961–78

I was brought up in Kuybyshev, a major river port on the Volga, in the heartland of the Russian Federation. Kuybyshev had been named for a hero of the Revolution, but most people called the city Samara, a name well known in Russian history. Both my parents were engineers. My father, Mikhail, was a technical manager at one of the city's aviation factories. My mother, Lydia, was a construction engineer at the Kuybyshev Hydroelectric Institute.

During the Great Patriotic War, when the Nazi armies threatened Moscow, Kuybyshev had become the temporary capital of the Soviet Union. Our aircraft factories had turned out thousands of combat planes. Assembly lines had worked day and night producing the Ilyushin-2, the famous Shturmovik that had helped defeat the Nazi panzers. And since then, military and civilian aviation manufacturing, as well as the precision-machine-tool industry needed to support those plants, had remained the economic backbone of the city.

The broad blue Volga had always been vital to the life of Samara, just as it still was to present-day Kuybyshev. My mother's institute had responsibility for an immense, multiyear and multibillion-ruble construction project, eventually meant to harness the power potential of the vast upper Volga system, which included the huge Kuybyshev Reservoir.

My father was a good amateur photographer and supplemented his salary by selling scenic pictures to a local postcard publisher,

55

by photographing wedding ceremonies and sports events, and by producing much better family portraits than available through the crowded State enterprise photo shops in town. We didn't have money for luxuries, but my clothes were not ragged, we ate well, and I always had five kopeks to buy a sweet roll after school. Every New Year's there were brightly wrapped presents under the decorated fir tree. We lived in a one-room, hundred-and-twenty-eight-square-foot apartment in an older building. I had my small bed in one corner of the room, and my parents slept in a curtained alcove. The kitchen was hardly big enough for all three of us, but as with so many Russian families, it was the heart of our home.

I had seen families living nearby, crammed into old wood-and-stucco tenements near the railroad station, sharing the same dirty kitchen and a smelly toilet in the courtyard. So I was happy my parents were engineers and we could live in a nice brick building.

The kitchen of our apartment, not school, was where I learned to read and write the year before I began first grade. My mother valued education highly, I imagine, because she had had to struggle for her own. She was the only child from her street to go on to a professional school. And I had been born while she was still in the technical institute. So she took great pride in her engineering degree.

But my mother understood the value of hard work in the classroom. "Sasha," she would often say as we sat at the kitchen table with my schoolbooks open before us, "the people who get ahead in life are the ones who work honestly and hard."

My mother was then a person of great optimism.

Her belief in the benefits of working hard in school had a direct impact on me. While other parents in our building made sure their children completed their lessons each night, Lydia Zuyev sat patiently at the kitchen table verifying that her son Alexander completed all of his calligraphy and arithmetic exercises letter-perfect. For her, no errors were permissible, nor was I allowed to cross out mistakes and start again on the same page. "We have sufficient paper," she would tell me, ripping up the half-complete sheet from my exercise book. From her I learned to concentrate on the task at hand.

In kindergarten my first classroom had been dominated by a

large framed painting of "Dedushka," Grandfather Lenin, smiling warmly down on the children. We'd first learned to sing songs about our patriotic duty from a book with pictures of "Valodynka" Lenin, a child just like us with golden curls above the starched white collar of his school uniform. Once, my mother had taken me on a long riverboat trip to Ulyanovsk, another port on the Volga, where we had visited the Lenin Home Museum. I was happy that Valodynka had been raised in such a nice big house, but surprised that his father had been a schoolteacher, not an engineer.

I was a pudgy boy, not at all athletic. On Sundays my mother would often take me on the long trolley ride out to my grandmother's house in Bezimaynka on the eastern edge of the city. Anna Vasilyevna Khatuntseva, my mother's mother, was a typical Russian babushka. She was stooped by years of hard work, but had a bright smile and kind eyes. Like many women of her generation, she smoked, and relished the luxury of a quiet cigarette.

She believed it was her duty to feed her grandchild as much as he could eat. To her, *blinchik* dipped in melted butter and filled with sugar, honey, or raspberry jam, or a steaming plate of *piroshki* filled with spiced minced pork, shredded cabbage, and hard-boiled eggs, were meant to be eaten right down to the last crumb. Naturally I loved going to her house. Even though she had no running water and heated her room with a wood stove, I never thought of her as poor.

She was close to her neighbors. On summer afternoons the old people would set tables under the shade trees, and the women would bring food. Everyone shared, everyone was equal.

I enjoyed all the attention I received at these picnics. I was the first grandchild in the family, and had come late in the first postwar generation. Children my age were doted on because we were the visible continuation of families that had been almost extinguished in the war.

And the war was a very strong presence in my childhood. At school we all learned Red Army songs, and the most exciting movies were all war films. One of my favorites was *The Chronicle of the Dive Bomber.* At the end the heroic young pilot dove his crippled plane right into a column of panzers and sacrificed his life for the Motherland. Sitting in the warm darkness of the Torch Cinema, watching those powerful old fighter-bombers howl through the sky of the Ukraine to blast the invaders, I felt deep pride to be a Soviet citizen. Then, riding home on the trolley, I gazed at the actual Shturmovik that sat atop the pedestal in a neighborhood memorial near one of the new *microrayon* apartment complexes. Its wide green wings and rugged tail were emblazoned with the red stars of the Soviet Army. That airplane had been built right here in Samara. It had crashed in a Baltic swamp and been carefully restored as a memorial. To me, it was a tangible link to a truly heroic time.

But there were stronger links to the war within my own family. My mother's father, Mikhail Stepanovich, had driven a truck before the war, then had become a chauffeur for a Party official. Like my father, he must have had some other talents, because he had apparently been fairly well-to-do. Grandmother had a framed photo of him standing on the porch of their own small wooden home, dressed in a handsome leather coat. In 1941 he had gone to war. At first, she told me, his letters had come regularly. Then, during the worst of the fighting in 1942, they had stopped. For months she received no news. She had joined thousands of other women, boys, and old men on the emergency construction of the aviation factories that had been moved east from Moscow and Leningrad after the Nazi invasion. Although she had been a village schoolteacher in her teens and had never before endured hard manual labor, Grandmother worked for months, hacking the frozen ground with a pick, digging foundations for the factories that were soon producing the Shturmoviks.

Those were terrible times, she told me. My mother and her brother, Vladimir, had only one pair of shoes to share between them. Then in the middle of the harsh winter of 1943, a dishonest salesclerk stole the family's three-month food ration book from my mother one day when she had gone to buy bread. With that ration book, the family was entitled to a basic allotment of bread, flour, and cooking oil. Without it, they faced starvation. That winter and spring my grandmother led my mother and uncle far out into the countryside, digging beneath the snow for damaged potatoes in the fallow fields. They had survived on rotten-potato cakes and a kind of soup Grandmother made from grass and willow buds.

But despite these hardships, she retained her basic humanity. She was assigned as a guard at a camp for German prisoners of war. Many of these POWs were hardened Nazis, but others, she told me, were just boys who had been drafted straight from school. One prisoner, she said, played the harmonica beautifully, and she rewarded him by sharing her own meager bread ration.

Then in the spring of 1944, they finally received official notification that my grandfather had been killed at the front. As sad as the news had been, this official notification meant the family was entitled to a small survivor's pension. And as war orphans, my mother and uncle also received a special food and clothing allotment from the American Red Cross. My mother was given a pair of yellow shoes with strong rubber soles. Uncle Vladimir received plaid wool knickers. Once a month the family was given a large can of powdered eggs, canned pork, and several thick chocolate bars.

"Sasha," my grandmother told me, "your mother and Uncle Vladimir thought it was New Year's when they opened those packages."

I understood why making sure children were well fed was so important to my grandmother.

But being a chubby boy of nine had begun to bother me when we lived in the old neighborhood near the center of the city. I could not run in the park or climb trees with the other boys. They laughed and called me "fatso."

Out in Microrayon 8, my new neighborhood, however, I discovered that being a pudgy, overfed kid was more than simply unpleasant. This district was a cluster of seven-story prefabricated concrete apartment blocks standing like dominoes among open parkland and playing fields. Few families knew each other here, so older boys could prey on kids like me as we walked to school each morning. My mother always gave me fifteen kopeks for sweets at the school buffet. But I often had to hand those three copper coins over to bigger kids who ambushed me along the way. They knew I couldn't defend myself.

Finally Grigori, one of the guys in my building who had rescued me several times, gave me some good advice. "If you're going to live out here," he said, looking around the open fields, "you're going to have to learn to defend yourself."

But I didn't know where to begin to learn this important skill. Then, that summer, I almost drowned while wading in a pond. My mother decided that I had to learn how to swim, even if I didn't seem otherwise athletically inclined.

She entered me in a swimming program for boys and girls offered at the SKA, Soviet Army sports complex, not far from Samarskaya Square in the center of the city. To get there, I either had to wake up early and ride in with my mother on the shuttle bus to the Hydroelectric Institute, or take the trolley. I almost drowned again before learning to swim. But within three months I was the best underwater swimmer in my group, which included boys as old as fourteen. I could dive in at one end of the long pool, swim underwater 150 feet, then turn and swim halfway back, all on the same breath. The coach, a pretty young woman, was impressed.

"Sasha," she told me one afternoon, "I could make a decent swimmer out of you."

I was selected for the advanced group, which trained for competition. But there was a problem I had not anticipated. At the SKA complex the boys and girls were expected to be well behaved and obedient to all rules. But I had discovered a real aversion to mindless discipline. One of the rules was no jumping from the high board, even during our twenty-minute "free" warm-up period. But I loved to jump from the board. Before I could make a name for myself as a swimming champion, I was caught leaping from the board and dismissed from the program.

"At least you learned how to swim, Sanya," my mother said.

I had learned to swim so well that I felt like a fish in the water. But I had learned more than just the skill. Although I was still pudgy, I knew that I had the coordination to be an athlete. And on my way back from the pool that afternoon, I had spotted an interesting poster from the trolley window. There were openings in the boys' wrestling program at the Spartak sports complex, which was administered by the city's trade union association. This complex, in a new building not far from the river, was a well-equipped sports center. At Spartak hundreds of boys and girls were taught wrestling, boxing, gymnastics, rowing, and team sports like volleyball and basketball. In the winter there was Nordic skiing and ice-skating.

My first day at the Spartak center was almost my last. I found the strength test to qualify for wrestling classes too challenging. The coach, Alexey Karanov, lined up all the ten-year-olds and had us attempt pull-ups, rope climbs to the echoing ceiling above, and tumbling on mats. He watched us like a peasant examining livestock. One of the most difficult tests was kneeling on a mat and bending backward until the top of your head touched the mat behind your ankles. Every time I tried, I collapsed. But I did manage the tumbling better than most boys. It was my natural limberness, which had developed during my swimming, that kept me in the program.

After I had fallen backward in a heap for the sixth time, Coach Karanov took me aside. He was a stocky, well-muscled young man in his late twenties with a wide, open face and the patience of a natural teacher. Alexey Karanov had been one of the city's best wrestlers and an honor graduate of the local Institute of Physical Culture. "You're just not strong enough to benefit from these classes," he said. "Go home and practice the back bend. Return in a month." He smiled to reassure me. "If you can pass the physical test then, you're in the program. If not, you'll have to wait until next year."

That summer my family moved again, to Microrayon 7, a raw new suburban neighborhood. The five-floor apartment blocks were surrounded by treeless, muddy lots. It was up to the people themselves to do the landscaping. Each building was organized around an individual *podyesd*, or entrance. On summer evenings and weekends the residents planted trees and grass, and dug ponds, which would one day be great for fishing and ice-skating. We now had a two-room apartment with a balcony and a kitchen you could actually walk around in. And we had a nice Caucasian rug with bright geometric patterns to decorate the living room.

It was on that oriental carpet that I practiced the Spartak back bend, hour after hour. I was clumsy but determined. That September, while other kids shoveled dirt outside after school or studied in their kitchens, I worked alone in our apartment, my knees planted firmly on the carpet, my arms arched behind me as

I bent, the muscles of my gut stretched taut. At first I piled pillows behind me to break my fall. Then I struggled without them.

Finally, after three weeks, I managed the back bend without falling. Two days later I could do three repetitions. But the test required five successful back bends. My month had expired. I rode in by trolley early one Saturday morning, then nervously walked the streets until the Spartak wrestling students assembled at nine. I felt ready for the test. But when Coach Karanov led me out to the middle of the gym, with the other boys lined up across from me, I was overcome by nerves. Then I forced myself into the exercise. To my amazement, the first three back bends went perfectly, and I flipped up each time with my knees still in place. On the fourth repetition, though, my right knee slipped and the leg gave way. I was on my back, staring up at the distant wood-paneled ceiling of the gym. I had failed.

Then something strange happened. I heard applause. The other boys were walking toward me, grinning and clapping as they came. They helped me up. Coach Karanov slapped me on the back. "Sasha," he said, "I've never seen anybody try so hard. If your knee hadn't slipped, you would have made your five. Tell your parents you are in the program."

Only later did I learn that it had been my mother who had convinced the coach to give me a second chance. She realized I was a boy who needed a healthy outlet for my restless energy. And she had been worried what kind of influence I could come under from the boys on the street.

Once I was in Spartak, my life changed. I was in the fifth year at School Number Two now, on the afternoon class schedule, which left my mornings free. So three mornings a week, and all day Saturday, I spent at the gym. The coach demanded a lot from us, but he was not a mindless disciplinarian. Wrestling, he taught us, was much more than the brute physical domination of a weaker body by a stronger one. The sport required a complete union of mind and body, brain, muscle, reflex, and tactics. That was a rather mature concept for eleven-year-old boys to grasp, but it made perfect sense to me from the outset. There were almost seventy juniors who began the program that autumn, and many were two years older than me. We were told that the final team cut in the spring had room for fewer than fifteen.

I was determined to work as hard as I could on my physical conditioning and to master all the basic match moves required of us that first year. To do so, I had to be in the Spartak gym when it opened at nine each morning. Coach Karanov had a rule, one of his few inflexible requirements: Morning instruction began at nine. To reach the city center from Microrayon 7, I had to ride with my mother on the institute bus that left our apartment complex at six-thirty. I hated waking up at that hour, when it wasn't even light yet. But my mother insisted.

"Lydia Mikhailnovna," my mother's colleagues would tease her, "why do you torture your son?"

But she would only smile, knowing the sport was helping shape my character. She realized I had found a sense of purpose in my life that many adolescent boys in our neighborhood clearly lacked.

And this was especially important now. For several years I had realized there were problems between my mother and father. I had come to understand that my father had been overcome by the turmoil of his life, and had found a solution in alcohol. The war had disrupted his schooling, and he had had to complete his engineering studies at night school while working days in the aircraft factory. This left him no time to acquire the Party affiliation and draw the notice of the factory's apparatchiks, all requirements to advancement in his career. Although he was professionally qualified for a better position, he was stymied. More and more he turned to vodka to ease his shattered pride. The year after I began the Spartak wrestling program, my father moved out, and my mother filed for divorce.

Although she felt equally frustrated by the politics that controlled her institute, she had not yet lost her Socialist optimism and surrendered to bitter despair. Year after year, she dutifully renewed her application for Communist Party membership. She sincerely believed that the Party was leading the Soviet Union and the world to a bright future of justice and universal equality. She also understood that the only way to improve conditions for herself and me was through professional advancement. The key to that advancement was held by the Party. But her application was formally rejected each year, supposedly because she had not yet achieved the proper level of "political maturity."

This was simply not true. She had studied Marxism-Leninism just as hard as solid geometry and physical chemistry. But the Party remained closed to her. Although theoretically open to all Soviet citizens, Communist Party membership was rigidly controlled. Eighty-five percent of members were industrial workers or *kolkhozniki* from collective farms. Because of their political naïveté, they were easily controlled by the ten percent of the Party members drawn from reserved positions among the military and government apparatchiks. Only five percent came from the intelligentsia, which included professions such as medicine, law, and engineering. The practical effect of this unofficial Party caste system at a large industrial complex like the Kuybyshev Hydroelectric Institute was that my mother stood little hope of membership.

Perhaps because of her experience, she never encouraged me to become active in Party youth groups in school. Anyway, by my second year at Spartak, I was far more interested in wrestling than in the Young Pioneers. And as my athletic skill increased, I saw no advantage to joining the clique of smug and ambitious young politicians who controlled the Komsomol branch at School Number Two.

You could always spot a Komsomol member, we joked, by the hole in the seat of his pants—worn by sitting through endless, deadly boring meetings.

At first I tried to balance my schoolwork with wrestling, mainly because there were many subjects that interested me, particularly the hard sciences. The teachers proudly emphasized the "Soviet" contributions to science, although I learned that many of the breakthroughs—such as Mendeleyev's periodic table—had been made by prerevolutionary Russians. Nevertheless, I was fascinated by mathematics and physics. Biology was also one of my favorite classes, although the textbooks seemed to waste a lot of time straining to link the laws governing natural processes with Marxism-Leninism atheism. And these books also strained hard to avoid the one issue we were all fascinated by, sex.

The school subject that I liked the best, however, was geography. My geography textbooks and atlas were endlessly engrossing. I could spend a whole evening curled up on the Caucasian rug reading about the tribes along the Amazon River or the gold mines and oil fields of the Siberian taiga. Sergei, a friend from school who lived nearby, also loved geography. He was in a motocross club, which took as much of his free time as the Spartak wrestling did of mine. But we always found a few hours each week to "study" geography together. Many winter nights we would sit at my kitchen table with the atlas open before us, playing a game.

"Find Atlanta in America," Sergei would challenge, staring at the second hand of his watch.

I would have fifteen seconds to find that city or river.

Playing the geography game with Sergei made me think about America. The teachers taught us that America was a large, rich country, which had been settled in the eighteenth and the nineteenth centuries just like Russia under the czars. I had a feeling that Americans were probably not much different from us. But then in history classes, which focused heavily on the Revolution and the Great Patriotic War, we were taught that American capitalists had tried to keep their country out of the war so that the Nazis could destroy the Soviet Union. After Pearl Harbor, the capitalists conspired with British imperialists to delay the Second Front until the Nazis had almost bled my country white.

In these same history classes, though, I learned that American lend-lease weapons, including the rugged P-39 Airacobra, flown by Soviet aces like Alexander Pokryshkin, had helped turn back the fascist hordes. And, of course, I remembered my grandmother's stories about the American yellow shoes that had kept my mother's feet from freezing, and the canned food, powdered eggs, and chocolate that had saved the family from starvation during the war. But I was taught that, although the whole world had been united to defeat the Nazis, the Americans' invention of the atomic bomb had renewed their imperialist ambitions. And now the Socialist Motherland was the principal target of those nuclear weapons. That made me both sad and angry.

But I couldn't really hate everything about the West, especially their music. Every Saturday night I tuned our shortwave radio to the Voice of America to listen to the rock music show. Although I didn't understand more than three words of English, I memorized the lyrics to songs by Three Dog Night, Blood, Sweat and Tears, and Creedence Clearwater Revival. Maybe the music was just propaganda, as the Komsomol leaders warned us, but it certainly was exciting.

However, politics really did not interest me much. In school we learned that Stalin had inherited the mantle of the Great Lenin and had gone on to lead our country to victory in the war. Then, we were taught, certain personal "excesses" had tarnished his place in history. Outside of school, people usually avoided talking about Stalin. And when they did, it was with a mixture of respect and fear, a strange, grudging reverence. Sometimes at my grandmother's house, I would overhear whispered conversations in the kitchen, when the older people would talk about the Stalin years. They might mention the "Black Raven," which was apparently a police car that had come in the night to take people away. Where it took them, I had no idea.

Later, my mother brought home a copy of *Roman Gazeta* that bore the yellow cardboard "Restricted" tag from her institute's library. When asked about this, she said the issue contained the famous novel *One Day in the Life of Ivan Denisovich* by a writer named Alexander Solzhenitsyn. I had never heard of him. He certainly wasn't mentioned in my literature books at school.

"What's it about?" I asked mother.

"It's not for you, Sasha," was all she said.

She didn't hide the book, despite the yellow label. I hoped there might be some sexy passages. So one evening when I got home early from practice, I sat down in the kitchen and began to read the book. I was shocked that my mother should choose such a work. The language was terrible, with all these crude, antisocial convicts and their prison guards exchanging foul insults like "fucker" and "shit face."

I read enough of the book to trouble me. Why would a major literary magazine in Moscow publish this kind of thing? Then I heard on the radio that Solzhenitsyn was "a disgusting person, who has sold his soul to imperialist circles."

But literature was less important than wrestling. I was now on the morning class schedule at school, so every afternoon I ran from the commuter train depot all the way to the Spartak sports complex. The coach had weeded out the habitual latecomers and had instituted a good-hearted punishment for those who were occasionally late. My group would line up in a double rank with everyone clutching a gym shoe. The latecomer had to run this gauntlet, once if he was less than two minutes late, two or three times if he arrived more than five minutes after roll call.

My first year I'd been able to master the standard tactics of classical Greco-Roman Olympic wrestling that Coach Karanov had such trouble hammering into the skulls of many of the other boys. And the linked sequence of grips, throws, and countergrips had come easily to me, long before the other guys understood them. In fact, whenever the coach needed someone to demonstrate new tactics in the ring, he usually chose me.

But when we finally began our interclub matches against teams from SKA, Dynamo, or Trud, I was consistently defeated in the ring. I knew *how* to maneuver, but I was just not strong enough to make my holds stick or to toss my opponent. Most of the fellows in my weight class were my height. However, they were a lot thinner, with taut, wiry muscles.

For the next two seasons, I muddled through with a mediocre record. Then one afternoon at the Spartak complex, I overheard two boys from the Metalurg team going over the roster for the matches.

"Who's this Zuyev?" a boy asked his friend.

"Oh, don't worry about him," the other fellow answered. "He's a weakling."

I stepped back in the hallway, my ears burning with embarrassment. And as if to prove their point, I lost both my matches that afternoon within three minutes.

That was a Saturday afternoon. All day Sunday I moped about the apartment, trying to decide what to do. I simply couldn't face the continued embarrassment of defeat, knowing deep down that I was potentially one of the best wrestlers at the Spartak complex. Then I made my decision. The Kuybyshev Aviation Institute had an excellent gymnasium, with a complete weight room equipped with bodybuilding apparatus. The next afternoon I was there, requesting use of the facilities. Officially you had to be sixteen to work with weights, and I was not yet fifteen. But the coach there was sympathetic and signed me on.

For the next six weeks I took the electric train to the Aviation Institute every evening instead of to the Spartak complex. As far as Coach Karanov knew, I had simply dropped out, another disappointed student wrestler. But I had another plan. Before, I had never tried systematically to increase my strength, muscle tone, and endurance. Now I worked at it. My mother even borrowed barbells from someone at her office for me to use at home. And one of the first things I did was stop eating sweets. Instead of chocolate pastries and honey rolls, I ate bowls of kasha, chopped beef, and salad, and I asked my mother to stock the refrigerator with fresh fruit and milk.

At the Aviation Institute weight room, I began with light barbells and worked myself up to heavy bench presses and long, multiple repetitions on the spring apparatus to build up my thighs and back muscles. Four weeks later the fat had shrunk to muscle. At the end of six weeks I could bench-press 130 pounds, which was 20 pounds over the norm for my group at Spartak.

Late one warm Tuesday afternoon after school, I found Coach Karanov in the locker room.

"I'm back, Alexey Ivanovich," I said. "Will you give me another chance?"

He looked at me thoughtfully, then nodded. "I will, Sasha," he said, "but only if you're serious this time."

And that I was. I never missed another day of practice. Every evening I stayed there after the training was over to work out with weights. When the coach gave us twenty push-ups, I did twenty-one. If we had to run a mile, I ran a quarter of a mile more.

And I began winning matches. I was chosen for the 150-pound class traveling team. It was a real honor to ride the train with my friends on the first road trip to Syzran, where we defeated the Spartak juniors in straight matches. As the wrestling program wound up at the end of that school year, I had the great pleasure of hearing opponents actually groan when they read the roster and saw my name matched against them.

But I wasn't so successful at School Number Two. The academic standards were high, but I just did not feel challenged intellectually. In fact, by the time I was fifteen, school bored me. I was only interested in wrestling and didn't have the time for my studies. This attitude, of course, kept me out of the political intrigues of Komsomol and put me in bad favor with the faculty.

Like other bored adolescent boys, I became rebellious and joined forces with two close friends, Vovka Ivanov and Igor Devyatkin, to harass the teachers. We always chose the last table at the rear of the classroom, which the teachers had dubbed "Kolyma," for the Siberian gold mine prison where the hardest tattooed criminals were banished. One of our favorite targets was a chubby math teacher we scornfully called Mishka. Vovka and Igor helped me make poor Mishka's life difficult. We booby-trapped his chalk pieces by drilling them hollow and put thumbtacks under the piled lesson forms on his desk so that he stuck his thumb. Once we used a stepladder to tape a chunk of ice on the glass lampshade hanging above his desk, so the water dripped steadily onto his head. But our best prank was when we pulled the pins from the hinges of the classroom door. As Mishka strode into the room, the heavy wooden door clattered on top of him and set off uncontrollable laughter.

He knew where to find the villains. A moment later he grabbed me by the collar and tried to slap me. I wasn't about to be hit by a butterball like him and twisted his arm behind his back. Ten minutes later I was standing at attention before our principal, "Rema" Alexandrovna, the tough, middle-aged woman who tried to run her school fairly for both faculty and students.

"Zuyev," she stated coldly, as if she were a State prosecutor, "your mother will be here tomorrow. You are to be expelled."

Somehow my mother managed to patch things up the next day.

Then my friends and I were caught sneaking wine into the school Red Army party. We shared a bottle with an old cleaning lady, but she informed on us the next day anyway. Again I was hauled before Rema. "This is what you want, isn't it?" She calmly lifted a printed Ministry of Education form from her desk. "This is your 'wolf's ticket.'"

It was a formal expulsion form, the "ticket" to a dead-end life. Any youth expelled from school was excluded from further training, either academic or vocational, condemned to a life of manual labor at best, or even a criminal career.

Again my mother intervened successfully. But my academic record itself was bad enough to keep me from the ninth and tenth years of academic study at the school. In fact, I had no interest in more school. I told them that I wanted to leave classrooms behind and get on with adult life. Rema noted that, in any event, my poor grades probably meant I would flunk the eighth-year exams.

My mother turned from Rema's desk to glare at me, her face set in anger. "I cannot believe that my son is this stupid."

"Evidently, Lydia Mikhailnovna," Rema said scornfully, "he is both stupid and lazy."

My pride was hurt, which, of course, was what they both intended. "If you give me a chance," I said, "I'll show you I'm not stupid."

For the rest of that spring, I cut back on my wrestling training and worked hard, preparing for the exams. I studied on the train when the team took road trips. I studied on the trolley riding to and from practice. I studied hard at home each night. And when I entered the test rooms that June, I felt confident. The math and science exams were rigorous, but I passed in the upper quarter. I scored high on geography. Soviet political history didn't interest me much, but I managed a passing grade. I liked military history, and I did very well on the section about the defense of the Motherland. I had made my point. Now no one could call me either stupid or lazy. But I'd had enough of this theoretical classroom study. I still intended to skip the final two academic years at School Number Two and to become an apprentice electrician at Kuybyshev's electro-technology vocational school.

Being fifteen that summer, I was expected to attend an organized vocational camp or to intern at an industrial institute in the region. Since I was always eager to travel, I managed to land a summer job with a geological survey team attached to the Hydroelectric Institute. The three-man, two-boy team, led by a friendly engineer named Yuri Sokalov, was assigned to the east bank of the Volga, covering a region over a hundred miles long. Our responsibility was to measure the electromagnetic potential in the bedrock so that a complete geological survey chart of the region could be drawn.

It was interesting work. I was just a helper, but I learned a lot about geology and about the grown-up world of men. Yuri took pride in his profession and made sure we did a thorough job. My responsibilities included unloading the heavy steel probes and coils of cable that we used to set up our measurement grids. The first day, the men let me swing the eighteen-pound sledgehammer to drive in the steel stakes and then hook up the insulated cable.

We worked outdoors, in the rye and wheat fields of the collective farms and sometimes along the sandy banks of the Volga. If we completed a day's assigned survey tract early, the team would go for a swim and fish until after sundown. Some evenings we cooked up our catch in a big sooty kettle over a campfire on the river beach. The men taught us how to make a delicately spiced fish soup they called *oukha*, which combined the essence of fresh bream and pike with a tang of woodsmoke.

They also taught me how to play cards and drink vodka. Only an idiot drank warm vodka straight from the bottle without food, they said. On the nights when we split a bottle of well-chilled Sibirskaya, I was responsible for laying out the plates of sliced pickles, boiled potatoes, rye bread, and butter. Then, when the thimble glasses were filled, we all made our toast, exhaled loudly, tossed back the cold vodka, and breathed in through a thick wedge of bread before eating a snack.

They never let me drink very much, though. And when I joined the ritual, I remembered the advice my mother had given me after the escapades of the wine at the school party.

"Sasha," she said, "I can't tell you not to drink. But always remember where, when, how much, and with whom to drink, and you won't have trouble in your life."

One Saturday night that August when we were staying at the dormitory on a dairy *kolkhoz*, I hiked over to a nearby summer camp that was having a Komsomol dance. This was the kind of camp where well-connected city kids supposedly worked side by side with the farmers to bring in the harvest, but actually wasted a lot of time on the volleyball court. When I entered the camp refectory, I spotted the red paper banners proclaiming the eternal solidarity between urban youth and the collective farmers. Another boring Komsomol affair. But then I saw there were two distinct groups: a handful of self-conscious city kids, including several pretty girls, outnumbered by a crowd of young *kolkhozniki* in shabby blue work trousers with a telltale wide seam on the leg. Some of the farm boys were drunk. They insisted on cutting in to dance with the city girls, even though the farmers had no idea how to dance to the Beatles or Pink Floyd records the students had brought to the camp.

I saw a pretty blond girl trying to dance with a city boy in a V-neck sweater, but a drunk, lanky farm guy who looked too old to be there kept pushing his way in. When the shorter boy from

Samara tried to stop him, the drunk *kolkhoznik* elbowed him aside and tried to get the girl in a bear hug.

I shoved my way in and told the guy to leave her alone.

He laughed, his mouth full of rotten teeth. "Sit on my dick," he swore, then threw a clumsy punch.

I dodged the blow, tripped him, and had him in a neck lock before he hit the dance floor. The guy was tall and had heavy shoulders, but he didn't know a thing about wrestling. Before I could really hurt him, the adult monitors intervened and hauled him off to sober up.

The girl's name was Marina. She thanked me, then jotted down her phone number in Samara. "Please call me before school starts again," she said. All in all, I thought hiking back to the dormitory in the cool starlight, it had not been a bad night.

When I went to see Marina back in Samara at the end of the summer, I took a bus to Microrayon 4, a neighborhood of well-made twelve-story brick apartment blocks along a broad, tree-lined avenue named for Cheluskin, a famous Soviet pilot. This was the nicest district in the city. People called it Micro-Israel, because many of the famous Jewish scientists from the institutes were supposed to live here. On the ground floor of Marina's building there was a row of nice shops and cafés.

When I went into Marina's *podyesd,* the babushka in the concierge box gave me a stern look, as if I had no right to be there. The elevator was clean and ran smoothly. The landing on Marina's floor had only four doors. I stood there for a moment, wondering if I had the right building. It seemed impossible that only four families lived on each floor of this large building. But I wasn't lost. Marina greeted me, led me into their long sitting room that faced the street. They had four tall, double-glazed windows and a balcony with a wrought-iron table and chairs. In the vestibule off the entrance, I saw the doors of two bedrooms and the open doorway of a kitchen that was almost as big as the main room of my apartment.

Marina's living room looked like something out of a European magazine: oriental rugs, Scandinavian furniture, and even a bar with tall swivel stools. Through the glass bar front I saw bottles of imported Scotch whisky, Italian liqueurs, and French brandy. A big Japanese tape recorder sat next to their color television set. When I'd peeked in the kitchen, I had seen a tall refrigerator with double doors. Nobody that I knew lived this way.

The men on the survey crew had joked scornfully about the *shishka,* the Party "bosses," whom you found at the top of any organization. Whenever the crew's work orders were fouled up or a piece of equipment was late in arriving, the men would blame the *shishka,* who were probably all too busy stocking their apartments with luxury goods to sign the paperwork. Now I was standing in one of those apartments, which I had only imagined were the fanciful subject of frustrated jokes before.

Marina offered me a whisky, but I settled for a stick of American chewing gum instead. She showed me her French and Italian fashion magazines, then told me she attended a special school where all the classes were taught in English.

"*All* the classes?" I asked. "Even physics and chemistry?"

"Yes," she said proudly. "We speak, read, and write English all day."

This was amazing. I wondered how far she had to travel to attend such a school. "What do your parents say about your going away?"

She seemed confused but then answered nervously. "Sasha," she said, "the school is here in Samara."

When you learned foreign languages, there were lots of interesting professions open to you. "How do you apply for this school? What's the exam like?"

"The school," she said, "is not like you think. Your parents have to have the correct position for you to enter."

I took in the silk Kirghiz carpets, the bar, and the Finnish furniture. "What does your father do?" I asked.

"Oh," she said, "he is on the city's Party Committee."

Riding the commuter train back out to my neighborhood, I felt a moment of regret that my mother did not have the *blat* needed to secure me a place in one of those special schools. The devil take all of them, I thought. I would become an electrician, land a good job in one of the aircraft factories, and make money on the side repairing the shoddy work the State construction enterprises did in all the new apartments.

But when I went back to School Number Two to collect my academic records before registering at the electro-technology school, I found Rema had locked up my files. She was gone for vacation. Then Coach Karanov called me down to the Spartak center. He explained that Rema Alexandrovna had asked him to talk sense to me. Apparently students in the vocational school were not encouraged to compete in sports competitions within the Russian Republic.

"Sasha," he said, "you've got a real chance at the 170-pound championship. The team needs you."

Once more I sensed my mother's hand in this conspiracy. But the chance of traveling to Moscow and winning a weight-division title was a lot more appealing than earning money as an electrician. I had struggled too hard to throw away my chance at a title. Most of the boys I knew wore their hair long, fashioned after the pictures of Western rock stars we sometimes saw in magazines. That was how you got the girls. But wrestlers could not wear long hair because that just gave your opponent another handle to grab. It wasn't fair, but I knew you had to give up one thing you wanted to have something else you wanted more.

That September I began the upper form of advanced academic courses to prepare students for professional institutes and universities. But my first love was still wrestling. I traveled with the Spartak senior team now, coached and refereed the juniors. Because I correctly assumed Rema had conspired with Coach Karanov to keep me in the academic program, I thought she would not mind if I missed a few days' classes traveling with the team. I was wrong. My homeroom teacher, Ludmilla—"the Rat with Glasses" to me and my friends—turned me in to Rema for unexcused absences.

Once more Rema dangled the dread wolf's ticket over her desk blotter. "It's not too late to throw you out."

I got her point. From then on, I had to be a student first and a wrestler second.

All ninth- and tenth-year boys were required to attend twice-weekly military training classes at the school. Our instructor was a rather indecisive retired Army lieutenant colonel named Nikolai Gusev. I didn't care for the mindless drill ritual in the school yard, but I enjoyed handling Kalashnikov rifles and hand grenades and studying famous battles like Stalingrad and Kursk. Still a rebel, however, I made it plain to the good comrade lieutenant colonel that military training was not my favorite class.

The next summer I was not eager to sweat through another

vocational camp, doing the same work as the men but earning only twenty rubles a month. Oleg, a friend of mine, said his father could get me in as a summer replacement worker at a local machine-tool factory that produced precision boring and milling machines and lathes for the aircraft plants and for export. When I took the job, I hoped to make contacts that might lead to an apprenticeship at the plant. Skilled professional toolmakers earned 500 rubles a month and had access to cheap vacations on the Black Sea or Baltic.

Even as a summer replacement, I would earn 150 rubles a month, a great salary for a kid of sixteen. Maybe I couldn't yet afford real blue jeans, but I had already ordered my first pair of bell-bottom slacks from the girls at the fashion design school.

A master tool and die maker named Alexander Konstantinovich was my mentor in the export shop. I had heard a lot about the high-quality work at the plant. Machine tools from this factory were exported around the world, where they earned hard currency and compared favorably to similar products from West Germany or America. So I was shocked the first day on the job to find the assembly floor practically silent with men lounging around in groups playing cards and dominoes.

My mentor explained the situation. It was the first workday of the month, in this case July. All the factories that supplied us parts and raw materials were also beginning the month. They would not be required to complete their month's quota under their ministry or directorate's all-important Plan for thirty days. Neither would we. So all across the industrial heartland of the Russian Republic, workers like these sat around the factories, watching the clock, smoking to kill time.

But at our plant the men eventually got bored with card games and used expensive machine-tool steel to make kitchen knives for their wives. Konstantinovich taught me how to weld beautiful stainless-steel anchors that I could peddle to men with small fishing boats on the river.

Then, in the third week of the month, our regular quota of metal stock and electrical supplies began arriving. Things got busy. But still the tool and die makers and assemblers only completed ten machines a day. That was the norm. They were paid the maximum rate to meet that norm. If they completed more than that number, they risked having the norm increased by the factory bosses. So we worked slowly to produce only ten machines every workday.

By the end of the summer I had lost any illusions about a satisfying career in Soviet industry.

But I certainly wanted to pursue some kind of profession to match my interest in technology. One Sunday that autumn I watched the weekly military television program, *I Serve the Soviet Union*. The entire hour was devoted to the Air Force (VVS) and the Air Defense Force (PVO). The program focused on young officer cadets undergoing pilot training at an air base in the Transcaucasus. Guys not much older than me were strapping themselves into the cockpits of jet trainers and taking off into the clear southern sky. That looked interesting. The next week's program was devoted to Soviet Army engineers, and my mother encouraged me to think about applying to a military institute specializing in construction engineering. But I couldn't forget the image of those young cadets flying jet aircraft.

I went down to the Army *komandatura* headquarters and inquired about the process of applying for an opening at a military aviation academy. Having done some preliminary research, as I usually did before approaching bureaucrats, I'd learned that this was the first day that application forms for aviation academies would be available. But the bored administrative officer I asked said there were "no more openings." Apparently he thought I wanted to try for a place at the military helicopter academy in nearby Syzran. I then realized that you even needed *blat* in the military. Only boys with influential families went to that academy, because there was plenty of high-paying work for civilian helicopter pilots after they finished their military obligation. And I learned that the Air Force's Kacha Higher Military Aviation School for Pilots near Volgagrad, which was nearest to home, was also inaccessible without *blat*. But the officer finally conceded that there were still openings at the PVO Higher Military Aviation Academy at Armavir down in the south of the republic. The PVO flew supersonic jet fighters, not lumbering transports or fighter-bombers. That prospect appealed to me.

In October 1977 I approached Lieutenant Colonel Gusev, my military training instructor at School Number Two.

"Comrade Lieutenant Colonel," I said respectfully, "can you

spare the time to help me with my application to the Armavir Higher Military Aviation School for Pilots?"

He was obviously shocked. "Zuyev," he exclaimed, "*you* are interested in the military?"

But he quickly overcame his shock, realizing that, even if I wasn't selected, my application was a sign of his good example and diligence.

Rema, the principal, was even more skeptical when I requested a formal transcript of my academic records. "Young man," she said scornfully, "you will never make it."

But Lieutenant Colonel Gusev was the secretary of the school faculty's Party collective. He was determined to see me placed at Armavir. In quick order, I became a member in good standing of the school's Komsomol *aktiv*, at least on paper. Then Rema got to work on the written evidence of my fine academic career. Her résumé of my academic record was a monument to bureaucratic cunning. To read her words, I was a brilliant, dedicated young Communist scholar and athlete, whose only fault was accepting too many challenges (which explained my less than stellar exam grades).

I discovered that over 100,000 tenth-year boys from the entire Soviet Union were preparing applications for the twelve aviation academies, 20,000 for Armavir alone. It was estimated that only about 2,000 would pass the physical and aptitude examinations, and from that group, only 300 would eventually be selected for the class beginning in September 1978. All that winter I worked on the tedious application process. Finally, in February 1978, I was ordered back to the *komandatura* to take my initial physical examination. I had passed the first hurdle. But I still had to pass a battery of written tests and at least three more increasingly rigorous physical exams.

In mid-February my energy and determination were shattered with the news that my father had died of a sudden heart attack. I was staggered by grief, and by remorse that I had not been able to understand him better.

After my parents' divorce, I had finally learned about my father's childhood during the war. As a boy of eleven, he had been caught in a Nazi round-up of villagers near Smolensk and shipped to Poland to work as a farm laborer. Luckily the family he worked for were kind. He ate at their table and was able to read a few

Russian books from their library. But when he finally was freed by the Red Army in 1944 and found his way back home, his village was devastated. He somehow traveled to Samara, where he had relatives. My father had never told me about all this because of the stigma the State placed on anyone who had been captured by the Germans and taken West. With typical paranoia, Stalin was convinced all former prisoners of the Germans returned as imperialist spies.

My mother had made sure I made no mention of his captivity on my academy application. And my father was gone before I could ever talk to him about his experience.

Only three weeks before, I had seen him standing outside a State liquor store one afternoon, like so many other Soviet men who had lost their way, waiting to find two others so that they could pool their money to "go three on a bottle" of cheap vodka. I had wanted to tell him of my plans to become a military pilot, but the shame of the circumstances kept me from approaching him. It was the last time I saw him alive.

I was still in emotional turmoil from my father's funeral when I took the second physical examination, this one designed to eliminate all but the fittest applicants from the Kuybyshev Oblast. The cardiologist discovered an irregular systole beat on my EKG. I explained that my father had just died and asked to be retested. Once more, Coach Karanov came to my rescue by arranging the EKG at a friendly sports-medicine center, where I passed the exam ten days later.

But I was not so lucky with the vestibular balance test, designed to provoke vertigo. I had to sit on a revolving chair with my eyes closed and swing my head back and forth. I immediately broke into a clammy sweat and the woman doctor stopped the test. I told her I had been training too hard and requested another test.

When I came back at the end of February, I brought with me a foil-wrapped block of dark chocolate from the city's best confection factory. This, I told her, was a small *prezant*, a gesture of thanks for her patience. It was the first bribe I ever gave. I passed the test. But the act left a bad taste in my mouth.

The written examinations were draining. And when I received the news I had passed them, I was almost too exhausted for elation. Which was just as well: These exams were simply a ticket to even more rigorous tests and interviews to be administered at Armavir itself in June.

I still was not certain of acceptance at the academy. But at least I had made it through the first two selections. And in the process, I had grown absolutely determined to become a fighter pilot.

— 4 —
Armavir Higher Aviation Academy
1978–82

O ver two thousand candidates for the academy arrived in Armavir by train in late June 1978. For me the three-day trip was pleasant and exciting. I had certainly been proud to visit Moscow the year before, but the idea of traveling to the South enticed me. Armavir was in the valley of the Kuban River, part of the Krasnodar Territory in the far southwest corner of the Russian Federation. And my Spartak teammates who had visited the city spoke highly of its grapes and cherries—*and* the pretty girls at the local nurse-midwife school.

Armavir's buildings were handsome stone, with red tile roofs. The city's name was Armenian for "valley of wind." And the residents included many wealthy Armenian and Kazakh merchant families who had somehow retained their wealth after the Revolution.

On Spartak road trips I'd learned the trick of using local taxi drivers as unofficial guides to a new city; they were always in the know, and seemed proud to share their inside knowledge with young guys from out of town. Riding the taxi from the train station to the candidates' reception camp with several other candidate cadets I'd met on the train, the taxi driver showed us the large nursing school and teachers' academy.

But it would be a long time before any of us could visit these girls. My train had carried boys like myself, mostly seventeen, with a few as old as nineteen. I had ridden in the same compartment with six young guys from Samara. At home we probably would have been rivals, but as the train rumbled south, we quickly became "Samarskiye," as the sons of Samara proudly called themselves.

I shared a huge tent with several of my new Samarskiye buddies and over a hundred boys from all over the Union. Anatoli Savelyev, one of my new friends, had a brother at the academy who was a cadet sergeant in his fourth year. His name was Valery, and he came to visit us with another, older Samarskiye cadet soon after we arrived. As new candidates, still dressed in civilian clothes, we were certainly impressed by these fellows. They wore their uniforms well and had an unmistakable disciplined confidence about them. Valery Savelyev was a husky, open-faced gymnast who had won many athletic prizes, but was also one of the academy's best students and the chief cadet sergeant. Yuri Krasin was tall, lean, and handsome. He had been selected for the academy from the ranks of the Kremlin detachment that formed the honor guard at Lenin's Tomb.

They quietly briefed us on the selection process. There would be four weeks of physical, psychological, and academic examinations, interspersed with less formal interviews. All the time we would be observed and ranked. At the end of the month, only 300 of the 2,300 candidates in this camp would be selected. The successful cadets would then undergo a month of tough basic military training.

"Be sure to obey *every* order immediately," Valery said. "And never answer back or argue."

Yuri warned us about trying to leave camp without permission. "That's a quick ticket home," he said.

I kept their advice in mind as we sweated through the endless tests, physical exams, and interviews.

The physical examinations and strength tests were our first hurdle. Although all the candidates had been screened by doctors in their home cities, the PVO aviation medical staff physicians had their own high selection standards. We had to have absolutely perfect vision and show no predisposition for eye problems. My EKG showed no irregularities, but other boys were disqualified for problems undetected earlier. I found it interesting that several of the real musclemen from the bodybuilding clubs were washed out; apparently they had used steroids, and the drugs had damaged their hearts. Our bones and muscles were carefully probed and examined to make certain we had never suffered from a poor diet. Overall, the guys from the country were in better condition than the city boys, both because there was more fresh food on the farms and because hard outdoor work had built them up. These honest, unsophisticated country kids were really eager because becoming a military officer was a chance to escape the dead-end drudgery of the State farms.

I was surprised how tough the strength tests were and glad I had worked so hard at Spartak. Our upper-body strength was tested with spring apparatus similar to the ones I had used in my weight training. I passed easily, but many likely candidates failed. Our endurance was measured by a timed 3,000-yard run, repeated 100-yard sprints, and a 100-yard swimming test. Again, fellows who had scored high on the academic exams were cut after the endurance tests.

Our reflexes, reaction time, and hand-eye coordination were tested over a three-day period in a very simple cockpit simulator that combined a control stick and a crude "gunsight." Sitting in a regular chair, you worked the stick to keep the gunsight ring aligned along a waving curve on a moving scroll. It was a tough challenge. We also had to follow rapid commands to write an endless series of 0's and X's in random patterns. These tests broke us down into four aptitude groups. The lowest group were washed out; those in group three could continue only if they scored well in the academic tests; and the top two groups qualified in motor skills. I was in group one.

Many of the candidates were obviously not up to the tough academic and practical-skill tests. They came from Central Asian republics like Kazakhstan and Kirghizia. Some guys ridiculed these "national heroes," because they had been selected as token candidates to demonstrate the fraternal Socialist bonds of the Union. In reality, there were almost no non-Russian or non-Slav pilots in either the PVO or the VVS.

And the demanding math, physics, and Russian language examinations weeded out some of the candidates from State farms whose rural schools had not prepared them well. The winnowing process continued through a series of personal interviews. Although all the officers on the panels wore the same uniforms, our Samarskiye mentors had warned us that there would always be a zampolit political officer present and sometimes a man from the KGB's Osobii Otdel "Special Department." Lucky for me, Lieutenant Colonel Gusev, my military instructor at School Number Two, had attached a glowing testimonial to the *Kharacteristika* "Personal Characteristics" record that accompanied my application forms.

The interviewers seemed satisfied that my family background did not include any "enemies of the people," criminals, or psychopaths. And they seemed genuinely impressed with my mother's academic and professional accomplishments. They verified that no one in my family was a member of a religious sect or ever traveled abroad or had been a prisoner of the Germans. Of course I did not reveal my father's captivity during the war. Since he'd been a civilian child, there was no military record. And, fortunately, both Ivanov and Rema had done a masterful job of disguising my delinquent attitude and rebellious behavior.

After a hot, exhausting month of basic training, I found myself standing in Armavir's Lenin Square with three hundred other successful candidates, taking the Soviet military's Oath of Loyalty. We solemnly promised to be "honorable, brave, disciplined, and vigilant" soldiers who would defend the homeland, sparing neither blood nor life if necessary to achieve full victory over our enemies.

"And if I should break this solemn oath," I recited in unison with the boys around me, "then let me suffer the severe penalties of Soviet law and the universal hatred and contempt of the Soviet people."

A young senior lieutenant shouted an order and we marched off the square with the band playing the Air Force Anthem. Our polished boots sounded with the drumbeat.

"We were born to turn fantasy into fact," we sang, referring to the miracle of flight. "Higher! Higher! Higher!" The brass instruments gleamed in the southern sun; the drums pounded. "Faster! Faster! Faster!" Our column marched down the broad avenue toward the walled Armavir Higher Military Aviation School for Pilots on the outskirts of the city. I was no longer a schoolboy. Now I was a Soviet soldier.

I was proud that my mother attended the ceremony. My selection for the academy was certainly proof that I was neither stupid nor lazy, as Rema had once scornfully suggested. My mother took me aside to explain that she hoped to marry again, to an engineer named Valentin. But she wanted my permission. My grandmother had already raised the subject with me. "Give her your blessing, Sasha," she'd said. "Your mother should not have to grow old alone as I have." Naturally I wished my mother happiness.

The academy was an attractive, well-shaded complex of dormitories, classroom blocks, and a military airfield that bore the call sign "Burav." First-year cadets were assigned to a long three-floored dormitory facing the cement-block wall that enclosed the front of the academy.

The top of this wall was studded with broken wine bottles set in the cement, a crude but efficient deterrent to cadets tempted to slip into the city without leave. "Actually," one of the older cadets joked, "the glass is there to keep all those horny, good-looking nurses from assaulting you handsome young fellows."

Jokes aside, we learned on our first day that we were expected to act like soldiers, not simply privileged students at a State academy. On our familiarization tour of the campus, the escort officer pointed out the *gaupvakhta,* the guardhouse manned by tough conscripts of the school battalion who performed the manual labor and administrative duties at the academy.

"They don't like you *kursanty* very much," the captain warned us.

I don't know who stared at my group with more menace, the guards or their German shepherds. Stealing State property, being absent without leave, or showing disrespect to a commissioned officer were all offenses punishable by time in the guardhouse.

The Armavir Academy, we learned, had an honored history. Founded in 1940, the academy had barely begun classes when it had to be evacuated as the Nazi armies advanced south toward the Caucasus. Once the Kuban Valley had been recaptured from the Nazis and the school reopened, cadets were pushed through accelerated training, and many flew their first combat sortie directly from the school's airfield. Legendary Red Army aces like Alexander Pokryshkin and the Glinka brothers had flown Shturmoviks and American lend-lease P-39 "Kobras" from our Burav runway. Among the aviation academies of the PVO and VVS, Armavir was known as the "Kuznitsa," the Forge of Pilots.

There were about eleven hundred cadets at Armavir divided into four classes. During any given academic year, two classes would be "in the South," at air bases in Azerbaijan, receiving flight instruction on L-29 jet trainers, or in nearby Maikop, taking the advanced flight course on MiG-21 fighters. The other two classes remained at the school taking academic courses or practice flying at the Burav air base. We were expected to complete forty-three academic courses in eight semesters to graduate with a degree in aeronautical engineering. Simultaneously we would train as jet-fighter pilots and receive our wings with our commission on graduation.

I was appointed the cadet sergeant of the 112th Platoon. Even though the rank doubled the basic cadet pay from seven to fifteen rubles, I had not sought this position and found the extra responsibility annoying, considering the punishing work load that first year.

Six days a week we were rousted out of bed by the national anthem blaring on the loudspeakers at 0600 and had forty-five seconds to pull on our uniform. After a quick stop in the latrine, we fell in on the parade ground for running and calisthenics at 0610. At 0700 we were given half an hour to wash up and prepare the barracks for inspection. I had to verify that the cadets in my platoon all wore presentable uniforms and that the linen liners sewn into the collars of their blouses were changed at the regulation two-day intervals. Some guys were lucky; they had skinny necks and could keep a liner looking clean for a week.

We sat down to a good breakfast that usually included eggs, skim milk, kasha, and fresh bread and butter. The dining hall atmosphere was always friendly and relaxed. Dmitri, one of my classmates from Leningrad, came from an influential family and had studied English at a foreign language school. He had read about military academies in America, where first-year cadets were harassed and hazed by their older colleagues. We found that a totally alien concept. Here we all needed mutual support to survive the rigorous work load. The idea that cadets would actually join with the faculty to harass newcomers seemed bizarre.

We soon found out just how important the guidance and support of our older Samarskiye friends actually was. They had cautioned us in general terms during the selection process about being punctual and well disciplined. Now they had a more important warning.

"Whatever you do," Valery Savelyev told us, "don't joke

about the Party bosses, the *shishka,* or keep any controversial books or Western magazines."

Even songs, he added, could be suspect. The best advice he could give us was to form a close circle of buddies and confide only in them.

"Who's going to inform on us here in the platoon?" I asked. "We're all in this together."

Valery shook his head sadly. "No, Shurka," he said, "there are *stukachi* here, 'knockers' who report to the commandant or even to the Osobii Otdel. Your sergeant's stripes won't protect you from those little bastards."

Valery explained that the Osobii would probably try to recruit first-year guys as informers who "knocked" quietly on their office doors to report, late at night when the other cadets were sleeping. "Don't do it," he said. "Don't even listen to those shitheads. Once you're in with the Osobists, they've got you by the balls for the rest of your life."

That was advice we all took to heart.

The older Samarskiye also helped us with another unanticipated problem. A few Armavir cadets had been selected from the ranks of Army conscripts who had completed a year of service before coming here. They considered themselves tough old soldiers deserving of special privileges, and they intended to sustain this privileged status, by brute force if necessary. If a younger cadet refused to polish their boots or change their collar liner after lights-out, they would gang up to knock some sense into him. This was *dedovshcina,* the brutalizing of recruits by *deds*— "grandfather" soldiers. The practice had become widespread in the Army, especially in units where one ethnic group dominated another. In some units where *dedovshcina* was left unchecked, victimized recruits had even been tormented and humiliated into suicide. There was certainly no place for this senseless cruelty at a higher aviation academy.

The Samarskiye collared the worst of the *deds* for a quiet conversation on the parade ground. The older cadets made it clear that unfortunate accidents could happen at any time during athletics or the upcoming parachute training all first-year cadets received. The *deds* got the message.

The combination of academic courses and military training was exhausting. None of us had ever taken such advanced courses in subjects like engineering, calculus, thermodynamics, and aerodynamics. We also studied military history and tactics. Our class schedule began after breakfast at 0830 and ran to 1400. After a good lunch that always included fresh vegetables and meat or fish, we had mandatory study halls and tutorials. Unlike the civilian schools we had come from, hard study was not an option taken by a few gifted students. Our instructors were officers, we were soldiers, and the officers gave us direct orders to learn a group of equations or memorize a list of aerodynamic terms. Everyone in class was expected to obey those orders. We were still only teenage boys, but we faced the responsibilities of soldiers.

That first year, we all looked forward to lights-out at 2200. And most of us had to force ourselves to stay awake during the mandatory group viewing of the Vremya television newscast from Moscow each night at 2100.

We were also required to take an active part in athletics and physical training. One of the most challenging routines involved a training apparatus called the *lop'ing*, a kind of rotating trapeze swing that prepared us for aerobatic maneuvers. The device looked deceptively simple, like a children's playground toy, and had been developed for the space program. It was said that cosmonauts that mastered it had no problem with weightlessness.

You stood on the metal trapeze, which was suspended from a high outdoor frame in the academy sports complex, your ankles and wrists attached by cuffs to the frame. The steel trapeze frame could rotate in a full vertical circle and also twirl around its own axis. So the cadet could perform the equivalent of a simultaneous loop and roll, one of the most disorienting aerobatic maneuvers. We all had to master a basic competence on this apparatus.

The most demanding routine on the device was a timed sequence of ten forward loops with one complete rotation of the frame for each loop. To accomplish this, you had to let your body completely enter the three-dimensional, fluid motion, flexing your knees as you rose in the loop in order to pump momentum into the falling limb of the circle, all the while keeping even pressure on your shoulder and torso to execute a smooth rotation along your own vertical axis. You could actually "pull" almost seven Gs on this simple rig, or three stomach-churning negative Gs at the top of the loop.

Parachute training was another challenge which came early

in the curriculum. Less than two months after we put on our new uniforms, we were strapping on parachute harnesses for practice jumps off a training tower. This was a standard D1-5U military parachute harness, complete with chest-pack reserve. But the risers were connected to a bar that slid down a slide wire that replicated the speed and angle of a parachute landing. We quickly progressed from ground training to our first jump.

Our drop aircraft was the reliable old An-2, a rugged, single-engine biplane originally designed for agricultural aviation. Seven jumpers sat in two rows of folding sling seats that faced inward from both sides of the cabin. The "Anushka" was an ideal parachute-training aircraft. Throttled back at the 2,500-foot jump altitude, the plane droned along at barely eighty knots. The exit door was on the left. All you did was hook up your static line to the overhead cable, follow the man ahead, and leap out the door, keeping your hands crossed on your reserve and your elbows well tucked in. There wasn't much prop blast from the Anushka.

My first jump was also my first airplane ride.

After our first two jumps, we received seven rubles parachute pay. The next jumps were paid at the rate of one and a half rubles. After twenty-five jumps we would earn five rubles each time we climbed aboard the Anushka. Parachuting a minimum of twice a year was mandatory for pilots. The rule was: If you don't jump, you don't fly.

Given the intensity of our training, we quickly formed close friendships. I found myself spending more and more of my precious free time with five classmates who had come to Armavir from widely separated parts of the Soviet Union. Vladimir Chizhov came from Uralsk, a new industrial city in Kazakhstan. His parents were both Russian factory workers, but from his lean intensity and obvious high intelligence, he seemed more like a member of the intelligentsia. He had come to Armavir from a technical college and was a year older than most of us. Because there were so many Vladimirs about, he quickly acquired the nickname Siskin, "lapwing," because he resembled that keenly observant bird of the steppes.

Vladimir Morozov we called Deep Freeze. He was a brilliant student who helped us all with our math and physics, but he was not a natural soldier. In fact, we all had to help him square away his uniform and sloppy bunk and locker before each inspection.

Sergei Mashenko came all the way from Sakhalin Island in the Far East. His father was a well-to-do manager in oil production and his mother was a schoolteacher. One of the first things he did at the academy was order tailor-made uniforms. He was well read and, like Dmitri, knew English. He took everything with a sense of good-humored grace. Nothing seemed to faze him. And as soon as we all trusted each other completely, Sergei was telling an endless series of witty political jokes, often at the expense of the stuffed-shirt zampolits.

Gary Tselauri came from Tbilisi in Georgia. His mother was Russian. His father, a Georgian, had died several years before. Gary was tall, husky, and a natural athlete, well trained in judo. Because of his dark good looks, we called him the Prince of Georgia. At first, Gary stubbornly refrained from rough barracks-room language and wouldn't say a vulgar word until parachute training. But after slamming into the ground on the slide wire, it was "fuck" this and "fuck" that.

And then there was Igor Karpov, Karpich. He was tall and gawky and had just made it under the six-foot height limit. His feet were huge, and with his eagle's-beak nose we told him he had a natural "pilot's profile." Karpich came from the city of Armavir and tantalized us with tales of all the good-looking lonely nurses across the town at their school. His father had a wonderful collection of Western rock music records and we later had some great parties at his family's apartment.

By the end of our second semester, we were deeply involved in preflight training, studying the systems of the L-29 jet trainer. My class was flown to the preliminary flight-training center at Pirsagat in Azerbaijan in August 1979. The base was on an arid stretch of Caspian Sea coast south of Baku. I was not prepared for the baking heat of the Azerbaijan summer. We slept in old wooden barracks with no mosquito nets, and a few slow ceiling fans moved the stifling air. The soldiers showed us the trick of sleeping under wet sheets so that the evaporation cooled us.

Like most of the cadets, I had just turned eighteen. We knew, of course, that the L-29 was only a jet trainer, not a combat fighter, but standing next to the gleaming three-ton aircraft and sliding my hands along the hot alloy skin of the thirty-two-foot wingspan, it seemed incredible that the State would give me the responsibility of flying such a complex and powerful machine.

Dmitri, the keen observer of the West, told us that student pilots in the American Air Force and Navy received their basic flight instruction on propeller planes, and didn't progress to jets for many months. When you considered that our American counterparts didn't even begin to fly until they had completed their university or service academy education, this meant they were almost twenty-three years old before they soloed in a jet. By that age, most of us would be line pilots in combat regiments with hundreds of operational sorties under our belts.

But first we had to learn to fly.

The L-29 was built by Aero Vodochody in Czechoslovakia, and was the standard basic advanced training aircraft of the Warsaw Pact. Over three thousand had been produced. The tandem twin cockpits, each with a complete set of flight controls, sat well forward of the straight wings.

At Pirsagat I was fortunate once again in the instructor I was assigned. Senior Lieutenant Anatoli Tveretin was demanding and meticulous, but personally relaxed in his approach to flight training. Tveretin, who seemed a young man of almost miraculous patience, never lost his composure. I was lucky because Karpich and I were the only cadets on the lieutenant's training crew that term. But he did expect us to study hard and not repeat the same mistakes.

Lieutenant Tveretin reiterated that flying was primarily a physical, not an abstract, exercise. "Zuyev," he told me that first day I strapped into the front cockpit, "get a good feel of that ejection seat. Pilots have to feel their airplane with their butts."

The Americans, he said, had supposedly once conducted an experiment in which they had injected pilots in the ass with novocaine, and none of them could properly land his plane. "The point," he added, "is that *you* control the aircraft. The aircraft does not control you."

Waiting to take off on my familiarization ride around the training circuits, Lieutenant Tveretin urged me to pay close attention. "If you don't understand something," he said, "ask me."

He started the engine and we closed and latched our canopies. I was immediately struck by the smell, which I later recognized as the distinctive odor of Soviet military cockpits, a combination of hot electronics, stale sweat, and rubber. It had a sour quality that almost made me gag. Before me, the instrument panel suddenly seemed completely unfamiliar, even though I'd

learned the systems perfectly in the classroom. Tveretin released
the brake and advanced the throttle. We were trundling along the
taxi ramp toward the end of the runway. Now we had swung out and
were square on the centerline, facing the broad concrete runway
rippling with heat mirage. I hated to admit how nervous I was.

In the closed cockpit, with the sun pouring in, the cloying
sour smell grew stronger. Luckily our Samarskiye mentors had
told us to carry plastic bags in our flight suits in case we got sick
on our first training flights. A cadet would be immediately grounded
if an instructor reported he had actually vomited in the cockpit.
"If you're going to puke," our friends warned us, "do it in the bag,
then hide the bag." That same harsh rule, I learned, applied to all
Soviet military pilots. This first flight in a jet was not starting well.

And then, as if telepathic, Tveretin reassured me. "Fear is
normal," he said calmly. "Don't be surprised to be afraid. The fear
will go away with experience."

On this first sortie I was to rest my feet lightly on the rudder
pedals and my hand loosely on the control stick to get the feel of
the controls. Now Tveretin opened the throttle to full military
power and released the brakes. We slid slowly down the runway.
The acceleration increased, but we were still rooted to the
ground. Only after a ponderously long, deliberate takeoff run did
Tveretin gently rotate the nose and we climbed. The gear came
thumping up and the flat brown horizon slid away. I felt the stick
in my right hand. The airplane was alive.

Tveretin put the plane through a series of steep quarter-rolls
as we climbed around the airfield approach circuit. He was doing
me a favor, pointing out the various landmarks below that I would
later need to recognize when I flew solo. But tilted way over on
the right wing, staring straight down through my canopy as we
sailed above the Azerbaijan desert, was not soothing to my
stomach. The hot rubbery smell of the cockpit grew worse. I
slipped the folded plastic bag from my flight-suit pocket.

Then, while Tveretin had me hold the controls on the
landing approach, I knew I was going to vomit. If I didn't hide it
from the lieutenant, my career as a military pilot was going to end
prematurely. "Please take over, Comrade Lieutenant," I managed, sliding the open bag to my face.

"What's the problem?"

"My kneeboard slipped," I said into the intercom micro-
phone. Then I vomited up my breakfast.

Tveretin was too busy flying from the rear cockpit to notice. I
knotted the bag and stuck it in my pocket.

After getting sick three more times—always unnoticed by
Tveretin—I learned to skip breakfast and lunch on flying days.
Eventually my stomach settled down. Although Tveretin never
acknowledged my airsickness, he did explain the Coriolis effect
that provoked dizzy nausea when you moved your head too fast
during banks and turns. From then on, I moved my head *very*
slowly, especially when we were steeply banked.

As we trained through that stifling Azerbaijan summer, the
Stavka high command in Moscow suddenly announced that the
Armavir PVO Academy was being transferred to the Air Force,
the VVS. This abrupt transformation, we were told, was part of a
general reorganization and modernization of the entire Soviet
military ordered by Deputy Defense Minister Marshal Nikolai
Ogarkov. The Air Force would be expanded with additional
regiments of advanced fighter aircraft, while the bloated and
inefficient PVO would be trimmed down to a proper size.

I had not understood the difference between the two services
as a schoolboy in Samara. But a year at the academy had taught
me that the PVO Air Defense Force provided much more comfortable duty than the VVS. Despite the dire warnings about the
guardhouse, Armavir was a quiet sanctuary from overly strict
military discipline. On the other hand, the VVS had a reputation
for rigid adherence to regulations and snap inspections by incor-
ruptible teams from the Ministry of Defense. In the PVO command, inspections were usually scheduled months in advance.

The PVO had evolved during the Great Patriotic War from
antiaircraft artillery units and had less of the traditional élan than
the VVS, which had descended from the colorful Hussar cavalry
regiments. Senior PVO officers had a reputation of being stolid
dolts, oxen not thoroughbred horses. One of the forbidden stories
at Armavir concerned an account of several PVO generals being
flown by helicopter on an inspection tour. When they kept the
helicopter crew waiting at one base several hours while the
generals enjoyed a long lunch, the pilot got revenge by claiming
his engine wouldn't start because the battery had run down.

"Comrade Generals," he said, "you'll have to get out and push."

The credulous generals climbed down, took off their bemedaled uniform blouses, and pushed the gawky Mi-8 along the runway until the pilot decided to hit his start button. Later, one general wrote a report condemning the poor design of the helicopter.

But we soon discovered that Air Force generals had both similarities and differences. A delegation of senior VVS officers descended on Pirsagat to look over their new charges. One tough, clearly arrogant colonel general named Gorelov, who wore the wings of a Sniper pilot, inspected our barracks. He seemed aghast that the floors and furniture were painted in pleasant shades of blue and green.

"In the Air Force," General Gorelov bellowed, hardly controlling his outrage, "we do not have *painted* furniture. Scrape it all to bare wood."

Once Tveretin was satisfied I had mastered the feel of basic flight maneuvers, he nipped any overconfidence I might have exhibited by setting out a more difficult challenge: precision flying.

"You can even teach a bear to fly," he said. "It's really not hard to fly dirty. But a good fighter pilot flies clean."

By "clean" he meant flying the aircraft with absolute control and certainty, so that you could consistently arrive at any given point in the sky with a minimum correction. Tveretin's approach to instruction combined multiple repetitions of basic skills like flying landing approaches with more challenging maneuvers.

All the cadets were required to keep a personal logbook to record their training sorties. But I had a separate, private logbook in which I carefully noted every phase of my training with brutal honesty. "Cannot manage power for climbing right. Lost 120 feet of altitude on 60-degree turn," I wrote. Two days later I noted, "Poor elevator trim on left-hand descent to final approach." The next week I logged, "*Huy ovo*, all fucked up," after a sloppy landing flare.

In early October, six weeks into our flight training, I was expected to be the first in my crew to solo. But Siskin, my skinny friend from Uralsk, was doing just as well with his instructor. We had each flown over thirty training sorties and could now accomplish the basic curriculum maneuvers required for solo flight. Lieutenant Tveretin, however, was not completely satisfied with my performance, although he assured me I wasn't a "giraffe," a student pilot with impossibly slow reactions, as if his hands and feet were too far from his eyes and brain. That was a compliment, coming from him.

On October 5, 1979, Siskin became the first in our class to solo after thirty-six sorties. Tveretin and I stood on the parking apron, watching Siskin complete his mandatory triple *krug* oval racetrack maneuver and descend onto final approach for landing.

"He's a little short," I commented.

Tveretin smiled. "So were you this morning."

As always, the lieutenant was right. Siskin had to add power and climb out of his smooth glide slope to make the runway threshold. But he did manage a beautiful touchdown.

"Tomorrow we practice landings," Tveretin said.

And practice we did. I flew five sorties that day and racked up three touch-and-go landings. After we put the airplane to bed that evening, Tveretin turned to me and coolly stated, "If the weather's halfway decent tomorrow, you will solo." That night it was hard to fall asleep.

And the next morning after one quick circuit of the course, my thirty-eighth training sortie at Pirsagat, the deputy squadron commander pronounced me ready to solo.

"Good luck, Zuyev," was all the lieutenant said.

Taxiing out to the runway felt completely familiar. But I didn't hear Tveretin's terse comments in my earphones. When I turned onto the centerline and ran up my engine for the instrument check, I somehow still expected to hear his voice. It was hard to believe that I was the only man in the plane.

I released the brakes. The L-29 was supposedly slow on takeoff. The fellows said you had time to smoke a cigarette before you reached rotation speed. But on this sunny autumn morning in Azerbaijan, the takeoff roll seemed impossibly quick.

I was climbing straight above the runway. The gear was up and I raised my flaps at 300 feet altitude, just as Tveretin had taught me, before I fully realized I was flying solo. Then I banked right and climbed to fly the oval three-circuit *krug* pattern at 1,800 feet without incident. Once I was level, I craned my neck to look in the rear cockpit to make sure no one was there. I burst into a loud rendition of the Volga folk song "Stepan Razin," which celebrated a brave and audacious rebel from czarist times. That was exactly how I felt, brave and daring.

I was less than three months past my eighteenth birthday, and I had just soloed in a jet aircraft.

When my class returned to Armavir that December, we found that the Air Force had ordered a complete landscaping of the parklike campus. The old laurel and plane trees that had provided pleasant shade in the summer—and welcome concealment for cadets following the "Ho Chi Minh Trail" to slip over the far wall and into town—were hacked down. The quaint old model of the MiG-15 rotating above the mossy fountain in the parade ground was demolished, replaced by an abstract sculpture of a missile, which the cadets quickly dubbed the "Monument to Hockey Players," because of its resemblance to stacked hockey sticks.

Our third semester began just after the Soviet military intervention in Afghanistan. Official publications, including *Red Star,* all proclaimed satisfaction that Party Secretary Leonid Brezhnev had allowed the Army to fulfill its "internationalist duty." In January a political administration colonel from the military district headquarters in Rostov lectured us about the events in Afghanistan. The colonel was unusually informative because he had helped plan the operation. He went through the predictable rationalization for the Soviet invasion, explaining that it had been our duty to protect Socialist democracy in that fraternal country, which was under attack by medieval Muslim fanatics, who had murdered many Soviet citizens struggling to improve backward conditions in Afghanistan.

Then the colonel described the actual invasion in great detail. He noted how Spetsnaz forces had been infiltrated into Kabul, the capital, where they had seized the international airport, which became an airhead for the Airborne intervention force. Our forces had completely overwhelmed the Islamic bandits who had resisted them. Hafizullah Amin, the Afghan prime minister who had betrayed his Socialist principles, had been "eliminated," the colonel added. Socialist democracy would soon be restored, despite the machinations of the imperialists, who were trying to stir up resistance among the bandits.

He reassured us that the Armavir curriculum would not be accelerated because of Afghanistan.

As I sat in the darkened auditorium, I marveled at the organization and precision of the operation. I was a member of a powerful professional military organization that acted with courageous resolve when necessary.

When we returned to Pirsagat for advanced L-29 training in March, the focus was on navigation, formation flying, and aerobatic and combat maneuvers, which prepared us to fly the higher performance MiG-21FM. This was a transition aircraft that would sharpen our skills for assignments to combat regiments equipped with the supersonic MiG-23.

Cross-country navigation over the Azerbaijan desert was a real challenge. Some guys got lost and made it back to base with only the proverbial "bucket of fuel" remaining in their tanks. In such cases, Soviet aviators could switch to radio channel 4 and request a radio-direction-finding (RDF) fix to guide them back to base. Our controllers at Pirsagat were often Central Asians who spoke with strong accents in Russian. But there was one fluent, unaccented Russian voice that sometimes answered on that frequency. It belonged to an Iranian who would try to guide an unwary young Soviet cadet over the border into Iran. We were told that he worked for the American CIA. That was one more pitfall to avoid.

Our training climaxed that summer with a formal maneuver competition among the cadets. We flew a set of increasingly difficult maneuvers over a three-day period, each sortie flown with a different judge in the backseat.

The first maneuvers were relatively simple, involving horizontal figure eights that had to be entered and exited at exact, predetermined headings and speeds. But as the competition progressed, we had to fly double spins and split-S's, again entering the maneuver at a precise compass heading and exiting at a prearranged altitude and speed. I had practiced this stage of the competition repeatedly. I knew exactly when to chop the throttle, how hard to pull back on the stick, and how much rudder pressure was needed. I scored well on the first two days.

But on the third day of the competition, we had to integrate the vertical, horizontal, and speed elements. I began the last series of maneuvers at an altitude of 9,000 feet and a speed of 270 knots. As before, I had mentally rehearsed the exact sequence many times. By the time I was in my second rolling climb to 9,000 feet, I realized I was almost finished with the hardest segment of the competition and that I had made very few mistakes.

That afternoon the instructors met to compile the cadets' cumulative scores. The unattainable perfect competition score totaled 400 points. When they posted the results that evening, I had scored highest with a tally of 380.

From my point of view, the positive result of our transfer to the VVS was the sudden announcement that the Air Force had chosen Armavir as the first pilots' academy for an experimental accelerated flight-training program. A select group of cadets from my class were to phase directly from the L-29 trainer to the MiG-23 advanced jet fighter. In the past, both PVO and VVS cadet pilots had to spend several years mastering the complexities of the high-performance MiG-21 before qualifying to fly a "third generation" aircraft like the MiG-23.

The fifty best-qualified cadets of the 250 who remained in my class were selected for MiG-23 training. Based on my performance at Pirsagat, I was in this group. So were my friends Sergei Mashenko, "Deep Freeze" Morozov, Dmitri from Leningrad, and "Boris" Bagomedov from Dagestan, one of the few successful Asian cadets.

The MiG-23 cadets were assembled on a ramp near the Burav runway where a variety of fighter aircraft were kept for familiarization purposes. The big gray MiG-23 parked there was almost twice as long and four times as heavy as the L-29 trainer. The MiG-23 evoked brute power and speed. Its tapered nose ended in the bullet tip of a gray radar dome, from which a titanium Pitot instrument probe extended like a lance. Just aft of the canopy, the two tall, rectangular engine air intakes gaped open, which explained why pilots of the smaller MiG-21 called the MiG-23 the Crocodile. This image was intensified by the widespread main landing gear, protected by the angled plate of mud deflectors, which gave the undercarriage the appearance of a crouching reptile's clenched legs. In turn, MiG-23 pilots scornfully called the MiG-21 *okurok*, "cigarette butt."

The massive Tumansky R-29 turbofan engine occupied most of the fuselage, terminating in the heavy segmented alloy ring of the afterburner. Thick, swiveling powered differential stabilizers and a hulking vertical tail over twelve feet high made it clear that this aircraft was designed for high supersonic speeds.

The MiG-23 was a variable-geometry fighter, and its wings

were the most striking feature of the aircraft. Set high on the fuselage, they had a tapered cross section, thick near the center and saber-thin at the tips. In flight the plane's wings could be swung back from the low speed configuration of sixteen degrees from perpendicular to the fuselage, all the way to a sharply swept falcon-tuck of seventy-two degrees for the top supersonic speed of Mach 2.35.

Like all high-performance fighters of its generation, the MiG-23 was a design compromise. To perform well at the high-G, supersonic end of the flight envelope, the airplane traded lift for raw power. With the wings tucked completely back, the stabilizers provided responsive pitch and roll control. However, even with the wings returned forward to the minimum sixteen-degree-sweep angle, the MiG-23 could become dangerously unstable at subsonic speed.

To demonstrate the power of the big afterburning Tumansky R-29 turbofan, an instructor climbed into the aircraft, started the engine, and ran it up to full military power. A deep, rasping roar hit us, and the ground seemed to tremble. There was a heavy concrete block resting on the slope of the steel blast deflector behind the aircraft's tail pipe. The block must have weighed three tons. When the pilot hit the afterburner, a pulsing tube of orange flame erupted from the tail pipe with a thunderous crack. On afterburner the engine developed over twelve tons of thrust. The concrete block was blown away, spiraling like a maple leaf in the wind, and landed twenty yards behind the blast deflector.

"That's your engine," a captain instructor shouted, once the roar had abated. "You will have to learn to control this machine, or it will control you . . . right into the ground."

Our MiG-23 ground classes were piled on top of our regular aeronautical engineering studies. There was a cadet saying, "blue nose, Red Diploma," which referred to the almost superhuman effort required to earn the coveted Red Diploma for academic excellence. All of us felt our noses turning blue that year. But we were old soldiers now and we knew how much slack to expect from the instructors, and what regulations we could bend or break. And the strict rule against unauthorized visits to town was the one regulation we most enjoyed breaking.

It was unrealistic for the academy commander, General Major of Aviation Nikolai Kryukov, to expect healthy young men like ourselves to remain stone-sober and celibate when there were nursing students, vodka, and beer virtually a stone's throw from the glass-studded front wall of the academy. Again the sense of losing the best years of our youth often overwhelmed us. And our restrictive life seemed so unnecessary when Dmitri informed us that cadets at American military academies actually had telephones in their rooms and were allowed to drive cars to visit girls in towns like Annapolis and West Point. By our second summer at Armavir, the members of my unofficial "crew" were all veterans of the Ho Chi Minh Trail over that wall.

Absence without leave was a guardhouse offense that meant at least three days' tough confinement, eating stale bread and drinking cold tea, and sleeping on a wooden plank with your *shinel*, greatcoat, as a blanket. But the tantalizing prospect of sleeping with those willing and experienced nurses overcame our fear. Once we had reconnoitered the town, "the Prince of Georgia," Sergei Mashenko, and I pooled our money and rented a small furnished apartment nearby from a kindly old babushka whose daughter had married and moved away.

Getting from the campus to that apartment and back was always an adventure. But even with the trees and foliage cut back severely, we found several good routes over the wall.

These routes were also our smugglers' trail whenever we brought back vodka for a party in the dormitory.

I was on a vodka run just before New Year's 1981. After making an uneventful sortie into town and returning late at night with my *shinel* pockets clanking with .75-liter "grenades" of Sibirskaya vodka, I hauled myself back over the wall and dropped down into the shadowy snowdrifts.

"Oh, how nice," a voice bellowed. "Those are fine trophies you've got there, Comrade Kursant."

It was too dark for us to see each other's face, but I certainly recognized the voice of Colonel Stonov, one of the battalion commanders. I was looking at a week in the frozen guardhouse.

"Hand it over!" the colonel shouted. "*Now!*"

I thrust out two squat bottles of vodka. "Comrade Colonel," I said, disguising my voice with a slur as if I were drunk, "I have more on the other side. Wait one moment, please."

Before he could answer, I was back over the wall and down on the gritty ice of the pavement on the city side. I dashed all the way around the walled compound and found the hole under the fence near the runway. Once inside the campus, I sprinted back to my dorm. My friends hid the vodka and brushed the snow from my uniform while I crawled into bed. The lights in our bunk room were out when Colonel Stonov came storming up the stairs. Given the time it had taken me to go all the way around the wall, he must have remained standing like a fool where I'd left him for at least five minutes.

He was not amused. But he was never able to prove who had tricked him.

All of us hated the idea of the guardhouse, which was the main deterrent that kept most of the cadets on campus. In the guardhouse the soldiers shaved your head, threw buckets of ice water on your wooden bunk, and generally made your stay there as unpleasant as possible.

Their favorite trick was screaming *"Otboy,"* "Go to sleep!" while the prisoners were outside in the exercise yard in the evening. At that command they loosed their vicious German shepherds. One cadet grabbed a shovel and clubbed the dogs to death. And the court of inquiry found in his favor and disciplined the sadistic guards.

As the cadet sergeant, I had to escort prisoners in my platoon to the guardhouse. It was a duty I despised. But at least it allowed me and the Prince of Georgia to pull one of the best ruses in the history of Armavir. Gary was caught AWOL in town and given five days' guardhouse confinement. I was responsible for both escorting the prisoner and handing over his paperwork. We took a true gamble instead. Gary crawled back over the wall and spent the five days in our apartment. I ripped up his charge sheet.

No one was ever the wiser. But the experience convinced me to relinquish my stripes as a cadet sergeant.

Luckily I was never directly involved in one of the most daring and eventually dangerous cadet escapades. My close friend Sergei Mashenko had shown a real artistic talent since our first days at Armavir. Using tools in the model shop, he made us beautifully crafted switchblade knives that we could use in an emergency to cut parachute shroud lines. And he could sketch freehand detailed engineering drawings that were far superior to anything others could achieve with compass and protractor. Sergei was also an excellent forger. Our military identity papers were a cardboard-faced booklet, with pages listing our particulars, including the all-important entry "Marital Status."

Using well-sharpened artist's pencils, Sergei assigned a number of cadets a wife and perhaps a child or two. This deception was invaluable to graduating cadets who had enjoyed the comforts of young ladies from Armavir, but who had no intention of marrying. These were girls who had been urged by their ambitious families to spare no pain in order to snag a new Air Force lieutenant in marriage. Armed with their newly acquired proof of marriage, the cadets would break the sad news to their girlfriends just before graduation. There was not much the girls could do, as bigamy was against the Soviet constitution.

But Sergei was not as lucky as the Prince of Georgia had been. One of his many girlfriends decided to go work as a prostitute in the international hotels on the Black Sea. The managers there let only married girls work as whores because they were supposedly free of disease. Sergei altered her internal passport. But the KGB picked her up and she informed on him. The Osobii Otdel at Armavir launched a full-blown investigation. Sergei was dismissed from the MiG-23 program and almost landed in prison.

During the October leave between my second and third years at Armavir, I was able to visit Leningrad, having saved money by working an unofficial night job in the city. Soviet factory managers were always looking for men eager to perform unpleasant work for high wages. My friends and I contacted the manager of a textile factory near the academy that produced the cotton wadding for quilted winter garments. Our job was to climb inside the huge ventilation conduits and clean the matted lint from the filters. We used our Army gas masks to protect our lungs. It was nasty work, but paid fifteen rubles a night, and the academy never knew about it.

It was common practice for greedy faculty members to barter cadets' labor for their own gain. Major Zheloudkov, my battalion commander, was one of the worst offenders.

"Well, comrades," he would say, "we need materials to refurbish our Lenin Rooms."

There was nothing wrong with the wall paneling or bookcases in the Lenin Rooms, but Zheloudkov had promised a local furniture company to supply cadets for weekend work in exchange for all the material he needed to refurbish his own dacha outside the city.

He never roped me into that flunky work because I represented the academy on the Spartak wrestling circuit, and the major was a great sports fan.

In June 1981 we finally completed our formal MiG-23 ground school and sweated through our theoretical exams. My flight instructor was Captain Vladimir Bogorotsky, a typical no-nonsense Air Force instructor, very businesslike and direct. I found him rather humorless, but completely honest and dedicated to his job. It was not surprising that he was the Communist Party secretary of his instructors' *kollectiv*.

Bogorotsky's crew consisted of five cadets. Lapwing Siskin and I were in the first echelon. Deep Freeze had the second echelon to himself. And Misha Soutormin and Anatoli Sarichev formed the third echelon of the crew. With our strong academic background and good record on the L-29, we were probably the best-prepared crew at the academy.

We had worked hard on MiG-23 cockpit simulators, and were completely familiar with the complexities of the afterburning engine, hydraulic wing-sweep control, pulse radar, and infrared search and track system (IRST). But the only way we would truly understand the new aircraft was to fly it.

Our first instruction was in the MiG-23UB, the *uchybno boyevoy*, a two-seat combat trainer version of the aircraft. As in all Soviet trainers, the instructor sat behind the student, both a reassuring presence and a reminder to the guy in the front seat to pay attention to business.

Our new G-suits had larger constricting inflatable air bladders on our thighs and abdomen to protect us more effectively from blackout during maneuvers than our L-29 suits had. This was good news because we'd been told our testicles could be damaged during high-G turns and banks. But cadets also believed that pulling a certain amount of Gs made you a better lover because your blood pooled in the "vital organs" of the lower body. The new KM-1 ejection seat was more powerful than the L-29's, and had a powerful, solid-fuel rocket that could save your life at zero altitude in the event of a flameout on takeoff. The instrument panel of the MiG-23 was crowded with electronics, including a radar sight for the 23mm GSh cannon-pod, air-to-air missiles, and a weapons-release panel for bombs and ground-attack rockets. The cockpit also had a Sirena 3-M radar-threat warning system and a SRZO Information Friend or Foe radar-interrogation system. And the TP-23 IRST actually displayed data on a clear Plexiglas head-up display (HUD) above the instrument panel.

If these complexities were not enough, management of the afterburning R-29 turbofan was a demanding task. An afterburner, we learned, could virtually transform the aircraft into a piloted rocket. But learning to control the variable-geometry wings through all the power-setting regimes of the flight envelope proved incredibly difficult for some students, even during ground school. The wings had to be swept back at least thirty-three degrees for transonic flight, but forty-five degrees was the standard setting. If you forgot this requirement and accelerated to 0.8 or 0.95 Mach in the denser air below 9,000 feet with your wings unswept, a sudden, dangerous "overswing" could occur, which caused rapid, alternating negative and positive Gs. The plane quickly became uncontrollable. In 1980 an instructor and student from Armavir were killed in just such a sudden overswing accident.

Naturally, for high-Mach flight, the full-rear wing sweep was necessary. This meant we had to learn to handle the throttle, the wing-sweep hydraulic lever beneath the throttle quadrant, and the control stick simultaneously—while also using the weapons system electronics and the radio. And, of course, the wing had to be in the full-forward position for landing. Clearly, even some of my group of fifty talented L-29 pilots were not yet up to this challenge.

Captain Bogorotsky believed in long flying days while the weather was good. Within two weeks I was handling my own takeoffs and landings. The takeoffs were no problem because of the generous lift of the upswept wings and the powerful engines. But landing the MiG-23 was never easy. The landing airspeed was high, 140 knots, much faster than the L-29. So you had to judge your flare altitude and speed on the landing threshold with precision. If you landed with too much airspeed, you might experience a dangerous condition known as the "progressive goat."

The overly springy landing gear exacerbated this problem. In any aircraft the actual flare maneuver was a near stall. But if you flared too fast and slammed down your nose gear, the MiG-23 would bounce back into the air in a nose-high attitude, at which point the inexperienced pilot would instinctively jam the stick forward and bring the nose gear back down to the runway. This was the start of the "goat." The nosewheel would slam down hard, and the aircraft would bounce again, this time higher, with the nose pitched even more steeply. The bounce and pitch back would progress, with the nose dropping and bouncing back more sharply on each cycle. By the fifth bounce, the tail keel would drag, killing the last of the airspeed. The plane would stall off on one wing, fall onto its belly, and explode. And, unfortunately, even our advanced ejection seat would not save a pilot at zero airspeed.

We read accident reports of both Soviet and foreign students, Cubans, Angolans, and North Koreans, who all experienced a progressive goat landing. Several of them had been killed. I was determined to avoid this potential trap.

I soloed in the MiG-23 on September 15, 1981. This was quite an accomplishment, considering I had been grounded for one month that summer as punishment for being caught in town, AWOL in civilian clothes. If I hadn't been in the advanced MiG-23 program, I probably would have done time in the guardhouse. But my deputy squadron commander, Major Nurokmiyetov, knew that, for me, being grounded was worse punishment than being chased by the guardhouse dogs. When I turned in the rags I had substituted for my real clandestine set of civvies, the major shook his head, realizing he had been taken. He had seen me in town before, but ignored the infraction because I was dating the daughter of his former flight instructor. Now he had to follow regulations and confiscate my civvies. "I'll never believe that you actually wore this shit," he said, fingering the old tennis shoes and warm-up suit I surrendered. My first American "Levi's" jeans and nice shirt were safely hidden at the apartment.

After I soloed on the MiG-23, my attitude toward life in the Air Force changed. I was twenty years old and had been given the responsibility of flying this powerful combat aircraft. We flew now several times a week and spent long hours in the classroom studying basic individual and formation air-combat tactics, designed to prepare us to counter known NATO combat maneuvers such as "yo-yo" ambushes from high or low altitude and high-G barrel-roll attacks.

At this time, several of my friends became candidate members of the Communist Party, a mandatory apprenticeship of at least one year before they could be considered for full membership. If you were a candidate, you had to watch your behavior; reprimands or a stretch in the guardhouse could kill your chances for Party membership, which, in turn, could stifle your career as an officer. I preferred to wait until after graduation to become a candidate member. That way I could still take chances sneaking off to town to see girls, and all I risked was the guardhouse.

Over the next year I mastered the Crocodile. While some cadets were still dreading every landing approach, I and a few others were practicing instrument-landing-system approaches. As I had anticipated, the members of my crew were near the top of our class. We had all conquered the terrible goat by learning to judge our flare attitude accurately before chopping the throttle.

During our combat training in 1982, we learned to fly with a wingman in a *para* two-plane formation. We all knew where this training was leading us. The war in Afghanistan had become a protracted test of wills between the Soviet Union and the imperialists—treacherously supported by the Chinese. When we graduated in October, we would probably be sent to an advanced combat-training regiment and then on to Afghanistan. So we concentrated on the deadly serious and complex business of flying a high-performance aircraft. My earlier romantic illusions about the life of a fighter pilot were tempered by reality. You simply did not hop into the cockpit of a jet fighter and roar off into the sky to do battle like a Hussar on his horse. Modern combat aviation was more a science than adventure.

Now my working days revolved around the mundane but essential problems of mission planning: fuel consumption, optimum climb angles, tactical navigation, multichannel radio communications, radar sights, and formation maneuvers. We also were given the additional complication of learning to evade surface-to-air missiles (SAMs) and antiaircraft artillery (AAA), just to make life more interesting. It was engrossing work, but it was not the mindless excitement I had once envisioned.

Then one morning I woke up in my comfortable two-man room in the upperclassmen's dormitory and realized I was about to graduate and be commissioned as a pilot lieutenant in the Soviet Air Force. I had passed all my final written and flight exams. The only unfinished business was our graduation party, the actual graduation ceremony, and, of course, the matter of my assignment.

Our experimental program had proved successful, and I was rated near the top of the group. But I still dreaded the possibility of being kept back here as a MiG-23 instructor. In early October the academy was visited by unofficial "agents," officers from advanced schools and combat regiments, recruiting promising graduates. I had already stated my preference for a Frontal Aviation regiment, and tried to make a favorable impression on the officers from combat units who came to observe our final flight exams.

One of the visiting officers who interviewed me was a major from the PVO's advanced instructors' school at Savaslayka. He had a list with the six most promising cadets in the MiG-23 program. Although I was still averse to the idea of becoming an instructor, he did pique my interest when he mentioned the instructors there would be trained for advanced "fourth generation" aircraft, such as the MiG-31 and the Su-27, that were just completing flight testing in prototype.

"Zuyev," he said, "we can certainly use a man like you. Think it over."

I promised the major I would and he left the interview room reminding me that the sign-up deadline for his program was the next afternoon.

That night we had our graduation party. I didn't go to bed until dawn, and I didn't wake up until midafternoon, my mouth dry and my head pounding. Still fuzzy, I rolled out of bed, now convinced that the opportunity of flying truly advanced fighters at Savaslayka was too good to miss. Wandering down the corridor in my hangover daze, I discovered that all six openings for the major's program had already been filled. The guys said that everyone with family connections had pulled out the stops to get on that list. If I hadn't enjoyed the party so much, I might have made the deadline.

The suspense about my assignment was finally broken when one of Sergei Mashenko's girlfriends, a typist in the commandant's office, revealed I was on the list of six cadets destined for Frontal Aviation regiments in the Transcaucasus Military District. That was good news. There were three MiG-23 regiments in

Georgia, the 176th at Mikha Tskhakaya, the 512th at Vaziani, and the 614th near Meria. Rumor had it that these regiments were training hard, preparing to send squadrons to Afghanistan. That was the kind of action I wanted.

Besides, I had visited Georgia on my summer leave with my friend Gary and knew what a pleasant place it was. The small republic was wedged between the high wall of the Great Caucasus and Turkey, bounded on the west by the Black Sea and the east by the mountains of Armenia and Azerbaijan. It had a mild, subtropical climate and lush vineyards and citrus groves. Georgian families were renowned for their hospitality and Georgian women for their dark-eyed beauty.

When my friends asked if I was pleased to be heading for Georgia, I quoted that old Air Force saw, "It's better to eat white bread by the Black Sea than black bread by the White Sea."

But the guys who were headed to isolated bases on the Arctic shores of the White Sea reminded me of the heat and food poisoning that had plagued us in the South. Deep Freeze Morozov shut them up.

"Look," he said, "it's better to wash the sweat off your balls than to have to defrost them."

At the graduation parade, I watched as Lapwing Siskin and Deep Freeze were presented with the coveted Red Diploma, signifying academic excellence. And their noses were definitely not blue. But I was more than satisfied with the citation on my own diploma, which noted my flying skills and dedication to duty.

"Staunch in aerial combat, prepared to give his life for the Motherland and the ideas of Marxism-Leninism."

— 5 —
Combat Training
1983–84

I spent my graduation leave at home in Samara, working on my grandmother's tiny apartment in the old wooden house in Bezimaynka. I had received a 540-ruble bonus after four years at the academy, and it gave me great pleasure to spend most of it on paint, plaster, and electrical fittings for Grandma's little room.

Life was certainly becoming difficult for elderly pensioners, especially those who lived alone. As a boy in Samara there had always been plenty of food on the shelves of the grocery stores and clothes on the racks of the State department store. But around the time I graduated from school, shortages of meat and cheese became more frequent. And I had been so busy with my flight training over the previous two years that I had hardly noticed the general deterioration in living conditions. Now people actually had to wait in line for staples like milk and flour. And I saw many more drawn, angry faces on the crowded sidewalks.

When I had visited home from the academy, I had always brought flowers and a small gift of cheese for my mother. Now I saw that the precious cheese, which was still available in Armavir, was even more appreciated than the flowers.

My mother and stepfather had been able to exchange their two small apartments for a comfortable larger flat in Microrayon 4. But even the food stores of "Micro-Israel" were no longer well stocked. My family, however, was able to build a tiny "dacha" on a parcel of land outside the city, which they could garden in the summer. They rented 450 square meters from the oblast, where they planted tomatoes, potatoes, and a variety of berries. They even planted a line of apple and cherry trees. This was still a hobby for them, but one that promised to see them through any real food shortages.

And now people were beginning to complain about the chronic, unexplained shortages. Their complaints, however, went unanswered, unless an important delegation of Party officials visited the city. Then, miraculously, the shops were always stocked with meat and dairy products people hadn't seen for months.

I reported to the 176th Frontal Aviation Fighter Regiment at Mikha Tskhakaya in December 1982. The base, known by its call sign "Ruslan," was just south of this western Georgian city. The Republic of Georgia was ringed by high, rugged mountains, with a hilly plateau in the east and the marshy Kolkhida lowlands running to the Black Sea in the west. Our base stood on this rich alluvial plain, not far from the Rioni River. The region was a citrus-growing area that had been reclaimed from stagnant marshland since the Soviet Union had annexed the republic in the 1920s. The city of Mikha Tskhakaya was the ancient Senaki, which like so many Soviet cities had been renamed for a local hero of the Revolution.

The area was historical. Known as Colchis to the ancient Greeks, the hero Jason and his Argonauts had struggled hard to journey there in search of the Golden Fleece. And judging from the bustling open-air markets beneath the towering eucalyptus trees and palms, there were still plenty of riches to be found. I had never seen such diverse and beautiful produce. The vendors' stalls were piled high with gleaming peppers, pyramids of huge oranges, and bunches of the season's last fat purple grapes. There were stacks of yellow squashes, mounds of big white onions, beets, carrots, and yams. Freshly butchered lambs and goats hung on hooks in the butcher stalls, and old peasant women in bright head scarves sold both plucked and live chickens. There was an exotic southern spice to the air. Beyond the snowy wall of the Caucasus to the north, there was winter.

Here the December sunshine was bright, and the air smelled of jasmine.

Riding the bus out to the base, I saw farm carts and trucks carrying even more produce to the city. Obviously the prosperity in Georgia was due to more than just the favorable climate of this protected, subtropical valley. The Georgians had a reputation for being energetic and enterprising. For every hectare of collective farm down here, there were two still held in private hands. I later found out that many of the "State" farms were actually run by Georgian families for their own profit. Probably the biggest difference between Georgia and the Russian Republic was the attitude of Georgians toward wealth. Where I came from, people were universally jealous of anyone who saved enough money to buy a car, for example. Here a wealthy person was respected. And people didn't mind spending money on themselves. The small, family-owned kebab stands and marketside canteens offered better food than most State restaurants I had seen elsewhere.

I came to Tskhakaya with five other lieutenants who had completed the accelerated MiG-23 training program at Armavir. Two of them, Yevgeni "Firefly" Svetlakov and Gennadi Zheleznyak, were good friends. Our enthusiasm at joining a real combat regiment was dampened by the reception we received. The commander, Colonel Homenko, was a sleek Ukrainian in his early forties. He eyed us warily as we stood before his desk. We were the first graduates of a former PVO academy to join his regiment. Leafing through our records, the colonel did not seem impressed by the progress we had made at Armavir.

Finally he looked up and frowned. "We do everything by regulations here," he growled. "All of my pilots obey official safety standards. You'll soon discover that the flying weather here is terrible. Just follow orders and you won't get in trouble."

We saluted and marched out of the colonel's office.

Firefly offered one of his sardonic grins. "That was a wonderfully inspirational message," he whispered as we left the regimental headquarters. "I definitely feel motivated to defend the Socialist Motherland."

As expected, we were assigned to the 3rd Squadron. In Soviet Air Force Frontal Aviation regiments, the 1st Squadron traditionally has the best-qualified and most experienced pilots and is usually called the Dogfight Masters. The 2nd "Ground Attack" Squadron is made up of less experienced pilots, while the 3rd "Training" Squadron is where new lieutenants are assigned to work with experienced instructors.

Once more, our reception was somewhat less than inspiring. The squadron commander and his deputies made it clear that safety, not combat readiness, was the major concern of all pilots. The 3rd Squadron was equipped with battered early-model MiG-23Ms. The damper system on the flight controls was less precise than on the newer aircraft we had flown at Armavir.

Colonel Homenko had decreed that flying would be suspended during "dangerous" weather. And it was the colonel himself, not the regimental meteorologist, who determined if the weather was acceptable on any given flying day. His methods were not overly sophisticated. He rose before dawn with a call from the weather office, pulled on a robe, and went out on the balcony of his apartment. If, for any reason, Colonel Homenko did not like the smell of the dawn air, the 176th Frontal Aviation Regiment's flying schedule was delayed while the colonel went back to bed for some well-earned rest.

"The less you fly," the colonel was fond of noting, "the longer you keep on flying."

In other words, you could not have a flying accident if you didn't take off.

We had both the lowest sortie rate and the best safety record in the division. This, of course, was what Colonel Homenko had in mind. To the chagrin of my friends and me, we discovered that the regiment was in fact an unofficial springboard to the 283rd Aviation Division located in Mikha Tskhakaya for regimental officers in search of comfortable staff positions. The way this system worked was that our regiment caused no headaches for the staff rats at Division, and they recommended officers from Ruslan to replace them when they climbed the ladder toward Moscow. Under the leadership of Leonid Brezhnev, this kind of cronyism had spread throughout the military. It was a cozy system, but had nothing to do with combat readiness.

But this attitude of almost paralytic caution would hardly help my friends and me to become rated pilots. We had graduated from Armavir as junior lieutenants and Non-Rated pilots, qualified to handle the MiG-23 only within a narrow range of flying conditions and maneuvers, which basically encompassed takeoffs and landings, formation flight, and rudimentary ground-attack and air-combat regimes.

Our immediate goal was to become Third Class pilots. This rating normally required a year's hard training after the academy, which included about 600 sorties or 350 flying hours. At Armavir we had already completed about 550 sorties, totaling around 230 hours. A Third Class pilot was qualified to fly day combat missions under minimum weather conditions that included visibility of at least one and a half miles and a ceiling of 750 feet, in formations ranging from four-plane *zveno* "links," up to a full squadron of sixteen aircraft.

Second Class pilots usually achieved their rating three to four years after academy graduation. Most of them had logged 770 sorties, with a minimum of 450 hours. They stood duty alert in combat regiments and flew both day and night. They were fully rated on instrument flying and were qualified for both ground attack and "maneuverable dogfights." Their daylight weather minimums were the same as Third Class, but their night minimums were three miles visibility and a 1,500-foot ceiling. The written and practical instrument flying examinations and night-formation flying made achieving Second Class rating the military pilot's greatest hurdle.

Becoming a First Class pilot required around 1,200 sorties and at least 550 flight hours. This usually took six years beyond the pilot's academy. A First Class pilot was fully instrument-rated and could fly any individual or formation combat maneuver both day and night down to weather minimums of 0.9-mile visibility and a ceiling of only 450 feet.

Both Second and First Class pilots received salary bonuses ranging from fifteen to twenty-five percent of their base pay. This bonus came at the end of the year, if the pilot met all the requirements of his rating during the year.

The next highest rating, Sniper pilot, was limited to a few highly experienced leaders who were selected for a long, demanding qualification process.

Our flying schedule was unexpectedly intensified soon after the New Year. Maybe, we thought at first, the Air Force had requested that the new MiG-23 pilots from the experimental

Armavir program continue their accelerated training, or perhaps the operational demands of the Afghan war overrode Colonel Homenko's habitual caution.

But we soon learned the real reason. There was a movement afoot to modernize the Soviet military. Younger, more dynamic officers were being promoted to general rank. One of them, Major General Gennadi Anosov, took over as commander of the 283rd Aviation Division. He was dissatisfied with Homenko's leadership of the 176th Regiment. One of the general's first acts was to send Homenko out to pasture as an instructor at an aviation academy. The general then named a bright, hardworking younger officer, Lieutenant Colonel Gennadi Torbov, as our regimental commander.

These changes reflected the political shake-up in Moscow. While I had been on leave in Samara after graduation, Leonid Brezhnev, the General Secretary of the Communist Party, had finally died. The joke at Armavir had been that he had actually died three years before, but the chest of his fine worsted suit was so encrusted with medals that it had taken him that long to slump over. In any event, Brezhnev was replaced by a leader with a much different style and agenda.

Yuri Andropov was an energetic and sophisticated career Party apparatchik, who had been chairman of the KGB for fifteen years. He was sworn in as Party Secretary only two days after Brezhnev's death and soon made it clear that he intended to clean house in the Kremlin and stamp out corruption and inefficiency in the Soviet economy.

By spring, his economic reform campaign had taken an interesting turn. Andropov specifically targeted "idlers, slackers, and drunkards" in Soviet industry and collective agriculture. The KGB was beefed up with thousands of plainclothes volunteers who cracked down on absenteeism and public drunkenness, especially during the official workday. Men and women found standing in line or lounging in the familiar groups near the State liquor stores were accosted by KGB agents who demanded their papers. Those found absent from their work place were arrested.

Andropov took the unusual step of appealing directly to the Soviet people via radio and television. The incipient decline of Soviet industry over the past thirty years, he said, was due entirely to the weakening discipline of the Soviet people. Socialist

Planning could only work to the benefit of all if the individual citizen on the shop floor or the farm took his job seriously. But absenteeism and tardiness, which led to drunkenness and widespread alcoholism, were sapping the vitality of the Soviet economy. These abuses, he added, had been tolerated in the past—a brutally frank, and accurate, aspersion on Brezhnev's decrepit leadership—but Andropov made clear there was a new leader in charge of the country.

The reform movement seemed to be sweeping the Soviet Union. People were afraid to leave work during the day, even if that was the only chance they had to buy scarce necessities. My mother told me that workers at her institute were encouraged to report anyone arriving even two minutes late. I felt great satisfaction at watching these events unfold. Andropov was exactly the kind of leader we needed: tough, practical, and resourceful. I knew from my own experience that the Socialist system rewarded those who worked hard. I had sworn to defend that system, with my very life if necessary. And I wanted everyone else to show the same level of dedication.

By order of the chief of staff of the VVS, all new lieutenants had to qualify as Third Class pilots within one year. This meant we had to work harder than Colonel Homenko could have ever imagined possible.

Our maneuver training circuits and weapons poligons— rectangular bomb, missile, and cannon firing ranges—were close enough to the Ruslan base that we could fly three or four sorties a day and at least two each night we trained. Ruslan lay in the middle of the flat Rioni delta, less than thirty miles from the coast, equidistant from the Great Caucasus to the north and the Maliy Kavkaz mountains to the south.

After our initial jet training in the L-29, the complex attributes of the MiG-23 combined to produce a seemingly sophisticated airplane. In effect, we had to learn three completely different sets of aerodynamic limits with their accompanying power-setting and angle-of-attack restrictions. The plane would behave one way at low speed with unswept wings and completely differently at another wing angle and throttle position.

At Ruslan I learned how this flawed design had been accepted as one of the Air Force's first-rank combat aircraft. Apparently

Marshal Pavel Kutakhov, the Air Force commander in chief, was a close friend of Brezhnev's. Kutakhov was also a crony of the heads of the Mikoyan Design Bureau. The marshal convinced Brezhnev to accept the bureau's new aircraft without submitting the design to a very rigorous competition among the combat aircraft OKBs, Mikoyan, Sukhoi, and Yakovlev. So the Air Force received thousands of MiG-23s, a design with many strong points, but one whose flaws had not been "wrung out" in competition.

Unfortunately the Sukhoi Design Bureau, which had done brilliant work during the war, fell out of favor in the late 1940s. Stalin was influenced by Anastasi Mikoyan, his foreign minister, and the brother of the Mikoyan OKB chief, Artem. The Sukhoi bureau was disbanded and its brilliant, forward-thinking designers and engineers dispersed throughout the Soviet Union. The Mikoyan OKB was now top dog in Moscow. Although their MiG-15 and MiG-21 were well-conceived and innovative aircraft for their time, the bureau lacked the vision of Sukhoi. Instead, they relied on political connections and *pokazuka* to push through their MiG-23 design.

Short-landing capability was one of the new aircraft's main requirements. The Mikoyan test pilots demonstrated this by a crude ploy. With PVO and VVS generals assembled at the test center, a demonstration pilot flared a prototype for landing and popped his drag chute with his wheels still three feet above the runway. Naturally the plane's landing roll was short. But the generals did not notice that the prototype had blown all three tires and damaged its gear. They were so impressed that they actually commented that the new aircraft should be considered a possible candidate for an aircraft carrier fighter.

As we trained that spring and summer on the Ruslan ranges, I had to constantly keep all of the aircraft's sensitive characteristics in mind. One afternoon of blustery showers when there was a fluky crosswind blowing on the active landing runway, I executed a missed approach only ten seconds from flareout. I rammed the throttle ahead to full military power, raised the gear and flaps, and climbed away.

"Bird," I called the tower, indicating that I had seen birds flying across the runway. This had not been the case. But I *had* recognized that for some reason, I had been just too fast to land and risked provoking a goat. I went around the circuit and set up for landing again. Once I landed, Captain Shalunov, my link leader, met me on the apron.

"What's going on, Sanya?" he asked. "I didn't see any flocks of birds out there."

I was stowing my helmet and oxygen mask in my flight bag and collecting my tactical navigation charts. I rose to face him. "Comrade Captain," I admitted, "for some reason I just felt that approach was not safe."

Instead of a reprimand, Shalunov smiled and slapped me on the shoulder. "Good job," he said. "Never forget, caution is not fear."

Even though the MiG-23 was a bastard of an airplane to master, I qualified as a Third Class pilot on the aircraft in August 1983. Our training shifted to Karachala, an isolated base in Azerbaijan. I had managed to rack up a full year's worth of sorties in only eight months.

After qualifying, we began to fly at night. I had no particular problem with the disorientation that can sometimes lead to hazardous vertigo, which afflicted some of the junior pilots during their early night flying. Again I was fortunate in having excellent instructors. Captain Shalunov helped me build on the skills that I had learned from Lieutenant Tveretin and Captain Bogorotsky. And, as always, I kept my own personal flight logbook in which I emphasized my shortcomings.

Then the Soviet military was rocked by a scandal of unprecedented scale. On September 1, 1983, a PVO Su-15 interceptor shot down a Korean Airlines Boeing 747 jumbo jet with 269 people on board over the Sea of Okhotsk between the Soviet Union's Sakhalin Island and the northern Japanese island of Hokkaido. There were no survivors. The plane had been en route to Seoul from New York with a layoveayover in Anchorage, Alaska. A number of important Americans, including a congressman, were among those killed.

Pr01 and the Vremya news broadcast from Moscow television stressed that the airliner had flown straight into Soviet airspace above sensitive defense installations and was flying in darkness without aerial navigation lights. According to Moscow, the Korean pilot also refused to respond to repeated warnings from both civilian and military Soviet air traffic controllers.

Marshal Nikolai Ogarkov, the deputy defense minister who

had tried to undercut the PVO in his reforms of the early 1980s, was now given the task of publicly defending the Air Defense Force. Ogarkov led an unprecedented internationally televised press conference at the Kremlin, which continued the same condemnation of the Korean pilot initiated by *Pravda*. Ogarkov's explanation for the Korean pilot's strange behavior was that the South Korean airliner might have been working in conjunction with an American Air Force RC-135 electronic spy plane. He stressed that the PVO radars had tracked the intruder all the way south from the heavily defended Kamchatka Peninsula, hundreds of miles to the north. The marshal used elaborate graphs and charts to demonstrate that the airliner had penetrated deeply into sensitive Soviet airspace despite repeated warnings from Soviet ground controllers to turn away.

After the widely publicized appearance by Ogarkov, Dmitri Ustinov, the Soviet Defense Minister, angrily chastised both the Americans and South Koreans for having endangered the civilian passengers so recklessly.

Most of the pilots in my regiment accepted the official version of this unfortunate event. But as VVS officers, we were scornful of the PVO pilot, Lieutenant Colonel Gennadi Osipovich, who had destroyed the airliner with two missiles. Osipovich's Su-15 was a typical PVO interceptor, a fast-climbing, rather unmaneuverable fuel guzzler with a short combat radius. The Su-15 was little more than a high-altitude missile platform. Some of my older colleagues dismissed PVO interceptor pilots as "robots" because they slavishly followed the radar vectors and weapons-release commands of the GCI ground controllers. Apparently this was the case in the Korean airliner incident.

My own reaction was that Osipovich certainly had not done everything possible to protect both Soviet territory and innocent lives. Then I began to hear a starkly different version of the events over Sakhalin Island. The Defense Ministry announced that a second Su-15 and a VVS MiG-23 had also been scrambled and were trailing Osipovich when he shot down the airliner. In fact, my link leader, Captain Shalunov, actually recognized the MiG-23 pilot on television. The officer was a friend of his named Litvinov. The pilots in my squadron began to whisper that there was something wrong with the official explanation of the airliner shoot-down. Nobody believed that the Americans would jeopardize hundreds of innocent civilian passengers for a routine espionage gain. The VVS base was in the north of the island. If at least two Su-15s and one MiG-23 had been scrambled, why was the airliner destroyed *south* of Sakhalin Island?

Later we discovered the shocking truth. A GCI officer named Andrei, reassigned from Sakhalin Island, came to our regiment for a familiarization course. Over dinner one night, he revealed what really happened to the Korean airliner.

Ten days before the incident, Andrei said, an Arctic gale had knocked down the early warning radar antennas on the Kamchatka Peninsula, depriving eastern Siberia and Sakhalin Island of the "air picture" needed to vector interceptors against intruders. Moscow put incredible pressure on the PVO to repair these antennas immediately to regain air-defense coverage for the Soviet Far East. Finally Far East PVO officers reported to Moscow that the radars were up and running. But the antennas were still lying broken on the tundra.

When the Korean airliner strayed into Soviet airspace, it passed right over the strategic peninsula and on toward Sakhalin Island without being properly tracked. One air base on the peninsula did scramble interceptors, but the GCI controllers could not give the fighters the correct vector or altitude for a successful intercept. The PVO on Sakhalin Island did not receive precise data on the "intruder." The first firm indication they had of KAL Flight 007 was when the airliner flew directly over the base in the center of the island. But the local radar operators did not speak English, so they couldn't talk to the Korean captain using the international distress radio frequencies of 121.5 or 243 MHz.

By the time they relayed this information to PVO Far East headquarters in Habarovsk in Siberia, the Korean Boeing 747 had already passed over Sakhalin and was on its way out of Soviet airspace. The order to destroy the unidentified *narushitel*, "violator," came from Habarovsk in a panicky attempt to conceal the fact that the northern early warning radars were still inoperable.

"They killed 269 people to save their own ass from Moscow," Andrei said bitterly.

I didn't know how to answer. Finally I replied, "Those PVO bastards are a bunch of dinosaurs."

Alexander Zuyev, age nine months, with mother, Lydia, Samara.

Alexander Zuyev, age
first day of school,
Samara, 1968.

Father, Mikhail Zuyev, teaching science class, Samara.

First-year cadet, Armavir Higher
Aviation Academy, 1978.

Parachute training,
Armavir, 1980.

MiG-23.

With Soviet Air Force Chief of Staff, Marshall Pavel Kutakhov,
Ruslan Air Base, Georgia, 1983.

MiG-23, military display, Red Army Day, Vasiani, 1985.

Discussing MiG-29 with Mikoyan OKB test pilot, Boris Orlov, 1985.

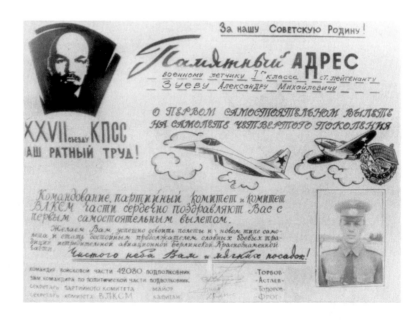

Certificate for flying "4th Generation" aircraft,
awarded after first MiG-29 flight, August, 1985.

Ankara, Turkey, May, 1989, after escape flight;
note wounded right arm cast.

America: with former Senator Barry Goldwater, 1991.

With American MiG-29 killers after Operation Desert Storm; Left: Lt. Nick "Mongo" Mongillo, USN, of VFA-81; Right: Capt. Chuck "Sly" McGill, USMC, serving as exchange pilot with USAF 33 TFW.

With the Navy's Blue Angels, Lt. John Foley, USN, San Diego Air Show, 1990.

USS *Abraham Lincoln,* welcoming ceremony af carrier landing, with F-14 Aardvarks Squadrc VF-114, 1991.

But I knew the fault lay deeper in our military system.

However, I soon had more personal events to consider than the poor leadership of the PVO and cover-ups in Moscow. On November 6, the eve of the annual celebration of the Great November Revolution, five of us from the Armavir MiG-23 program received transfer orders to the 512th Regiment at Vaziani, southeast of Tbilisi. The 512th was definitely *not* a Potemkin's village charade, as Colonel Homenko's unit had been. My new outfit had earned the proud designation "Combat Leadership Regiment." Almost all of its pilots had First Class ratings, and the unit's overall combat readiness and skill level was outstanding. Much of this was due to the efforts of our new division commander, Major General Anosov, who worked closely with the talented and energetic regimental commander, a full colonel named Boris "Bimba" Rinchinov.

My new commander was exceptional in many ways. He was a Buryat, one of the Siberian Mongol ethnic groups who lived around Lake Baikal, and had been raised in a State orphanage. Some Buryats had mixed Russian blood and did not appear especially Asian. But Colonel Rinchinov was a pure Buryat. With his big head, flat nose, and barrel chest, he looked like a Mongol horseman from the Golden Horde. For him to have reached the rank of full colonel in command of a Combat Leader Regiment in the VVS—a service that had only a handful of non-Slav pilots— was a testimony to his abilities and dynamism. He was a Sniper pilot in his early forties who had graduated near the top of his class from the Kacha academy. His advancement had been rapid, and his career had prospered from combat service as a MiG-21 adviser in Egypt during the protracted Arab-Israeli wars.

Bimba Rinchinov was both a terrific pilot and a popular leader. But unlike Homenko, he was blunt and demanding. He recognized that pilots were basically hardworking and ambitious, and wanted nothing more than the opportunity to fly. During our first meeting with him at Vaziani, Richinov made it clear that we would, indeed, get that opportunity.

The colonel demonstrated his leadership style by dispatching a four-engine An-12 transport from Vaziani to Tskhakaya to pick up the new lieutenants, their families, and their household effects. When we landed, late at night, the entire regimental senior staff was there to meet us. They had trucks laid on to transport our furniture and trunks to our new quarters. This was a far cry from the 176th.

After we came back to Vaziani from our mandatory annual leave, the colonel himself greeted us in his office.

"I know you fellows," he said, smiling as he looked us over. His expression was much more open than the habitual cunning blandness of Homenko. "You love flying more than sex. But I promise you that you're going to be flying so much here that you won't have any energy left to chase women."

That was exactly the kind of reception we'd been hoping for. This was the real Air Force, not a holding tank for staff rats.

I was assigned to the 3rd Squadron along with four of my Armavir colleagues. The squadron commander was an energetic young major named Nikolai Kuchkov. He was one of those rare men who are literally natural pilots. Where other experienced pilots might have to sweat through a tricky ground-attack or air-combat maneuver, Kuchkov could perform effortlessly with near perfection. He was an intense, demanding taskmaster, who expected absolute precision from all his pilots, including the new lieutenants who were struggling through their rating sorties toward Second Class.

The 512th Regiment had an excellent simulator center, where we carefully rehearsed all our training maneuvers before actually flying the sorties. Here Major Kuchkov often displayed his incredible flying skill. The simulator had a cockpit mock-up with a computer analysis station beside it. Using an electronic stylus, he could trace the flight path of a desired maneuver—anything from a shallow landing approach to a high-speed spiraling climb to an intercept. Then the students were expected to "fly" the simulator, following the optimal flight path as closely as possible. The only pilot who could actually match the original tracing, *every* time, was Kuchkov himself.

I was determined to do my best for this brilliant officer. So every free moment I had I spent in the simulator building working on my combat maneuvers. The young lieutenants in my squadron began calling me "Spare Parts" Zuyev because of the time I spent in the darkened simulator cubicle.

"Perfection is impossible, Sasha," Kuchkov told me one day

when I had been sweating in the simulator for over an hour. "Excellence is good enough."

Major Kuchkov was just as good, if not better, in a real cockpit. Most pilots occasionally experienced varying degrees of disorientation, especially flying at night while working "inside" the cockpit, adjusting the radar or arming weapons systems. We were prepared for this and always recovered quickly, usually by focusing outside the cockpit on the horizon. But Kuchkov seemed always aware of his aircraft's altitude and position.

He also always appeared aware of the other aircraft in the formation. Pilots swore he could swivel his head 360 degrees. And if you weren't tucked up in the proper *zveno* formation, be it combat trail or line-abreast, Kuchkov immediately let you know about it.

The older pilots in the squadron called him "the mind reader." To us young lieutenants, he was "the Professor."

However, he was certainly not unnecessarily critical or needlessly sarcastic. Within a year, we could all be in combat. Our regiment's 2nd Squadron departed for combat duty at the big Kandahar Air Base in Afghanistan while I was training for my Second Class rating. Kuchkov realized he was working us hard, virtually pushing us to our limits. But he also understood that combat would be tougher than any training.

One day in the squadron ready room, he held up a sheet of stationery in one hand and a smaller notepad in the other. "This is the division safety inspector," he said, hefting the stationery page. "And *this*," he said, hiding the notepad behind the larger sheet, "is combat readiness." He looked at us hard. "Safety will always get in the way of combat training." He reversed the sheet of paper and the small notepad. "We're going to turn things around and the devil take the safety inspector."

From that day on, we began flying in almost any weather, day or night. There were no safety inspectors on the forward bases in Afghanistan, Kuchkov assured us, and the Mujahedin did not wait for good weather to attack our troops. Some days we flew below minimum ceilings through the dense smog from the local steel mill, shooting ILS landings in visibility so poor you couldn't see the runway until almost touchdown. The division was always on our backs, but we flew anyway.

A typical flying day began at 0530, with an orderly banging

on the door of our two-man rooms, announcing that we had good flying weather. Unlike his counterpart at Ruslan, Colonel Rinchinov trusted our professional meteorologist to predict flying conditions. In this regiment we began flying much closer to minimums of visibility and ceiling than they did in the 176th. And as our hectic training schedule progressed, we were soon flying in marginal conditions that were often well below the minimums. Major Kuchkov was fond of pointing out that the Afghan Mujahedin preferred cloudy weather and snowstorms for their rocket attacks.

At 0600 we sat down to a "light" breakfast in the officers' dining room, a meal that always included fresh eggs, sausage, cheese, and rolls. As in other VVS regiments, the pilots' flight ration was very substantial.

We drew our Makarov 9mm pistols at 0620. I was very proud of my Makarov, having made sure that the gun was a top-quality specimen when it was issued, and having adjusted any minor flaws with the armorers after I had practice-fired it several times. I knew that the light automatic was not a match for an infantry weapon, but I wanted to be able to hit what I aimed at.

The regular flight-day medical test was next on our schedule. The regimental doctor examined every pilot flying, verifying blood pressure, temperature, pulse, and respiration. Any pilot suffering from a cold or the flu was automatically excused from training. We knew that the doctor also checked us for signs of drinking. Each regiment had its own traditions about alcohol, but most frowned on any drinking whatsoever during a period of flight training that could last as long as a month. The doctors were always prodding and probing us to make sure we had not suffered internal damage from high-G flight and giving us theoretical instructions on how to prepare for the stress of high Gs. But Major Kuchkov gave me much more practical advice, based on his own years of experience in jet fighters.

"During a training cycle, Zuyev," he told me, "don't drink a drop of alcohol. And stay away from sex, even a little bit."

"I'm not sure what a 'little bit' of sex is, Comrade Major," I replied with a straight face.

"Get the hell out of here," Kuchkov said with a smile.

His point was well taken, however. Drinking dulled your reflexes, and the effects of a hangover could last well into the next day. I was surprised to discover in intelligence briefings that

NATO pilots, especially the Americans and British, almost ritually frequented their officers' club bars every evening after flying. They apparently considered drinking a sign of masculinity. At the same time, we were told, they believed Soviet pilots suffered from serious alcohol problems. Certainly we drank in groups, but only during stand-down periods to celebrate the completion of a successful training cycle. Here in Georgia, excellent cognac was cheap and bountiful. But we stayed away from it while we were flying. If the regimental doctor even suspected smelling alcohol on your breath on a flight day, you would be grounded and severely disciplined.

My friend Dmitri, who had studied the American military so closely, was now with us in Vaziani. He explained that U.S. pilots were forbidden to take a drink twelve hours before flying. But, he said, they were notorious for drinking hard right up to that deadline, and were often badly hung over when they strapped themselves into their cockpits. In the Soviet Air Force a pilot would be grounded for even sipping a beer a full thirty-six hours before flying.

Air Force medical staff had more authority than their counterparts in the ground forces. Although a doctor might only be a captain, regimental commanders always accepted their doctor's "suggestion" about grounding a pilot found to be physically unfit to fly. The doctors also made sure we got the mandatory eight hours sleep each night. If a man was seen outside his building late at night, the doctor might ground him the next day. And Air Force medical regulations about the maximum number of flying hours or sorties in the training month, as well as mandatory annual leave, were strictly enforced. Every pilot on an active flight status was required to take a full forty-five days' leave each year. This was recognition that flying high-performance aircraft was both mentally stressful and physically debilitating. Under the same regulations, every year served on active flight status counted as two years toward retirement. The same regulations covered Navy submariners.

The pilots flying met with the meteorologist and tactical operations officer for a thorough weather briefing and a detailed walk-through of the objectives and maneuvers of the day's planned sorties. This was not a static rehearsal of an inflexible procedure, but rather an assessment of the training goals and skills required.

At 0800 the regimental commander briefed the pilots as to what he expected out of the day's sorties. At Ruslan, Homenko had usually stressed safety. In Rinchinov's fast, precise briefings here at Vaziani, he normally told us to keep our eyes open and to work hard. The ground radar controllers then gave us our GCI briefing as to the altitudes and vectors we would follow to our training circuits or weapons poligons. We also received the daily codes for our SRZO aircraft-recognition equipment.

The final squadron briefing came at 0830. It was a precise military formation rather than a friendly chat. Major Kuchkov spoke personally to each pilot, both chiding and urging him to concentrate on improving his skills.

We pulled on our G-suits and drew our helmets at 0845, just before conducting our walk-around inspection of the aircraft parked outside on the squadron apron. The maintenance officer in charge of that aircraft always accompanied us to answer any questions we might have about the condition of the machine. These guys had been up and working even longer than we had. In their black coveralls, greasy berets, and neckties splattered with hydraulic fluid, they always had a mournful, harassed look about them. But they were all graduates of first-rate engineering academies and were good at their work.

By tradition, takeoff came precisely at 0900. This was more than just an empty ritual. By insisting on an exact takeoff time, a regimental commander could be sure all the complex, interrelated elements necessary for a successful flight, from pilots' briefings to maintenance procedures, would be completed in proper sequence.

Because the training circuits were near the base, the first sortie was usually over by 0940. We ate a second breakfast after this first flight and held a quick debrief with the flight leader and the GCI officers to make sure the flight and ground controllers had no communications problems. Takeoff for the second flight of the day was usually around 1020, with the same postflight debriefing at 1100. We took off on our third flight by 1140 and had our final formal debrief an hour later.

Lunch was always a good meal. But we did not linger at the table. At 1300 we normally had a postflight analysis with our immediate training officer and began planning the next day's flying. The fellows needing extra work then flew a training sortie with an instructor in a two-seat aircraft.

In theory we were required to carry out some kind of political work, which included writing in our personal political essay book for an hour or two each week. But most pilots found this irksome and often stuck a flight manual inside the cover of a Marxist-Leninist text. About this time I discovered a handy expedient. I had dutifully copied out a tract essay on the virtues of the proper Communist officer and submitted it to the squadron's zampolit soon after I had arrived at Vaziani. He gave it high marks. Then, on a hunch, I resubmitted the same essay the next week in my spring binder, changing only the title page. Again he praised this work. From then on, I just revamped the same tired old essay, always adding a new title sheet. So much for the "keen interest" all zampolits were supposed to show in the pilots' political development.

Like all good Air Force leaders, Major Kuchkov recognized that we could only take the stress of such intense training for so long. He was extremely well organized and made sure we had regular physical training and sports events. He organized passionately played soccer tournaments, which certainly took our minds off the strain of flying. Kuchkov also held Saturday small-arms practice on an outdoor range as a substitute for sports.

Air Force fighter pilots in a combat regiment were just as keen gamblers as their military forebears, the cavalrymen of the czar's Hussar regiments. We bet on chess, cards, billiards, and even pistol marksmanship. One of our favorite games was "Watches."

The fellows in my squadron introduced my group of young lieutenants to the game one bright spring Saturday afternoon.

"Here," Captain Shalunov said, hanging his personal aviator's wristwatch from a nail on the pistol-range target. "Take your chances, one ruble per bullet."

Aviators' wristwatches were probably the best timepieces made in the Soviet Union and worth a lot of money. But the captain believed we were either too poor to risk hitting it or were just plain bad marksmen.

I waited while the other guys bought a few chances. They all missed. After Shalunov had retrieved his watch, I hung my own up and challenged my fellow lieutenants to have at it for only a ruble per shot. After I had earned an easy nine rubles, I turned to Firefly, who was beginning to puff with frustration.

"Hang on," I told him, "I'll be back in a minute with a grandfather clock."

Watches became one of my favorite games of chance. If my watch were hit, I'd have to replace it at my own expense before I flew again, but a watch was a very small target at twenty-five yards range. And someone with the guts to risk his watch repeatedly could win fifteen or twenty rubles on a good afternoon.

Such traditions, of course, cemented our loyalty to the Air Force through a proud and genuine sense of esprit de corps. Russian pilots are very superstitious. We had no aircraft or dormitory rooms numbered 13. Young lieutenants quickly learned never to use the word *posledniye*, "last," when describing the final flight of the training day. Instead, all Air Force personnel, pilots and ground crew alike, said "ultimate" flight, *krainiye*.

Our other main diversion, of course, was drinking. When we completed an intense training cycle and were not scheduled to fly for several days, the squadron's pilots would usually gather for a party in the regimental *banya*. As junior officers, we were responsible for organizing the *zakuski*, typically the kind of small dishes served with beer. And the older pilots brought the beer.

At dinners celebrating someone's promotion, we usually toasted with excellent Georgian cognac. Often the second toast of the party was the standard *za bezopasnost*, "safe flying," to honor men killed in accidents or in combat in Afghanistan.

We always stood around the table when toasting. The man offering the toast touched his glass, about halfway down from the rim, on the table edge and said, *"Kontact."*

Each of us in turn repeated the gesture, saying, *"Yest, kontact,"* as if we were a flight of Kobra pilots lined up on a grassy strip during the Great Patriotic War.

The man making the toast would then reply, *"Ot vinta,"* the command for the ground crew to clear the prop and start engines.

We would all then hoist our glasses, with our elbows at a precise ninety degrees from our torsos, exhale loudly, and drain the cognac.

But these parties became increasingly rare events as we dug into our serious training schedule. The weather on this eastern Georgian plateau held good through the spring and summer of 1984. And we were soon flying three or four sorties a day, four times a week. This meant our wake-up time was shifted from 0530 to 0400. As we were required to get at least eight hours sleep a night, we were usually in bed immediately after dinner. The pace was exhausting, but no one complained. As always, Colonel Rinchinov had been right: Young fighter pilots loved flying more than anything else. We would have gladly flown seven days a week, if Air Force regulations had permitted.

And as the pace of training got tougher, we broke the stress with practical jokes and humor. Just before pulling on our G-suits every morning, someone would always crack a new joke that would keep us laughing until we climbed into our aircraft.

One day, during a particularly rough training cycle, Boris Bagomedov, the usually serious Dagestani, had us practically rolling on the tarmac.

"All right," he said with his hoarse accent, "what's the difference between an American, an Israeli, and a Russian pilot? An American pilot jumps in his cockpit and sits on a thumbtack." He plucked at the seat of his flight suit to extract the imaginary tack. "'Shit! What the hell is this?' So he throws the tack out and gets on with his job.

"An Israeli pilot climbs into his F-16," Boris continued, repeating the same gesture. "He cries out in pain, pulls out the tack, looks at it, and sticks it in his pocket. 'This may be useful someday,' he says."

Boris folded his arms across his chest in a typical Russian posture. "A Soviet pilot sits down in his MiG-23 and gets a tack in his ass. He pulls it out and swears, '*Blyat!* What's this?' Then he thinks for a moment. 'Maybe it's supposed to be there.' And he sticks it back in his ass."

Like all good jokes, Boris's story had a core of truth.

In July pilots from the 2nd Squadron came back to Vaziani on leave from Afghanistan and filled us in on the realities of combat in that particularly nasty war. The Mujahedin were a murderous bunch who took pleasure in torturing and butchering any unlucky Soviet pilot that they shot down and captured. And the Kandahar Air Base was often brought under mortar or rocket attack, so the air crew were not tempted to stray into town.

But they flew an intense schedule. There were no dogfights, of course. And the air-defense tactics of the Mujahedin were relatively primitive, at least for the moment. The enemy forces had American Redeye shoulder-fired missiles, which were not very effective in the hands of the Afghans. But their 12.7mm and 14.5mm antiaircraft machine guns could be dangerous below an altitude of about 4,500 feet. This happened to be the bomb-release altitude we were currently using for our ground-attack training. So we listened intently to the veterans from the 2nd Squadron.

Colonel Rinchinov immediately shifted tactics and tailored our attack training to meet these new conditions. Most of our bomb and rocket-attack training was conducted on a dedicated range of the sprawling Karachala Air Base in Azerbaijan. This was an ideal location to test our new tactics. Now we flew steep, fast, high-G bomb runs, dropping like an old Luftwaffe Stuka from 21,000 feet and releasing our 1,000-pound fragmentation bombs at about 9,000 feet before hitting the air brakes and executing a savage, seven-G pullout. After a bit of practice we could hit targets on a sixty-degree dive angle and consistently pull out above 6,000 feet.

Then our intelligence officer reported that the Mujahedin were receiving new American Stinger shoulder-fired antiaircraft missiles. These were far superior to the Redeyes. Major Kuchkov studied the specifications of the Stinger and concluded that he could develop bombing tactics to overpower the missile's maneuverability and tracking. His new ground-attack maneuver was brilliant. Basically the four aircraft in a link would roll in on their target from four separate directions if possible, in a slightly staggered sequence. After weapons release at about 3,000 feet altitude, each plane would pull up steeply at a sixty-degree, six-G climb. The dive would be made with enough energy to allow the initial climb with the throttle at idle to minimize infrared emissions. In the climb, the pilot would begin a complete roll while simultaneously popping decoy flares. The roll would end with the aircraft back in level attitude, only 300 feet above the ground, with the nose turned toward the target and the tail pipe shielded from the enemy's Stinger positions. The pilot would then hit his afterburner and speed away on the deck.

It was one hell of a maneuver to master, even on the simulator. But we all recognized how effective it would be in combat against the Stinger.

We became so proficient in our ground-attack training that our 3rd Squadron was selected to represent the regiment in the division weapons competition that summer. Kuchkov led us into the bombing run on the poligon, using his dazzling anti-Stinger maneuver. No sooner had he recovered than the division safety inspector was screaming on the radio, "Stop this gross violation! Stop this hooliganism immediately!"

Kuchkov was called on the carpet, but was not seriously reprimanded. The worst outcome, however, was this new innovative maneuver, which could have saved many lives in Afghanistan, was never added to the combat training syllabus.

In September 1984 I was one of five new lieutenants in the regiment to pass the written and practical flight examinations to qualify as a Second Class pilot. I was less than two years out of the Armavir Academy when I crossed this difficult hurdle, an achievement that usually required four years of regimental flying. This was less of a tribute to me than to the excellent leadership of Colonel Rinchinov, Major Kuchkov, and their subordinate officers.

The 3rd Squadron had received the warning order to prepare for deployment to Afghanistan after the New Year. We became even more serious about our training. No one was reckless, however. Major Kuchkov and Colonel Rinchinov trusted our individual judgment in any given situation. They recognized that self-preservation was a strong motivating force, even among hot young fighter pilots. Rinchinov always gave us the old Russian tailor's advice, "Measure seven times and cut once." This did not mean to act timidly, but rather to exercise mature prudence.

During this period the regimental Party secretary advised me that I was probably now ready to submit my application for membership in the Communist Party. I had been a candidate member since coming to Georgia. In any given Air Force regiment every active pilot and most of the maintenance officers were Party members. Party membership was not quite an automatic privilege, however, and there was a certain traditional ritual to follow. Men with reputations as heavy drinkers were excluded and brand-new lieutenants were rarely accepted. Several of my fellow lieutenants also received the secretary's nod at this time. They consulted their Komsomol manuals and submitted standard answers to the most important question on the membership application form: "Why do you wish to become a member of the Communist Party of the Soviet Union?"

The stock answer always had something to do about the Party being in "the vanguard of the proletariat." As long as you used some combination of that tested formula, your application was usually endorsed by the unit's Communist *kollectiv.*

But I decided to write another answer. As long as I was going to become a Party member, I wanted to take the matter seriously. I understood that fewer than fifteen percent of Soviet citizens were granted this privilege, and I saw the Party as an elite group that could help bring about the needed fundamental reforms that Chairman Andropov had begun, but which were stagnating under his elderly successor, Konstantin Chernenko.

"Since becoming a military pilot," I said to the members during the regimental Partkom meeting called to consider our applications, "I have gained increasing responsibility. I now feel that I am ready to take on an even greater responsibility, membership in the Communist Party of the Soviet Union."

The secretary seemed thrilled by my answer, and Partkom wrote a glowing endorsement to my application.

A few weeks later I boarded a transport that flew my group of successful new applicants to division headquarters in Mikha Tskhakaya. Dressed in our pressed uniforms, we stood before the red banner of the Soviet Union and the standard plaster bust of Lenin as we took our oath as full Party members. Normally I wasn't much for sentiment, but I felt real pride as I spoke those solemn words.

That autumn, Colonel Rinchinov offered us new Second Class pilots a radical proposal for earning our First Class rating. Instead of taking our mandatory forty-five-day annual leave, we would take a minimum one-week stand-down from flying duties that would permit us to delay the long leave for three months. In those three months, he said, he would guarantee us the flying time and instructors to have us qualified as First Class pilots before New Year's. In short, he proposed compressing a year's training into ninety days. Naturally we jumped at the chance.

On the last day of this brief leave, a squadron runner told me to report to Colonel Rinchinov as soon as convenient. The colonel's secretary immediately showed me into his office. Given Rinchinov's expression of gravity and excitement, I thought I was about to receive immediate replacement orders for duty in Afghanistan. This was great news. But I was wrong.

"Tomorrow," the colonel announced, "a transport will arrive to take you to the Air Force test center in Lipetsk."

I looked at him quizzically.

"You have been selected for training in the MiG-29." He looked at me hard, then smiled broadly. "Congratulations," he said, rising to shake my hand. "This is a real honor."

"Comrade Colonel," I asked, "does this mean I'll be leaving your regiment and not going to Afghanistan with my squadron?"

"Yes, it does," Rinchinov said gruffly, brushing back his thick black hair.

"Comrade Colonel," I said, looking into his frank, open face, "what if I don't want to go to Lipetsk?"

"Comrade Lieutenant," Colonel Rinchinov said with a gleam in his dark eyes, "it's not your job to make such decisions."

I was on my way to Lipetsk.

— 6 —
MiG-29
1984-85

In the first week of December 1984, I joined a group of Air
Force officers boarding an An-26 "Curls" transport at a military
airfield near Tbilisi. We were en route to several other bases in
Georgia to pick up more officers and eventually fly north to the
VVS Fourth Flight Tactical Advanced Training and Test Evaluation Center at Lipetsk. My group was the core of a regiment to be
equipped with the new MiG-29. The Lipetsk training center had
already given the MiG-29 orientation course to two similar groups,
one from the prestige fighter base at Kubinka near Moscow, and
the other from a Combat Leader Regiment in the Ukraine. There
were only a few production-line MiG-29s already in service, and
our assignment, once we received the new aircraft, would be to
complete the complex, and rigorous, combat evaluation tests.

Igor Novogilov and I were the only two lieutenants selected
from Vaziani. The other three officers from our base were First
Class pilots; two were captains, the other a major. Major General
Shubin, the VVS deputy military district commander, and two full
colonels from his staff made up the Tbilisi contingent. At Tskhakaya
we picked up three captains from the Meria regiment and a
colonel who was division deputy commander. Late that afternoon
we landed at Gudauta on the Black Sea, where four more
experienced pilots climbed on board to round out our party.
Novogilov and I exchanged glances as these officers settled in for
the long flight north. We were the only two Second Class pilots

132

on board. Apparently our performance had rated high enough to merit selection. I certainly appreciated the honor, but I knew a lot of hard work lay ahead.

Whatever other advantages came from this assignment, the selection of Igor and me to fill senior pilot slots in the new regiment was a pleasant surprise. This guaranteed us promotion to captain at the earliest opportunity. Even as an experienced First Class pilot, a senior lieutenant could not be promoted in military rank unless he filled an appropriate position. So most junior officers in established regiments had to accept flying as wingmen. Only a senior pilot could lead a two-plane formation. In fact, there were some fellows at Vaziani who had been serving as senior lieutenants for years. Now I was going to become a captain well ahead of my peers.

As the plane droned along, the late afternoon sun lit the high glaciers of the Caucasus off to the east. I could distinguish the twin white cones of Mount Elbrus, the tallest peak in Europe. In the Abkhas language Elbrus meant "untarnished virgins' breasts." My regiment's young pilots joked that Elbrus was the only virgin with tits in the whole Transcaucasus. The mountain's lower slopes were thick with snowfields glowing pastel peach in the sunset. I was scheduled to take my delayed mandatory annual leave after New Year's up at the Terskol military ski resort on the slopes of Mount Elbrus, where I'd learned to ski the year before. This was a nice prospect, which had kept me going through the rough training at Vaziani. But now I was more excited about what lay ahead at Lipetsk.

Listening to the senior officers banter back and forth as they played poker and *preferans* in the transport cabin, I learned that we would receive an intense one-month orientation on the new aircraft's systems, but no actual flight training. We would then return to our own bases and only report to the new regiment when at least one squadron of MiG-29s was available. The regiment would be formed at Gudauta, a base which had bounced from the PVO to the VVS under Ogarkov's reorganization. The last PVO Su-15 regiment at Gudauta was transferred to Anadir in the Arctic in only three days, after an American SR-71 overflew Soviet Far East. A Yak-28 regiment was then transferred to Gudauta. That was fine with me. Gudauta was close to the resort town of Sochi, which had some of the best nightlife on the Black

Sea, including beachside discos with authentic Western music. It was a splendid town to visit as a single fighter pilot. Some of the married fellows from Transcaucasus regiments also patrolled the pebbly beaches and swimming pools. And the flying weather was less humid than in central Georgia.

Lipetsk was a fast-growing industrial center in the Don Basin. Some of the most modern Soviet iron and steel works and related machine-tool and chemical plants were clustered here. In turn, a number of aviation enterprises and support factories for the big military design bureaus were located in Lipetsk. The town had a reputation of being very hospitable to visiting pilots.

And I discovered just how friendly the people of Lipetsk were, the very first night when Igor and I went for a walk after dinner. We were on the way to the telephone office to call our parents when two good-looking young women in stylish fur jackets approached us on the icy sidewalk. Because there were so few single Russian women in Georgia, I was always attracted to pretty girls when I traveled. Usually I checked out their legs first, but on this occasion I was mesmerized by one of the girls' luminous blue eyes. To my surprise those innocent blue eyes were fixed just below my waist. She was blatantly inspecting *me*.

After the girls passed us, I turned to Igor. "I feel like she just opened my zipper with her eyes," I said. "I've never seen a woman so bold."

Luckily I still had a good supply of high-quality condoms from my years in Armavir. Besides being the site of an illustrious VVS pilots' academy, Armavir had the only condom factory in the entire Russian Republic. We had so many condoms that we even decorated our New Year's trees with them. And before I left, I had laid in a good stock of their products.

Condoms were as valuable as gold in the Soviet military. They were the only form of contraception available—besides abortion, of course. And the venereal disease rate in towns like Lipetsk was quite high, so I made sure to bring a good supply of Armavir's best-quality condom with me. It was a real shame that the Defense Ministry wasn't prepared to outfit all the troops so well. Apparently our imperialist enemies were more generous. Intelligence officers had told us that the American Army was so rich that they actually gave their "boys" two condoms and a handkerchief for every weekend pass. They were supposed to use the handkerchief to blow their nose to show they were gentlemen.

But I knew there wouldn't be much time to use up my condoms. And I also realized it was prudent to get to know a town better before seriously chasing after the local women. Many of them had more than just sex on their minds. In some cities, girls ran a clever racket. They'd meet a pilot at a local dance, encourage him to drink heavily, then invite him back to their room. When the fellow woke up early the next morning, he was always in a hurry to return to his base. Then he would discover that his Communist Party card and military identity papers, embossed with gilded missiles and comets, were missing. The girl would offer to organize a search for these precious documents. Sometimes the "bonus" required for the return of the papers went as high as 750 rubles. They knew what our salaries were and how much they could squeeze out of us.

Even the senior staff officers in our group did not know much about the MiG-29 before we got to Lipetsk. The new aircraft had a definitely mysterious aura, which angered many of us. We knew that the MiG-29 had already been discussed in Western military journals, but we pilots who would have to quickly master its complexities had been told absolutely nothing about the new fighter. This was more of the same old rigid secrecy that had hamstrung the Soviet military in many ways. It was a sad state of affairs if Moscow couldn't even trust *us* with some hint about the new MiG fighter.

At Vaziani a friend of mine had brought back some photocopies of Western technical publications, which had vague artist's sketches of the new fighter. These sketches confirmed our expectations: The MiG-29's configuration followed the same pattern as similar fighters being developed in the West. Like the American F-15 and the F-18, the MiG-29 pictured was a two-engine fighter with twin vertical tail fins.

In my first year at Armavir, Alexander Fedotov from the Mikoyan Design Bureau had briefed us on the new generation of aircraft. But all he had told us was that the new MiG and Sukhoi fighters "will be just as good as the Americans' F-15 and F-16."

From reading the Soviet publication *Foreign Military Review,* I knew that future combat fighters would be powered by reliable twin afterburning turbofan engines that needed gaping, low-slung air intakes. To operate at the extreme ends of the flight envelope— slow and low, and high Mach at high altitude—these new aircraft would combine a sculpted, lift-generating fuselage with thin wings that were only slightly swept. Twin vertical tail fins and large one-piece horizontal tail stabilizers were the logical solution to highly maneuverable flight control across the entire envelope. It was no wonder that all these modern combat planes—Soviet and Western—had a similar configuration.

But Soviet combat aviation doctrine was almost exactly the opposite of the NATO air forces. We did not have a global chain of modern bases. Our Frontal Aviation regiments operated from relatively primitive bases like Tskhakaya and Vaziani, each with a single large runway and simple maintenance facilities. The Soviet military was not a primarily volunteer force like those in the West. We did not have a limitless supply of technically talented young career sergeants to maintain our planes in the field. Many of the conscript mechanics I'd worked with could barely read Russian and had to be taught their tasks with the rote techniques you'd use with a child. *Kolkhozniki* with the cow manure of the State farms still wet on their boots could not be expected to repair radars and fire-control computers like their American counterparts, who had grown up with their own cars and—we heard on the Voice of America—their own home computers. Instead, we relied on a small cadre of professional maintenance officers trained in academies, supplemented by *praporshchiki*, warrant officers who could keep the conscript mechanics from destroying the planes.

Our military planners also faced another challenge when they wrote the design requirements for new Soviet aircraft. The Great Patriotic War had taught us an extremely valuable lesson: the tactic of offensive and defensive *zasada*, ambush. To survive, combat aircraft had to be dispersed as widely as possible—often to simple airstrips with steel matting or even roads for runways and no electrical power or maintenance hangars. In June 1941 the Nazi Luftwaffe had destroyed both the PVO and the VVS on the parking aprons of their elaborate bases in Byelorussia and the Ukraine. After that, we'd learned to disperse down to primitive grass strips, often hiding our aircraft in stands of birch and maple trees.

You couldn't fly a modern combat jet off a muddy grass strip, of course. But we built our modern planes to operate in conditions almost as primitive. If a regiment was using a potholed highway as an emergency dispersal strip, the pilots were even instructed exactly how much to reduce the air pressure in their tires. Soviet fighters also had to be simple, reliable, and robust— "soldier-proof." We planned to counter the Western lead in precision-guided weapons by spreading our assets thinly across our vast territory. I had seen plans for training exercises in the Far East, for example, where MiG-23 regiments would disperse down to squadron or even *zveno* level and operate off steel-mat strips, supported only by a small convoy of fuel and ordnance trucks. All Soviet combat planes could start engines with their own internal battery and be rearmed by a pair of mechanics working with simple tools.

So all of us who arrived at the Lipetsk training center understood that the MiG-29 would combine some design features shared in common with Western planes. But we also knew that the new fighter would have to meet our particular Soviet requirements. And we all expected that the airplane would combine both unprecedented thrust and maneuverability.

When my friend Pashka Goleitszin read in a European aviation magazine that the Mikoyan OKB had simply "plagiarized" Western designers in the configuration of the MiG-29, he exploded in indignation.

"Those damned capitalists," he yelled. "Who do they think we are, a bunch of ignorant Mongols? We've been building fighters for seventy years."

Pashka was an avid patriot, and what he said was certainly true, but I knew that the long conflict between the Soviet Union and its enemies, in both the East and the West, had reached a critical stage. Where we had been able to employ minimal technology in large numbers in the past, we now faced a critical advanced-technology challenge in the new generations of Western aircraft.

NATO had already assigned the MiG-29 the code name "Fulcrum," *tochka opori*. Most VVS pilots were pleasantly amused by the NATO designations for our aircraft: "Fishbed" for the MiG-21, "Flogger" for the MiG-23, and all the others. These English words had an exotic sound in Russian, and it made nicknames to the fighters a lot easier. But I especially liked Fulcrum. It was pure coincidence, of course, but the new fighter did represent a pivotal point in Soviet aircraft design. Either we were going to meet the Western technology challenge, or we would slip into the status of a second-class military power. And I knew our leaders would never allow that to happen, no matter what sacrifice was required.

Even before we received our first briefing at Lipetsk on the new MiG-29, I had learned something of its capabilities, which were developed to meet this new Western threat. During the air war in Vietnam, the Americans had lost hundreds of fighter-bombers to the Soviet air-defense system the PVO had installed and managed in North Vietnam. The combination of radar-controlled high- and medium-altitude surface-to-air missiles deployed in dense concentric circles around important targets—the same system we used in Soviet territory—had forced the Americans to adopt new tactics. They had learned to fly under our radar in small dispersed formations, which arrived on different headings simultaneously at important targets in order to saturate the defense forces. Since then, they had applied the same logic to their attack plans against Soviet forces. Current American and NATO doctrine called for multiple low-altitude strike "packages" flying below the radar horizon.

Their fighter-bombers and new cruise missiles all employed this tactic, as did their large strategic bombers. This would neutralize our air-defense missiles and effectively counter the old PVO GCI defense in which interceptors with relatively weak on-board radar would be strictly vectored to their targets by radar controllers on the ground. Our battle management officers could not spot F-16s or NATO Tornados streaking along at transonic speed just above the treetops. And interceptors like the Su-15 or the MiG-23 lacked the radar detection or fire control to shoot down such intruders. Traditional mono-pulse airborne radar could not detect a low-level aircraft against the clutter of the ground below. And at low altitude, passive jamming with chaff—ultra-thin hairlike strips of aluminum foil—could make a plane invisible to radar. Only pulse-Doppler radar, which detected relative motion, was capable of managing the so-called "look-down, shoot-down" fire-control system. But this radar depended on sophisticated computers, a technology that our designers had managed to avoid dependence on until now. The MiG-29 reportedly had this radar.

Naturally I was eager to see the new airplane firsthand. The winter cold and blizzards, however, had closed down the Lipetsk test-flight lines, so I didn't even glimpse the new fighter during the first week of intense classroom orientation.

Our instructors immediately made it clear that the MiG-29 was a revolutionary departure from traditional Soviet aircraft design. And production models of the new fighter were being built and delivered to combat regiments at a much quicker pace than previous planes.

"The MiG-29 is a fourth-generation aircraft," the colonel instructor lectured from the front of the classroom. He tapped the display board to illustrate his point. "The MiG-15 through MiG-17 subsonic jet fighters represent the first generation." He tapped the diagram of the familiar MiG-21, with its distinctive delta wing, and the American F-4. "These Mach 2 aircraft, equipped with radar-guided missiles, are the second generation.

"The variable-geometry MiG-23 and the American F-14 are the third generation."

Now the colonel strode to the large engineering model of the MiG-29 mounted near his lectern. "Comrades," he said proudly, "this is the fourth generation."

The colonel proceeded to highlight the new fighter's principal characteristics. As the officers around me in the overheated room listened intently, I realized that my new aircraft did, indeed, represent an entire new generation of technology. And I was astounded that the plane incorporated so many advances in a single aircraft.

The conceptual sketches in the Western publications had not done justice to the plane's streamlined aerodynamic contours. The airframes of the MiG-23 and Su-17—the last of the third-generation Soviet fighters—jutted with sharp, drag-producing angles. But the MiG-29 was a smooth flow of wing, lifting fuselage, and raked tail fins, blended around the long parallel tubes of the RD-33 turbofan engines. Certainly the plane evoked graceful power. But an experienced pilot could also see its inherent maneuverability.

Then our instructor began to recite the performance data. With a normal combat load, the plane had a sea-level rate of climb of 65,000 feet per minute. And the MiG-29 also had tremendous maneuverability. When we were told the acceleration rates, the rate and radius of turns, many of the officers around me whispered to each other to verify they had heard correctly. Then the instructor noted that, with combat fuel and weapons loads, the MiG-29 had a thrust-to-weight ratio of 1.35.

This was accomplished, he noted with obvious pride, by using ultra-light alloys of aluminum and lithium in the primary airframe and incorporating composite material such as graphite and carbon fibers in control surfaces and honeycomb stiffening in the twin tails. The colonel assured us that the space-age composite materials were stronger than titanium-steel alloys, but as light as cardboard. The fighter, he explained, had been built to perform nine-G maneuvers, the maximum safe aerodynamic stress that a veteran pilot could tolerate without blackout or injury. The airframe itself could pull over twelve Gs, so we obviously would have to be aware of the fighter's incredible potential.

When the instructor pointed out the key structural elements of the model, he noted that over forty percent of the generated lift was produced by the aerodynamic fuselage. This meant the plane could maneuver at unprecedented angles of attack.

"Comrades," the colonel said, "all you MiG-23 pilots will be happy to note that in our test programs to date, we have not been able to spin the MiG-29."

Flying a MiG-23 at a high angle of attack was a sure way to enter an often fatal flat spin. There was a murmur in the classroom.

"Let some young unrated lieutenants fly it," a senior colonel said gruffly. "*They* will find a way to spin the airplane."

"No, no," the instructor replied. "Our test pilots have been very thorough. This is an inherently stable aircraft."

The instructor proceeded to note that the MiG-29 had a greatly improved hydraulic flight-control system that was augmented by a computerized cross-control system and devices that transferred primary control among the ailerons, rudders, and horizontal stabilizers during high-speed air-combat maneuvers. I was just beginning to grasp the level of sophistication of the new plane.

"What about true fly-by-wire controls?" another senior officer asked brusquely.

"The Mikoyan OKB is working on such a system for the later models," the instructor explained.

Now a major general broke in. "I understand the Sukhoi OKB already has fly-by-wire for their Su-27."

The instructor nodded patiently. The Sukhoi Design Bureau

was renowned for its innovation. If it hadn't been suppressed by Stalin after the war, Sukhoi probably would have surpassed Mikoyan.

He smiled. "You fellows know those wizards in the OKBs," he said frankly. "If they added all their planned modifications and improvements to the first model of a new aircraft, they couldn't keep their contract pipeline open. You'll get computerized flight controls in two or three years."

He conceded that a fly-by-wire control system had its advantages. In American aircraft like the F-16, computerized controls allowed the pilot to fly to the maximum possible degree of maneuverability before encountering dangerous stalls and spins. This also made the airplane very forgiving of pilot error. But a fully computerized fly-by-wire flight-control system had one major disadvantage: It was vulnerable to the powerful electromagnetic pulse (EMP) of a nuclear blast.

"And we all know," he said gravely, "that any full-scale engagement with NATO forces will take place on a nuclear battlefield."

"You'll be happy to note, comrades, that the MiG-29 is just as maneuverable as the F-16C." He consulted a sheath of technical data, then smiled. "The MiG-29 has a 360-degree turn-rate time of only seventeen seconds."

Now the murmur in the classroom was excited.

The two RD-33 turbofans, he noted, each produced 18,300 pounds of thrust, which meant they were dramatically more powerful on afterburner than the engines of similar Western fighters. And because the MiG-29's overall weight was relatively low, the plane could fly at a near-equal thrust-to-weight ratio on "dry" power—without resort to the fuel-draining afterburners.

As the instructor noted the principal engine characteristics, I again heard a murmur of surprise in the seats around me. The performance of these big turbofans far exceeded that of the Tumansky R-29 in the MiG-23. Again the colonel smiled. "You will read in the 'well-informed' Western press," he said, "that our new aircraft is powered by the 'Tumansky' RD-33. Such an engine does not exist."

These engines, he said, were designed and built by the Leningrad/Klimov scientific group, which had taken over from the Isotov Engine OKB. The RD-33 was an entirely new undertaking, which incorporated optimal thrust-to-weight, fuel economy, reliability, and simplicity of maintenance. This was *not*, the colonel stressed—as the Western aviation press had reported—simply an improvement of an earlier Tumansky engine.

The instructor smiled. "But don't you fellows think that we might be capable of helping this misconception?"

When our laughter subsided, the colonel presented some highlights of the new fighter's weapons and fire-control systems.

"The NO-193 pulse-Doppler radar," he read from his data sheet, "can search for and track moving targets above or below the fighter's flight level out to a range of almost sixty miles."

"Computer-assisted?" a colonel asked.

"Of course," the instructor replied. "The fire-control computer automatically sorts out ten targets and presents them on the head-up display."

"And the IRST?" a major asked.

"A complete new system from what you had on the MiG-23," the instructor noted, citing figures from his data sheet. "And this search and track system is interfaced with the laser range finder and the helmet-mounted sight."

I was jotting notes as fast as I could, but then realized all these systems would be broken down and taught to us in great detail during our stay at Lipetsk.

"The great advantage of this multisensor system," the colonel noted, "is that the MiG-29 pilot does not have to use his radar constantly, which renders him invisible to enemy radar warning receivers."

He flipped a page in his data book and cited speed and range figures for the new radar-homing Alamo and infrared-seeking Archer missiles the aircraft would carry.

I had been trained to fly a difficult, relatively low-performance fighter armed with obsolete missiles. But I saw at once that this new aircraft—with its multiple weapons sensors and powerful missiles and cannon—was the equal of anything in the Western inventory. I couldn't wait to begin to study the fighter in detail.

For the next week, we sat in brightly lit, stuffy classrooms, sweating over a mounting pile of MiG-29 technical data sheets. The aircraft was so new that neither the Mikoyan OKB nor VVS Frontal Aviation had been able to produce final printed manuals for the fighter's systems. Instead, we were issued loose pages, most of which had to be carefully hand-corrected to incorporate the latest equipment modifications and performance information from flight-test data. It was hard, painstaking work, but all of us had a sense of being involved in a revolutionary endeavor. The more we learned about the MiG-29, the more we realized the colonel delivering that orientation lecture had been understating, not exaggerating, the plane's potential.

Then late on our second Friday afternoon, my group was escorted by armed guards to a nondescript inflatable hangar near the main Lipetsk flight line for the first personal inspection of the new fighter.

My first impression on entering the nylon igloo of the hangar was of the fighter's lean, sculpted contours. I went forward to stroke the cool gray alloy panels of the lifting fuselage and the thin swept wings. Although the MiG-29 was slightly longer than the MiG-23 Crocodile, the new fighter was much less chunky. On the ground the Crocodile was a clumsy brute. Even in this small hangar, the MiG-29 appeared powerfully agile, fluid, yet deadly.

I passed around the left wing and inspected the sweeping blade of the one-piece powered stabilizer. These big horizontal tail surfaces were half as wide as the wings. And they could swing through an unusually wide deflection arc above and below the horizontal. Melding such powerful control surfaces with the massive thrust of the two turbofans would produce unprecedented maneuverability. Each of the twin raked vertical tails supported a large one-piece slab rudder, made of composite honeycomb material, that extended beyond the fin's trailing edge, again evoking sensitive flight-control response. I was surprised at the thin airfoil sections of the wings and tail surfaces. These new alloys looked flimsy, but were stronger than steel.

My hand rested on the cold segments of the left engine's afterburner nozzle, which consisted of an inner and outer ring of tapered alloy sections.

"This is a two-chamber bypass system," a maintenance officer told me. "You can fly on maximum afterburner safely with no fear of nozzle overheating." These engines delivered more thrust and better fuel consumption.

The maintenance officer showed me the engine air inlets that were protected by hinged, folding metal screens that dropped down the moment there was pressure on the landing gear struts.

"On taxi and takeoff," he said, "the engines are protected from ingesting debris, like ice or gravel."

Obviously this meant the new fighters could be safely flown from dispersed forward airstrips. With these protective doors in place, the engines breathed through the big louvered "shark gills" beside the fuselage on the upper wing surfaces.

At the nose I stared up at the clear-glass dome of the IRST sensor, which shielded the smaller shiny black globe inside, the actual sensor head. It was cooled by liquid nitrogen and was reportedly accurate for search, track, and lock-on out to a range of over fifteen miles. When coupled with the look-down pulse-Doppler radar, I realized, the IRST gave the pilot a choice of sensor options not yet available in several advanced Western fighters. NATO fighters like the F-16 or Mirage F-1 lacked this dual sensor system, and relied instead on target acquisition from airborne radar planes like the American AWACS. That was all well and good in peacetime, when the AWACS could orbit unmolested up at 35,000 feet with its huge antenna sweeping the battlefield far beyond the horizon. But in war, one well-placed missile would blind the AWACS, and the Western planes would have to resort to their own radars, which would reveal their positions on our radar-warning receivers.

"How easy is all this electronic gear to work on?" I asked the maintenance captain.

He grinned, and pointed at an electronic diagnostic cart coupled to the fighter by a single green cable. "That computer checks every system after each flight. This is a very easy plane to service. If I have the right mechanics, I can change an engine in thirty minutes."

Intelligence had taught us that it took top American ground crews a full hour to change an engine on an F-15.

I waited my turn to climb the orange steel ladder to the open cockpit. When I sat on the surprisingly comfortable K-36D ejection seat, I felt like a king on a throne. This new fighter had been designed with a combat pilot in mind. Perched out here high on the nose, the view was unobstructed back past each wingtip. The instrument panel was dull gray with white instrument lights, unlike the MiG-23's green panel that had dim red lights, which

were hard to read. And the clear Plexiglas HUD was well placed
and did not block my view forward. My hands automatically went
to throttle and stick, where they would be in a dogfight. Even in
this cramped temporary hangar, I could sense how the plane
would feel alive, in its natural environment, the sky.

I was impatient to fly this splendid new fighter.

My group's classroom orientation lasted most of December.
And we only made it back to our bases in Georgia a day or so
before the New Year's holiday. But I had not minded the tedious
hours with the engineering manuals. I was now firmly convinced
that my country's full scientific and technical potential had been
brought together in a combat aircraft. The MiG-29 was not a
compromise born of political intrigue or Moscow cronyism. It was
a weapon equal to anything in the Western inventory.

But I would have to swallow my impatience to fly the new
fighter. The regiment then forming around my original cadre of
officers would not receive their first aircraft for several months. In
the interim I had two obligations to fill. First I had to complete
my mandatory forty-five days' annual leave off flight status. Then,
I hoped, I would have time to finish my qualification training for
my First Class pilot rating. Before leaving Lipetsk, I had stood in
line for an hour to buy a nice New Year's tree to bring back to
Tskhakaya. Pine trees were a novelty in Georgia. I planned to
host a large party for my friends in the regiment. This might be
the last time I saw them for a long time. They were going to
Afghanistan, and I was to be transferred to the MiG-29 unit.

On January 5, 1985, I flew Aeroflot to Mineralnyye Vody and
took an Army bus for the Ministry of Defense ski resort at Terskol
on the slopes of Mount Elbrus. The Air Force ordered that I
would forget about flying and devote myself to skiing through the
deep powder snow and cedar groves on the steep slopes of that
huge extinct volcano. The implication was that I was to relax
completely. This I certainly intended to do.

But then when I returned to Vaziani, I would have to throw
myself fully back into my qualification training. If I didn't make
my First Class rating before transfer to the new MiG-29 regiment, I would have to repeat a lot of the tedious training that I
had already sweated through at Vaziani. And I knew the new unit

would be too busy qualifying pilots on the MiG-29 to devote aircraft and instructors to me. I either had to make my grade before leaving Vaziani or be stuck as a Second Class pilot for the indefinite future.

I was tucked into a comfortable seat on the well-heated Defense Ministry bus, chugging slowly up the icy switchback roads toward the white dome of Elbrus. I had a reservation at the Terskol resort hotel and a canister of good Armenian cognac in my duffel on the luggage rack. Since coming to Georgia, I'd learned that cognac was as valuable as hard currency. A liter of Armenian cognac cost me five rubles when I dealt with a certain unofficial "Socialist Enterprise": an acquaintance named Otar—an amiable Georgian with a pirate's mustache—who had family connections in Armenia. The same high-quality cognac in the State liquor store cost fifteen rubles, and was almost unobtainable in the Russian Republic.

I had spent part of my annual leave here at Terskol the previous winter, and had learned how to ski the hard way, after accidentally taking a lift to the top of an expert run on the mountain's eastern shoulder. After a couple near-fatal falls, I stopped to "adjust my bindings," when a pretty girl took pity and showed me how to escape the dangerous slope by riding the chairlift back to the bottom.

My first year at Terskol I had also made friends with three interesting young fellows who would join me on this vacation. When I had met them in the men's dormitory of the resort the year before, they'd explained they were students. One of them was an ethnic Abkhas named Zaour. His tall friend Oleg was from Sochi with the precise diction of a television announcer. Vladimir, who appeared in his mid-twenties, was a Russian born in Georgia, but he spoke with a slight Baltic accent, as if one of his parents might have been Latvian or Estonian. They originally had a cramped, cold attic in the hotel annex, and I managed to get them into my bigger room, which we soon took over as our private domain. I had managed to bring three liters of cognac on my first ski vacation. Vladimir had a Toshiba stereo and a good assortment of Western rock cassettes. Zaour came equipped with a huge sack of oranges. Soon we had a nonstop party running every evening when the lifts closed. Oleg called it our "après ski" classes.

And the girls from Moscow Medical Institute and the professional schools in Georgia certainly seemed to enjoy the lessons.

When the bus dropped me at the snowy steps of the Terskol resort, Oleg, Zaour, and Vladimir were already there, all grinning broadly. It seemed that the resort's equipment manager, another Abkhas named Hamid, had been able to reserve us a pair of comfortable two-bed rooms which opened into a suite. The liter of cognac I'd given Hamid the year before was certainly bearing fruit. A senior lieutenant in the VVS and three students were going to live better than a lot of senior officers.

One afternoon, Oleg told me that the three of them planned to pay their respects to the base commander, the lieutenant colonel who managed the resort. He wore a blue VVS uniform, replete with pilot's wings, as if being up in the mountains was the same as flying duty. I wondered why students wanted to meet this officer.

I turned to Vladimir. "What institute is it exactly that you fellows attend?" When I first met them, they had seemed a little old for students, but I hadn't thought too much about it.

Zaour looked at his pals and they nodded silently. "Frankly, Sasha," he said, "we're with the Committee for State Security."

I tried not to show my surprise. To me, the KGB was a vaguely sinister institution; certainly most of my pilot friends both disliked and distrusted the KGB Osobii Otdel meddlers found in any regiment. But I was also deeply curious to learn more about their organization. I only hoped that I hadn't inadvertently told any political jokes during our late-night parties. Then, looking at their smiling, open faces, I realized these fellows were a lot different from the humorless Osobists whom I had met in the Air Force. Certainly Oleg and Vladimir were not here to spy on me, and Zaour was hardly sinister.

In fact, they were so close to me in age and education that I understood at once that we were actually colleagues, each defending the Rodina in his own way. The KGB had a reputation as the "Fighters on the Invisible Front," which meant they protected the Motherland from spies and saboteurs. And from what I had read in *Pravda* and *Red Star,* there were a lot of foreign espionage agents loose in the Soviet Union. The television series *This Is America* had focused one show entirely on the CIA spies among us. They had cameras in their shoes, electronic listening devices shaped like watches, and ballpoint pens that could fire bullets. With characters like that in our midst, I knew the kind of challenge my new friends faced. And I was glad that I had strictly followed Defense Ministry directive number 10, in my answers to their questions about my assignment:

"What airplane do you fly, Sasha?"

"A MiG."

"How high do you fly? How fast?"

"Very high. Very fast."

Even if I had drunk my fair share of cognac at night, I had never revealed any secrets.

The next night, the three of them spoke about their assignments. Zaour ran the KGB's communications room at their regional headquarters. It seemed to be an inherited job, as his father was the local KGB commander. Oleg was an operations man who worked in counterespionage in the major Black Sea ports and resorts. Vladimir was a newly appointed KGB officer who had trained as a physicist in Moscow. Once he completed his field orientation in Georgia, he would undergo intense training for an overseas technical espionage assignment, probably as a member of an "immigrant" group.

"You are one of us," Oleg told me. "You understand our work, Sasha. But keep it between us."

When I got back to the regiment in February, my squadron was very busy. The base had been selected to host the Central Committee of the Georgian Communist Party for the February 23 Red Army Day military exposition. And I had been chosen as the representative young MiG-23 pilot.

This was my first official encounter with high Party officials. My unit zampolit, Major Vladimir Novikov, gave the younger officers direct and simple instructions as to how to respond to the visiting delegation: "To any question about conditions, you will reply *Otlichno*. Excellent."

I was positioned at the nose of a well-scrubbed MiG-23 that had obviously never been flown hard. Its tires were brand-new. Laid out before me on the tarmac—which had been scrubbed clean of oil stains—was a fan-shaped display of all the missiles and bombs the aircraft could carry.

We had been told that the Georgian Party delegation would be led by its chairman, Eduard Shevardnadze, who was reputed to have good connections in Moscow. So PVO and VVS fighter interceptors were given the most prominent positions among the combat aircraft. This was in keeping with the Party and Defense Ministry policy line that the Soviet military was basically a defensive force, protecting the Socialist Motherland from imperialist aggression.

But after six weeks away from the regiment, the exposition's hypocrisy grated on me. Certainly everything was not *otlichno*. The officers of the habitually understaffed maintenance sections, for example, were forced to work almost fifty straight hours to prepare for the show. Then at the last minute they were issued new black coveralls to replace their stained and ripped regular uniforms to make it appear they had merely supervised the clumsy and inept conscripts assigned to them.

The engineering officers were also ordered to clean up the frayed, cast-off cloth earphone helmets, which the pilots had given the mechanics to jury-rig as improvised hearing protection. This was a glaring example of the gap between *pokazuka* and reality. Ever since I'd been flying, ground crews had complained that they were never issued protective helmets against the deafening whine and blast of jet engines. Indeed, "deaf as a mechanic" was a common phrase. So, whenever they could, pilots retired the close-fitting nylon and leather earphone liners worn under the hard flight helmets and gave them to the mechanics, who stuffed the earphones with thick cotton wadding.

Now these mechanics and engineers had to pretend the helmets were State issue.

The only people really looking forward to the exposition were the conscripts. They knew that whenever an important *kozyol*, "goat," of the Party visited the base, the food in the soldiers' dining halls would dramatically improve and the kitchens would be scrubbed spotless.

But it was unlikely Comrade Shevardnadze's delegation would perform a white-glove inspection searching for rancid grease in the soldiers' kitchens. Sometimes, though, apparatchiks—trailed by zampolits snapping pictures—would sit at the soldiers' dining tables to enjoy a bowl of rich, meaty soup, the only fresh beef or lamb the soldiers might see for months.

However, as I stood in my best winter flying suit waiting for the Zil limousine to come to a stop near the honor guard at the far end of the ramp on that cloudy February morning, I knew it was more than unlikely that the Party delegation would inspect the bachelor and married officers' housing compound two miles from the base. When I had first arrived in Vaziani, Bagomed "Boris" Bagomedov and I had shared a dingy room in the bachelors' quarters. But Boris was a hard worker and helped me make the quarters livable. We both felt sorry for the married fellows living in the shoddy, two-story brick building across from us. Their families were jammed into single rooms without toilets, equipped with a small sink and a single, cold-water tap. Every morning we saw the wives in their housecoats trudging across to the latrines on the ground floor of our building, lugging their sloshing chamber pots. Their husbands would be flying twenty-million-ruble aircraft while these women were obliged to scrub out stinking slop buckets with cold water.

After Boris got married to a girl from his home village in Dagestan, I had the room to myself, but could hardly enjoy this dubious privilege. I ate all my meals at the officers' dining room on the base, two miles away. This meant that on weekends I had to spend hours waiting for the single shuttle bus, just to eat breakfast, lunch, and supper. So I studied the situation carefully and planned a campaign to win the support of Major Novikov, my squadron zampolit.

"Comrad Captain," I told him, "I need my own apartment if I am to successfully complete my training."

"Lieutenant Zuyev," he said, "this is a most unusual request."

I had expected that he would respond that way and was prepared to put him on the defensive. "You know, of course, Comrade Captain," I reasoned, "that I am in a very intense training schedule and need all the sleep I can get as well as nutritious hot meals. Surely you realize our flight surgeon, Major Blustein, has recommended this regime."

Novikov nodded neutrally.

"Captain Novikov," I added, playing my trump card, "the flight surgeon suggested I see you to find a quiet apartment where I can sleep during the day when I'm on night training flights, and where I can prepare my own meals without wasting hours traveling back and forth to the officers' dining room."

Again, Novikov was noncommittal. Finding an apartment for a single junior officer would be a real challenge.

I let the silence between us deepen. "Well, Major," I said, filling my voice with disappointment, "I'll manage somehow. If you can't help me, I understand. I probably made a mistake in troubling you."

Novikov stared at me intensely. I could see he was intrigued by the challenge. "I will do what I can for you, Comrade Lieutenant."

Going to the zampolit with my problem had not been an act of desperation. The major took his duty seriously. The welfare of the officers and men certainly was his primary responsibility. And like most of his kind, he was a Communist zealot, who believed fervently that the Marxist-Leninist system provided answers to all human problems.

If a soldier's mother was sick or his father died halfway around the world in Siberia, the zampolit counseled the boy with suitable Communist condolences and arranged an Aeroflot ticket for compassionate leave. If a mechanic's wife complained he was spending his pay on a girl in town, the zampolit would call the man on the carpet for a lecture on Communist morality. When a soldier showed up drunk for duty, part of his discipline was a counseling session with the zampolit. I had read there were equally dedicated priests and ministers serving in Western armies as chaplains, men who rode the tanks or even parachuted into battle with their men. These chaplains served the same function as zampolits in the Soviet military. Or perhaps, given the sequence of history, the situation was reversed. All I knew was that a well-motivated zampolit was a good friend to have, even if he couldn't fly an airplane worth a damn.

The zampolit made a strong case for me with Major Kuchkov, who in turn took my request to Colonel Rinchinov. A week later I was given the keys to my tiny apartment in an old two-floor wooden building in the military housing compound. Two weeks after that, I discovered that the Voyentorg military exchange actually had a big brand-new Minsk refrigerator available, one that had been shipped by mistake, with no officer waiting to buy it. I told the clerk to hold it for me and he insisted I have my zampolit endorse my order. I was back at Major Novikov's office in a flash, presenting the order form for his countersignature. Novikov looked at me a bit strangely: It was unheard-of for a senior lieutenant to obtain both an apartment and a new refrigerator within weeks of each other. But he did sign the order form.

The Voyentorg closed for the weekend in three hours. And I had to hurry to withdraw the 470 rubles from the State savings bank. As a bachelor, I had managed to save more than 2,000 rubles since leaving the academy. But I resisted splurging and buying a good used Gorizont or Taorus television to complement my Minsk refrigerator. My savings were paying almost three percent interest. If I kept depositing a quarter of my monthly salary, I would have enough to buy a decent used Zhiguli sedan in six or seven years. So I installed the big white refrigerator in my tiny parlor, the place of honor usually taken by a television set. After that, when my friends asked me if I had seen some particularly interesting television program, I always told them, "No, boys, that show hasn't been shown on my Minsk station yet."

I was thinking about all these matters while standing like a store-window dummy in my pressed flying suit before the nose of the aircraft. But my reverie was interrupted by the sudden arrival of Lieutenant General Igor Buravkov, the district's VVS commander. I snapped to rigid attention and saluted in the best Armavir manner. But the general told me to stand easy.

"All set for the delegation, Zuyev?"

"Absolutely, Comrade General."

Buravkov looked over my display and briefly inspected my uniform. "Let's have a look at your cockpit."

He climbed the ladder ahead of me, and to my surprise sat down in the fighter's ejection seat. The general's hands slid over the throttle and stick, and lingered on the weapons' control panel. Then he looked at me frankly, one pilot to another. "You know, Lieutenant," he said quietly, "they don't let us general officers fly anymore, ever since those accidents in the Ukraine. I miss it. I envy you young fellows."

His openness had disarmed me completely. I nodded in sympathy. What could I tell a lieutenant general?

Finally he looked up from the instruments and assumed his normal role. "How's your training progressing, Lieutenant Zuyev?" The regimental zampolit was down there on the apron with his camera, and I was expected to smile respectfully.

For a moment I considered mouthing the standard reply, but

then I realized I had a unique opportunity to cut through the bureaucracy. "Speaking frankly?"

"Of course." General Buravkov frowned now.

I explained that I had been selected for the MiG-29 program and had been pulled out of the group undergoing intense training for First Class pilot rating. "I'm afraid, Comrade General, that I won't have the chance to make First Class."

Again Buravkov frowned, then climbed down from the cockpit and turned to speak to his aide, a dandy of a young captain with a Guards' tab on his epaulets. "Don't worry, Lieutenant Zuyev," the general said gruffly, "you'll receive the rating before your transfer."

Five minutes later Shevardnadze's delegation made its way down the line of planes, pausing before each one to ask the appropriate questions of the pilot or maintenance officer.

After I saluted the chairman and shook his hand, Shevardnadze turned his bright brown eyes on the array of weapons displayed on the tarmac. "Any shortcomings or deficiencies the Party should be aware of, Comrade Lieutenant?"

The question was pure *pokazuka*. "Certainly not, Comrade Chairman."

I caught General Buravkov's eyes as the Party leaders moved past me. The old pilot was smiling.

At the squadron briefings the next morning, Colonel Rinchinov glared at me and pushed back his thick black hair in an angry gesture. "Zuyev," he said, "I didn't know you could jump rank so high." He was furious that I had raised the training issue with the district commander.

"Comrade Colonel," I answered, "the general asked about my training and I replied."

Rinchinov glared a moment longer, enjoying my discomfort. "So I understand, Comrade Lieutenant."

The colonel had received a message directly from General Buravkov. The regiment was to guarantee that Igor and I would be granted the aircraft and instructors necessary to complete our First Class training before transfer to the MiG-29 program. And like everything else he did, Colonel Rinchinov organized this effort well.

He selected Captain Griek, who was also due for transfer to MiG-29s, as our chief instructor. And Rinchinov consulted his engineering deputy to locate four well-maintained aircraft, a two-seat MiG-23UB for dual instruction, and three single seaters to be flown only by Igor, me, and our instructor. Most of the training remaining on the syllabus was at night, so Rinchinov organized the entire regiment's flying schedule around ours, keeping the simulator, the runway, and the weapons poligons free for our use.

Four nights a week we flew. On Saturdays and Sundays we used the simulator and studied manuals. After forty-five days of this intense instruction, Igor and I passed our First Class pilots' examinations on April 25, 1985. I was two years and three months out of the Armavir Academy and had just reached a milestone that normally required seven years. The next night in the officers' dining room, Igor and I paid for the cognac.

The fellows in the 1st Squadron presented each of us a framed "Air Force Regulation" describing the duties of Third, Second, and First Class pilots:

> Pilot Third Class: knows it all, but can't fly worth shit.
> Pilot Second Class: knows a little bit of everything and can even fly a little.
> Pilot First Class: doesn't remember shit, but can fly anything, anywhere, anytime.

To me, that crude declaration was worth more than a thousand-ruble bonus.

I had been so focused on my training that I hardly had time to consider the political events shaking Moscow. In March, Communist Party General Secretary Konstantin Chernenko died—or at least the Central Committee acknowledged his death: Chernenko, an elderly zombie like Brezhnev, had been absent from Party meetings for over a month, so the official announcement of his death was hardly a shock. People were used to these fossilized old politicians dropping dead. But the Politburo's speed in naming his successor was a surprise. Only hours after the solemn music began droning on Radio Moscow, the announcement came that Mikhail Sergeyevich Gorbachev had been named Party General Secretary.

Despite the hectic pace of my schedule, I took the time to read both *Pravda* and *Izvestia* that week. Gorbachev was like no leader the country had ever known. For the previous year, as a new young member of the Politburo, he had often appeared on television, speaking frankly, with obvious conviction, about the need for reform and reorganization in the Soviet Union. It wasn't just his relative youth and enthusiasm that made him so different. Gorbachev spoke candidly, without resort to the text of a prepared speech or even notes. And when he addressed the people, he looked directly into the camera lens, in a way that riveted his listeners.

Mikhail Gorbachev had been a protégé of Andropov, and believed deeply that our huge, rich nation could reach its great Socialist potential if the people were well led and motivated. I shared his optimism.

"Finally," I told Pashka and Igor one night in the sauna, "we have a man in Moscow who will shake things up and get this country back on track."

That spring the regiment's 1st Squadron left for Afghanistan to replace the 2nd Squadron in Kandahar. Boris Bagomedov was now a member of the 1st Squadron, and I was with him on the apron the morning the squadron prepared for takeoff on the first leg of the flight east.

I had known Boris for six years; we had shared that huge tent of candidate cadets in the sweltering selection camp at Armavir. Even then, he had looked older than the other boys. His face had a definite Asian appearance, with sharp, clean-cut features and smooth olive skin. Unlike most Muslim men, he did not wear a mustache. But he spoke with the distinct accent of the Dagestan mountains, swallowing his consonants and rounding out his vowels. However, none of the Russian guys in that tent had mocked him as a "national hero." Boris had the thick chest and wide shoulders of a classical wrestler. He was incredibly strong and could do 140 pull-ups on the chinning bar. And when he moved, it was with a certain slow grace.

Neither the academy's academic course nor the flight training had come easy to him. But Boris ground along, the tortoise to the flashy hares like Sergei and Karpich. It hadn't surprised me when Boris was selected for accelerated MiG-23 training. People made a real mistake when they confused his native reticence and quiet manner with stupidity. It was only in our last year in the academy that we were able to convince Boris to taste vodka and enjoy the forbidden pleasures of pork sausage.

I certainly recognized this ethnic aspect of my friend more clearly after Boris went home to his village in Dagestan on his first annual leave from Vaziani and returned with his new wife, Sultanat. In his matter-of-fact way he announced that this shy young girl who matched his chiseled features and olive complexion had been selected to be his wife when she was a child. After Boris went to the academy, Sultanat studied to be a primary school teacher so that they would be social equals.

Boris was inordinately proud when he announced that Sultanat was expecting a child. Almost nine months to the day after their wedding, she gave birth to a healthy boy, who we all joked would naturally be named Bagomed Bagomedovich Bagomedov Bagomedovsky.

"No," Boris said, his serious face knit in a frown, "we will call him Bulat."

Only when we broke into loud guffaws did Boris realize we'd been having him on. That night he bought the cognac and helped us drink it.

But three months later no one in the regiment was laughing. It was a clear winter Wednesday morning, and we had already flown two training sorties, when the zampolit sent the commander's GAZ and driver racing out to the flight line to pick up Boris. There had been an accident with Boris's baby in the military housing compound, and Boris had to meet his wife and child at a civilian hospital in Tbilisi. Boris didn't even change out of his flight suit before clambering into the vehicle.

He did not return to the regiment for several weeks. But we all had heard the story by afternoon. Sultanat had been feeding the baby his first solid food in their tiny apartment. And this young Muslim girl, far from her home village, was too shy to ask other women how to best prepare food for an infant. The baby spit up on a piece of fruit and began choking. Soon the baby was turning blue.

When Boris reached the hospital, the baby was still alive, but was failing fast. To his shock and bitter dismay, he and his family were kept out in a crowded waiting room. No one brought an oxygen bottle; no doctor appeared to perform a simple tracheotomy. The Georgian nurses were indifferent.

By the time Boris forced his way past the nurse station and physically accosted a doctor, his baby son was dead.

He took his wife and the body of their child back to Dagestan and returned alone three weeks later to Vaziani.

When I saw him again, his smooth, composed face was a mask of grief and torment. Colonel Rinchinov had explained to him what went wrong in the hospital.

"Down here in Georgia," Boris said through his clenched teeth, "you have to either know the doctor or pay a bribe to be treated."

Boris's face was still set in mournful anger. "How could they refuse to treat a baby? Is this the Socialist morality the zampolits are always preaching?"

He walked away before I could find some suitable answer.

Boris changed after that. Now he drank with relish. Where he had stolidly worked on his professional skills in the past, he now simply did minimal preparation for each training flight.

And here he was, signing the maintenance officer's logbook to take possession of this MiG-23 for the flight to Tashkent and on to Kandahar. Around us on the tarmac, wives were hugging their husbands as children clung to the knees of their fathers' flight suits. All the women and kids were crying. The war in Afghanistan was in its sixth year and showed no sign of ending. Luckily the 2nd Squadron had returned from their combat tour with no casualties. But no one expected the 1st Squadron to preserve this run of luck.

The signal came to clear the aprons for engine start. I grasped Boris's hand, then hugged him. "I wish I were going with you, Borya. Be careful out there."

"Sanya," he said gravely, "if you only knew how much I hate going there."

— 7 —
Glasnost
1985

S oon after the 1st Squadron left for combat duty in Afghanistan, word came down that the new MiG-29 regiment in
the Transcaucasus Military District would not, after all, be
established at Gudauta. I was in my squadron ready room reading
a new intelligence report on the American F-15 when Colonel
Rinchinov came in and broke the news to Igor and me.

"Zuyev, you'll be happy to learn that you'll be returning to
the garden spot of Georgia, Mikha Tskhakaya."

The colonel explained this sudden change of plans. It seemed
that a second regiment in the district was going to receive another
model of fourth-generation fighter, the new Su-27 interceptor,
which was very similar in configuration to the MiG-29, but
heavier, longer and wider. Recent Defense Ministry doctrine
required that all combat aircraft be hangared in hardened concrete aircraft shelters against possible enemy surprise attack.
These shelters were also needed to perform maintenance on the
new planes' sophisticated electronics. That was one of the reasons
Gudauta had been selected as the site for the new MiG-29
regiment. As a PVO installation, the 182nd Regiment's big Su-15s
had all been kept in these supposedly bombproof hangars. Each
of the Gudauta hangars was big enough to accommodate one of
the smaller MiG-29s.

But the structures were too small for the Su-27, which had a much wider wingspan than either the Su-15 or the MiG-29. This meant that concrete aircraft shelters for the Su-27 would have to be built at some base in the district. The bureaucratic wizards in Tbilisi and Moscow, however, had decreed that the new Sukhoi interceptors would be based in Gudauta and that my old unit, the 176th Regiment in Tskhakaya, would be equipped with MiG-29s. This decision was illogical. It meant that brand-new concrete aircraft shelters would have to be built at *both* bases.

According to our Stroybat construction officers, their battalions could build *one* apartment building for officers and their families for the cost of three of those shelters. I mentioned this fact to Igor.

"Well, my dear comrade," Igor said, grinning bleakly as he always did when breaking the news of some gargantuan bureaucratic stupidity, "you've no doubt heard that in the Soviet military the medics perform tonsillectomies by going through your ass."

"How can a system *this* fucked up possibly work?" I asked.

On the ready room table lay a copy of *Red Star*, in which the Army chief of staff had written an article that General Secretary Gorbachev's sweeping reforms were going to completely transform the Soviet military into the world's best-equipped, most efficient fighting force. I thought for a moment of the military housing complex here at Vaziani. Again I could picture the pilots' wives in their shabby flowered housecoats, lugging their sloshing chamber pots across the gravel walk each morning to empty them in the bachelor officers' latrines. And then there were the young pilots themselves, living seven to a three-man "apartment," plagued with broken windows and crumbling plaster. But at least they had a toilet and a tap with a sink that drained. In my apartment I had a water tap, but no connection to the sewer. My friends joked that I had become an "English gentleman," shaving and washing each morning from a metal basin.

"Well," I told them, "at least Englishmen don't have to stand in line for soap and razor blades."

"What's a razor blade?" Pashka had asked, completely deadpan.

As I hung up my flight suit, these images melded with that of the smooth curved flanks of the MiG-29 in the Lipetsk hangar. It did not seem possible that a nation capable of producing such a beautifully designed and engineered weapon could not find some means to house its military officers in decent conditions.

I slammed my locker door. Gorbachev will kick those bureaucrats in the ass, I thought. He'll straighten things out.

When I arrived back at the 176th Regiment at the Mikha Tskhakaya Air Base in late June, the changes under way were apparent, but some of the old patterns persisted. The regimental commander who had replaced Homenko, Lieutenant Colonel Gennadi Torbov, complained about inspectors from division staff scrutinizing his flying schedules too closely and safety officers "trying to jam the regiment's gears" with needless petty regulations. But replacements from my MiG-29 orientation group at Lipetsk and from other regiments were arriving every day to fill up the 1st with First Class pilots.

One of the first problems we had to overcome in making the transition to the new fighter was the lack of UB-model two-seat trainers. Naturally the Mikoyan OKB had designed a dual-cockpit training version of the MiG-29. But when they began producing this model at their factory in Gorkiy, they encountered problems with the large one-piece canopy.

This was part of the general growing pains any new aircraft experiences during its early production. For example, the test flights at Gorkiy revealed that the fighter's autopilot could develop a violent, dangerous aerodynamic overswing on passing through transonic speed to Mach 1 at low altitude. A crew from the regiment at Kubinka had almost been killed when their two-seater went out of control in such an overswing. Luckily their new K-36D ejection seats worked perfectly at low altitude, demonstrating that the system did indeed live up to its reputed high-speed, low-altitude capability. We all felt good that the ejection seat worked so well, despite the widely held myth in the West that the Soviet Air Force cared more about precious equipment than the lives of its pilots. The test model MiG-29UB, of course, was destroyed.

The net result of these shakedown problems for us was a lack of two-seaters for dual-pilot instructor training. But we were all First Class pilots and appreciated the challenge of flying the new jet without a nanny riding behind us. Our first model 9-12 MiG-29s were not due to arrive at Tskhakaya until July. Meanwhile, we read our manuals, constantly updating the loose-leaf pages with revised data, and practiced flying MiG-23s.

For the first time in over two years, I was not on a high-speed treadmill toward the next scale on the pilots' rating ladder, and I could afford to spend more time with my friends. So I was pleased that Valery Tallokonikov, with whom I'd been very close at the Armavir Academy, had completed his second combat tour in Afghanistan and had been reassigned for training as a GCI battle-control officer at Tskhakaya. Valery had been a year ahead of me at Armavir. Although not a Samarskiye, he had befriended my group and saved our ass on several occasions when the instructors were about to discover our vodka caches or schedule a snap bed check when we were AWOL. He was an open-faced, husky guy, with long arms and deep-set blue eyes. His face was very Russian, and even at Armavir as a young cadet he seemed to have that typical ageless Russian patience that you often saw in old people in the country.

In his last year at the academy, Valery was washed out of the MiG-21 flight-training program because of repeated safety violations. Valery was the kind of fellow who did not take well to mindless discipline. He was grounded after buzzing his girlfriend Rita's house in a nearby village. He switched to the GCI course and volunteered for the toughest section: forward ground strike controller. These were VVS officers who traveled with the ground troops or paratroopers and coordinated close air support.

He had originally been assigned to a motorized rifle regiment guarding a sector of the Kabul-Herat highway in the mountains of the Hazarajat. But the ground controller working with a parachute regiment's reconnaissance group had been killed and Valery volunteered to take his place. This was a long-range unit that operated independently of the regiment's main force, traveling by foot or helicopter deep into hostile territory to locate enemy bands.

I brought a bottle of Armenian brandy to Valery's small apartment in the base housing compound and sat down to talk about old times at Armavir. My first impression was that he had aged decades in the four years since I'd seen him. Valery's close-cropped brown hair had turned gray at the temples. His face was furrowed with lines of strain, and deeply tanned up to the midpoint of his forehead, where the flesh was dead white from constantly wearing a field hat or helmet. But the biggest change was in his eyes.

Valery didn't want to talk about the war at first, and I refrained from asking. But after a couple of drinks, he seemed to loosen up. Soon after I arrived, I saw him slip a small plastic bottle from his jacket pocket and palm a little green pill, which he washed down with brandy.

Another thing unusual about the evening was that Valery kept his small Toshiba shortwave radio tuned either to the Russian language service of the Voice of America or to Radio Liberty, America's Russian language shortwave service station. When the news came on at the hour and half hour, he would wave me silent and sit listening, his face fixed in interest.

"They're the only guys you can trust anymore, Sasha," he said, pointing at the small radio. "Out there"—his chin tilted toward the east—"nobody listens to Moscow or reads the State press. They're all packed with shit. And besides, the reception is terrible."

Valery certainly had a point. Secretary Gorbachev had announced a new policy he called *glasnost,* "openness," in the official news media. This strategy seemed intended primarily to expose corrupt bureaucrats and Party officials who were blocking economic progress. But Gorbachev also appeared willing to look honestly at our own history. On the fortieth anniversary of the defeat of Nazi Germany, for example, Marshal Dmitri Yazov, Gorbachev's Defense Minister, spoke of the "thirty million" who died during the Great Patriotic War. When I listened to that speech on May 9, I was sure he had made a serious mistake; I had always been taught that twenty million Soviet citizens died during the war. But later, *Pravda* confirmed Yazov's figures. I wondered what other surprising revelations glasnost might bring.

But despite glasnost, I had certainly noticed that Soviet television and newspapers never mentioned catastrophes such as fires or plane crashes. The few times that I had listened to Radio Liberty, I had been surprised at the number of coal mine disasters, apartment building collapses, and similar calamities they reported from all over the Soviet Union. And it wasn't just natural disasters, either. The month before, I had taken a chance to listen to a Radio Liberty report about a prodemocracy demonstration in Moscow's Pushkin Square that had been broken up by the Militia.

That report was repeated on West Germany's Deutsche Welle, so I knew it was probably true.

Technically a military officer could be severely disciplined for listening to foreign radio propaganda. But Valery knew I would never inform on him. At nine that night, Radio Liberty broadcast a summary of the recent heavy fighting along the Afghan border with Pakistan. It was as if he had never left the war.

The brandy and the pills had started Valery talking about the war. Now he did not seem able to stop. Twice, he told me, his small unit had been surrounded and Valery had had to fight hand-to-hand in the steep, snowy mountains. On his second tour he was assigned to Kabul, but once more he was sent to a forward unit in the mountains when another ground controller was killed. The duty was among the most hazardous facing Soviet forces in Afghanistan. The Mujahedin guerrillas—*dushman,* "bandits," to Valery—had been taught by their foreign advisers to search for the telltale twin radio antennas of the forward air controllers section. Killing the Russian soldiers in this unit was a sure way of stopping the cluster bombs and rockets from the sky.

When he finally stopped talking, Valery presented me with a handsome set of silver and turquoise Afghan prayer beads that had to be quite valuable. At first I tried to refuse them, because I knew that his wife, Rita, and their little daughter were due at the base soon and the beads would make a nice present for one of them.

"No, Sasha," Valery insisted, "I want you to have them."

"They're too valuable," I argued.

Valery grinned and slipped a long-bladed Damascus fighting knife onto the table between our brandy glasses. "I didn't pay money for them," he said. "The *dushman* who had them paid *me* with his blood."

He shoved the beads across the table and fingered his knife blade thoughtfully. Obviously these were not a suitable gift for his wife or child. Turquoise was supposed to be a good-luck stone, but the beads had not been very lucky for that Afghan. Later, when I rolled the beads between my fingers, I often thought of the Afghan guerrillas in the steep mountains who were defending their homeland as they aimed their Kalashnikovs at the young Soviet soldiers sent there to fulfill their "internationalist duty."

For a few minutes we sat in silence. Then the woman

speaker on Radio Liberty announced in the precise diction of the Moscow intelligentsia that the percentage of Afghan territory controlled by Soviet and government forces had decreased dramatically during the course of the summer fighting. Valery chuckled, as if at some private joke. The Soviet military, he said, controlled less than a third of the country. And the towns they did manage to hold on to always reverted to the *dushman* after dark.

I flipped through the pile of photos that he had brought out. Several were of Valery on patrol with his small section. They were strung out along a steep ridgeline of bare, broken rock jutting at crazy angles between beds of rotten old snow. Each man carried a heavy rucksack with a bedroll slung beneath it. Valery kept his AKM assault rifle hanging close to his chest. He had a new long forty-five round magazine, an innovation of the Afghan war. To a soldier, this evoked desperate, close-range engagements in which the normal thirty-round magazine was not adequate. He stared up at the camera, his eyes crusty from the snow glare and exhaustion.

Finally I broke the silence between us. "What was it really like?"

Valery took the picture from my fingers and squinted at it through his cigarette smoke. "That was going toward the pass above Nayak," he said thoughtfully. "We crossed three valleys on that march. Each one took us half a day up and half a day down. When we got to the phase line for the assault, those two boys"—he tapped his thick finger on the photo—"stepped on mines. We had to drag them halfway down the mountain to find a usable landing zone for the medical helicopter. By then, one of them was already dead."

I nodded. "It must have been rough."

"We were ordered back up the ridge," Valery said, still peering at the grainy black-and-white photo. "When we finally got to the line of departure for the assault, the *dushman* had pulled out." He laughed. "Their camp was empty, just a few brass shell casings and some horse crap in the snow."

"Yeah," I sighed. "That's hard."

Again he snorted with brittle laughter. "Two men died to capture a handful of horse manure." He tossed the picture on the pile. "Sasha, when we came off that ridge, I spotted one of the butterfly mines lying on the edge of the snow. You know the little plastic ones?"

I nodded.

"I stood there, staring at the mine," Valery said, his voice wooden. "Then found myself walking toward it. My leg was up, my boot was right over it. I had to really struggle with myself not to stamp on that mine and finish the whole business right there."

Valery lit another cigarette, his fingers shaking.

"Well," I said, "you've done your time out there. They won't send you back."

He cocked an eye. "Oh, but they will, Sasha. There aren't many of us left, the old-timers who know the ropes."

"But you won't have to go for a third tour, Valery," I assured him. "They can't force you."

"I'll go if they ask me," Valery said quietly. "Someone who knows the score has to take care of the young boys they drop out there, fresh from the training barracks." He shook his head sadly. "I've replaced six lieutenants who died in those mountains. I've learned how to stay alive."

Valery's wish to protect the young soldiers was only one reason. He had also become as much addicted to the war as he apparently was to those little green pills. Back here, serving routine peacetime duty, he felt old and empty. It was only out in those heartbreaking mountains of rock and ice, where death could come at any moment of the day or night, that he could still feel alive.

The long war in Afghanistan was changing more than just brave combat soldiers like Valery Tallokonikov. When the 512th Regiment's 2nd Squadron returned to Vaziani from Kandahar, the commanding officer, Major Nikolai Gorbunov, received a much-deserved decoration. He had led his men for a year in some of the worst of the mountain fighting, without losing a single pilot or aircraft. In fact, Major Gorbunov was ordered to help revise the ground-attack tactics manual, based on his successful experience. Then suddenly one Monday morning, the Osobii Otdel descended on the regiment and the major was placed under investigation.

Apparently some Osobist "knocker" had informed on Gorbunov, revealing a relatively minor but embarrassing indiscretion. It was reported that, in Afghanistan, the major had quickly acquired a mistress, a reasonably good-looking waitress in the officers' dining room in Kandahar, and the major treated her well.

The Voyentorg at the Kandahar Air Base was one of the best in the entire Soviet military, stocked with a rich variety of contraband: Japanese electronics, blue jeans, and cigarettes seized from Afghan smugglers. And the prices were incredibly low: A soldier or airman paid in military script, which meant that a pair of Levi's or a Sony video recorder often cost less than a hundred rubles. Gorbunov, not an especially handsome man, was said to have been generous toward the woman with his Voyentorg bounty, so she was generous with her own favors. Their liaison was open. This was a common practice, one of the advantages of rank. No one complained, because Gorbunov was a brave officer who always flew the most dangerous strikes and never departed the target area until the objective had been hit. And he was always the last man to drop his bombs or fire his rockets, which was the most dangerous slot in any attack formation.

But Gorbunov had gone too far toward the end of his tour. He decided to reward the waitress by taking her along as a backseat passenger in a MiG-23UB on a routine strike. She was thrilled to see the bombs impact far below in the steep gorge and to glimpse a few orange and green tracer rounds sparkle against the overcast winter sky. And that was the end of the indiscretion.

Gorbunov probably saw the incident as a minor diversion in his long combat tour. But he inadvertently broke an important Soviet Air Force taboo: putting women in the cockpit. Unlike Western air forces, neither the VVS nor the PVO had women pilots in combat or transport aircraft. The most important position a woman could obtain in the VVS was control tower dispatcher; most were clerks or waitresses. During the Great Patriotic War, there had been the famous Night Witches "bomber" squadron, in which women pilots flew night milk runs in old Po-2 biplanes, dropping small harassment bombs in safe areas behind German lines. Stalin made a lot of these women pilots, and even decorated several personally with major medals for valor. He understood that the image of women in combat would encourage men in the front lines toward even greater sacrifice. But since this small propaganda unit was disbanded, no Soviet woman had ever flown a military aircraft.

Certainly the waitress's "combat" mission was an innocent

fluke. But when the Osobists were finished with their dirty work, Major Gorbunov was stripped of his decoration and cashiered from the Air Force—discharged onto the street with no pension and no possibility of finding work as a civilian pilot. But one year later his small pension was restored under a new regulation meant to protect the rights of Afghanistan veterans who had committed infractions during the stress of combat.

What made all this even more distasteful was the fact that staff officers from Kabul routinely earned combat pay and presented each other decorations by flying as backseat "observers" on such routine strikes. They knew full well there was little danger on these missions, so it was obvious that Gorbunov had not "risked" State property or the life of a noncombatant Soviet citizen, as he had been charged.

When I told Valery about this, he merely shook his head and smiled. The logical explanation, he said, was that some senior staff rat had been pissed off at Gorbunov for stealing his girlfriend and had sent the Osobist mice out to nibble at crumbs. Russian girls in Kabul, Valery said, were earning a lot of money by performing "extra duty." Some of them even received decorations from their patrons among the headquarters staff.

"Those girls earn the Order of the Red Banner for lying on their backs," Valery said. "But you know what a young paratrooper gets for leading a charge?"

I shook my head.

"The Order of the Dick in the Ass." Valery laughed bitterly. That particularly "decoration" was very familiar to the "Afghansti," as the veterans had come to be called.

I could have dismissed Major Gorbunov's sad story as an aberration if it hadn't been for a sensational news story that exploded that summer. One of the first stories to appear in military journals in the civilian press concerned drug smuggling among the military in Afghanistan.

Valery had told me about finding burlap-wrapped bundles of opium and pasty white heroin base in the camps of Mujahedin his unit had overrun. The official policy was to burn this contraband. But some enterprising Soviet troops—in both the Army and the Air Force—had another disposal technique. Soviet soldiers killed in the war were embalmed in primitive field mortuaries and sealed in zinc coffins for air transport home. But some of these coffins did not contain the eviscerated body of a young Soviet soldier, but rather forty or fifty kilos of opium, hashish, or heroin.

No one knew how long this practice had been going on. That summer, however, a family in Leningrad insisted on opening their son's coffin. Inside were bundles of hashish and opium sealed in plastic wrapping, but no body. The KGB investigation eventually led to a smuggling network centered on an Air Force transport squadron. Normally the caskets arriving in the Soviet Union would be secretly opened in a hangar, the drugs removed, and a suitable weight of sandbags put inside before resealing. Somehow, this one slipped through.

In the middle of the summer, a message came to the 283rd Division in Tskhakaya that my friend Boris Bagomedov had been shot down and was missing in action. Three days later a second message confirmed that he had been killed. A week later we received a briefing on the shoot-down from the division intelligence officer. After the briefing I was both shocked and saddened. And I began to better understand Valery's point of view.

Boris had been flying number four position in a four-plane strike, which included two Su-17s from another regiment. A squadron commander from that regiment led the mission, because his unit had more experience. The strike had been planned as a routine daylight bombing attack on a suspected Mujahedin village high in the Panjshir Valley northeast of Kabul. The intelligence on ground offenses indicated the enemy had only a few light machine guns and small arms.

The two MiG-23s from the 2nd Squadron rendezvoused with the Su-17s and proceeded to the target area. The weather was perfect, clear and warm. Boris's friend, Eduard Igorov, flew the number three aircraft and reported that Boris was in good spirits that morning. Even though the squadron commander had almost a year's experience in the war, he accepted the intelligence report on face value and planned a simple straight-in approach on the target. The planes were to strike from one direction only.

That would have been acceptable tactics, I suppose, if the Mujahedin had only been armed with Kalashnikovs. In fact, the rebel "village" turned out to be a major fortified staging area, a warren of bunkers, caves, and air-defense sites. The enemy had DShK 12.7mm machine guns, at least one ZU-23 twin-barreled

23mm antiaircraft cannon, and American Redeye and Stinger shoulder-fired infrared homing missiles.

The flight lead made his bomb run without receiving ground fire. But by the time the second and third aircraft rolled in, heavy red tracers looped and twisted around the target zone. Eduard Igorov's plane was hit in the tail, but he retained control. Boris must have known the situation when he rolled in on his own bomb run. The enemy was wide awake and had definitely gotten the range. They were so confident of shooting him down that they didn't even use one of their valuable missiles.

Boris's plane exploded even before he pulled out of his dive. The tumbling fireball smashed into the ridgeline across the valley from the enemy fort. Eduard saw the ejection seat fire from the tumbling mass of debris. But he couldn't be sure Boris's parachute deployed before impact. The surviving pilots definitely saw an orange and white parachute canopy crumpled on the rocks not far from the smoke of the crash site.

They called in an Mi-8 rescue helicopter and requested more fighters to suppress the ground fire. Two helicopters answered the call. After the surviving MiG-23 and the Su-17s made strafing runs on the enemy ridgeline, one of the Mi-8s flew across the valley to strike the enemy bunkers with its own rockets and machine guns while the second helicopter flew straight toward the parachute on the ground.

The helicopter pilots had a grim responsibility. According to Soviet military regulations, a man's family did not receive death benefits or a pension if his body was not recovered from the war zone. Soldiers' statements that they saw a comrade fall in battle were not considered sufficient evidence of his death. This cruel regulation stemmed from the desperate days early in the Great Patriotic War when some men had gone missing from their units in the thick of battle, but had actually deserted to the Germans or been captured. A soldier was meant to fight to the death if surrounded. To surrender willingly was a serious offense, punishable by years in prison.

But few of us actually considered surrender as an option in battle. All our intelligence briefings had stressed the fact that the NATO forces would torture Soviet pilots savagely to extract as much military information as possible. Then the poor devil would be either executed or killed in one of their horrible medical or drug experiments. Apparently the Westerners had carried on this barbaric tradition with the assistance of their ex-Nazi allies. No one in his right mind would surrender to the Afghan Mujahedin. Their torture methods were less sophisticated than the Americans', but even bloodier.

By Soviet doctrine, pilots who are shot down are "transferred" to the infantry the moment their boots touch the ground and their parachute collapses. They are then bound by the same orders to fight on as the ground troops. Many of the fellows in Afghanistan carried hand grenades in their flight suits, and strapped a paratrooper's folding-stock AKM Kalashnikov to their ejection harness.

Whatever the origin of the body-retrieval regulation, the crewmen of rescue helicopters knew they had an obligation not just to the airman on the ground but also to his family.

The rescue helicopter was halfway across the valley when it took a direct hit from a Stinger. Luckily the aircraft did not explode, but it did smash onto the side of the ridge several hundred yards below the wreckage of Boris's aircraft. The sky above the ridges and valley was suddenly crisscrossed by streams of heavy-caliber tracers. At least one missile was fired, but exploded among the helicopter's decoy flares. The pilot bore in to try to rescue the crew of the first Mi-8. But the valley was a death trap. The second helicopter went down on the lower slopes of the ridge. Now there were two helicopter crews on the ground and possibly an injured Soviet pilot.

By this time, rotating flights of strike aircraft were laying down an almost continuous bombardment on the enemy-held ridges. They dropped cluster bombs and napalm, fired rockets, and strafed with their cannons. The next morning a ground force of Spetsnaz commandos arrived in light-armored vehicles and rescued the helicopter crews. But the fire from the enemy positions intensified. Now the Air Force used powerful fuel-air explosives to neutralize the Mujahedin gun positions in the caves and bunkers. These were cruelly effective weapons. A mist of fuel droplets was dispersed from a canister by compressed gas and allowed to seep into the enemy positions before being ignited by a delayed fuse. The resulting explosion literally ripped the caves and bunkers apart, killing everyone inside. But the Mujahedin had devised means to counter even these bombs.

The fight dragged on for three days before the enemy fell

back in good order. When the Spetsnaz finally reached Boris's airplane, they found his burnt and mangled remains near the ejection seat. He had been dead before the parachute deployed. But at least Sultanat, his widow, would receive the pitiful death benefit of 120 rubles a month. Maybe back in her home village, I thought, as the major ended his briefing, she would be able to live on that shamefully small pension.

Walking down the corridor of division headquarters from the intelligence office, a picture suddenly rose in my mind. The previous winter in Vaziani, Boris had come down with the flu, and I had visited his small apartment to cheer him up. He had been newly married then. And Sultanat had been too shy to go out alone in the officers' housing compound. When I entered the apartment, Boris was sleeping in bed, propped up with pillows, wheezing hoarsely. The room was almost dark except for a small reading lamp at the bedside table, where Sultanat had placed a tea tray. His young wife sat straight on a stool, six feet away, gazing intently at her sick husband, the way a faithful servant guarded her master's sickbed in the old novels. Even though Boris only had a case of the grippe, the young woman's face bore an expression of forlorn misery. In their world, he was more than just her husband. Boris was her lord and protector.

Now I could picture Sultanat sitting on a stool in the whitewashed parlor of a village house high in the pine mountains of Dagestan, staring at a zinc coffin on a tripod, draped in the red banner of the Soviet Union. What good had Boris's faithful service to the Rodina done this unfortunate young woman? By marrying him, she had lost her firstborn son, a calamity that could never be extinguished. And now she was a widow with a baby daughter. And all she had in compensation was a pension that equaled a street-sweeper's salary.

Two days later I found myself seated in the regimental officers' dining room near the new division commander, Colonel Mikhail Popov. When Popov had finished his meal, I followed him outside. The colonel, who had replaced Major General Anosov, had a reputation for openness. On an impulse, I stepped beside him.

"Comrade Colonel, I'd like permission to speak," I told him. "We've all heard of the death of Senior Lieutenant Bagomedov, and I know the division will be sending a replacement for him. I want to be the man who replaces him."

Popov looked serious, then shook his head. "Zuyev," he said, "I can't do this. You have a more important mission here learning to fly the MiG-29."

"With respect, Comrade Colonel," I persisted, "Boris was my friend. I feel an obligation to the other men in the squadron. They need good pilots out there, and also, I'm a bachelor."

Again Colonel Popov paused, as if to make sure I wasn't speaking from empty bravado. "They need a lot of things out there, Zuyev, including good pilots." He stopped himself before speaking too frankly. "I know how you feel, captain. The war will still be there when you finish your training."

The colonel's words echoed in my head. I hoped he was right. The week before, I had been at the personnel office of the Transcaucasus Military District in Tbilisi, making inquiries about eventually applying for test pilot school. The old colonel in charge of the section was friendly and helpful. Then he asked if I had served a tour in Afghanistan yet.

"No, Comrade Colonel," I told him. "I hope to go as soon as I complete training on the new aircraft."

The gray-haired officer shook his head. "I wish you luck, young man. If you only knew the type of pilot I have to send out there to the war. They're mostly brand-new Third Class pilots, six months out of the academy, who don't know a combat turn from a barrel roll. Putting young boys like that into the cockpit of a Su-25 and sending them against Stingers is like sending sheep to the slaughterhouse."

While we waited for the first MiG-29s to arrive in Tskhakaya, I was able to pay attention to other matters than flying for the first time in months. And once I was able to lift my nose from the training manuals and mission plans, I discovered there was only one topic of discussion among my military colleagues and my fellow citizens. Mikhail Gorbachev—affectionately known as "Mishka" to many people—had launched an anti-alcohol campaign that threatened to careen off course.

In quick succession, Gorbachev had addressed the Politburo, the Supreme Soviet, and in an unprecedented, unscripted television speech, the Soviet people themselves, warning all who would listen about the danger of alcohol in our national life. He named alcohol as the root cause of the nation's economic stagnation.

Drunkenness, he said, provoked absenteeism and low productivity in the work place; alcohol destroyed families and sparked crime. In his speeches Gorbachev repeatedly made reference to a report of the Novosibirsk Scientific Academy that presented a dizzying array of statistical evidence on birth defects, domestic violence, and dismal industrial productivity caused by the presence of bountiful, cheap alcohol. This was a national scandal that had to be met face-on in the new spirit of glasnost.

Naturally the Party *apparat* all across the Soviet Union echoed the Moscow line. At the very next meeting of our regimental Partkom, the zampolit urged that we join the Communist officers of the division staff in voting that our dining room and sauna become completely abstemious.

"Not even beer?" Lieutenant Colonel Torbov asked, echoing the uneasy skepticism of his pilots.

"We have to set an example," the zampolit answered, parroting the division line.

Luckily the commander was able to defer that vote.

At first I agreed with Gorbachev's approach, because I had seen firsthand the destructive force of alcohol on our society. Certainly you could never ride a train or visit a city center on a weekend without encountering drunken hooligans. In recent years it had become very unpleasant to travel in civilian clothes. Every train station was full of drunken hoodlums, ready to curse and fight with strangers. And if you went to the summer open-air dances every town organized in their Gorky Park, you were sure to be challenged by a gang of drunks.

And the clumps of pathetic, burnt-out alcoholics forming in front of the State liquor stores every morning to "go three" on a seven-ruble bottle of Pshenichnaya were, indeed, a national disgrace.

But under Gorbachev's lead, the government seemed to have lost all sense of proportion on this issue. The Politburo ordered the Ministry of Planning, Gosplan, to slash the production of all alcoholic drinks, and the Ministry of Finance to triple beer and vodka prices. Gorbachev had decreed that moderate wine consumption was still acceptable, so naturally wine prices immediately shot up. To make matters worse, the Gosplan order to abruptly limit alcohol production was interpreted by zealous apparatchiks in the South as a mandate to destroy valuable vineyards. Night after night the Vremya newscast from Moscow showed Crimean and Ukrainian vineyards, and even some plum orchards, blazing, while the obviously glum *kolkhozniki* were forced to smile grimly beneath unfurled anti-alcohol banners.

But as Gorbachev's anti-alcohol campaign rumbled ahead mindlessly, driven by the clumsy bureaucracy, I began to realize he was not the perceptive, astute, and decisive young leader I had imagined. With vineyards destroyed, wine was in short supply, so moderate consumption was not an option. Either people stopped drinking completely, or bought home brew, *samogon*.

And after a short visit home, where I saw crowds of sober, angry people in the streets of Samara after a football match, I realized that Gorbachev had no valid insight to the mood of the people, as he had claimed.

Here in Georgia, where many of the vineyards and fruit orchards were in private hands, the bootleggers were having a field day. In Russia scarce vodka at the State liquor stores had become very expensive, a bottle of Siberskaya jumping to ten rubles. But in Georgia there was plenty of liquor, wine, and champagne in State stores. And there was always some friendly Vasily or Antanasy willing to sell you black market cognac. A sudden black market in bootleg alcohol began to spread from the South throughout the Soviet Union. Drinking was just too deeply ingrained in Soviet life to be abolished by decree. Gorbachev should have understood this. But he obviously did not.

One dramatic result of Gorbachev's anti-alcohol campaign was the rapid spread of criminal trafficking in aircraft alcohol among the maintenance personnel of the PVO and VVS. All our jet fighters used grain alcohol in their air-conditioning and electronics cooling systems. The more modern the aircraft, the more refined the grade of cooling alcohol that was used. In fact, some of the most highly distilled alcohol—far "smoother" than the cheap grain vodka sold by the State—was used in PVO Sukhoi interceptors. And in Lipetsk, I'd learned that the new MiG-29 used an even purer cooling spirit officially called "SVS," which some wag immediately dubbed *spirta vodochnaya smes*, "pure alcohol mixed with vodka."

During my training at Lipetsk, several officers had commented about the large quantity of super-pure alcohol in the plane's cooling systems. An instructor had noted the comments of the

MiG OKB designer Comrade Belosvet on the subject: "This is the MiG-29. If necessary, we'll use five-star Armenian brandy."

There had always been a problem in the PVO and VVS with maintenance officers and soldier mechanics siphoning off a little alcohol, for their own use or sale on the black market. And pilots in remote regiments in the Arctic or the Far East occasionally played a devastating drinking game called Polar Bear, in which they drank aircraft alcohol. The pilots playing sat around a table with a shot glass of alcohol in front of them. They bet money on each shot, which went into the bank. At regular intervals, someone shouted, "Polar bear." They all downed their shots and jumped under the table to hide from the imaginary bear. This could go on for hours. The winner was the last man who could still climb out from the pile of drunken pilots passed out beneath the table.

But these excesses had been rare, and usually limited to dead-end PVO regiments.

Now not just burnt-out maintenance officers but some squadron and regimental staff began stealing and selling aircraft alcohol. The *shpaga* "fencing foil" alcohol from MiG-21s and Su-15s was so rough that it had to be mixed with fruit juice to be palatable. But some PVO units flying the big MiG-25 interceptors—known to pilots as the "flying cocktail lounge"—had access to almost unlimited quantities of much better refined alcohol, which could be diluted slightly with distilled water and sold in vodka bottles with counterfeit labels at an incredible profit. MiG-25 pilots also used this alcohol as *valuta*, hard currency, to buy construction materials to build small dachas, garages, or as bribes to place their kids in a decent kindergarten. That summer the aviation regiments in the Transcaucasus began using much greater quantities of cooling alcohol than ever before, even though the weather was not noticeably warmer. We all knew what was going on, yet the zampolits and commanders ignored the matter because no one wanted to stand up to expose the glaring policy failures of the new leader.

Another unanticipated result of Gorbachev's anti-alcohol campaign was a spreading disrespect for State authority, the Militia, and the KGB. Because no Party official was willing to admit the campaign had boomeranged and had spawned a huge new bootleg-alcohol black market, the black marketeers began to flourish, unmolested by authorities. They quickly branched out into other fields, including luxury goods such as video players, pornographic cassettes, and hard currency. So while the Politburo was proudly announcing the rapidly spreading popularity of temperance groups in government offices and State factories, an entire new criminal class was getting rich.

And apparently Gorbachev was unaware of the problem. Obviously he was unaware of the growing food shortages undercutting morale in many regions. Still maintaining his popular image, he often visited factories and State farms, and even joined the people on the street to offer encouragement about the bright future. In one widely broadcast embarrassing encounter, Gorbachev waded into a crowd of disgruntled workers in the Siberian city of Krasnoyarsk, an industrial center, which unlike Lipetsk, had not managed to guarantee its supply of food at State subsidized prices. Several angry and frustrated men and women harangued Gorbachev about shortages and high prices.

Gorbachev shook his finger in their faces in mock reprimand. "You're making such high salaries out here," he told them, "that you're buying too much food. There's just too much buying going on for the supply to keep pace."

The faces in the crowd stared at him with a mixture of amazement and disbelief. But the General Secretary merely grinned confidently and proceeded along the pavement, reaching out to shake hands with whomever he could touch.

When I watched that scene on the television in my squadron's Lenin Room, I felt a sagging sensation. Just like all the other *shishka*, Mikhail Gorbachev seemed unable to see the reality around him.

Our new airplanes began to arrive in July. The first delivery flight was led by Boris Antonovich Orlov, one of the chief test pilots of the Mikoyan OKB. Orlov was a tall rangy man in his late forties with the chiseled features of a Moscow movie star. He *looked* every inch the test pilot. But we all knew there was much more to him than looks. He had earned one of the few legitimate Hero of the Soviet Union decorations for his long service developing new aircraft. In 1973 he had set a world time-to-altitude record of less than three minutes to 60,000 feet, which stood for over a decade.

Orlov addressed the regiment's assembled pilots, speaking softly with slow precision. He knew we had all studied our aircraft system manuals and assured us that he would be available for individual consultations with every pilot before he attempted his first solo in the MiG-29.

"Comrades," he said, "this is a beautiful airplane to fly. Even though you have no cockpit simulator yet, I'm confident you'll have no problems."

Orlov then climbed into the cockpit of his aircraft and strapped into his ejection seat prior to the demonstration flight. As I watched him, I was again taken by the powerful, fluid lines of the fighter. The louvered engine air inlets on the upper extended wingroots had the definite appearance of a shark's gills. This airplane was a true predator.

We stood on the edge of the apron watching Orlov taxi the gray fighter to the end of the runway. Under his expert touch, the plane seemed to move quite nimbly on the ground. As soon as he swung onto the centerline of runway 09, Orlov lit the afterburners and the fighter sprang ahead as if on an invisible catapult.

Like the men around me, I was counting silently, "One, two, three . . ."

The throaty rumble of the afterburners seemed smoother than the roar of other fighters. There was no rasping, crackling edge to the noise, just pure power.

"*Blyakha Mukha!*" the man beside me exclaimed. "Wow!"

In less than six seconds, Orlov had rotated the nose and was climbing away at a steep angle, the afterburners glowing bright orange. The takeoff roll had been only 900 feet. As he climbed, the fighter's nose rose to the vertical, then past it. He topped off his takeoff loop at only 3,000 feet and was diving vertically toward the runway. We all cringed instinctively as Orlov seemed to delay his pullout far past the safety margin. But then the gray fighter snapped out of the dive and roared past us at an altitude of 300 feet, straight and level on military power.

Just as the fighter passed our position, Orlov lit the burners again and rotated the nose straight up. He climbed in the vertical, relying on raw thrust instead of lift. We had never seen a jet perform this maneuver. But then when Orlov reached 1,800 feet, we saw the molten glow of the burners wink out.

"Oh, *nyet*," another man squawked. "He's in compressor stall."

Everybody on the apron stared at the vertical gray dart as it decelerated and peaked out, then slid back horribly on its tail like a dud rocket. Orlov was about to suffer a fatal compressor stall at only 1,800 feet. He had to eject or die.

But then the airplane sprang alive again. Obviously Orlov had not suffered a compressor stall, but merely throttled back his engines. He now lithely pitched the nose forward, below the horizon line, while simultaneously giving the machine full thrust. The result was a graceful descending spiral that ended in a high-G turn back to reverse his flyby course 300 feet above the runway.

Now Orlov rotated the nose to an impossibly high angle of attack, almost thirty degrees above the horizon, and wagged the aircraft slowly back and forth to graphically demonstrate this astonishing high-alpha maneuver regime. We could clearly see vapor vortices spiraling back from the wings in the dense morning air. The extended forward wingroots, not the wings themselves, provided much of the lift in this flight attitude. Any other airplane that I knew of would have to either stall or go to burner and climb in such a position. But Orlov proceeded leisurely down the entire length of the runway, maintaining a steady speed of less than 150 knots.

Again, as he passed our position, he lit the afterburners and blasted into another vertical climb, this one complicated by a series of snapping aileron rolls. When he topped out, he again dove to that heart-stopping low-altitude flare and flashed by us in a half-roll on afterburner. But this rapid acceleration, which took him to transonic speed in less than three seconds, ended with another sudden spiraling climb.

The entire demonstration flight was being executed within the 7,200-foot length of the runway and below an altitude of 2,400 feet. It seemed impossible that any airplane could be pushed through such violent maneuvers so precisely. But then Orlov demonstrated the aircraft's maximum, high-G turning rate. With the afterburners laying down a tight, smoky circle of exhaust, he threw the MiG-29 into a turn that stayed well within the narrow oval of the runway traffic boundary. His maximum-rate turn must have pulled more than seven Gs, but was completed in only seventeen seconds. The maneuver reminded me of a graphic image on a computer screen. The airplane obviously delivered whatever Orlov wanted from it. There were no skids or slips, no hesitation. Then he snapped through a series of rolling, climbing split turns that shifted heading every two seconds and topped out, inverted, at 2,400 feet. When he rolled back to level flight, his gear was down and he was set up on final.

Orlov put the fighter gently down almost exactly on the skid marks where he had begun his takeoff roll only six minutes before. The moment his nosewheel touched the runway, his tan, clover-shaped drag chute popped.

All of us stood silently, staring at the fighter as it trundled by and slowed to a stop. Then, quietly at first, the men began to clap. In a second we were all applauding wildly and cheering, like the little kids I had sat with at the Torch Cinema, cheering the brave Shturmovik pilots.

I had been flying jet planes for over four years. And I had just completed perhaps the most demanding flight-proficiency curriculum in the Soviet Air Force. But never in all those years of intense training had I ever imagined an aircraft or a pilot that could perform the display we had just witnessed.

For the first time since being named to the MiG-29 program, I did not regret being diverted from combat duty in Afghanistan. I had wanted to be a fighter pilot for many years. But only now did I understand that *this* was the fighter I had dreamed about flying.

On the morning of August 8, 1985, I sat with Boris Orlov at a trestle table in our open-sided summer classroom, completing my final briefing before my first flight in the MiG-29. The day before, I had finished my taxi and takeoff roll tests. The MiG-29 was an extremely easy airplane to maneuver on the ground, with the engines providing smooth power at thirty percent throttle, and the nosewheel steering fast and precise using only my left index finger on the steering button on the inboard throttle knob. Because the nose gear strut was mounted aft of the cockpit, the plane turned in a narrow, precise arc. On my practice takeoff roll, I slid the throttles full forward to military power and released the beavertail brake lever on the control stick. The two RD-33 turbofans delivered more acceleration with "dry" thrust than the MiG-23's RD-27 produced on burner. After only three seconds, I was at seventy-five knots and popped the drag chute to stop short of rotation speed.

Orlov verified that I understood the parameters of my first solo flight envelope. I was to rotate the nose at 126 knots and lift off the runway two seconds later at 153 knots. My climb angle would be limited to thirty degrees, and I had to be sure to retract gear as soon as I cleared the ground.

"Be careful on takeoff, Sasha," Orlov said in his calm, precise manner. "You'll find the stick quite sensitive at rotation speed."

He went on to explain that the automatic retraction of the hinged engine intake protective screens caused a slight aerodynamic fluctuation that produced an abrupt nose-down angular "moment." This had to be parried with a single light backward tug on the stick. Too much and the computer-controlled hydraulic stall limiter would knock the stick forward; too little and the pitch-down might delay airspeed dangerously so close to the runway.

I carefully printed his instructions in the exact sequence he gave them on a clean page of my personal flight log.

"This is not a major problem," Orlov assured me. "In fact, many of the test pilots ran multiple takeoffs before they ever detected the pitch-down." He smiled. "But I know you young fighter jockeys like to look good on your first takeoff with a new aircraft."

I grinned back at the famous test pilot. Suddenly it occurred to me that he had perhaps the best job in the world. He traveled widely in the Soviet Union, demonstrating new aircraft and tactics at combat regiments like mine. And Orlov and his fellow Mikoyan test pilots also spent part of each year at air shows in the West. Since leaving Armavir I had been able to indulge some of my insatiable hunger for travel, but I knew visiting the West was not an option open to me.

Almost three years before, when I had first come to Tskhakaya from the academy, Lieutenant Colonel Trubinin, the deputy regiment commander, had flown with me on several check rides. Apparently he had been impressed by my control of the aircraft and by my habit of careful note-taking.

"Lieutenant Zuyev," he had told me, after we had debriefed on the last check ride, "you should seriously consider applying for test pilot school. That's a good career move for a pilot."

At the time, I was much more concerned about becoming a pilot Second Class than a test pilot and had only made preliminary inquiries. But now, sitting here with Boris Orlov, about to solo in a MiG-29 without benefit of simulator or dual-cockpit instruction, the option of one day becoming a test pilot was definitely on my mind. These model 9-12 MiG-29s were the first production aircraft, the "A" model that would equip fourteen regiments. Already, I knew, the Mikoyan OKB and the VVS had plans for a steady, evolutionary modification program on the MiG-29s, one that would lead to a fly-by-wire flight-control system and a cathode-ray-tube "glass cockpit" instrument array, as soon as computers immune to the electromagnetic pulse of nuclear blasts were developed. And an entire new generation of air-combat missiles beyond the Alamo and R-73 was already in development.

In other words, the Air Force would definitely need a new generation of young test pilots for this ambitious MiG-29 modification program. There was no reason why I couldn't be one of them.

And showing Boris Orlov my professional skill was a good place to start.

I recited the response sequence to the aerodynamic aberration he had mentioned. "I am prepared for my flight, Boris Antonovich," I said, standing up.

He rose slowly and smiled again. "Have fun," he said.

I silently reviewed my takeoff checklist, making sure the caution and warning panel showed no red lights, that the canopy was closed and locked, and that my twin-engine RPM needles were stable and matched at seventy percent, "GI," ground idle. My right hand touched the three lock points on my ejection seat harness and I breathed deeply twice to verify the flow gauge of my oxygen mask. I knew that all the pilots in my squadron were out there on the apron watching. There was no sense waiting. I slid the throttles full open to military power and counted to ten waiting for the engines to stabilize thrust RPM.

Then the fingers of my right hand tripped the brake lever on the stick and the wide runway began to slide past my canopy. I sagged into the seat with the even acceleration. The thrust was so even that the aircraft stayed glued in the center of the takeoff lane without any control input whatsoever.

Eight seconds after brake release, my airspeed passed 124 knots and I gently rotated the nose. The main gear lifted at exactly 150. A soft tug on the stick kept my nose at the proper climb angle.

With the fighter aerodynamically clean, both the altimeter and the rate-of-climb dials spun as if in a fast-forward video. I wanted to level off smoothly at 3,000 feet, without chopping power too quickly and going through an ugly porpoise bounce. As Orlov had briefed me, I simultaneously slid the throttles back to seventy-eight percent while easing the stick forward. The airplane responded with an even precision I had never known before. But I still popped through 3,000 feet and had to shove the nose down hard to level off at the proper altitude.

"Shit," I whispered.

This first flight was a simple double *krug* around the runway circuit, out to the nearby maneuver range north of the city, then back to the ILS beacon marking the glide path to Runway 09. As I set up for the long final approach, I was again conscious of the plane's precise balance and control. I slid the throttle back to eighty percent and tripped the flap button to landing. The aircraft settled into a steady sink rate. The landing flare and touchdown were easier and softer than any I had ever experienced.

I was grinning inside my oxygen mask as I gently squeezed the brake lever and turned toward the taxi ramp. This was a fighter pilot's airplane.

A week later the regimental zampolit and Lieutenant Colonel Torbov held a ceremony for the first group of pilots to fly their solos on the MiG-29. Even though this was the expected *pokazuka*, we were all proud of our achievement. Our certificates were photocopies of the originals that had been ceremoniously mailed to the XXVIIth Session of the Communist Party of the Soviet Union, "dedicating" our labor to their greater endeavor. Under a bold headline, "For Our Soviet Motherland!" the certificate pictured a stylized MiG-29, "Fourth Generation Aircraft," beside a rather whimsical drawing of an old first-generation prop fighter. We were, the message noted, "carrying on the proud traditions of a Red Banner combat unit" of the Great Patriotic War. My photo, a rather ugly mug shot, was pasted in the right-hand corner, above the cheerful message "Clear Sky and Soft Landings."

We were all so excited about flying the new aircraft that no one managed to slip in any whispered sarcasm at the blatant and sickening propagandistic language of the certificates as we lined up to face the zampolit's camera.

— 8 —
Mary and Akhtubinsk
1985–87

The flying weather was good for most of the summer and autumn. Every week ferry pilots delivered new MiG-29s to our regiment. The beautiful gray aircrafts remained an exciting novelty for most of the summer. Each ferry flight from the factory at Lukhovitsi drew soldiers and pilots outdoors to watch the fighters come in.

Our transition program was structured to move smoothly and rapidly toward mastery of the aircraft. The pilot had to successfully complete forty-six flights, beginning with simple *krug* oval circuits of the base area to make sure he understood all basic systems and procedures, and leading on through increasingly higher performance missions, first dogfights and ground attacks, then onto night and poor-visibility flying with ILS landings.

According to this schedule, all the regiment's First Class pilots were to be combat qualified on the MiG-29 within five months. No later than seven months after we received our first aircraft, the entire regiment was scheduled to take its unit combat proficiency test at the VVS evaluation center at Mary in the Kara Kum Desert in the Turkmen Republic. We were the third fighter regiment to receive the MiG-29, and would be undergoing the demanding Mary center process after the Guards regiment from Kubinka and the Ros regiment from Ros in the Ukraine. They were certainly our greatest rivals, especially the "Royal" regiment from Kubinka Air Base outside Moscow, where all the Party bosses were taken to be shown the latest Soviet military achievements.

After a few orientation flights, I found myself advancing rapidly up the ladder of this transition program. The MiG-29 permitted skilled pilots to easily fly with the kind of precision required in modern air combat or ground attack. I did not have to worry about the plane remaining stable as I progressed through increasingly higher performance maneuvers. Flying loops, high-speed barrel rolls, and split-S dives was a real pleasure.

And the plane was so forgiving that even a timid, sloppy pilot could perform basic maneuvers with responsible precision. But I also realized that only a highly qualified fighter pilot could push the MiG-29 to its true potential. In effect, this fighter was going to sort out the natural pilots from the fellows who had to sweat through every combat turn, gritting their teeth and hoping that somehow they would get it right.

Although I was absorbed in flying each training sortie that autumn, the issue of my future as a military pilot became increasingly important. For several years I had been unofficially exploring the possibility of becoming a military test pilot.

Test pilots probably had the most interesting assignments in the Air Force. And they usually were stationed near Moscow, where they were assigned comfortable apartments. The very best of them traveled overseas, demonstrating new planes at air shows. To a young junior lieutenant just out of the academy, these were dazzling possibilities.

Two years before at Vaziani, an Air Force celebrity delegation visited the base as part of a "Bridges Between Generations" morale-boosting tour meant to cheer up units bound for Afghanistan. The group included a couple of cosmonauts, an old Hero of the Soviet Union Shturmovik pilot, and even a woman veteran of the war, who had flown with the famous Night Witches, the Po-2 biplane squadron. One of the senior members of the delegation was Lieutenant General Stepan Mikoyan, son of the famous designer. After the usual patriotic speeches, I privately asked General Mikoyan the best approach to eventually becoming a test pilot.

"Civilian or military?" he asked, looking me over.

"Is there much difference, Comrade Lieutenant General?" I asked.

He smiled, a suave Moscow operator. "Well, my young friend," he said, "I think you're best qualified for the military program."

Without being explicit, Mikoyan indicated that family connections were a prerequisite for the civilian test pilot school at Zhukovsky near Moscow. But the military test pilot school at Akhtubinsk, south of Volgagrad, was open to the best-qualified Air Force and PVO pilots.

After learning about Akhtubinsk, I informally queried the Ministry of Aviation and Air Force Personnel Command in Moscow when I was there for a physical exam at the Central Aviation Hospital. The officers I had spoken to had not been very forthcoming.

When Boris Orlov delivered the first MiG-29 to Tskhakaya in July, I asked him directly how I could cut through the red tape to make a formal application to Akhtubinsk.

"I want to become a test pilot," I told Orlov. "I've already been briefed on the process in Moscow. I just need advice on how to best prepare for the exam. I hear it's a rough one."

Orlov nodded and smiled with the same knowing, sophisticated expression as General Mikoyan. Orlov folded his thumb. "Study *everything* about every airplane you've flown." He now folded his index finger. "Practice your technical flying skills. They are very important. A test pilot must fly with smooth precision in all flight regimens."

He explained that the public image of the test pilot as a rough-and-tumble fighter jockey was completely inaccurate. Military test pilots were obliged to accurately apply engineers' requirements, day after day, month in, month out.

"In test aviation, Sasha," Orlov told me, "there's no substitute for precision. The engineers fill the aircraft with data recording instruments. They soon find out who can produce, and who cannot."

I was developing these skills, but I certainly did not have the *blat* necessary for nomination to the Zhukovsky civilian test pilot school. So that autumn I began assembling the seemingly endless stack of command endorsements and flying and education records that I needed to submit with my preliminary applications to Akhtubinsk.

* * *

Even in the intense MiG-29 transition program, we could only fly so many sorties a week. But I didn't travel much during this period because I wanted to be among the first in the regiment to qualify on the new aircraft. My social life was rather tame. When I wasn't studying aviation manuals, preparing for test pilot's school, I'd get together with friends to watch a soccer match on television or perhaps go fishing in one of the nearby lakes. When I'd first come to Tskhakaya, I had met Alexander and Yuri Olmelchenko, two brothers from Siberia who were maintenance officers at the base. Like many Siberians, they were physical culture enthusiasts. Their particular sport was weight lifting, an activity I practiced irregularly to stay in shape for high-performance flight.

Alexander had a girlfriend named Yelena, who had an apartment in the same building as our deputy division commander, a colonel named Alexander Baglai. He lived one floor above on the same *podyezd*, the mutual "staircase," which made them all neighbors. Yelena was a friend of Colonel Baglai's oldest daughter, Jana.

That's how I met Jana Baglai. Yuri and I were drinking tea at Yelena's apartment one Saturday afternoon that summer when Jana came over to have her hair set for her school graduation party that night. She was eighteen, a remarkably good-looking girl, tall with long dark hair and blue-green eyes. When we shook hands, I tried not to stare too obviously at her figure, but that was difficult. Even in blue jeans and an old sweater, she was a head-turner.

But I was just as impressed with her manner. She seemed unusually mature and responsible for her age. And I wasn't surprised to learn she was going to begin the State University in Kiev that September as a chemistry student. Her father had been a MiG-23 regimental commander in Hungary, one of the best assignments in the Air Force. In the "fraternal Socialist republics" of Eastern Europe, you received double pay and the Voyentorgs were stuffed with luxury goods unobtainable back home.

But Jana Baglai didn't give the impression of a shallow young girl simply interested in Levi's and Toshiba stereos. Chatting briefly that afternoon, I learned that Jana, as the oldest child, had been responsible for her younger brother and sister since she herself was a little girl, which probably explained her own quiet maturity.

At the Armavir Academy I had first experienced the matchmaking that was so prevalent in the Soviet professional military officer corps. Young lieutenants with good prospects were courted by single girls in military families, with the active encouragement of their parents. An Air Force pilot was an especially valuable catch. Unlike ground force officers, pilots were rarely heavy drinkers, they had solid engineering degrees, and their prospects for assignment overseas (where pay was double and luxury goods readily available) were good.

I had been dragged into one of these romantic intrigues almost by accident. My last year at the academy I met an attractive young fashion design student named Svetlana at a dance club in Armavir. She was there on a blind date with one of my classmates, but quickly latched onto me. We chatted as I walked her home that night. Her father was a senior VVS colonel stationed in Tbilisi, who had just returned from overseas. She made a point of mentioning that her family had come back from their year abroad laden with luxury goods they had purchased with their hard currency. When I told her of my assignment in Georgia, we exchanged phone numbers and addresses.

To my great surprise, Svetlana showed up in Samara as an uninvited guest when I was home on my postgraduation leave. My mother and I had been working on Grandma's little apartment, and when we returned home that night, my grandmother said we had a "surprise guest." It was Svetlana, who had come to Samara to take a course and had simply moved in with my family. Since we had to sleep in the same small room, she was obviously hoping a romance would develop quickly. But I kept her at arm's length. Then she followed me to Georgia and told everyone we were "probably" going to become engaged. This was awkward for me because her father, an important senior officer, had insisted I stay with his family in Tbilisi while I was processed into the district.

Before I knew what was happening, I had a fiancée, and her parents were sending out wedding invitations. Luckily I had followed the advice my mother had given me at the end of my leave. "Whatever you do," she warned, "don't sleep with her."

I had not. And that was fortunate. When I finally realized the unnatural pressure Svetlana and her family were subjecting me to, I bit the bullet and told her the engagement was canceled. Her family raved and shouted, but at least they couldn't claim I had dishonored their daughter by seducing her and then canceling the wedding.

I had never met Jana's parents, Colonel Baglai or his wife, and I knew for certain that my first meeting with Jana had been an accident, so I didn't think about her much that summer. I was also preoccupied with my qualification flying on the new aircraft, so dating a good-looking young university student was not my top priority.

But then Yuri's girlfriend, Yelena, let me know that Jana was definitely interested in seeing me again. She came home to Tskhakaya on her fall vacation late that autumn and asked Yelena to invite the two of us to dinner. As luck would have it, I had just completed my qualification flights on the MiG-29 and had sneaked off to the mountains to celebrate. When I returned to the base, Jana's brief autumn vacation was almost over. But we did manage to join Yuri and Yelena for dinner the night before Jana went back to Kiev.

Again I was taken by both her good looks and her calm maturity. She seemed to have adjusted well to university life, but like all students, complained good-naturedly about the dormitory food.

"And none of the girls have any decent music," Jana told me. "I've got a tape deck, but I've listened to all my old tapes until they're worn out. I was hoping I could copy something new..." She scowled theatrically. "But who wants to copy Bulgarian 'disco'?"

"I've got a whole collection of American rock tapes," I told her. "And Yuri's got a great machine to make dupes."

Jana smiled and stared at me with those luminous blue eyes. "Could you possibly make me a few copies?"

She wrote her university address and the dormitory telephone number with a neat hand. Before I realized exactly what was going on, we had exchanged addresses and agreed that I would write her when I sent the tapes.

After Jana left that night, Yelena, a good Air Force matchmaker, was radiant.

"She's a wonderful girl, Sasha," she said. "A young officer

could do a lot worse, you know. Her father will be a general soon."

I shrugged. "I'm not interested in her father," I told Yelena honestly.

"Ah," she said, "but are you interested in Jana?"

I knew how these girls worked among themselves. If I said no here, that would be the end of it. Again I was honest. "Yes," I said. "I certainly am."

That autumn Jana wrote every week, and I replied as often as I could. I also made sure that Yuri copied my best tapes on good blank cassettes. Jana appreciated the gesture and we agreed to see each other for the New Year's holiday.

When Jana came back to Tskhakaya in late December, there was a subtle difference in her attitude toward me. Now she revealed in small ways that she had been too busy with her first-year classes to attend any dances. In effect, she was saying that she was available for me, if I chose her. But I knew enough about Air Force etiquette to avoid the obvious temptation of seducing a senior colonel's young daughter. If I was going to see much more of Jana Baglai, we were going to have to become engaged.

I was only twenty-four, however, and, as much as I was attracted to Jana, I wasn't ready for marriage. And she wasn't even nineteen yet. I decided to delay any decision. For the moment, we both had full agendas.

By early March 1986, all the regiment's pilots had qualified on the MiG-29, and we were ready for our combat proficiency test at the Mary center. We all understood how much depended on our performance out there. Both the Kubinka Guards regiment and Ros in the Ukraine had failed their ten-day test at Mary that winter. Obviously, if the glory boys from Kubinka couldn't charm the humorless judges from the Defense and Aviation ministries who scored the Mary test exercises, our chances of passing the test were not good. But on the other hand, if we somehow *did* manage to score well, we'd become one of the hottest units in the Air Force.

When a regiment went to Mary, the entire unit deployed, right down to clerks, cooks, and drivers, and the civilian waitresses in the officers' dining room. Our intelligence officers had briefed us on the Red Flag air-combat exercises the American Air Force conducted out in their western desert bases. Apparently only those pilots deployed with their planes; the maintenance and administrative personnel remained at the home base, presumably reading *Playboy* magazine, or however such people amuse themselves.

That was hardly a realistic test of a unit's combat proficiency. So, when the 176th Regiment deployed to Mary, our entire ground support structure flew ahead of us aboard several Il-76 jet transports. Our armorers, mechanics, meteorologists, and maintenance officers would be there to meet us when we flew in, just as if we had deployed to a Warsaw Pact base during a real military operation against NATO.

Our first success came when all forty of the regiment's MiG-29s, plus two MiG-23UB trainers, took off from Tskhakaya right on schedule. This was a tribute to our maintenance and engineering staff who had worked around the clock all week to prepare the aircraft. Our second success came late that afternoon when all the aircraft had landed at Mary West Air Base in four-plane *zveno* formations. We had flown the nine hundred miles from Tskhakaya to the Kara Kum Desert of the Turkmen Republic, making one refueling stop at Sital Chay on the Caspian Sea, without incident. The other two MiG-29 regiments that had failed the Mary center test had come straggling in like wounded ducks over a period of several days, due to maintenance aborts en route and, in the case of one sad pilot from Ros, landing with his gear up.

The weather was good throughout the flight. And once more I marveled at the comfort and stability of the aircraft. After crossing the Caspian, we flew almost due east, leaving the snow-crusted mountainous frontier with Iran well off our right wingtips. Ahead the even higher white ramparts of the Hindu Kush rose above the dark browns and charcoal gray of the flat Kara Kum, the "Black Sand" desert. Mary was an oasis town sprawled among vegetable plots on the banks of the Karakumsky Canal, a geometrically straight irrigation and barge channel that provided one of the few landmarks in the featureless desert.

The Mary base complex spread across a wide area north of the dusty, mud-brick civilian town. Mary Two, the smaller of the two airfields, was a regular VVS Su-17 base and transport stopover for flights to and from Afghanistan, which lay over the steep ridges of the Paropamisus Range on the southern horizon. That unit had dropped bombs on the very first day of the Afghan war seven years before and was still flying combat missions.

Mary One was a much more elaborate base, with extensive maintenance facilities and ordnance depots to service the VVS regiment permanently stationed there, which flew a variety of aircraft to simulate NATO formations.

It was nice to fly into such a big, well-equipped base surrounded by hundreds of square miles of empty desert, completely free of ground obstacles or air navigation hazards. But when I flared for landing on the broad concrete runway, I was surprised to see crusty snow beside the taxi ramp. Then, pulling onto the apron with my canopy open, I saw that the snow was actually crystallized salt, caked on the sooty gray sand.

The weather at Mary was typical of the high Central Asian desert in early spring, sunny hot at midday, and chilly dry at night with a vast unbroken dome of stars. Outside the barbed-wire perimeter fence, Turkmen tribal people, the men in turbans, the women veiled, herded shaggy two-humped camels, donkeys laden with bright carpetbags, and endless herds of sheep and goats. But the base itself was definitely part of the twentieth century.

The Mary center regiment operated an unusual variety of aircraft types. They flew modified MiG-21s and MiG-23s that registered the same type of radar profile as American F-15s and NATO fighters. Heavy turboprop An-12 transports and Mi-8 helicopters were used as electronic countermeasure (ECM) platforms to jam the radar of "friendly" aircraft like our MiG-29s. Other Tupolev and Ilyushin multi-engine aircraft had been rigged to duplicate the function and electronic signature of American AWACS and British Nimrod airborne radar planes. During our two weeks at Mary, we would eventually fly large engagement exercises involving the entire regiment against an equal unit of "NATO" planes.

Our first afternoon at the center we met with the base test officers and the high-ranking evaluation staff from Moscow. The mood of the meeting was formal and professional, with none of the typical sardonic Air Force humor exchanged among the pilots from the two groups.

In all the tests we would have to demonstrate the ability to fly the MiG-29 to the limits of its performance envelope. This meant low and slow, low and supersonic, and all the way up to stratospheric high-Mach flight. The air-combat tests would all be closing engagements, ranging from two opponents to a huge two-regiment melee spread across a hundred horizontal miles and thousands of feet of altitude. The rules of engagement for these dogfights gave our opposition MiG-23s the close to performance as American F-15s, supported by AWACS. These MiG-23s would be escorted by pairs of MiG-21s and Su-17s carrying active ECM jammers.

A separate *malchi-malchi* "hush-hush" technical delegation from Moscow would test my first squadron on a tactical nuclear bombing mission. We would drop the standard six-foot-long dummy nuclear bomb that we trained with on the Special Weapons poligon in Georgia. This particular test could come at any time and would involve close scrutiny of our ability to correctly and rapidly enter the secret unlocking codes into our aircraft weapons systems in the precise sequence needed to arm and drop a nuclear bomb.

The next day the test commanders presented their first surprise. Cool high pressure with minimal turbulence was the forecast in the morning. So, instead of the scheduled dogfight exercise, we were given our maximum airspeed test. Although everyone tried to take this assignment in stride, we were excited by the prospect.

Speed, of course, is what fighters are built for. But most people did not understand the full ramifications of a maximum airspeed test in a modern high-performance fighter. High Mach numbers were not always the equivalent of high airspeed.

Our maximum airspeed test would be flown on full after-burner at an altitude of 3,000 feet above ground level. Here the air was quite dense, so the speed of sound—Mach 1—was much faster than in the stratosphere. The maximum safe speed for the MiG-29's airframe at 3,000 feet was 805 knots. None of us had ever flown supersonic so low. Now we were ordered to do so.

As forecast, the next morning's weather was cool and windless, with a vast blue dome of desert sky, rimmed with the distant snowcapped mountains. We took off in pairs from the broad runway and flew straight out to the speed test range twenty-five miles north in the empty desert. I was in the first group to fly the seventy-five mile course. The process was relatively simple, but required a sure hand and rock-solid nerves. Even though the MiG-29 was a stable aircraft, a sloppy maneuver at maximum speed could prove dangerous.

I set up on my compass heading, flying straight and level on full military power at an altitude of 6,000 feet.

"Three seven four," ground control ordered. "Proceed."

"*Ponyal,*" I replied. "Roger."

I cupped my left hand over the throttles and clicked them forward to afterburner. At this altitude the acceleration was tremendous, pushing me firmly back into the padded ejection seat. Then I eased the stick forward to a ten-degree dive angle and accelerated down to 3,000 feet. Just as I leveled out, my Mach meter twitched through Mach 1 and all my instrument needles jumped with the snap of the supersonic shock wave. My ears popped and the throaty rumble of the engines went suddenly quiet, as if someone had piled feather pillows around my helmet. But I saw the airspeed needle winding steadily up. I remembered to apply strong forward pressure to the stick to parry the supersonic pitch-up "moment." At this speed the fighter's lift became so great that I had to push my stick forward to maintain level flight.

But in straight, level flight with the burners devouring 704 pounds of jet fuel per minute, I had to slide the throttles back to minimum afterburner, not to exceed the maximum airspeed of 805 knots. A powerful moaning, whooshing noise rose around the cockpit, as if I were somehow flying near a waterfall. Then I realized that bizarre sound came from the curved airframe slicing through the dense air like the blade of some fantastic cutting machine.

Looking straight ahead, the horizon seemed stationary. But when I glanced down on either side of my line of flight, the dark surface of the desert flowed past in a blur. I knew the cone of my sonic boom cascaded down behind me, battering the desert floor. Local tribesmen sometimes left camels out here to graze. I hoped none of the poor creatures were down there today.

After eight minutes at this incredible speed, I carefully eased off the burners and climbed into a gentle oval to return to base. Before I set up for landing, I rolled and banked the aircraft to make sure none of my flight controls had been damaged by the supersonic run. My aircraft performed perfectly.

But some of the regiment's planes did not escape the maximum airspeed test undamaged. They landed with alloy panels ripped away from the air brake section of the lower fuselage between the engines. When I stooped beneath one of the planes to inspect the damage, I was amazed. It looked as if someone had removed the panel with a precision rivet cutter.

Potentially this aerodynamic damage could have grounded those aircraft for the duration of the regimental test, which would have doomed us to failure. But the Mikoyan OKB rose to the occasion. That night an Il-76 carrying factory technicians and spare parts arrived from Moscow. They worked until dawn with our own engineers, repairing the damage. The next morning we again had forty-two fighters ready to continue our regimental evaluation.

And it was a very good thing that we did have a full complement of aircraft. The ministry evaluation team sprang another of their little surprises. Instead of the standard ground-attack mission we had briefed for, the early morning quiet of the parking apron was suddenly shattered by the warbling siren of the nuclear-strike alarm. We would be bombing that day, all right, but with mock RN-40 nuclear bombs, not the 1,100-pound fragmentation bombs our ground crews were preparing to load.

When the "Special Weapons" alarm sounded in a Soviet Frontal Aviation regiment, an intricate and demanding sequence of carefully timed procedures began. As I dashed toward the regimental briefing room, per standard orders, I saw Major Tereshenko, my squadron leader, and Colonel Torbov trotting toward me from the other direction. Their faces bore the mixture of strain and excitement we all felt when rehearsing a nuclear strike. But today their stress was intensified by the unsmiling silent faces of the two Moscow officials trailing them. One of these officers represented the VVS Strategic Forces; the other was a representative of the Central Committee. Such "twins" shared the responsibility for supervising nuclear strikes throughout the Soviet military. Now they would be officially evaluating our use of nuclear weapons with the new aircraft.

The regiment had a maximum of two hours and ten minutes to launch its strike force. In that time, a number of important events had to occur, all in the proper sequence. First, the regiment's base defense force—an enlarged combat air patrol, which included most of the 3rd Squadron—had to be launched to protect the airfield from enemy air strikes while the rest of the strike force was briefed and armed. This defensive patrol was launched within twelve minutes, despite the fact that most of the pilots were young lieutenants who had just achieved their Second Class rating.

As the fighters screamed away, into the pale morning sky, their afterburners cutting orange holes in the winter sunrise, the rest of the regiment's pilots sat attentively in the briefing room, their mission notebooks open. The target, Colonel Torbov announced, was a series of four secondary NATO fighter-bomber bases located within a dense ring of Hawk air-defense missiles and defended by multiple Stingers. Torbov's face was set with sober determination, and his voice sounded with harsh precision as he read from the careful mission order he and his operations officers had so meticulously written in anticipation of exactly this nuclear strike sortie.

Our strike force, he said, would be composed of eight MiG-29s, each carrying an RN-40 boosted fission bomb with a yield of more than thirty kilotons. Each enemy airfield would be struck by a two-plane force. The eight aircraft would breach the enemy SAM ring at transonic speed and low altitude, while the balance of the 1st Squadron and half the 2nd Squadron would engage the "NATO" combat air patrol overhead.

I swallowed when I saw my name on the strike roster, leading a two-plane formation to hit "Karlsruhe East" F-16 strip, forty miles inside the enemy defense belt. Captain Andrei Shelomtsev, a new First Class pilot, would be flying as my wingman. Our strike force was led by my *zveno* leader, Captain Vladimir Petrukhin, a bold and skilled pilot.

While the strike force and the escorts attacked almost due south—after a diversionary feinting loop to the north—the balance of the 2nd Squadron would conduct a maximum-range low-level sweep, far to the southeast, covering the four-hundred-mile dogleg to swing back on the enemy "AWACS," an An-12 flying at 27,000 feet and escorted by six MiG-23s. This was our trump card. NATO air forces, especially the Americans, were used to the luxury of their so-called "God's eye" radar coverage from the orbiting AWACS. They were not accustomed to suddenly losing that coverage.

Deprived of their radar target vectoring the AWACS provided, the enemy combat air patrol would be relatively blind. If they relied on their own active radar, our escorts would be able to locate them on our SRZO radar-warning receivers. For the actual close combat, the escorting MiG-29s would rely on their passive IRST systems, which gave no telltale radar illumination for the enemy to detect.

This was the bold concept of the mission. Now we broke into squadrons to brief on our particular assignments. While we were engaged with our navigation charts, the regiment's attached Radio Tecknitsky Brigada, our *malchi-malchi* nuclear weapons unit, was loading the eight RN-40 bombs to the reinforced inner left weapons pylon of each strike aircraft. These tapered six-foot gray cylinders with their swept, movable tail fins were identical in every way to the real weapon. In fact, on combat proficiency drills such as this, we never knew whether the "dummy" bombs were actually training devices or the real thing. Our exercise clock would be stopped after the arming sequence so that these elaborate training bombs could be demounted and replaced by the cheaper sheet-aluminum replicas for the actual drop at the poligon.

I immediately followed Captain Petrukhin and the other strike pilots to the parking apron. The RTB mechanics had just finished loading the *spetz podviesky*, "special loads," as we informally called the bombs. My weapon was a two-tone, gray and black, aerial bomb, over six feet long. The nose cone was brown plastic, the color of cheap chocolate, a combination radar and barometric fuse sensor. I noted that the preflight pins with their fluttering yellow caution flags were all in place on the pylon attach points and on the bomb's tail fins.

While we had been in the briefing room, the regimental chief of staff for operations had retrieved our State Secret coded orders from the cryptographic room and removed the matching Secret arming code envelopes from the regimental safe, which had traveled all this way to the Kara Kum Desert under armed guard.

Our squadron deputy chief of staff followed his superior, carrying a black fiberglass satchel with nuclear weapons instructions, and the special tools needed to complete the arming process. A senior maintenance officer and an officer of the RTB unit stood beside each aircraft, next to the squat electronic arming code apparatus, a rectangular metal box with a ten-digit keypad, connected to the nose of each bomb by a snaking blue cable.

I received my arming code envelope and opened it immediately, as per standing orders. Now I climbed into the cockpit, but did not connect my ejection harness. Instead, I warmed up my instruments and tuned my radio to the regimental operations frequency. Finally I tore open the red plastic seal of my arming envelope and read the word: *Zvezdachot,* "Star Counter." This was the Secret mission designator. In a moment, this word was repeated over the radio net by the regimental ops officer.

"*Ponyal,*" I replied. "Four nine seven is standing by to receive."

One by one, the other strike pilots checked in. I held my arming code card in my left hand, with my mechanical pencil poised in my right. This was a solemn moment. The State was trusting me with its most delicate secrets.

"Be prepared to receive," the regimental headquarters called.

Thirty seconds later the number sequence began:

"3 5 7 4 9 6 3 7 5," I carefully wrote, centering each digit below the similar digits printed on my code card.

Now I subtracted the line of lower digits I'd just received from the upper numbers, matching each pair in its vertical column. If the results had produced any 9s or 0s, the code transmitted by the regiment would have been false and invalid. I had neither 9s nor 0s If any top number had been smaller than the number below, I would have followed our cryptographic procedure and added ten to the upper number.

Down on the apron, the RTB officer showed me his own code card, which he had tallied, using his own separate communications links leading eventually back in an unbroken line to the Central Committee in Moscow. The vital dual, separate-channel code sequence was now complete. My code had been transmitted by the military, his by the civilian leadership. It was time to arm the bomb.

While the RTB officer watched intently, the maintenance captain entered each of the ten digits on the code apparatus keypad. He punched the wide enter key after each digit. When all ten had been completed, a green light flashed and the words "Code Entered Unblocked" appeared in a narrow Plexiglas window. Had he made a mistake, he would have been able to correct the problem once; any further attempt would have rendered the bomb inoperable.

As I climbed back into the cockpit, I considered the flexibility and flawless security of this system once more. Neither a renegade general nor a deranged politician could commit Soviet forces to a nuclear attack. Yet, the arming sequence was completely practical and worked well, even under realistic field conditions.

All nuclear-capable fighter regiments practiced loading their bombs at least twice a month. This process was always conducted at night, inside a hangar, in order to avoid American spy satellites. During one such training exercise at Vaziani, I explained to a young weapons officer from the RTB that our superiors had never revealed to the pilots just how powerful the RN-40 actually was. I felt we had a right to know.

"The yield is slightly over thirty kilotons," he said casually. The young man wore plain dark coveralls, with no rank on his epaulets or branch insignia on his sleeve. From his tone, he could have been discussing the performance of a truck engine.

When I commented on the well-conceived arming process, he went on to tell me some fascinating information.

"Soviet forces adopted this system in the 1970s," he said, stroking the gray flanks of the practice bomb. "It's the Americans' own system, but we've added some improvements."

He must have noted my confused expression. "The American methods," he added, "we obtained from several U.S. Air Force 'guests,' nuclear-qualified pilots our fraternal Socialist comrades in Vietnam provided us during that Imperialist war."

At the time, I had not wanted to consider the methods the GRU had used to extract such information from professional military pilots. This was a cruel side of war that I hated, but I knew the Americans would do the same to me if I were to parachute into the hands of one of their "fraternal" Imperialist allies. All that could be said was that the unfortunate American pilots had probably died painlessly soon after they had revealed this vital information.

Or maybe not. I had grown up watching television reports of the endless anti-war demonstrations on the streets and university campuses of America. Clever Soviet intelligence officers might have manipulated images of the demonstrations to persuade American prisoners to remain *voluntarily* in the Soviet Union, convincing these battered, vulnerable pilots that they would be imprisoned as traitors if they ever returned to their country.

It was not surprising that Soviet interrogators had used whatever methods necessary to extract secret nuclear weapon arming procedures from captured American pilots. Prisoners of war were held in contempt by the Soviet military. During my years at the Armavir Academy and the constant training in the regiments, I was never instructed in the Geneva Convention on the Treatment of Prisoners of War. Never; I didn't even know it existed. No Soviet soldier or officer was ever told that the Imperialist enemy had signed binding international treaties guaranteeing humane treatment of prisoners. I first learned about the Geneva Convention during my debriefings in America. Throughout years of Air Force service, I was constantly taught that my oath of duty to the Motherland bound me from ever surrendering, as long as I was physically capable of fighting. And then, we were told, it was better to use the last bullet or grenade for suicide than to surrender. Many young Soviet soldiers in Afghanistan had chosen death rather breaking this sacred oath.

My strike force took off in two-plane elements beginning at 0921 hours, exactly three minutes after the escorts. This timing was vital. Our AWACS killers were flying at the extreme limit of their combat radius. We could not enter the wide circle of AWACS radar coverage, and betray our presence, until the AWACS was destroyed. So we flew our doglegs to the north and west, as briefed, then my strike force dropped to the deck, and the escorts fanned out above, on either side of our route.

Captain Petrukhin was not hesitant about leading us across the sooty brown desert at .9 Mach, only 250 feet above the sand. This was even more visually spectacular than the supersonic run we had flown two days before. At this altitude the ground below sailed by in a crazy blur. Twice Petrukhin bounced us up to 400 feet to clear massive power lines. Then we were down on the deck again. At transonic speed, well below the radar horizon of the Hawk defense belt ahead, we were invisible, but closing fast on the enemy.

Then my earphones sounded with the unmistakable terse radio calls of the dogfight unfolding between 9,000 and 30,000 feet above us. Our escorts were engaging the enemy combat air patrol. I could hear the calls of *"Rubege odin,"* quickly followed by *"Pusk . . . Pusk.* Launch . . . Launch."

Obviously the enemy air cover had been caught off guard, and this probably meant their AWACS had been destroyed by our "back door" attack.

I followed the lead element, half a mile ahead, glancing occasionally in my mirror to make sure my wingman, Andrei, hung behind my right wingtip. My briefing notes told me I was three minutes from the Hawk zone and nine minutes from weapons release. In the next ninety seconds my SRZO threat receiver whined and blinked alarmingly, a real New Year's tree of colored lights. But the enemy sweeps were ineffective at this altitude and speed. A minute later we were past the Hawks' effective range.

Now it was time to prepare the weapon. On my weapons-control panel, I flipped the ordnance switch to *spetz,* and verified it was centered. Then I selected *tormos,* "drag," which meant the weapon's retarding parachute had been armed. In the low-altitude toss-up bombing mode, I would release the weapon in a high-speed loop back over the target. The parachute would slow the bomb until I sped away on afterburner from the immediate lethal blast and radiation kill circle. Next I depressed the lock-on button on the inner throttle knob and a clear white circle appeared on my HUD, perched atop my straight vector line.

Two minutes to release. I carefully verified that my oxygen system was on 100 percent, emergency pressure, and that the outside airflow was completely closed. No one wanted to breathe a mouthful of plutonium dust. Next I dropped the smoked-glass flash filter on my HUD and lowered my dark helmet visor. As I was preparing my cockpit, the other three elements split away, and I eased my aircraft onto a heading of 195 degrees true and climbed to 600 feet.

Suddenly I saw the target, a small shed of rusty metal sheeting with a squat antenna tower, centered in the middle of a six-hundred-foot white circle painted directly on the gravel pavement of the desert. I saw Andrei peel away on his own target off my right wing. Now I concentrated on the HUD as the seconds to pitch-up and weapons release pulsed on the left margin of the screen. When I pulled up hard, my G-meter immediately registered "5" and I was forced deep into my seat. The horizon fell away and I was climbing vertically on afterburner. The seconds to auto release blinked silently to zero, and I felt the weapon lurch as I crested through a loop angle of 120 degrees at 3,600 feet.

Now I had one minute to make my break before that gray monster exploded. Had this been a real nuclear mission, I could have been buffeted by a hellfire flash, a brutal shock wave, and an invisible but powerful electromagnetic pulse. Now, on this realistic training sortie, I prepared my cockpit for the EMP, knowing that all my computerized instruments would be rendered inoperable by the pulse and I would have to navigate back to Mary by analog instruments and magnetic compass alone.

When I touched down and taxied to the apron, I saw a line of smiling faces among our maintenance staff. Preliminary strike results had just come in: All targets destroyed. Only one aircraft lost. The regiment had "killed" the NATO AWACS and shot down nine of their twelve F-16s. This was a spectacular success.

That afternoon Colonel Torbov cautiously suggested that we might actually become the first regiment in the Soviet Air Force to be judged combat operational with the MiG-29.

Like all successful tacticians, my commanders had played our strengths into the enemy's weakness. And high-level intelligence briefers had stressed that NATO in general, and the American Air Force in particular, underestimated the new tactics of the VVS, which were grounded in our new equipment.

In fact, we had learned, the Americans judged us based on a series of myths. According to American military intelligence, Soviet wingmen were helpless without their leaders; this was false. We were all taught to fly independently and were free to maneuver and select our own targets. The Americans also believed we were totally dependent on our GCI battle-control officers. In fact, we worked with them to build the total threat picture, and were actually more independent of radar control than the Americans, who relied so heavily on their AWACS. The U.S. Air Force also taught its pilots that their Soviet counterparts were simply interceptor pilots trained to fire missiles from poorly maneuverable aircraft. They were confusing the PVO with the VVS.

American myths about rigid Soviet tactics and training procedures were based in part on the poor performance of Soviet clients, especially the Arabs, in air combat against the Israelis.

The Americans somehow believed that we provided the Arabs with our best tactics and training methods when we sold them our airplanes. And, for some strange reason, the Americans also chose to equate Syrian and Egyptian pilots—who usually gained their assignments through family connections—with professional Soviet Air Force pilots who underwent stiff competition to win their place at academies like Armavir.

As the GRU colonel who briefed us on this scornfully indicated, the Americans had somehow put things *cherez zhopu,* "ass backward." Training in the Israeli Defense Force was based almost entirely on the Soviet military. In fact, during the Israeli War of Independence in 1948, their ground and air officers had been Red Army veterans of the Great Patriotic War. And today, Israeli pilots were trained exactly as I had been: selected as teenagers right out of school, and flying jets in their second year at an academy.

If anything, the amazing record of success Israeli pilots had achieved over their Arab opponents was an endorsement of Soviet training doctrine, not a condemnation of it. But, as our GRU colonel reminded us, if the Americans chose to believe differently, so much the better.

On a foggy afternoon two weeks later when flights were grounded at Tskhakaya, Colonel Torbov was summoned to division headquarters. When he returned, he presented the compliments of the division commander and the Air Force chief of the military district. The Moscow evaluators had scored us: 4/5 "*Horosho,*" Good. This was not a 5/5 "Excellent" rating, but it was quite acceptable compared to the 2/5 the Kubinka and Ros regiments had scored. The 176th Frontal Aviation Regiment had become the first combat-ready MiG-29 unit in the Soviet Air Force, beating out two better-known regiments, including the famous Guards of Kubinka.

Even more exciting, Colonel Torbov continued, was the news that the Ministries of Aviation and Defense had selected our regiment to be the official test evaluation unit for the new fighter's air-combat tests.

The colonel declared a regimental holiday, and we all unearthed our private caches of good brandy.

*   *   *

Home in Samara on leave in early May, I noticed a small article on the inner "Regional News" page of the local *Izvestia*. Apparently there had been a fire at a nuclear power station near the town of Chernobyl, sixty miles north of Kiev in the Ukraine. The story was only two paragraphs long and concluded with the reassurance that there was no danger of radiation spreading because "the situation was quickly brought under control."

Sitting on that park bench near the Volga with the laughter of children ringing in the sunshine, there was certainly no reason why I felt the sudden stab of alarm. Under Mikhail Gorbachev's policy of glasnost, the Central Committee of the Party and the Politburo had unanimously endorsed complete openness in the news media. Indeed, I had actually read a few unusually frank stories on Aeroflot accidents and industrial explosions over the past year that never would have been printed before glasnost.

Still, there was something in the bland, neutral language of that page-four story about the power plant fire that nagged at me. Perhaps it was the phrase "under control" that triggered my inner alarm system. I suddenly remembered my Afghansti friend Valery's cynical advice. "Sanya," he'd repeatedly told me, "never believe the shit in the official press. If you want to know what's really happening, listen to Radio Liberty."

Unfortunately I didn't have my shortwave radio with me on this leave. But friends told me that both the Voice of America and Radio Liberty had been suddenly subjected to incredibly thick jamming, as if Moscow was intent that no details of the accident would reach the Soviet people. I asked my mother if she'd heard of the accident at the Chernobyl nuclear plant.

She nodded, her face set, as always when she spoke of disasters. There had been a notice posted at the Hydroelectric Institute, she said, requesting "volunteers"—concrete construction specialists, carpenters, and structural engineers—to work at Chernobyl. "Do you know the kind of salary they're offering?"

I shook my head.

"Three hundred and fifty rubles," she recited, "per *day*."

We looked at each other for a moment in silence, both grasping the implications. If the authorities were willing to pay volunteers a month's salary for every day they worked at that plant, the situation could hardly be "under control."

"Some people," my mother said, "have already signed up to go."

I immediately thought of Jana. A fire in a nuclear power plant might easily spread radiation more than a hundred miles. But if the city of Kiev, the capital of the Ukraine, was in danger of radioactive fallout, surely there had to be more in the news than that brief article.

The next day there was in fact more mention of Chernobyl. Now the newspapers and television commentators spoke of the "incredible sacrifices" of heroic fire fighters who had battled a stubborn blaze in the power plant's reactor number 4.

Whenever the Party ordered the press to speak of "sacrifice," there had to be some serious problem. I decided to find Jana and convince her to leave the city.

The Kiev airport was chaotic, crowded with hundreds of families sleeping on the floors of the big modern terminal. I noticed that many of the thousands of passengers waiting uncomfortably on this warm spring afternoon were small children, flocked together in groups supervised by tired and frustrated women.

Two miles from the airport the motorway divided, with one road turning right, north toward Chernobyl. Here there was a military roadblock and a small convoy of GAZ field cars with long whipping radio antennas. The soldiers on station between the steel spike pads of the roadblock wore nuclear warfare gauntlets and rubber boot covers. They carefully examined every vehicle arriving from the north, pushing the long snouts of their battlefield Geiger counters under the hoods and chassis. Anyone carrying produce or poultry for sale in the city had their load confiscated.

I had never been to Kiev before and was excited to be driving along the riverbank, then climbing up the long curved motorway toward the high bluff of the Upper Town above the river. Kiev was the first capital of the Russian nation, dating from the Dark Ages of the tenth century. The gilded domes of St. Sophia's cathedral glittered through the budding beech and maple trees around Bohdan Khmelnytsky Square. But after seeing the city half-deserted, I lost my enthusiasm for tourism.

At the Hotel Ukrainia I tried Jana's phone number again, but there was no answer at her dormitory. Then I contacted a friend named Ivan who worked at the Antonov plant in the suburbs. He and another friend, Alexi, had been reserve maintenance officers

at Tskhakaya and were now engineers working on the huge
An-224 Ruslan transport. Ivan invited me for dinner that night.

I was impressed by the high quality of the seven-story
buildings in Ivan's *microrayon* near the northern ring highway.
But once more it was obvious that something strange had happened.
I saw men on the sidewalks between the buildings, but few
women and no children. The playground with brightly painted
swings and slides stood silent and empty in the warm spring
twilight.

Over some good Armenian brandy, Alexi and Ivan told me
frankly what they knew of the "accident" at Chernobyl. In the ten
days that had passed since the first alarm, my friends had used
their contacts within the Kiev scientific community to learn the
truth.

"It was a complete fuckup," Ivan said bitterly, shaking his
head. "They were behind schedule running some kind of a test for
the ministry in Moscow."

Alexi continued. "To speed up the results they wanted, the
plant engineers actually disconnected the safety systems, then
shut down most of the circulation pumps for the reactor coolant
water."

He stared bleakly out at the sunset on the rows of suburban
high-rise apartments. "The reactor went wild . . . uncontrolled
reaction. Nothing they could do would stop it."

"And the fire?" I asked.

"The entire reactor exploded," Ivan said flatly. "It blew the
roof off the building. The fire was the graphite control blocks
burning, and hydrogen from the chemical reaction between the
fuel rods and the coolant water."

We refilled our glasses, but this time did not bother with
the typical toasts. Good engineers that they were, Ivan and
Alexi fully grasped the relentless progression of the Chernobyl
catastrophe. Once the tons of uranium fuel were deprived of
coolant and exposed to the atmosphere, they explained, the
zirconium fuel rods melted, and the fuel pellets themselves
formed a molten slag that reacted with steam pockets in the
reactor vessel and the burning graphite to churn and bubble for
hours. There was little the heroic fire fighters could do to
extinguish such a blaze.

"Every second during that period," Alexi said, "extremely

radioactive fragments were being carried upward on the smoke
and steam."

"Picture a volcano, Sasha," Ivan added. "But instead of lava
you have molten uranium, and instead of normal ash you have
radioactive cinder."

"*Blyat*," I whispered.

Ivan laughed hollowly and pulled a large bottle of amber
liquid from the china cabinet. "I hope you haven't been drinking
tap water. We ran a Geiger counter test. The stuff is definitely
hot. So now we drink *kagor* communion wine. There's a lot
available here in the Ukraine."

"It's supposed to clear your thyroid of radioactivity," Alexi
said. He drank down a glass and poured more.

I then realized that they were both drunk, the kind of
intoxication that came from steady drinking over a period of days.

Ivan filled his own glass. "When we die, we will have blessed
thyroids."

I drank a glass of sweet *kagor* with them in silence, watching
the last light drain from the sky above the river, and the streetlamps
blink on along the opposite bank.

Finally Ivan spoke in a different tone, cold anger, not fatal-
ism. "You should know about the Party officials from Pripyat and
the other towns around the Chernobyl plant," he said, reciting a
story he had obviously told before. "They evacuated their own
families *immediately*, even before dawn on April twenty-seventh."

"That was a Sunday morning," Alexi continued. "Kids were
out playing in all the villages. The Party got their own people out
by plane and helicopter. But they didn't begin the public evacuation until Tuesday, fifty hours after the explosion."

Ivan sipped his wine. "And when they did evacuate the
people, the buses crossed a bridge through a terrible fallout zone
only two miles from the plant, much closer than the route the
Party families had taken."

I was weighing the implications of this when Ivan broke out
laughing. "Well, Sanya," he said, clapping my shoulder, "don't
look so shocked. The Party finally was able to prove that it was
the *Vanguard* of the Proletariat."

Jana and I finally met the next day. We climbed up to the
medieval ramparts of the old city for the view down to the river
beaches and of the sports complex on the island opposite the bluff.

I tried my best to convince Jana to leave Kiev, to come with me to Moscow. But she couldn't understand the extent of the danger here.

"There's no reason to panic, Sasha," she said, taking my hand in the bright spring sunshine. "The authorities have measured no unusual radiation here in Kiev."

"Why did they evacuate all the children, then?"

Jana looked untroubled. "That's just a precaution. We have to be sure children do not drink milk from cattle in the danger zone, which profiteers might try to sell."

Obviously Jana had fully accepted the official version of events, which, of course, did not mention the early evacuation of the Party families. There were young men sunbathing on the beach. A few were even splashing in the shallows. Like Jana, they did not seem concerned about the water flowing south from the Chernobyl Reservoir.

I persisted. "Jana, just come with me. I can get you a plane ticket."

She smiled, pleased over my concern for her, but shook her head. "No. I called my father, and he called his colleagues here in Kiev. They assured him there was no need for panic, no reason for me to leave."

I studied Jana's young blue eyes. Her trust was complete. Nothing I could say would convince her to leave. Her father had reassured her.

Looking away at the river below, I tried to understand the mentality of a man like Colonel Baglai. He had certainly been an officer long enough to realize that no military colleague would dispute the official party line and warn him of true danger. And her father, a deputy division commander, also understood the invisible menace of radioactive fallout.

The night before, I had experienced some of this invisible hazard. I'd woken up before dawn, with a vicelike headache searing my temples and forehead. As I sat on the edge of the bed, I was suddenly seized by a bout of explosive nausea, and vomited all over the floor. (Later, my flight surgeon told me these were the unmistakable symptoms of light radiation poisoning.)

I said goodbye to Jana the next day at the airport bus terminal. She stood there smiling among the forlorn ranks of schoolchildren carrying their small satchels, as if they really were just going to camp. Jana was the only one smiling.

It was not until May 14 that Party Secretary Mikhail Gorbachev finally broke his silence and spoke about the Chernobyl accident on national television. I was in Moscow staying with friends, and anxiously watched Gorbachev's message, hoping for reassurance about the situation in Kiev, or at least some facts about the accident.

But instead of the "timely and frank information" that Gorbachev had promised two years earlier would be the hallmark of his government's "trust in the people" and respect for their intelligence, the General Secretary was tight-lipped and defensive, belligerent toward the nations of Western Europe and the United States, which had demanded an explanation for the dangerous radioactive fallout spreading across their territories. It had not been until the French released detailed satellite pictures, showing the roofless Chernobyl reactor number 4 building with the terrible molten glow of its burning core, that Gorbachev reluctantly acknowledged the true scale of the disaster. But he avoided any concrete details, and instead fell back on crude xenophobia to berate the foreigners who had criticized the actions of the Soviet government. Watching Gorbachev's speech, I realized that glasnost might be just another device that the authorities in Moscow cleverly manipulated to maintain themselves in power. I decided to take my friend Valery's advice and began listening to Radio Liberty late at night in the kitchen of my tiny apartment in the military housing complex at Tskhakaya.

My pessimism about the validity of glasnost, however, certainly was not a preoccupation that summer. The regiment's assignment to conduct the air-combat evaluation of the MiG-29 kept us all much too busy to dwell on politics. Even though we were flying multiple sorties every day, and pushing the aircraft to the limits of its envelope, there were still certain safety standards that none of us dared breach. I knew that a number of MiG-29s had crashed during the OKB and factory-production test phase, but no operational fighter had crashed yet, and Colonel Torbov made it clear that he did not want the first accident in a line regiment to happen at Tskhakaya.

So we were forbidden from low-altitude maneuvers until the regiment had its own instructors officially qualified to teach us. These two officers were the deputy regimental commander, Lieutenant Colonel Anatoli Antonovich, and the commander of the 2nd Squadron, Lieutenant Colonel Nikolai Semonich, a former PVO Yak-28 pilot who had spent most of his career in the Far East.

When Semonich came to Tskhakaya the previous autumn, he gave the impression of definitely being a hard-assed fighter pilot. He quickly let it be known that he had been named a squadron commander twelve years before, when he was only a senior lieutenant. Speaking in a rough, deep voice, Semonich also let all the younger pilots know that he had flown thousands of sorties in some of the worst flying conditions possible.

At the time, I guessed that this bluster was a defense mechanism; Semonich had made the transition from the clumsy old Yak-28 to the MiG-23, then to the MiG-29. He might well have flown thousands of "elevator ride" sorties as a PVO interceptor pilot under tight GCI vector control, but that fact had little to do with his true ability as a fighter pilot.

The officers were sent to Lipetsk for a one-month low-altitude maneuver course. On their return, they had to fly a series of structured sorties and then would be officially qualified to become our low-level instructors. Antonovich was a natural fighter pilot, a short Byelorussian who really could fly anything with wings. We were all pleased that he would be one of our instructors for dangerous low-altitude air combat. Most of us reserved judgment about Semonich; if he flew as well as he talked, he'd probably be satisfactory.

Monday, July 14, 1986, was one of those summer days of low overcast and oppressive humidity that often afflicted the coastal region of Georgia. My squadron was scheduled for ground-attack training on the poligon near Kulevi, but we all realized the first sortie would have to be delayed until the overcast lifted. Antonovich and Semonich had the last of their low-altitude aerobatic exercises to complete. And they had to fly them that day because the mandatory forty-five-day limit since their Lipetsk instruction was almost over.

We all knew that Colonel Torbov wanted them qualified. In the briefing room it was obvious that Lieutenant Colonel Antonovich was resigned to returning to Lipetsk for a refresher course. But Semonich seemed determined to fly his aerobatics, despite the low ceiling.

By takeoff time, the ragged gray cloud deck was below the minimum 3,000 feet required for their aerobatics exercises. The safety norms were set with a minimum recovery altitude of 600 feet for vertical maneuvers like loops and split-S's, and the initiation altitude had to be 3,000 feet—clear of any cloud deck.

Antonovich took off first, flying a MiG-23UB on a weather check, to make sure they had their minimums. Semonich followed at exactly nine o'clock in a MiG-29. The weather report was not good: Antonovich called that he had a ceiling of only 1,800 feet when he flew the length of the aerobatics oval, just north of the base. But when Semonich turned into the oval, he called out that he had exactly 3,000 feet and was about to commence his first maneuver.

We were all lined up on the parking apron, watching the two planes lace in and out of the gray cloud tendrils. I expected the safety officer in the tower to recall Semonich. Always the tough fighter pilot, he'd made his point. But no recall was sounded. Semonich flew two circles to verify the exact level of the ceiling, then performed his first maneuver, a combat turn. Unfortunately the cloud base was uneven, at some points billowing down to a mere 2,700 feet. The next scheduled maneuver was a wingover, in which Semonich would perform a two-thirds roll to inverted flight, left wing down, then haul back on the stick, still inverted, and whip back into a steep dive—similar to the bottom leg of a loop—and recover to a climb without breaching the 600-foot safety limit.

The moment he began his wingover, rolling into inverted flight, he sliced into the cloud deck for several seconds.

Flying inverted in clouds was dangerous. Even the best pilots could experience vertigo. And we watched with mounting alarm as Semonich—still inverted—sank out of the cotton-thick base of the ceiling.

"Roll over, you fool," a pilot down the line shouted.

We all expected Semonich to snap back to level flight and discontinue the aerobatics. But he held his course, in inverted flight, as if he could not decide whether to pull his stick back to begin the maneuver or not.

Finally his nose dipped and he swung the plane sluggishly down into a vertical dive toward the runway. To execute a proper wingover, you had to handle your throttles precisely, going to military power before entering the base of the pendulum loop and climbing into your recovery. But as we watched in stricken silence, Semonich's plane fell, still inverted, straight toward the ground across the runway. He slowly pulled up and his nose began to rise in the round-out maneuver. But he simply wasn't climbing.

"Climb... now... *now,*" I shouted. "He's too low. He's too damn low."

Semonich was through the base of the maneuver, still nose-high for his climb out. But the aircraft continued to sink inexorably, as if being dragged to the ground by invisible wires.

"*Forsazh!*" someone shouted nearby. "Afterburner!"

But we saw no orange burner flame and heard no throaty boom. Instead the aircraft continued sinking, almost gently, like a flat pebble in water. When the MiG-29 hit, there was no loud explosion, only a soft, muffled puff. The red and black fireball was strangely silent. We waited, frozen in place, for Semonich's ejection seat to blast through that greasy mushroom of smoke. It never came.

The board of inquiry from Moscow was led by MiG-29 Chief Designer Mikhail Waldenburg and Chief Test Pilot Valery Menitsky. They determined that Lieutenant Colonel Semonich had left his throttles on idle throughout the entire maneuver. They also discovered that he had spent the weekend drinking heavily on fishing trips to the nearby lakes. The blood alcohol level in his body was beyond acceptable limits. Unfortunately our regular doctor, Major Blustein, who never would have allowed Semonich to fly, was not on duty that morning.

And the accident board discovered something even more disturbing. Many of the "thousands" of training sorties in Semonich's logbook had been faked. He really had been just a mediocre PVO pilot who had taken the risk to fly aircraft far beyond his ability.

Instead of celebrating my twenty-fifth birthday that week, we buried Lieutenant Colonel Nikolai Semonich.

There was no mention of the accident in either the civilian or the military press.

That autumn I received orders to come to the military test pilot school at Akhtubinsk for my first official interview. If I successfully passed this stage of the process, I would be invited to take the formal written and oral examinations the next summer.

But even for this preliminary screening, I'd had to assemble eighteen separate documents.

I took the train from Sochi to Volgagrad and then traveled south along the river by bus. Once we were clear of the city's industrial suburbs, the countryside became bleak and marshy. This brackish floodplain of the Volga River had never been prosperous, and the number of large, ill-conceived drainage projects had failed. The solid concrete highway stretched on toward the flat horizon, seemingly a road to nowhere.

Then we passed the guard posts and barbed-wire fences marking the entrance of the Kapustin Yar military space center. This was one of the Soviet Union's chief missile test ranges. The uniformed KGB guards I glimpsed through the bus window were all heavily armed. Akhtubinsk lay twenty-five miles south of this strange highway through the salt marshes.

This desolate area, however, was not completely deserted. Twice we passed through villages. The log houses stood at crooked angles among the winter-brown reeds, their thatched roofs sagging like swayback horses. These were some of the poorest towns I had ever seen anywhere in the Soviet Union. A few rusty tractors and a battered farm truck with three flat tires were the only vehicles I saw. The only people in evidence looked old and lost. They wore the faded, threadbare work clothes of hopeless *kolkhozniki* collective farm workers for whom all promises had been broken. An old woman stood at a well, drawing water with a crudely patched rubber bucket. As the bus rolled by, I stared into her eyes, but saw no flicker of recognition.

Half an hour later, we rolled into Akhtubinsk, a closed military city of 35,000. After the desolation of the nearby villages, the modern town seemed incongruous. I didn't have to report to the center until the next morning, so I had the afternoon and evening free. After I checked into the officers' hotel, I strolled into the city center, looking for a café or a restaurant. But block after block, all I found were featureless office buildings and standard seven-story apartment units. Finally I located a *produkty* State food store. If I couldn't eat a hot meal, I thought, at least I'd buy some sausage and cheese to take back to my room.

Inside I found two women clerks in soiled white smocks, chatting quietly at the cashier's counter. The shelves and refrigerator cases were almost completely empty. The only food I discovered was a heap of one-kilo white bread loaves that were stale and hard, a few sacks of rice, and a forlorn row of pickled green tomatoes in dusty jars with rusty lids. Those were the total "food products" available in the store.

"Excuse me," I said, approaching the clerks. "Where can I get something to eat?"

The heavier of the two women glanced at me, taking in my uniform. "So," she said rudely, "not from here, I suppose."

"No," I said, "I'm just visiting the center."

The second clerk wrinkled her nose. "Don't they feed you, then?"

I shook my head.

The first clerk yawned. "Well, this is all we have."

"Is it always like this?" I asked, looking at the bare, dusty shelves.

The fat clerk shrugged. "Sometimes we get shipments, but it all goes fast."

Outside it was almost dark, a cold, windy twilight. People were hurrying by, bundled against the chill. I looked back at the two clerks. "Where can I find a restaurant?"

The thinner clerk laughed so loudly, spittle formed on her lips. "Are you kidding with us?"

That night I went to sleep hungry.

The next morning I did manage to find an acceptable breakfast of sweet rolls and tea at the officers' canteen on the base. This was fortunate because I didn't want to face my interviews with an empty stomach.

Colonel Yuri Rizantsev, who chaired the three-officer panel, seemed friendly enough. The officers slowly verified my Armavir Academy records and my training certificates. They noted that I had never had an accident and that my overall record was excellent. The thin engineering major on the right read his questions from a notebook. He seemed interested in the aerodynamic damage my regiment's planes had suffered at Mary One. But before anyone asked any truly challenging questions, the colonel was on his feet, thanking me for my visit.

"You will be notified in a few months when to return for your formal examination," he said, stacking my papers.

That was it. I had just become a finalist for the biannual Akhtubinsk selection exams. I knew that over four hundred candidates among the ten thousand fighter pilots in the VVS had applied this year and that there were only forty-eight chairs in the examination room. Now I would sit in one of them.

"Try not to become complacent, Zuyev," Colonel Rizantsev warned me. "Work hard, study, and keep up your flying skills. They will definitely be tested next summer."

On the bus back to Volgagrad, I sat beside an electronics instructor, a jovial middle-aged lieutenant colonel. He revealed how the staff of the Akhtubinsk center managed to eat. Every day, he said, a Tu-154 jet transport flew a regular shuttle route from the Akhtubinsk Air Base to Pushkino airfield near Moscow, a round trip of over thirteen hundred miles. And every day, officers and their wives were on board, carrying plastic panniers and string bags. They shopped in Moscow and returned each night lugging their salami, sacks of potatoes and macaroni, and their clinking tins of condensed milk.

"It's an unusual system," the officer admitted. "But so far, we get by."

I nodded. If men with families could manage, I decided, I could certainly do so as well. The bus rolled north through the brown salt marsh toward civilization.

For a while I thought about the kind of country that could build a city like Akhtubinsk but could not put bread or milk on the store shelves. Then I fell asleep.

— 9 —
Perestroika
1987–88

I was promoted to captain in January 1987, four years and three months after graduating from the Armavir Academy.

During the spring of 1987, the regiment was well into the long, complex process of the MiG-29's combat evaluation. As a lead pilot, I often flew independent two-plane sorties out to the air-combat range over the Black Sea or to the weapons poligons. After each flight, there was always a heavy load of paperwork that most of my friends grumbled about. But I welcomed the demanding and detailed engineering and aerodynamic evaluation reports: Flying these evaluation flights was excellent preparation for my formal examination at the Akhtubinsk test pilot school, scheduled for June. In fact, we had several test pilots and engineers from the Akhtubinsk center at our base who kindly gave me tips on taking the exam.

Mikhail Gorbachev had been Party Secretary and President for two years. His policy of glasnost was expanding rapidly, and he had just announced another major reform: *perestroika*, the "restructuring" of the entire Soviet economy along modern lines. The reform seemed aimed at hacking down the thick bureaucratic deadwood that was strangling the Soviet economy. In speech after speech, "Mishka" spoke directly to the people, urging them to throw off the shell of mindless habit, to work harder, to streamline, to innovate.

This was exciting. Gorbachev constantly stressed that we were a great nation of immense potential, graced with almost limitless natural and human resources. He intended to kick a number of well-rounded asses among the lazy and corrupt apparatchiks and the smug *nomenklatura*, the affluent class of members who held positions of authority all across the Union that were delineated by the Party. The combination of efficient modern Socialism and the inherent energy of the Soviet people, Gorbachev confidently proclaimed, would be invincible.

As I watched his televised speeches and read his long policy statements in *Pravda* that spring, I felt a swelling optimism, a confidence that this strong young leader was really going to lead my country to its true destiny.

Certainly the process of glasnost seemed to be expanding rapidly. The scandalous corruption trials of the Central Asian leaders were reaching a sensational climax. The Uzbek Party secretary Sharaf Rashidov had led a truly corrupt mini-empire for decades. After his death in 1984, his successor—a seemingly bland Uzbek with the tongue-stopping name of Inamshon Usmankhodzhavev—and his republic's Interior Minister were convicted of gross corruption and abuse of power. They had lived like oriental pashas; now they would learn the life of convicts in a corrective labor camp.

Over the months that followed, the scandal spread inexorably out of Central Asia to wash up on the red brick moats of the Kremlin itself. Yuri Churbanov, Leonid Brezhnev's son-in-law, and the former first deputy minister of the interior (one of the top policemen in the Soviet Union) were implicated in the Uzbekistan morass and faced a stunning list of corruption charges, including accepting huge bribes from Rashidov and raking off millions of rubles from State enterprises. Every day, the Vremya newscast provided more sensational details of the Churbanov trial.

Sitting with my squadron mates in the duty-alert dayroom, watching our big color television, I was both fascinated and disgusted by the Churbanov trial.

My *zveno* leader, Yuri Petrukhin, now a major, aptly caught our mood. "That son of a bitch," Petrukhin swore, pointing at the screen where Yuri Churbanov sat smirking at the courtroom camera. "He's the type of leech that's been bleeding this country white for years."

The trial seemed to be glasnost at its best; Gorbachev appeared determined to rip apart the rotten old Brezhnev system of corrupt cronyism, to sack all the "bloated parasites" who were dragging our country into stagnation. But many of us began to wonder if such deep-seated corruption existed elsewhere in the Soviet Union; were former Brezhnev officials the only ones guilty of such gross abuse of power? Like the rest of the Soviet people, we had to wait for Moscow to shed more light by opening more doors to the unvarnished truth.

Then people began whispering rumors about shocking revelations by Western historians concerning the brutal execution of Czar Nicholas and his family by the Bolsheviks in 1918. According to accounts, the royal family had been butchered with bayonets, their bodies dissolved in acid and the bones thrown down an abandoned mine shaft. The zampolits dismissed these rumors as slanderous provocations. But confirmation came from a strange source. Major Yuri Petrukhin, our intelligence officer, a great pilot and a loyal Communist, told several of us in the ready room one afternoon that the reports were true.

"How do you know this, Comrade Major?" Nikolai Saratev asked. He was a Siberian country boy, a Party zealot with an "admirable" Komsomol record.

Petrukhin merely reached in his pocket and pulled out the beautiful little transistor radio receiver he had built himself from spare parts. "Radio Liberty" was all he said.

Nikolai gaped but did not challenge Petrukhin.

It was against State Security regulations to listen to Western radio broadcasts, which were known to contain coded messages for spies and saboteurs. But Petrukhin was never without his transistor radio these days. It was as if he had appointed himself an unofficial monitor of glasnost, whose duty it was to verify the accuracy of the State news media. Petrukhin had always been just as loyal a Party man as Nikolai. But something had changed in the major's perspective. He now seemed obsessed with learning the real truth, not just the official glasnost version of events.

In many ways Petrukhin symbolized a barely perceptible schism between the hard-line Communist senior officers, who had staked their lives and careers in supporting the official status quo, and the restless junior officer corps, senior lieutenants, captains, and majors like Petrukhin who were beginning to have fundamental doubts about the Party's leadership of our nation.

These were uncertain times, so I decided to keep my own counsel. One thing I knew for certain, however, was that glasnost certainly was *not* anywhere near as "open" as Moscow would have us believe. This was dramatized a few days later. I was talking to Peotr Tutakin, a visiting engineer from Akhtubinsk. We were alone in the squadron dayroom, so I decided to ask him about an accident report we had received the month before. Apparently a civilian aircraft had been destroyed in a "mishap" involving a combat plane on an Akhtubinsk poligon. The VVS report had been sketchy at best.

"What about all this?" I asked. "What actually happened?"

Peotr smiled grimly. "Last November Major Viktor Stepanenko was flying a MiG-23 on a live-fire test of our new anti-helicopter missile," he explained, then gave the details.

The weapon's radar sensor was tuned to detect the Doppler rotation motion of a helicopter's rotor. There was an old Mi-6 drone flying twenty miles downrange when Stepanenko fired his missile.

"But no one had informed the regional Aeroflot office of the exercise," Peotr added. "Instead of striking the helicopter drone, the missile locked onto the propellers of a civilian An-26 and destroyed the airliner."

"Shit!" I said. "How many were killed?"

"Twenty-six. All civilians . . . women, kids."

"There was nothing in *Pravda*, not a word on Vremya," I blurted out, then suddenly realized I sounded naïve. "There wasn't even a vague token report of an Aeroflot accident."

Peotr nodded again. "Glasnost is a very *flexible* policy, Sasha." He shook his head. "Missiles are dangerous. Remember the American U-2 flown by Gary Powers?"

"Sure."

"Well," Peotr said, "we shot down one of our own MiG-19s before we got the Americans that glorious May Day."

That night I thought more of the missile accident. It reminded me of Chernobyl, not in magnitude, certainly, but in the cover-up that followed. At least in the aircraft, the people died quickly.

In each case, gross bureaucratic bungling had resulted in the tragic death of innocent Soviet citizens. But, despite glasnost, neither tragedy was reported to the Soviet people. Obviously, old habits died hard. But Mikhail Gorbachev had solemnly pledged during his All-Union television speeches that glasnost was more than token propaganda, that the new policy of openness was not simply a sophisticated variation on the old deceit of *pokazuka*, the official sham that pervaded all Soviet life.

Now, like Yuri Petrukhin, I was beginning to harbor serious doubts, not just about cautious bureaucrats sabotaging Gorbachev's bold policy, but about the popular Gorbachev himself.

Valery was off on his third combat tour to Afghanistan and had graciously given me the keys to his flat. I had planned to use this quiet sanctuary away from my fellow pilots to study for the Akhtubinsk center examination. Sitting alone at night in Valery's small, comfortable apartment, I found myself pushing aside my aerodynamic and electronics manuals and turning my own transistor to Radio Liberty.

Valery, a bitter, traumatized Afghansti, had recommended I learn the truth from Radio Liberty, not *Pravda* or *Red Star*. Major Petrukhin, a New Communist Man if there ever was one, had implicitly given the same advice. I began to listen to the American radio station each night, alone in the center of Valery's small kitchen, the radio before me on the table, sheltered by my spread arms and shoulders so that no one in the staircase behind me could hear.

I heard a steady litany of reports on train crashes, mine and factory accidents, and increasingly, civil strife among rival ethnic groups in the outer republics. None of this was reported by the official Soviet media. I could believe either the American radio station or my own government. Finally I came to believe the Americans. And learning this privileged information gave me satisfaction; I knew things my comrades did not.

One reason I had lost faith in my government's honesty was the hollowness of perestroika that was becoming more obvious as each month passed. Apparently the much touted "restructuring" of perestroika was just a shifting of the same old inefficient structures of the economy. Gorbachev was taking the same apparatchiks from ministries like Gosplan and Agriculture and shuffling them around into new "super ministries" that were supposedly much more efficient. All that looked wonderful in Moscow, but it had absolutely no impact out in the provinces or the distant republics. Yet month after month, Gorbachev appeared on All-Union television, gazing earnestly into the lens to assure us all that perestroika would soon dramatically improve our lives.

He began to sound like a zampolit.

Under perestroika, apparatchiks who *earned* their living mouthing platitudes—Gorbachev and the Politburo included—still had their fine apartments, their Volga sedans, and access to Beryozka hard-currency stores. They lived in a separate world from the millions of normal "toilers" whom they supposedly cared for so deeply. I saw no future in these splendid reforms.

But glasnost itself was a fascinating concept. I came to realize that there were actually two forms of glasnost evolving simultaneously: the official warmed-over *pokazuka* glasnost, and a parallel, more authentic and deeper process of national awakening. Once Gorbachev had opened the door to the truth a narrow crack, the doorway itself could never be completely blocked again. For example, his most recent admission that at least thirty-five million Soviet citizens had been killed in the Great Patriotic War—almost twice the previous official number—raised immense questions about other "official" versions of major historical events. New magazines such as *Ogonyok* and *Argumenti i Facti* had seized the opportunity presented by glasnost to conduct valid historic investigations, actually based on eyewitness accounts, not the dictates of the Party.

Books by banned authors such as Alexander Solzhenitsyn and Anatoli Rybakov were now available in photocopies of printed editions. Growing up, I had never actually seen a *samizdat* "self-published" carbon copy of an illicit book manuscript, although I'd heard they had been popular among Moscow intellectuals. But now with glasnost there seemed to be much greater access to copy machines, so that even if Moscow tried to suppress a newly legal magazine by limiting the publisher's paper supply, the important articles quickly spread throughout the Soviet Union, and were even quoted on news broadcasts in the republics.

Perestroika, I knew, was doomed from the beginning. But glasnost, I suspected, had the potential to transform my homeland.

*   *   *

That spring I received my orders to report to Akhtubinsk in June for the week-long official examination and interview process. A few days later the 1st Squadron was unexpectedly ordered to fly to Akhtubinsk for several months' intensive combat evaluation of the MiG-29. I immediately grasped the potential benefits from this order. The new fighter would be the star performer at Akhtubinsk, and flying as a member of my elite squadron would put me in daily contact with the test pilots who would conduct my formal examination in June. As every Soviet pilot knew, when you sat in a sauna drinking beer and talking airplanes with another aviator, you had a friend for life.

But my sudden good fortune was just as suddenly stymied. Colonel Torbov, my regimental commander, personally assigned me to a four-plane *zveno*, standing indefinite duty alert at the Vaziani Air Base near Tbilisi. When I requested an appointment with Torbov to appeal his decision, he curtly dismissed me.

"You have your orders, Captain Zuyev," he said coldly, hardly looking up from his embossed-leather desk set.

"But, Comrade Colonel . . ."

"Dismissed, Captain."

Now he looked up, his sharply chiseled features set in a scowl. He was lean and tall, a true "Hussar" of a fighter pilot who could display a definite aristocratic hauteur when he chose to. The colonel was a graduate of the prestigious Gagarin Academy in Moscow and came from a well-connected military family. There was no arguing with his decision.

Walking back to the flight line, I had to face the bitter logic of his order. Colonel Torbov was exacting revenge, a prerogative of senior Soviet officers. A few months earlier Torbov had been unusually friendly and highly complimentary of my performance. I had quickly discovered the reason for the colonel's pleasant attention. His wife had a relative named Tamara, an attractive woman of thirty, who had just been divorced and had sought refuge on their doorstep. Although Torbov was a regimental commander, with an ample supply of *blat*, he couldn't find an apartment or job for this domestic refugee. So he had to marry her off to free the sofa in his small living room. Apparently he and his wife sorted through personnel files of all the bachelor pilots, and my name was on the top of the pile.

They invited me to dinner, then to tea, then encouraged me

to escort Tamara to the November Revolution Day reception at the officers' dining room. I declined. The blatant, passionless manipulation of the situation was distasteful. Tamara seemed an attractive and pleasant enough woman, but I found the crude matchmaking degrading for both of us. The whole situation was embarrassing. What the hell kind of country was this that could equip Colonel Torbov's regiment with the world's most versatile combat aircraft and forty skilled pilots to fly them, but could not provide decent housing for a young divorcee? Instead, an intelligent and energetic senior officer like Torbov was reduced to playing the role of a village babushka, trying to snare a valuable husband for his relative.

As soon as Torbov realized I was not interested in Tamara, he turned cold toward me. Within days his lavish attention was focused on my friend Yuri, one of the twin Siberian maintenance officers. Three weeks after that, Yuri and Tamara were married, and Yuri received an unexpected plum assignment to a regiment in Germany. This was his reward for marrying Tamara. But it was also a breach of the unofficial policy not to split up twin officers who had joined the service together. In fact, Yuri's assignment drove a wedge between the two brothers and eventually destroyed their close relationship. Once again, the sordid reality of everyday Soviet life had a destructive effect on normal human relationships.

But at least Tamara had found a husband. We all knew terrible stories of divorced couples who were forced to continue sharing the same small living space because there were no other apartments available. In some cases, a divorced man or woman brought the new spouse or paramour back to the one-room apartment where they "lived" on a cot or sofa separated by a curtain from the former spouse—and usually a child or two. And yet the editorialists in *Pravda* lectured us about the weak moral fiber of those who turned to alcohol to escape the brutal reality of their lives. I couldn't blame Yuri for snatching up Tamara; her unofficial dowry—orders to a VVS regiment in Germany—made her a very attractive bride.

These foreign assignments paid at least double salaries in convertible currency. After five years in Germany, a young captain could return home with a houseful of furniture and enough money saved to buy a Zhiguli. Real "overseas" assignments to third world Socialist countries like Syria, Angola, or even Cuba were still more prized. There a man got five or six times his normal salary, paid in hard currency. "Frying your ass" three years in Africa or the Middle East set you up for the rest of your life. Colonel Torbov had dangled such a prospect in front of me, before I made it clear I didn't want to marry Tamara.

The lesson of this sequence was clear: If you cooperate with the system, you will be rewarded. Conversely, I had to be punished for resisting Torbov's pressure.

In May the 1st Squadron flew off to Akhtubinsk, and I went to Vaziani.

Both glasnost and perestroika were subjected to bizarre scrutiny on a bright afternoon in early May, when a teenage West German pilot named Mathias Rust flew a rented, single-engine Cessna 172 across the Gulf of Finland from Helsinki, on across the coastal plain, all the way through Moscow's ultra-modern air-defense zone—which even included antimissile weapons—and landed on a bridge near the Kremlin. He then proceeded to taxi the light aircraft directly into Red Square, where he hopped out and began signing autographs. Before glasnost, this would have been a nonincident; official Moscow would have staunchly denied it had ever happened. Reports of the intruder aircraft would have been dismissed as imperialist provocation, just as Moscow had refused to admit that the Korean Airlines Flight 007 had successfully penetrated our most concentrated air-defense sector in the Far East. But under glasnost, Western journalists and tourists were allowed to videotape the landing and even chat with the young pilot, who stated he was on a peace mission and wished to meet with Mikhail Gorbachev.

Unfortunately Gorbachev and his new reformist Defense Minister, Marshal Sergei Sokolov, were at the Warsaw Pact conference in East Berlin when Rust landed. With much fanfare, Gorbachev had just announced that the forces of the Warsaw Pact were undergoing their own perestroika, based on a new military doctrine that was purely "defensive" in character. Efficiency based on high technology, not the brute force of numbers, was to be the hallmark of the Socialist nations' military, a restructuring to be led by the Soviet Armed Forces. Unfortunately for Marshal Sokolov, the penetration of Moscow's vital airspace by a light plane flown by a young civilian was hardly a tribute to this newly efficient defense. Gorbachev summarily dismissed Sokolov, replacing him with a mere general of the Army, Dmitri Yazov. The head of the PVO Air Defense Force, Marshal Alexander Koldunov, was also fired. In the official announcement he was referred to simply as "Comrade Koldunov," without his name or patronymic, a cutting insult to a Marshal of the Soviet Union.

My *zveno* was on duty alert at Vaziani when Mathias Rust landed. At first we thought the news was just another of the rumors or weird jokes that had mushroomed since glasnost, but we quickly learned that the Defense Ministry was boiling with angry embarrassment over the incident. That night the deputy military district commander, Major General Shubin, drove his own car out to the base from Tbilisi after midnight in a personal attempt to assess our readiness to intercept similar provocation flights down here in Georgia. The scared conscript guard at the gate waved the general through without even checking his identity papers. Shubin drove right to the control tower and the parking apron of the duty-alert section. He called the hapless duty-alert officer on the carpet, bellowing that—like Mathias Rust—he could have a "powerful bomb" in the trunk of his Zhiguli.

The next morning General Shubin returned with a delegation of senior officers from the district to conduct a formal readiness inspection. Because my *zveno* had the duty alert, we were in the full glare of his scrutiny. Either we had to prove we were capable of intercepting light aircraft intruders, flying low and slow, or Shubin would "squash shit" in our personal dossiers.

Luckily the resourcefulness of a wily Soviet pilot did not fail us. My former instructor, Captain Yevgeni Griek, had been up half the night drawing up elaborate diagrams—all convincingly postdated—of the squadron's interception maneuvers against low and slow intruder flights, including enemy "deception" missions flown on civilian light aircraft.

Shubin and his staff of angry bears were visibly impressed. They left after half an hour to report to Moscow that at least *one* unit of the regiment of the VVS was prepared to intercept and destroy such provocation flights.

After the general left, Captain Griek rolled up his bogus diagrams and grinned sardonically. He then quoted a very appropriate old Red Army aphorism: "The more paper you use, the cleaner your ass."

As it turned out, the PVO had certainly not used enough paper. My friend Sergei Rastvorov had a pal who flew a MiG-23 in the PVO regiment that had tried to intercept Mathias Rust north of Moscow on that sunny afternoon. That pilot had, in fact, conducted an effective visual intercept on the small plane droning only 120 feet above the budding orchards and muddy fields of the coastal plain. But when he called in his "visual contact," to GCI, the battle-control officers said he was seeing things. He was informed that the radar blip he had been sent to intercept was just a "flock of birds." Frustrated and short of fuel, he returned to base and was angrily trying to convince the GCI wizards he had seen a light foreign aircraft when the news of Rust's landing came in.

Over the coming days, there was only a curt mention of Rust's flight in *Pravda,* and no pictures on Soviet television. For those we had to rely on videos from West German TV recorded by friends based in East Germany and on photocopies of Western magazines.

So much for perestroika in the military; so much for official glasnost.

I did not arrive at Akhtubinsk until mid-June, and came via the long train and bus ride from Georgia, rather than flying in with my squadron.

The first interesting news I received when I signed in was that the center's test pilots and engineering staff had finally gone on strike earlier that spring in protest of the chronic food shortages. A high delegation from Moscow had eventually appeased them with promises to restock the base Voyentorg. And the officers' dining room was certainly well stocked with food. My first morning I ate a typically "light" Air Force breakfast that included a plate heaping with fried sausage and eggs, cheese, roll and butter, and a block of real chocolate, all washed down with cups of coffee. But I was told there was still no food in town, and most of the Akhtubinsk officers remained angry and frustrated.

I was one of approximately seventy-five applicant fighter test pilot students. There were two other similar groups, one for bombers, the other for helicopters. We represented the top 0.5 percent of the 30,000-odd Soviet military pilots in the VVS, PVO, and Naval Aviation. Most of my competitors were fellow captains, but there were also a large number of young majors, many with experience as squadron commanders. I even recognized a couple of my former instructors from my academy years. At least I was in good company.

My squadron mates confirmed what I had already suspected: They had become friends with the test pilots of the fighter division, but I did not have time to socialize with the center staff. Colonel Torbov had indeed extracted his revenge.

The tests began the next day. We were told that the week-long examination would be divided into five days of separate tests: theoretical aeronautical engineering tests; medical exams; physical fitness and dexterity; practical flight tests; and, finally, personal interviews before a board of center instructors. As my fighter group assembled in a school amphitheater to receive our test schedules, I could see that most of my colleagues—like me—were anxious to do well. Fighter pilots are a competitive lot by definition, and we were all acutely aware that we represented the cream of the Soviet Armed Forces.

The eight hours of theoretical exams went well. Glancing around me in the brightly lit test room, I saw my fellow applicants literally sweating over their exam sheets, some nervously rapping their slide rules on the varnished tabletops in frustration. They had not taken the months to prepare, alone each night in an empty flat, as I had. My investment in the big Minsk refrigerator, rather than in a distracting color television set, was now paying dividends.

The medical and strength and dexterity tests were rigorous, but I knew I'd done well. Unfortunately I walked back from the sauna in a cold breeze and came down with a sinus infection the morning of my practical flight test. A blocked sinus throws off your vestibular balance, which makes precision flying difficult. As luck would have it, the first of the two flights was with the test pilot school commander, Colonel Migounov. By definition, he was a pilot's pilot, who had probably forgotten more about precision flying than most Soviet fighter pilots ever learned.

The flights were in a two-seat MiG-23UB, a well-equipped and very well maintained aircraft. I rode in front, with the colonel perched behind in the narrow instructor's rear cockpit. He had a full set of instruments back there and could accurately assess how well I executed the demanding maneuvers he ordered. I had been flying such precision tests since preparing for the L-29 aerobatics competition years before in Azerbaijan. But this morning I was simply not in tune with the aircraft. One particularly exacting sequence, a descending sixty-degree spiral at exactly three hundred knots down to a precise altitude of 6,000 feet was needed, I was way off the required speed and dive angle.

But Colonel Migounov remained silent behind me. All I heard was his slow, rasping breath in his oxygen mask.

My second test flight was scheduled for 1500 hours that afternoon with Colonel Rizantsev, the school's deputy commander for curriculum. Instead of fretting about my shaky performance that morning, I went back to the officers' barracks, undressed, climbed in bed, and slept for almost three hours. Luckily I had been used to catching such "combat naps" while standing duty alert day in, day out at Vaziani. When I awoke, my blocked sinus was clear, and my headache was gone.

That afternoon's flight was flawless. And climbing down from the rear cockpit on the apron, Colonel Rizantsev smiled broadly. "It's not often I get to tally a ten-for-ten perfect score, Captain Zuyev."

I knew I had more than compensated for my poor showing that morning.

Two days later when I faced the formal personal interview panel, I felt calm and confident. The interview took place in a conference room at base headquarters. I stood before a long table where Colonel Migounov occupied the center seat, flanked by his deputies, including a benevolently smiling zampolit and a typically silent representative of the Osobii Otdel.

"You've done very well, Captain Zuyev," Colonel Migounov began.

I felt a stab of anxiety. If I had made the final selection, he or the zampolit would have begun, "Congratulations, Comrade Captain..."

My eye shot to the right-hand end of the table where an intricate rank-order diagram of all the fighter pilot applicants lay, its pink cover sheet pulled back. Even from this distance I could see that the name "Zuyev, Alexander M. Captain/176FAR" filled the number seven line. I had missed selection by just two places.

My cheeks felt hot and I had to suppress an urge to turn and leave the room. Colonel Migounov was still speaking.

"...So you see, Zuyev," he said. "We managed to get another opening from our helicopter colleagues." Now he pointed toward the diagram as if I had not yet seen it. "We've ranked Major Safonov number six to take advantage of this extra opening, even though the two of you had almost identical scores."

I must have frowned, because Colonel Bazlevsky, the school's flight operations director, now spoke up to explain.

"Safonov is thirty-one years old, Zuyev," he said. "This is his last chance to enter the school."

I nodded glumly. All those months of hard work, all those long nights of dry study.

"We'd like you to apply again for the next selection in two years, Zuyev," Colonel Migounov added. "It's the best solution for all concerned. This way we will gain two good officers in two years, instead of losing Safonov."

Obviously my interview was over. My arm felt wooden as I reached across the table to shake the colonel's hand.

Colonel Bazlevsky followed me out of the conference room to the small smoking garden on the gravel path between the two wings of the headquarters building. He sensed my deep disappointment. I stood politely while he lit his own cigarette.

"How old are you, Captain?" There was a sympathetic glimmer in his eye.

"Twenty-seven, Comrade Colonel."

He wrinkled his sunburnt nose. "This is June. When's your birthday?"

He had me there. "In July, Colonel Bazlevsky. "I'm *almost* twenty-seven."

Now the colonel smiled. "And not married yet?"

I shook my head. Had Torbov somehow poisoned the water with this panel? Then I realized that Colonel Bazlevsky was speaking of another matter altogether.

"This is an isolated post, Zuyev. We like our student test pilots to be married. It's a sign of mature stability."

"I understand, Comrade Colonel."

He clapped me on the shoulder. "Find some nice girl, Zuyev. Get married. Come back in two years and we'll have a place for you."

Normally the prospect of marrying a pleasant young woman and embarking on the exciting career of military test pilot would have overcome my disappointment. But I just could not feel good about the way these events had come together.

I still had a few days' special leave accrued before returning to Tskhakaya, so I took the train home to Samara to visit my family. My mother's fiftieth birthday was coming up and I hoped to offer her a suitable present: ten days at the Pearl Hotel in the Black Sea resort of Sochi. My KGB friend, Oleg, ran security for the resort, and I called him to confirm that he had landed me a reservation for my mother and young brother, Misha. Mother certainly needed a rest and a change of scene.

She looked worn, indeed haggard. Life was becoming harder every day. She toiled away in her demanding position as an irrigation project construction engineer, working on complex plans and blueprints for huge earthen dams, canals, and pumping stations, with little recognition and certainly poor pay. Twenty-five years before as a young engineering graduate, she had earned 120 rubles a month, enough to support her family. Now her monthly pay was only 180 rubles, and her and Valentin's combined salaries were hardly sufficient. Luckily they had their small garden plot and packing-case "dacha," to grow some fruit and vegetables each summer.

When I surprised her with the news of the Black Sea vacation, she was pleased but wary. "Where did you get the *valuta*, Sasha?"

She understood how the system worked, and knew such resorts were reserved for hard-currency clients. To my mother, the existence of luxury resorts on Soviet soil, open only to high Party apparatchiks and foreign tourists, could somehow be explained within the reassuring dogma of Socialist Economics. She looked forward to her holiday.

I arrived back at Tskhakaya the day after Jana Baglai returned from Kiev to begin her summer holiday. Sasha Olmelchenko's girlfriend, Yelena, mentioned that Jana had asked after me.

That first weekend I invited her to an outdoor restaurant on the slopes of Senaki Mountain dominating the vineyards and orange groves north of Tskhakaya. Over a glass of good Georgian white wine, I plunged right into the subject.

"Well, Jana," I said, taking her hand across the table, "maybe we should think about getting married."

Her response was immediate. "Yes, Sasha, I want to."

We had not had much of a romantic courtship. But this was often the case for Soviet military officers. Whatever romance there was would come after the engagement.

I sipped my wine and looked across the plastic tablecloth at this beautiful young woman. I felt lucky. It was common knowledge that many pilots' wives were "noncultured," but attractive rural girls whom the officers had snapped up out of desperation when they got an assignment to the deserts of Central Asia or the endless forests of eastern Siberia. This was usually an embarrassment because, by definition, the pilot was an educated man with four rigorous years of a service academy under his belt, while his wife was often a school dropout with only the minimum eight years of education.

But Jana had already completed a year of university toward her degree in biology. By the time we were ready to have children, I'd be a major, an established test pilot, and she would be a member of the intelligentsia with her university diploma. The more I imagined the lovely dark-haired girl sitting across the table from me in the shade of the grape arbor as my wife, the more desirable she became. Jana was exactly the kind of partner I wanted, not one of the nagging, frowzy military wives you saw in the lines at the Voyentorg, bloated fat at a young age, their hair in plastic curlers, wearing a stained housecoat instead of a proper dress. The only interest such women had was material possessions, and they drove their long-suffering husbands half-crazy with impossible demands for cars and household appliances.

But Jana and I would be different. We would have more in common than just sexual attraction and gluttony for possessions. I smiled. I was trying to be so logical about this engagement, but gazing at Jana's face, it was exciting to realize that this beautiful girl would soon be my wife.

We sat under a shady arbor, sipping our cold wine and discussing the pleasant details of our wedding plans. Outside on the terrace, I saw a table full of noisy, drunken officers from the base. The group was hosted by the most corrupt staff officer at

Ruslan. He had probably sold so much aviation alcohol and gasoline to the local black marketers that he was hosting this lavish luncheon to reward those other crooked officers who had helped him. This criminal even had soldiers cut the grass around our runway for sale as fodder to local dairy farmers. Men like that were a dishonor to their uniform and their country.

I turned back to Jana. We had decided to have our wedding in August, when my mother passed through Tskhakaya after her Black Sea vacation, and before Jana's parents had to begin packing for their new assignment; Colonel Baglai was scheduled to become a senior military adviser in Syria. I was honest with Jana about my finances. After five years as an officer, I had managed to save just over 4,500 rubles, although I had already agreed to spend almost 500 on my mother's fiftieth birthday holiday. So I suggested we plan a very small wedding with only our immediate families and then take a two-week honeymoon on the Black Sea ourselves. That would leave us with around 3,000 rubles to furnish the new apartment I was sure we would be assigned, once I announced our engagement. To me, the compromise represented a proper balance between the practical realities of Soviet life and the pleasant occasion of a family wedding.

Jana reluctantly agreed to convince her parents that this was what we both wanted.

But her parents would not hear of it. When I met them formally in their four-room apartment in one of the better buildings of the military housing compound, Colonel Baglai came right to the point.

"My daughter will not have a shabby little wedding, Captain," he said, speaking with his deep, brusque "command" voice. "Her mother and I have many social responsibilities and obligations. Jana is not just some factory girl, and you are not some truck driver who runs off to the wedding palace, then drinks warm beer in the railway station buffet."

I clenched my teeth, torn between speaking frankly to my future father-in-law and deference to an influential senior officer. By tradition, the families of the bride and groom shared equally in the wedding expenses. And the groom's family was expected to pay for the wedding dress, shoes, and flowers, plus all the other expensive decorations required for a "proper" ceremony and reception. Colonel Baglai assured me that we would split the real costs of the reception—champagne, wine, brandy, and food—equally.

"Don't worry, Sasha," he said, clapping my shoulder and addressing me informally, "all the senior officers we invite will load you down with generous presents."

When I attended weddings of junior officer friends, I always presented the couple with an envelope containing five new red ten-ruble bills.

"We have so many close friends," Jana's mother, Yevgenia Vasilyevna, added. "And, with my husband's important position, we simply can't avoid offering a large reception. After all, Jana is our first child to marry."

"Perhaps," I conceded. I nodded silently, appraising my new in-laws.

The colonel was a typical professional Soviet officer, stocky but energetic, with dark hair and even darker, intelligent eyes, a face rendered just short of handsome by a broken nose squashed like a potato by years of wearing tight-fitting oxygen masks. He was known as a good pilot and a forceful leader. I quite liked him, although I resented his bulldozer decision about the wedding.

Jana's mother was another matter. She was in her late forties, several years older than her husband, chunky, rather coarse-looking. As a younger woman, I imagined she had been quite sensually attractive, but she had aged badly; her skin actually looked stretched, like a sausage casing. And she tinted her hair and wore it in tight, springy curls. I realized that she had been one of the plastic curler matrons I'd seen on the Voyentorg.

I saw that there was no sense arguing with a woman like this. It was clear from the determined glint in her eye that the opulent wedding reception of their oldest daughter to a successful fighter pilot would be Yevgenia Vasilyevna's crowning achievement at Tskhakaya; they could depart for Syria at a high point, the perfect Air Force family.

I was already deeply worried about the expense of all this empty ceremony, and had to hold back from speaking my mind. The Baglais' apartment gave me some indication of the kind of family I was joining. They had inherited the flat from the former division commander, General Anosov, who had "hijacked" an additional room from the next-door unit by ripping down a wall when the other apartment was temporarily empty. Jana's mother boasted of Anosov's clever ploy, oblivious to the hardship it placed on their neighbors, a hapless maintenance captain and his wife who had to share a small room with two children, while the Baglais enjoyed the luxury of a storage room.

With a sinking feeling, I suddenly knew that this spacious apartment and the shelves of decorative books epitomized the Baglais' heartless materialism. Jana and my wedding would be just another decoration; acquiring an Air Force captain with a promising career would be one more enviable possession.

This was *not* a good way to begin married life.

But I had no choice in the matter. The wedding date was set for August 15, 1987, and the ceremony would be in the big hall of the ZAGS State Wedding Palace in the city. Colonel Baglai was inviting friends and colleagues from all over the military district and from several Soviet bases in eastern Europe. Jana's mother gave her a list of wedding clothes. It was my responsibility to locate these scarce items and, of course, to pay for them.

Naturally the Voyentorg had nothing we could use. They could hardly provide milk and eggs, so it was unrealistic to imagine they stocked full-length wedding gowns with lace veils, silk stockings, or satin shoes.

Instead, I turned to my resourceful Georgian friend, Malhaz. He ran an unofficial private shop, among other profitable enterprises. His small store was stacked with imported Dresden china, Polish and Romanian sport clothes, and a good collection of Japanese electronics and videocassettes. We had become friends the year before, when I greeted him in the shop with the formal Georgian salutation, *"Gamargoba,"* a courtesy few Russian soldiers ever learned.

When I had asked Malhaz how he managed to obtain all the import permits for his rich selection of goods, he'd replied silently with a gold-toothed grin, rubbing his right index finger and thumb together briskly. There was a large framed photo of Gorbachev prominently displayed on his wall. Then he had added: "Our Party leaders are very reasonable men." Under Gorbachev a man like Malhaz got along "like a cheese rolling over in sour cream," as the old Russian saying went.

A man like Malhaz probably had to pay some of his profits under the table to local Party officials. I was only slightly surprised at the admission. With glasnost, news of such "Socialist enterprise" arrangements was spreading. After I got to know Malhaz better, he dropped his pretenses and referred to his local Party patrons simply as "the Mafia." At the time, I had thought this was a rather colorful aspect of the irrepressible Georgian character.

Malhaz picked us up in his shiny new Volga sedan the next afternoon and drove us to a seemingly run-down industrial quarter of the city. We stopped on a muddy lane past the railway switchyards, and he led us to a nondescript concrete-block warehouse. Inside the rusty steel door, we found an incredible stockpile of luxury goods. Half the warehouse was a "special" clothing store, owned and managed by two of Malhaz's smiling relatives. There were racks of imported suits and dresses, piles of authentic American blue jeans, and British Reebok shoes. On the other side of the aisle, there were cases of canned Hungarian goulash and German chicken. Several locked glass display cases held perfume, imported televisions, and Japanese stereo sets.

Jana was stunned. I was impressed, but tried not to show it because I hoped to drive a reasonable bargain on anything we bought. As it turned out, I didn't have to. The owner took us to a rack of stylish East German wedding dresses fringed with delicate lace. The first one he selected fit Jana perfectly. The smiling Georgian businessman threw in a silk floral wreath with the price of the dress, only 132 rubles.

The next day Malhaz took us to a similar private warehouse, this one near the smelly State stockyards. But the goods inside were unaffected by the odor of sheep and cattle. Jana selected white satin wedding shoes with stylish high heels, a luxury never seen in the Voyentorg. All told, her wedding dress, shoes and an attractive sundress with matching jacket for the honeymoon cost me less than 300 rubles. Malhaz was a genius.

"Perestroika," he said, "is very good for business."

That weekend Colonel Vladimir Prozukhin, the deputy division commander for political administration, paid a call on the Baglais while I was at their apartment. As chief zampolit, Prozukhin had more than a personal interest in our wedding. The marriage of a reasonably presentable and successful young fighter pilot to the beautiful daughter of a senior Air Force officer gave Prozukhin the chance to promote the virtues of Socialist morality in the

Soviet military. And the occasion also presented him the opportunity to win favor with the pro-Gorbachev reformers in the Ministry of Defense. He planned to do so by staging a "sober" wedding reception at which no alcohol would be served.

"This is a great opportunity, Alexander Vasilyevich," Prozukhin told Jana's father, then turned to me. "Think of the example this would set, not only in the division but in the entire Air Force."

He went on to explain that he could arrange a special photo feature in *Aviation and Cosmonautics*. It would be a great propaganda victory in Gorbachev's sputtering anti-alcohol campaign, Prozukhin implied. If a MiG-29 pilot and his virile comrades drank only tea and mineral water at the wedding, Prozukhin argued, we would set a "splendid example" that would not go unnoticed in Moscow. Naturally Prozukhin's role in the affair would not go unnoticed either.

This time I didn't defer to Colonel Baglai before announcing my true feelings. "No," I blurted out. "Absolutely not, Comrade Colonel, I would like to have spirits at my wedding party."

Jana's father nodded emphatically. He was known as a man who liked his brandy. "Out of the question, Prozukhin," he said.

As things turned out, I wish I would have accepted this sycophant Prozukhin's offer.

The following weeks were hectic. I flew during the day. At night and on weekends, I worked—slaved was more like it—on the tiny apartment the housing office had assigned me as a wedding present. The place was a shambles; the window with broken panes was jammed shut and the intact window would not open. Half the plaster had fallen down. The toilet backed up when it did flush, which was sporadic at best. And the electric wiring was like an elaborate booby trap. Slowly I made progress. But these home improvements were expensive. Even with Malhaz helping, the necessary plumbing, carpentry, and electrical supplies were damned expensive and difficult to find. I worked "like an Ethiopian," as in the derisive Russian adage, and spent several hundred rubles just to make the apartment habitable. And I hadn't even started looking for furniture.

"*That*, my friend," Malhaz warned, "will be more difficult still."

Then Colonel Baglai broke the cheery news on the cost of

the wedding reception. There would be over 120 guests invited to the officers' dining room. What with food, *prezanty* for the kitchen and serving staff, a stereo discotheque for music, and an ample supply of alcohol, my share of the expenses would be two thousand rubles. He may as well have hit me in the face with both fists. When I handed over the thick packet of bank notes, I had less than eight hundred rubles left in my savings account.

But Colonel Baglai assured me we were getting high quality at a bargain price. He had an Osobist friend at Vaziani who had a colleague in Yerevan, the capital of Armenia, where the State brandy factory was located. Baglai ordered forty liters of the best five-star Armenian cognac to be delivered for the reception.

"Don't worry," he assured me, "we won't drink that much and you and I can split what's left."

By ordering in this volume, he explained, we were getting a bargain price. He had a point. Such high-quality Armenian cognac was extremely valuable. And by ordering through a KGB connection, we were buying at cost.

"Actually," Jana's father explained, smiling like a rug merchant in the bazaar, "we're getting it well below cost."

He elaborated. Apparently one of the plant foremen had constructed an actual secret pipeline directly from the aging room of the factory to a shed in the backyard of his small house just outside the distillery walls. While the casks were being filled for the aging process, a steady stream of this expensive brandy was trickling unnoticed through a copper pipe, across the factory grounds, through the wall, and into a collection vat. The man paid off the KGB with a portion of his product and sold the rest. No wonder good Armenian brandy was hard to find north of the Caucasus.

When I tallied up my savings account book that night, I also estimated that I would have at least five liters of good cognac left over to sell after the wedding, which might fetch forty or fifty rubles each. At least that would be some compensation.

My relations with the Baglai family remained cool, at best. After the first, formal visit to their apartment to discuss the wedding plans, I returned several times. These visits certainly were *not* formal occasions. But they were revealing of the family's character. One day Jana's mother asked if I was hungry, then simply said, "There's food if you want to eat."

She then returned from the kitchen with a pot of macaroni, slapped it down on the table, and proceeded to spread newspaper as a tablecloth. I was shocked. Even the bachelor officer pilots I had roomed with over the years had better manners than this. At first I thought she was staging some elaborate joke. But then I realized I was expected to eat this way. I politely declined.

A few minutes later Jana's sister Marina and her little brother came home and went directly to the kitchen stove to eat standing there, spooning the food right from the same greasy pot Jana's mother had presented me. Clearly that was their habitual practice. So much for close family life.

I could have dismissed these quirks as a minor irritation, but I knew they typified the home that had shaped Jana's character. If a family didn't care about properly forming their children's manners and public behavior, what did they care about? I remembered Jana's father's action after the Chernobyl disaster. His calling a colleague in the Ukraine to make certain there was no problem with a perfunctory gesture. No father who loved his daughter would have accepted this.

A few nights later I had to wait at the Baglais' apartment quite late because they had a phone and I was trying to get through to my mother at the Pearl Hotel in Sochi to verify some details of the wedding. Jana's mother didn't even offer me a cup of tea. She merely pointed to the couch, then tottered off to bed herself. I lay there for hours trying to get comfortable without a pillow, brooding on the irrevocable step I was about to take.

Then, two days later, I had a real blowup with Jana. I had finally gotten our apartment repaired and cleaned up. Although it was sparsely furnished, the walls were intact and nicely papered and everything was clean. While I was flying, Jana came over to spend the day to get ready for the Air Force Day dance that evening, which was going to be a kind of unofficial engagement party. When I got back from the base, it looked like the apartment had been ransacked. There were wet towels strewn on the bathroom floor, half-eaten plates of food on the floor of the small living room, and the kitchen was filthy. But Jana looked great, well scrubbed, her hair in long, loose curls, and her sleeveless summer dress beautifully pressed. She was ready to go to the dance.

I looked around the apartment and shook my head. She knew I had scrubbed the accumulated filth of years off the kitchen walls and tile floor, yet she had carelessly spilled food and tea and not even bothered to wipe up the mess.

"Hurry, Sasha," she said. "We don't want to be late."

I glared at her. "You go ahead without me."

Her young face clouded. She was genuinely confused. "Why, Sasha?"

I clenched my teeth to keep from shouting. It had been a long day. "I have to clean up this apartment."

She came back around eleven, a few minutes after I had finally wrung out the mop and put away the broom. I didn't hesitate. "Jana," I said, "I think we should wait. I think we should postpone the wedding at least one year."

Her lovely, suntanned face lost its color. "Why?" she gasped.

"I don't think you're ready to be married."

Finally she realized what had happened. She came and sobbed on my chest. "Oh, Sasha," she moaned, "I'm so sorry..."

But I remained noncommittal, saying only that I needed time to consider the matter of our engagement. Because I was still so angry, it wasn't wise to keep talking. Maybe her sloppiness had just been a fluke, or perhaps it was a clear indication that she was impossibly self-centered. I was torn between desire for this beautiful young girl and a nagging inner voice that told me we were completely unsuited for each other.

When my mother returned from her vacation on the Black Sea on August 13, she still seemed tired and strangely subdued, although Misha was deeply suntanned and merry. On an impulse, I told her of the fight with Jana, then expressed my revulsion for the Baglai family. "I want to just cancel the whole thing," I finally admitted.

Mother was standing at the window, fingering the clean gauze curtains I'd hung there. Her face was strained. "No, Sasha," she whispered. "We can't have another canceled wedding." She reminded me of the embarrassing uproar when I had spurned the blatantly engineered "engagement" with Svetlana in 1983.

"Sasha," she said, turning to face me, "you can't escape this time. The plans have gone too far. Be patient. Jana is young and her parents are leaving. You can change her."

I remained silent for a moment. Maybe she was right. Finally I nodded agreement.

The wedding was certainly everything the Baglai family wanted. Saturday, August 15, was a rainy southern day, with drizzle and low overcast. Colonel Baglai's colleagues provided the shiny Volga and Skoda sedans for the entourage. The cars were decorated with bright balloons, and everyone was smiling. Jana looked fantastic in her lace wedding dress, which her mother brazenly implied *she* had selected.

In the grand hall of the ZAGS State Wedding Palace, the woman registrar solemnly read the official vows, then pronounced us husband and wife, "in the name of the Soviet people and the Union of Soviet Socialist Republics." When I kissed Jana, I looked up at the huge realistic mural on the wall above, the Ideal Socialist Family, handsome, burly husband, demure wife, and radiant blond children, all nicely dressed, surrounded by the bounty of the Workers' Paradise. Turning, I faced Jana's own, somewhat less than ideal family. They looked plump and content, as if they had just eaten a satisfying meal. It was not as if they had gained a son, but that they had just managed to legally abandon the responsibility for their oldest daughter. The bust of Lenin gazed down on us, silent and aloof.

The motorcade to the base was boisterous, even by Georgian standards. The citizens of Tskhakaya, like all Georgians, knew much more about the Russians in the military than we knew about them. They always crowded the streets when a senior officer's family held a wedding, as if to demonstrate their deep affection for their protectors. By tradition, the crowds would block the road until the best man—my squadron mate, Sergei Rastvorov— showered the kids with handfuls of kopeks and hard candy.

The staff of the officers' dining room had done their best to provide a true banquet for the deputy division commander. I certainly couldn't complain about the quality of the food, the wine, or naturally, the brandy. Even the DJ who ran the stereo discotheque had some brand-new Western music.

But our wedding night was grim. Jana and I counted the

pitiful contents of the gift envelopes, less than eight hundred rubles, not even enough to buy a proper set of dishes. So much for the presents that Jana's father had assured me would replenish my empty savings account. One of the deputy regimental commanders had set the tone by presenting his own lavish gift: a book bound in imitation leather with thirty or so color pictures of antique china and place settings at the Hermitage Museum in Leningrad. It was the kind of giveaway volume presented as tokens to visiting official delegations, handsome but virtually worthless. Jana and I did not need *pictures* of plates and serving bowls, we needed the actual items.

Some guests had given us five single-ruble notes, no more. But they certainly hadn't held back at the buffet table or the bar. And I had seen Jana's father slipping full bottles of the precious cognac to the sleek clutch of senior men from military district headquarters. This expensive party was just a way to cement his *blat* connected to these big shots.

"Jana," I said, shaking my head, "I'm sorry, but we'll have to skip our honeymoon."

She nodded soberly, also stunned by the poor selection of presents. "I know," she whispered.

Late that night I lay on our improvised wedding bed—two soldiers' cots I had lashed together—watching the breeze billow the moonlit curtains. Somehow I still had to find the money to furnish this apartment.

The week before Jana was scheduled to return to the university in Kiev, she finally transferred all of her belongings to our apartment from her parents' flat. Helping her unpack, I noticed she had no winter clothes.

"Where are your boots and your heavy coat?"

"Oh," she said, "Mother kept them for Marina. I'll need money to buy new things."

By the time we finished yet another shopping spree through Malhaz's warehouse, my savings account was completely empty. For the first time in my life, I had to borrow money from friends. It was a disgusting experience.

In late September Jana suddenly returned from Kiev and announced she had managed to enroll in the university's correspondence program. She had brought several boxes of books and laboratory manuals, so I took her at her word. But two weeks later, those boxes were still unopened.

One night I got back late after an exhausting instrument flying sortie and blew up at Jana for yet again leaving the kitchen full of filthy dishes. She broke into tears and confessed that she was not, after all, enrolled in a correspondence course, but had simply left the university because she was "lonely."

This was a disaster. I knew her parents would blame me for her quitting the university. And I also realized that, if she did not return now, she never would. The next day I managed to secure a five-day leave and pulled some strings to buy Aeroflot tickets to Kiev with borrowed money.

The next morning we were in the university rector's office. I wore my best parade uniform with polished wings and the two decorations I'd earned. The old comrade was sympathetic when I explained that Jana had abruptly left the university after I had received a sudden overseas assignment. Now, I told him, that assignment had been just as suddenly canceled. It was imperative that she be allowed to enroll as a correspondence student.

Although the official enrollment deadline was weeks past, I somehow managed to slash through the red tape. When we left Kiev, Jana was glum and pouting, but she was enrolled.

Over the coming months, I learned another painful lesson about the reality of Soviet life. I had always eaten my meals in officers' dining rooms, where the food was free and plentiful. But now I was a married man and was supposed to buy groceries in the bazaar, where the prices were at least three times those in the Voyentorg. But the Voyentorg was always empty these days. And, unlike Akhtubinsk, we had no transport available to whisk us off to Moscow for shopping trips. On a salary of 350 rubles a month, two healthy young people with normal appetites simply could not eat properly. I now understood why the staff of the Akhtubinsk center had staged their strike.

Because Jana was only making a token effort in her correspondence study, I suggested she find a part-time job to help our finances. Before her father left for Syria, he managed to land her a well-paying position in the division meteorology office. But two weeks passed and she still had not reported for work. When I confronted her, Jana complained that she hadn't "felt well." In fact, she had merely slept all day.

Only three months into our marriage, and I was beginning to face the bitter truth that I had probably married Jana for the wrong reasons.

That December my squadron had duty alert when the huge, devastating earthquake struck Armenia. The Ruslan base became a staging and refueling point for Soviet transport aircraft hauling international relief supplies to the victims. Big An-12 and An-22 turboprops were landing and taking off every few minutes, and the convoys of fuel tanker trucks stretched along the apron halfway back to the main gate. The Air Force was doing its best to support the international relief effort.

The television coverage of the disaster had been heartrending. Not only had thousands of people died in the collapsed buildings, but thousands more were at risk from the blizzards that swept down after the earthquake. I was proud to do my part, helping to turn the transports around quickly. And it was encouraging to see the massive outpouring of international aid for the victims.

Then one rainy afternoon, I was talking to a tired crew of the An-22, who had just flown in short of fuel from Yerevan. The pilots were unshaven and their eyes were hollow; they had been flying practically around the clock. When I asked how the victims were holding up, the copilot, a lanky senior lieutenant, suddenly laughed bitterly.

"They are dying, of course, Comrade."

His aircraft commander, a shorter captain my age, shot the man an angry glance.

But the copilot ignored him. "All that food and medicine," he said flatly, "the tents, the blankets . . . the sleeping bags for the children . . ."

Now the captain spoke. "The whole republic of Armenia is controlled by *maroder,* pillagers."

"Pillagers?"

The two officers explained. As soon as the relief effort began, armed gangs of survivors—usually aided by the local militia—set up bogus landing zones for the relief helicopters that ferried the supplies from the main airports. When the Mi-8 cargo helicopters set down, the looters rolled up their trucks and loaded the supplies on board. They even had colored landing panels, strobe lights, and radio beacons.

"Obviously the local Party is in it too," the captain said bitterly.

The copilot added that women and children were literally starving in the ruins while the bands of looters were getting fat on canned Polish ham and French biscuits. They only took the most valuable goods; Army patrols had found boxes of medical equipment dumped in the frozen mud near the landing zones. The looters had thrown away the portable X-ray equipment and kept material that was easier to sell. Already, he said, the thick winter parkas flown in from Finland were for sale in the street bazaars of Baku to the north.

I tried to grasp what all this meant. "What about the Army? Isn't anyone trying to control this?"

The copilot scowled. "The soldiers are, of course. They have their own methods. They caught a man cutting rings off the fingers of the dead. They led him into the ruins, then knocked down a wall on top of him. But he was just a free agent. They can't do anything against the organized groups."

"But who's protecting those gangs?" I demanded.

The tired young captain slurped his sweet tea and shook his head. "The KGB . . . the Party . . . who knows? They call them the Mafia."

The term "Mafia" had first appeared during the Uzbekistan corruption trials to describe the crooked network established by the local Party officials. Since then, there had been other reports of secret criminal alliances among Party officials, State Security, and profiteers. This Soviet Mafia was not an American-style secret underworld group of pimps, drug dealers, or hijackers, as we had seen in so many gangster films, but rather an unofficial network of corrupt Socialist "entrepreneurs" who abused their positions of authority. And now these officers had affirmed that another absolutely corrupt *banda* existed in Armenia, a gang so cruel that they would strip relief supplies from the hands of starving women and children.

In a speech that winter Gorbachev had accused the Mafia of brazenly sabotaging the Armenian relief efforts. But the last thing successful criminals wanted was such notoriety. Then I realized that Party officials themselves had to be involved with this criminal enterprise. The only reason they singled out the Mafia was to divert attention from their own crimes. Indeed, corrupt officials seemed to use the Party's own Union-wide organization to extend their tentacles.

And the corruption seemed to be spreading like a cancer. I wondered where it would end.

— 10 —
Repression
1988–89

One of the few pieces of good news in the spring of 1988 was the announcement of our new regimental commander, Lieutenant Colonel Anatoli Ignatich Antonovich. He was a great leader and a very popular officer. Short and wiry, like many fighter pilots, he had a sharp nose and bushy brows above lively, deep-set eyes. He smiled easily and showed none of the cold brooding of Torbov. Antonovich was not carefree, however. He worked us hard, but always explained the purpose of orders in his precise, almost comically basso voice, as if the words were echoing from a railway station loudspeaker. Above all, he was an excellent pilot, and being in his mid-thirties, was much closer in age to his officers than Torbov or other regimental commanders had been.

I got along with him well. Lieutenant Colonel Antonovich made it clear from the beginning that he expected us to hold up our high flying standards, and complete the combat evaluation of the MiG-29 in record time. But he also worked hard to improve the officers' housing conditions and was continually fighting the bureaucracy—often unsuccessfully—to increase the food supplies in the Voyentorg.

Early that April, when I was due for my annual leave, Antonovich telephoned me at the duty-alert room.

"Shurka," he said, "people tell me you're the world's expert on ski resorts. Can you arrange a vacation package for me?"

I hadn't known he was a skier, and as it turned out, he was a novice eager to learn. "I'll try, Anatoli Ignatich."

"You'll do more than try, Shurka, because you're coming along to teach me how to ski."

That was, indeed, an incentive. I'd been flying hard and my troubling marriage was in one of its sporadic truce periods. Although Jana had not seriously tried to hold a job at the base, she had turned back to her studies with something like enthusiasm. Now she was in Kiev completing her second-year spring examinations, and I hoped to reward her effort by taking her along to the Terskol resort with me and the colonel.

That afternoon I called the military travel office; they called Moscow, and we had three packages in hand before the office closed. Next I called my friend Hamid, who lined up the best skis and rooms for us.

"Ignatich" was a skilled pilot, but did not make much progress in his large class of beginner ski students. So I promised to teach him parallel skiing quickly. The next morning we rode the lift to a remote shoulder of the mountain and I made real progress, using aviation terminology like "thrust," "bank," and "pitch" to explain the proper angles for his skis. By afternoon he was progressing well. And the next day he was actually skiing the steep slopes of Cheget, the hardest mountain.

But Jana was a problem. She resented being left behind in her beginners' class, and clearly she was jealous of the attention I devoted to the colonel. Jana insisted on joining the colonel and me, but complained about the cold and whined that she didn't have a pretty ski suit like the other girls. Imported ski suits cost three months' salary, and I told her crossly that she could have paid for one herself if she had kept her job.

When she lashed back at me, I responded in turn. "If you wanted a nice ski suit, you should have brought one from Hungary.'"

For months she had been harping on the wonderful trove of luxury goods her family had amassed during their long years in Hungary, and implicitly criticized me for not providing the same.

For the first time she swore at me and stomped away, her shoddy ski boots clomping on the ice. That night we slept in separate beds and were hardly speaking in the morning.

*   *   *

We didn't have a chance to reconcile. I received an emergency telegram to call my stepfather, Valentin, in Samara. When I finally got through to him on the poor interurban phone lines, he explained that my mother was in a psychiatric hospital, having become unstable and actually attempting suicide. I was shocked. She had never before shown any symptoms of emotional instability, although she had seemed nervous and subdued when she returned from her Black Sea holiday the previous August.

Colonel Antonovich immediately gave me a week's leave, and the resort commander helped with plane reservations to Samara. I arrived home at nine that night and wanted to go immediately to the psychiatric clinic. But Valentin explained that visiting hours were severely restricted. If I was lucky, I could see her for half an hour the next morning.

We sat in the kitchen, drinking tea late into the night, as he explained the situation. Mother had been taken directly from the Hydroelectric Institute to the psychiatric clinic, after her superiors and coworkers had signed commitment papers stating she had become "irrationally paranoid and dangerously depressed." This was her third week in the clinic, and Valentin said she was making no progress.

"Why didn't you call me sooner?" I had been skiing and drinking hot mulled wine while my mother was locked in some psychiatric ward.

"We didn't want to worry you, Sasha."

The next day I walked through the center of the city and onto a street of old brick offices dating from before the Revolution. The psychiatric clinic was one of the oldest of these narrow, two-story buildings. The heavy steel front door was flecked with rust, and there were thick, rusty grates on the windows. The wooden stairs were worn and creaked badly as I climbed to the second floor. The place smelled of damp and there were stains on the walls and ceilings from leaking steam pipes. When I got to the reception, I had to pound on another steel door to get someone's attention. Finally the door slammed open to reveal an inner steel grate. I was staring into the eyes of a fat nurse whose gray-blond hair was pulled tight against her skull. She scowled severely.

"Name?" was all she hissed as a greeting.

After a while they brought Mother to the stuffy narrow visiting lobby. Dressed in a robe and slippers, she looked stooped and old. The skin of her face was both pale and strangely flushed. Her eyes moved slowly as if searching for focus.

"Only fifteen minutes," the nurse snapped.

After embracing my mother, I held her at arm's length, searching her face. Obviously she was under sedation. Her eyes were languid, her voice flat and slow. And she constantly licked her dry lips and slurped the water I brought her in an enamel cup.

But she was just as obviously glad to see me. Her main concern on that first morning was that Misha was all right. She was deeply concerned that my little brother be dressed properly for school and get a good meal in the evening. When I tried to question her about her emotional problems, she fell silent and stared down at the worn linoleum floor.

The next day I brought her a basket of fresh fruit from the bazaar and a casserole of fish soup that I had simmered long in the kitchen. But again, she made no direct reference to the condition that had brought her here. When I probed her, Mother became visibly confused, as if she had no clear memory of those events. She absently rubbed the flesh of her forearms, sliding back the sleeves of her robe. I saw the small scarlet welts of hypodermic marks. But when I demanded to speak to her doctor about the sedation, the nurse scornfully told me to write for an appointment.

It was Mother herself who managed to secure her temporary freedom. When she told her doctor—a shadowy woman psychiatrist—that her son, "a senior Air Force pilot," was here to help her, the clinic allowed her to return home, on the proviso she visited the clinic as an outpatient, "for regular therapy."

The first thing I did when she came back to the apartment was to confiscate the brown glass medicine bottles and check their contents. Unfortunately the prescriptions for the capsules were partially written in a special Health ministry code. So I spent a morning seeking independent medical advice. Through friends, I contacted a senior psychiatrist at another clinic. I made a point of wearing my best uniform to the doctor's office. He took one look at the brown bottles and picked up his phone to call Mother's clinic.

When she returned for her treatment the next day, the staff

was less brutal. For the first time in weeks, Mother was not given an injection.

That night her eyes and mind seemed to clear, as if a curtain was lifting. Again, we sat at the kitchen table, the steaming teapot between us. She began to talk, first in disorganized spurts, then more slowly, with the logical reasoning of a trained engineer. Over that long night and during the next day and evening, the strange story of her "illness" slowly emerged.

What she told me began as a description of an innocuous bureaucratic process. Her story ended as a nightmare.

Under perestroika, Gorbachev's Politburo had decreed that the resources of the entire Soviet Union be accurately surveyed. In the military this had meant exhaustive inventories of equipment and detailed tabulations of troop strength. Factories had to list every machine and vehicle, registering their serial numbers. Tens of thousands of State enterprises were engaged in the process. In the spring of 1987 the Kuybyshev Hydroelectric Institute had been ordered to produce a complete survey of all the farmland in the oblast that was part of the region's large, complex irrigation scheme.

Mother had been honored when she was given the task of supervising the survey brigades and tabulating their findings. At first the job seemed relatively straightforward, she explained. There were some minor discrepancies between the new survey sheets and the existing boundary lines of the *kolkhoz* collective farms and the *sovkhoz* State agricultural units. But this was to be expected; the new survey instruments were much more accurate than the old equipment that had been used just after the war.

"Then, Sasha," Mother explained gravely, "a strange pattern began to emerge."

The new surveys revealed that *every* collective farm and almost all the State farms were much larger than the official land records indicated. In many cases, a collective farm that was listed as having five hundred hectares of irrigated pasture actually had a thousand. The same pattern held for the *sovkhoz* vegetable enterprises and orchards. Mother was annoyed.

"So I went out with them, Sasha," she said, sweeping her hand across the tablecloth. "You've worked with survey crews. It's a straightforward process. Either you use the instruments correctly and tabulate, or you shirk your task."

"Then I saw the true situation," Mother said, her voice clipped and somber. "Over a third of the State land in the institute's irrigation scheme was not officially listed on the records."

I frowned, not sure where all this was leading.

Mother quickly explained. "It was theft on a scale I never imagined, Sasha." She shook her head, as if she still could not believe her own words. Somewhere between a third and a half of the agricultural production of the oblast did not officially exist. This meant that the managers, and the government and Party officials responsible for agricultural production, easily and consistently met their monthly and annual quotas, and were generously rewarded with medals, promotions, bonuses, luxury apartments, and holiday packages. But that was only a minor benefit. The actual milk, fruit, meat, and vegetables produced, Mother added, "disappeared" into an intricate illegal distribution network.

"What happened when you presented your findings at the institute?" I was beginning to understand the evolution of Mother's "mental illness."

Her face clouded. "At first, they said there were errors in my calculations. Then I made a formal presentation, using the original surveyors' figures and detailed plans of the land itself, with all the accurate coordinates clearly marked." She smiled bitterly. "The chief engineer and the institute director thanked me and formed their own study committee to consider the matter."

"They told me I was working too hard and needed a rest." She shrugged. "The next day they suggested a holiday at the children's resort at Anapa on the Black Sea for me and Misha." Mother's face clouded. "Sasha, I'd had enough of those *luxury* seaside resorts. The Pearl Hotel in Sochi was filled with black marketeers, entire families of them, flashing rolls of dollars and deutsche marks, buying *everything*... even the poor girls who came to the terraces every night to sell their bodies."

"I've seen those girls," I said. "They can't make a living with their university degrees, so they drift down to the Black Sea. They like to be called courtesans."

Mother shook her head in distaste. All her life she had been taught that Socialism had abolished evils like prostitution. Now she looked up and spoke again, her voice stronger. "There was another reason not to go back down to the Crimea. Isolated at that resort, I could have easily had an 'accident'."

My first impulse was to reassure her. Then I remembered the tight control the KGB maintained over those hotels.

"I took two days away from the office," Mother continued in the same dry tone. "When I returned, the chief engineer called me into his office to reexamine my findings. He said there were many errors. Sasha, someone had changed the figures. They had used correction fluid and simply altered the original calculations to make the land area conform almost exactly to the official records.

"They told me I was suffering from stress and had made serious errors."

Mother continued her grim recitation. When she went to the Party secretary to protest, she brought her own copies of the original surveyors' figures to show that documents had been illegally altered. Instead of helping with a formal investigation, the Party apparatchik scolded her for insubordination and meddling.

She realized the entire institute was aligned against her. Obviously they were either all party to the massive fraud or had been intimidated into silence.

"They kept saying I was emotionally unbalanced," Mother said. "I was angry, certainly. But I was not deranged."

Then the resistance to her one-woman campaign took a cruel turn. "Misha was out on the neighborhood playground," she said, her jaw trembling with outrage. "A man stopped his car and called him. 'Hey, *malchik*, do you want a ride?'" Mother smiled. "But Misha remembered I had always told him never to take a ride from a stranger. He ran, and the man tried to catch him. Sasha, that man chased him almost to our *podyesd*. That incident was not an accident. I am sure of it."

"That is terrorism..." I sputtered, too outraged to speak clearly.

"Under Stalin," Mother whispered, "our parents warned us about 'Dark Forces,' the Black Raven van from the NKVD that came in the night. Sasha, I realized after they tried to kidnap Misha that these same forces still exist."

Two days later when Mother raised this issue with the chief engineer, demanding a criminal investigation, the institute director arrived with two big ambulance attendants. The director insisted she was suffering emotional stress and ordered her to receive a medical evaluation. Only when she had been examined and returned with the proper health certificate, he said, would she be readmitted to the office. Mother was taken directly from the institute to the clinic.

She refused the capsules the first psychiatrist offered her. When he insisted, Mother demanded to leave. She had come for a health evaluation, not sedation.

Then the drug treatment began. She was forcibly injected with antipsychotic drugs, mixed with more common sedatives. This "therapy" left her in a stupor for days.

Mother had her hands around my fists. "Sasha," she whispered, sobbing now, "all my life I believed that if I studied hard and became an engineer I would earn respect. I would help support my family and do honorable service to my country and to Socialism. Now..."

None of us spoke. The spring sunshine fell through the window, warming the kitchen.

Mother wrung her hands in anguish and stared out the window. "It wasn't just the institute or the Party, Sasha. This does sound crazy, but there's an invisible *apparat* out there that we never knew about. The Party is in it, State Security..."

Through other patients at the clinic, Mother had learned there were entire warehouses jammed with meat and produce from the *kolkhoz* and State farms. All this bounty was controlled by the local Party bosses and their accomplices. They not only took this booty free of charge, they shared in the profits from the sale of the goods on the black market. The authorities responsible for stopping this corruption were part of the *banda* who profited from it. It was a perfect criminal system, until Mother—a good Socialist—tried to derail their train. She had to be stopped.

And they succeeded. "By the time they took me to the clinic," she added, again shaking her head as if stunned by a blow, "even the *original* survey records had been altered. There is nothing more any of us can do." Now Mother grimaced at some private memory. "All those terrible people in Sochi," she said, "they are part of their own network elsewhere in the Union."

"Mama," I said, taking her hand, "I'm afraid you are right. Those famous corruption trials in Moscow have just skimmed the surface. If you read *Ogonyok*, you will see the scale of this... *octopus*." It was difficult trying to explain the sheer size and brazen nature of this enterprise. "In Georgia the State jewelry factories lose half their production. Half the gold from the mines in Kolyma is never counted. It's the same for the caviar from the Caspian and the sable furs at the collectives in Siberia..."

I raked my hand through my hair in frustration. "Mama," I said, "they call them the Mafia."

Before I left Samara, I went back to the senior psychiatrist at the clinic. It was not necessary to detail the criminal abuses to which my mother had been subjected. Glasnost had already exposed the corruption of Soviet psychiatry. The previous autumn, *Komsomolskaya Pravda* had sparked an official investigation of these repressive "medical" practices. Without being specific, I alluded to friends in the Ministry of Defense in Moscow and the KGB who would be interested in how the mother of a Soviet Air Force pilot had been abused. The psychiatrist seemed terrified that the scandal of my mother's treatment might become public. He assured me all drug therapy had been canceled. She would be granted an indefinite convalescent leave at full salary.

It was a small victory. But I felt no elation.

Jana reluctantly agreed to fly to Samara and help in my mother's recovery. Mother was still too weak from the weeks of heavy sedation to cook and clean, and she certainly couldn't face the long food lines. I had requested additional emergency leave, but Division refused. The MiG-29 combat evaluation was more important than minor personal matters.

But after three weeks, Mother called and said Jana was returning the next day. Instead of helping, Jana had simply whined and complained, often sleeping until past noon. When she went out to buy food, she usually returned empty-handed. Jana did not have the patience to stand in line. They were better off without her.

That summer the original trickle of information about officially sanctioned corruption became a steady flow in publications such as *Argumenti i Facti*. Now everyone knew the true meaning of the word "Mafia." But aside from the politically motivated and well-publicized ongoing trial of Brezhnev's son-in-law, Yuri Churbanov, there was constant public outrage, but almost no official action. When the newly independent magazine *Ogonyok* suggested Gorbachev and the Politburo themselves were beneficiaries of the Mafia, the magazine suddenly was found to have exceeded its authorized quota of ink and paper.

I read all I could, keeping my own counsel. There was no sense even mentioning the subject to Jana. She was a true daughter of her family. To her, anyone who found the means to acquire wealth—no matter by what method—was to be admired.

That summer I became more familiar with *Argumenti i Facti* and *Ogonyok* than with my aircraft manuals. I spent more time alone in the kitchen hunched over my small Riga transistor receiver listening to Radio Liberty than writing engineering reports.

Stories of corruption and rumblings for real democracy were no longer sensational news. Another, much more historic issue gripped the Soviet Union. Under glasnost, Gorbachev had made repeated references to the cruelty and "excesses" of the Stalinist period. But he had carefully restrained from specific detail.

Now that the floodgate was open, however, other, unofficial groups came forward to provide that terrible detail.

One of the most prominent was a private organization simply called Memorial. It began as a small gathering of middle-aged intelligentsia in Moscow, determined to rehabilitate the reputations of good Communists who had been unfairly persecuted under Stalin. But once intellectuals like Yevgeni Yevtushenko and Andrei Sakarov joined with the group, the new, freer news media ran story after story about the repressive decades of Stalinism. For the first time, the official acronym *gulag*, Central Administration for Corrective Labor Camps—which exiled writer Alexander Solzhenitsyn had apparently made infamous in the West—became fully understood among millions of Soviet citizens. In fact, "gulag" quickly became a common noun, not just another meaningless bureaucratic term.

Week after week, the stories ran with numbing authenticity. I learned about the purge trials of the 1930s. Thousands of senior Red Army officers had been unjustly executed. Thousands more had been sent to the gulag. Millions of innocent citizens had joined them in those bleak camps, their only crime an accusation by some faceless informer that they were "enemies of the people." An unofficial historical colloquium in Moscow estimated that somewhere between twenty and forty *million* Soviet citizens had died in the four decades that the gulag had existed.

This holocaust now had a name: the Great Terror. This wholesale murder had been ordered and managed by Communists. Millions died in the name of Communism. The proof was undeniable. Memorial demanded that the KGB open the archives, and offered a victim-tracing service. The group's small Moscow office was quickly overwhelmed by hundreds and hundreds of letters from relatives of innocent people who had disappeared, victims of the "Dark Forces" my mother had mentioned.

One issue of *Ogonyok* offered a detailed analysis of the holocaust in the Ukraine in which at least seven million peasants died of starvation. Stalin had sealed the borders of that republic to keep food out while his NKVD troops confiscated every grain of wheat, every apple, every egg. It was no wonder the Ukrainians hated us. Chernobyl had only been the latest disaster of the Soviet system.

I simply could not keep silent about this. But when I tried to discuss the Great Terror and its impact on the Soviet military during the regimental Party meeting, our chief zampolit, Lieutenant Colonel Dovbnya, muttered that this was inappropriate and "irrelevant." *Ogonyok*, however, had already presented a quite relevant, two-part series proving that the disastrous initial military reverses during the first year of the Great Patriotic War had been a direct result of Stalin having decimated the professional officer corps in the late 1930s. When the zampolit refused to allow a legitimate discussion of this important issue, I simply posted the *Ogonyok* article on the "Local News" section of our regimental dayroom bulletin board.

What made the clipping especially provocative was the reproduction of the painting *Requiem*, by Alexander Lozenko, which ran the full width of the page. The painting showed a long line of boxcars curving across the bleak steppes, shrouded beneath a plume of coal smoke from the distant locomotive. Superimposed on the battered slats of the windowless railcars were the ghostly faces of the victims: intellectuals, workers, women, boys and girls, soldiers just like us.

In all our years of school and training, we had never been told. Now we had to face the truth. Our nation was built on a dictatorship much crueler than the Nazis we had defeated in that heroic war. We had been taught that the Nazis had murdered six million Jews, Gypsies, and other "subhumans"—including Soviet war prisoners—in extermination camps like Auschwitz and Treblinka. But now we learned that our own Organs of State Security had killed at least three times as many citizens of the Soviet Union, all of them just as innocent as the victims of the fascist terror.

The Nazis had used their perverted scientific techniques for mass murder, herding the victims into gas chambers.

The Soviet methods had been cruder, but equally effective: Beginning in the 1930s, NKVD execution squads had simply loaded suspected "enemies of the people" into their Black Raven vans, driven them to the forests outside the cities, and shot them through the head. Those who were not immediately murdered were automatically convicted in Peoples' Courts, and sentenced to hard labor in the frozen Siberian taiga or the "death mines" like Kolyma.

Only the strongest of these prisoners survived. If you worked people twelve hours a day cutting timber in forty degrees of frost and only fed them a "harsh regime" food ration calculated to result in starvation, the outcome was inevitable: death. Reading the carefully documented reports from the Memorial organization, I finally understood the plight of the helpless *zeks*, the political prisoners of whom Alexander Solzhenitsyn had written so eloquently in his searing novel, *One Day in the Life of Ivan Denisovich*. In his monumental *Gulag Archipelago,* which was now being privately circulated in photocopy, Solzhenitsyn dramatized the institutional barbarity of this system. One third of the population had been sent to the camps to work as slaves. Another third of the Soviet people closed their eyes to this cruel reality and lived reasonably well on the production of the gulag economy. The top stratum lived in luxury. Solzhenitsyn had dared to expose all this. He had been the conscience of our entire nation. And when the Party finally deported him, men like Andrei Sakarov stepped forward to fill the void. Now we all knew the dirty secrets of the past. And the Dark Forces who had tormented my mother with their illegal treatment could not deport an entire nation. But they were not yet ready to relinquish power.

The foreign fascists had been vanquished. Unfortunately the ones who had survived were not alien to our Motherland.

*   *   *

One hot bright morning in late July, I was in the squadron locker room pulling on my G-suit. We had a long day of flying scheduled. But I could hardly remember the details of the first training sortie, which Colonel Antonovich had just briefed us on. My mind was focused instead on the dark image of those thousands of unmarked mass graves, stretching like an invisible crescent scar all the way from the pine forests of the Polish frontier to the ancient larch groves on the granite bluffs above the Pacific. That terrible image was not just remote history. Now I saw the steel door of the psychiatric clinic in Samara, I felt the rusty grate in my hands, and I smelled the dank despair of the prisoners who had been held there for "treatment." Then I saw the sunlit pool terrace of the Pearl Hotel in Sochi. The profiteers sat around the outdoor bar, smearing oil on their hairy chests, leering at the pretty young girls who came forward to sell themselves. Those criminals always reminded me of half-boiled crayfish, cold, predatory.

Suddenly it came to me, as I bent to zip up the legs of my flight suit. I could no longer defend the fascist system that ruled my country. Somehow I would leave the Air Force. I no longer wanted the exciting career of a test pilot. I no longer wanted *any* of this. I no longer wanted to be married to Jana, a true daughter of the system.

I slammed my locker shut. For the first time in months, the way ahead looked clear.

When Jana returned from Kiev after her summer examinations, I decided to confront her.

"I want a divorce," I told her, pulling back the shade to flood the room with morning sunshine.

I had to catch the bus to the base in five minutes, and, as always, it had taken a long time to wake her up. As she sat on the edge of our makeshift bed, wincing at the early morning sun, I wasn't sure she had understood my words.

"Be ready this afternoon at three," I told her. "We are going to the ZAGS to file the papers."

Now Jana had definitely understood. She gripped the sleeve of my flight suit. "No, Sasha... no. We can find a way..."

Angrily I pulled back. Jana was completely unrealistic. The night before, I had tried to discuss our country's bloody history and the criminal class that now controlled every aspect of our lives. But she had moped and pouted, finally haranguing me for not having enough money to buy a proper television set or a car. We would find no "way" to reconcile our differences.

"Be ready at three" was all I said in reply.

It took two more days to convince her. But on a rainy Thursday afternoon we went to an office in the large ZAGS building in central Tskhakaya to file our first divorce petition. By Soviet law, we had to attend regular counseling sessions for a month, attempting a reconciliation. Only then would our formal divorce petition be forwarded to the courts.

I tried to spend as much time as possible at the base during this period, and actually volunteered as a replacement duty-alert officer so that I wouldn't have to sleep at my apartment. All I wanted was for this marriage to end.

But, despite her childlike demeanor, Jana had inherited much of her mother's native cleverness. Although she signed the preliminary divorce papers, Jana was bound to resist the process in any way she could. Luckily her parents were already in Syria, which deprived her of powerful allies. I hoped there would be enough time to complete the divorce before her family tried to intervene. But this was a gamble.

When we completed our first divorce papers, I knew the news would reach Colonel Baglai in a matter of days. And he would be sure to retaliate. It really did not matter, however. I no longer planned ahead for an Air Force career.

But Jana actually struck the first blow herself. She had confided in the wife of Colonel Prozukhin, the division zampolit who had tried to stage the alcohol-free wedding. His wife, Nadezhda, another chunky matron with even tighter ringlet curls than Jana's mother, was the head of the division officers' wives' committee. This was a powerful position, which gave her as much authority over family matters as her zampolit husband had over our "political maturity." In addition, Nadezhda was a close friend of Jana's mother.

One evening when I returned from the base I found Jana serving tea to Colonel Prozukhin and his wife. Obviously they had hatched a plot, because for the first time in weeks the bed was properly made, the apartment was neat, and the kitchen was actually clean. From all appearances, Jana seemed the perfect young wife.

Colonel Prozukhin came directly to the point. "Are you serious about this divorce, Zuyev?" He tried to sound like a real officer, a man used to confronting troops and making hard decisions. But his voice broke into a squeak.

Prozukhin's wife glared when she saw me smile.

"Yes. I am serious." I had not invited these people to my home, so I neglected to add the courtesy of "Comrade Colonel."

"Alexander Mikhailovich," Prozukhin's wife said, her voice more authoritative than her husband's, "how *can* you talk of divorce after all of us witnessed that wonderful wedding only last summer? That was a tribute to the Socialist Military Family."

Only a zampolit's wife would still use such brazenly false terms.

I shrugged. "People get married. People get divorced. Jana and I are going to get divorced."

Nadezhda Prozukhin scowled at her husband and nodded. He had his orders.

The zampolit sighed and visibly braced himself. "Captain Zuyev," he recited from memory. "If you persist in this matter, I'll see that you rot in some lost desert in Central Asia."

He had made his speech. We all knew it was not an idle threat. Prozukhin's wife sneered openly as I pondered his words. The division zampolit did have the power to cripple any officer's career. That spring, Major Ivan Matushkin, an able pilot in the 2nd Squadron, had run afoul of the zampolit and his wife. Matushkin was moving dishes from his apartment to the officers' dining room for the Air Force Day party. But he had broken the rules by driving his old Zhiguli right up to the door of the *podyesd*. It was a weekend, and no one cared except Prozukhin. On the urging of his wife to reestablish his "authority," Prozukhin came down the staircase, grabbed Matushkin's car keys, and ordered him to report for a reprimand on Monday morning.

"You bastard," Matushkin had sworn, "I'll show you some authority." He snatched back his keys and threw the colonel against the side of the car.

Prozukhin had written a report that the major had attacked and beaten him. The VVS grounded the major, reduced him in rank, and ordered him reassigned to Central Asia as a GCI officer.

Like my mother, this honest pilot had also been sent for a psychiatric "evaluation."

"My personal life is my own affair, Colonel Prozukhin," I finally answered.

"And your professional *kharacteristika* is my affair, Zuyev." He had gotten his full nerve and spoke with real menace now. "If you persist in this, your career is dead."

I shrugged. How could anyone want a career serving officers like this? But if Prozukhin acted quickly on his threat, I might find myself isolated in some Asian outpost where it would be difficult, if not impossible, to petition for a discharge.

Finally I answered him. "Let me consider this matter carefully, Comrade Colonel."

Word of the divorce spread quickly. Two days later I was ordered to Lieutenant Colonel Antonovich's office to discuss my marital problems. I stated my case as best I could, and added that giving in to the division zampolit's threat might preserve the marriage, but certainly would not resolve the conflict between me and Jana.

"You can't *force* people to be happy, Comrade Lieutenant Colonel." I said. Antonovich nodded sadly. "That will just put more stress on me, and flying with stress is dangerous."

Antonovich sighed loudly. "At least try to work things out, Shurka. I'll keep you on the ground for a while."

"Like you did Major Matushkin?"

Antonovich squared his shoulders. He had no doubt received direct orders from Division. "Zuyev, you will withdraw this divorce request, or I'll ground you permanently. What's your decision? Can you try to work things out with your wife?"

"I'll try," I finally conceded.

A week later I told Antonovich that Jana and I had withdrawn our divorce petition.

But we had not. The lie was just a ploy to gain breathing space in which to make some concrete plans.

So I told Jana that we should both think about our future carefully. The next divorce counseling session at the ZAGS was not scheduled for a month. At least this gave me time to think.

But instead of thinking clearly, I sank into a numb lethargy, an ambulatory depression that seemed endless. I skipped the scheduled meeting with the ZAGS counselor. This suspended our divorce process. But I had no intention of canceling it. Jana became a distant figure, even though we still shared the same small apartment. She knew she had lost, that I was willing to sacrifice my future in the Air Force to be free of her. We hardly talked to each other; it was as if we had both witnessed some terrible accident and were too stunned to speak.

With my divorce proceedings in limbo, I was able to reach a truce with Lieutenant Colonel Antonovich. He put me back on flying status. But I still felt deep revulsion at wearing this bloodstained uniform.

Then, in December, the somber weather broke for a few days. The southern sun flooded the green valley, and the air was fragrant with the blooming citrus groves. Instead of returning home from the flight line one afternoon, I walked up the slopes of Senaki Mountain alone, trying to break the black vise that had seized my emotions by exercise in the sunshine.

Time disappeared. I trudged through the orchards and beside pastures full of bleating sheep and goats. The sun was almost down and long shadows hung in the valley below. I heard the sweet chime of bells. At first I thought they were from the livestock. Then I realized I was walking beside the fieldstone wall of a church. I entered the courtyard beneath the high wrought-iron gate and stood just outside the door of the vestry. Inside there were old women and a bearded priest. I could see the yellow glow of candles and smell incense. Soft chanting echoed from inside. Again the bells rang. Birds flew through the sunset and landed on the gilded, onion-dome steeple.

All at once, I stood upright, feeling the muscles of my legs and back unclench for the first time in months. The weight of depression had been lifted.

My life as a Soviet Air Force pilot was finished. But now I saw that there were other careers, other lives, to live. And, I realized, there was another country to live in, America, the nation of refugees and immigrants. For almost two years I had been listening to the American shortwave station, Radio Liberty, and to the Voice of America. That exotic country now seemed more hospitable to me than my own nation. After I somehow found a way to resign my commission and leave the Air Force, I would find a way to leave the Soviet Union itself.

State Security would never approve an exit visa for a former fighter pilot, especially one with my background. So I would have to "emigrate" unofficially. Everyone I knew thought this was impossible. But I knew our borders were hardly airtight. There had to be a way to escape to the West, where I could live in freedom.

I stopped in the twilight, halfway back down the mountain. Unconsciously I had been marching straight toward my apartment, as if preparing to simply pack my bag and leave. Once I had made my decision, it seemed absurd to remain here, wearing this uniform, living this false life. But it was obvious my future would not unfold so simply.

One thing was certain: I could never simply slip out of the Soviet Union while still an Air Force officer. Almost every minute of my day, every day, week, and month of the year, my movements were officially noted. So a discharge was my first priority. Then I would consider the safest way out of the Soviet Union.

For the next two weeks the problems of a discharge and an escape route were constantly on my mind. I soon realized that leaving the country would be easier than resigning my commission. I had once shared a train compartment with some KGB border guards, traveling from Sochi to Tbilisi. Over a bottle of cognac, they'd revealed that the entire mountainous southern frontier of Georgia was a warren of smugglers' trails. The Turkish tribesmen on both sides of the frontier crossed the border continually, with donkey trains of contraband. I knew from my training in Azerbaijan that the same porous frontier existed with Iran. A determined man with a few thousand rubles to spend could easily escape to the south. Then there were our "fraternal" Socialist allies of the Warsaw Pact: Czechoslovakia, Hungary, and East Germany. Each of those countries bordered the West. And my friend Sergei Salamov who had served in Hungary told me that a handful of dollars or deutsche marks would see you across the border into Austria. So escape from the country would not be impossible.

Escape from the military itself was another matter.

A few weeks later Gorbachev himself offered the solution to this problem. It was early on a Friday evening, and most of the regiment's pilots had gathered in the sauna to mark the end of another training week. I was in the duty-alert dayroom completing some paperwork when the announcement came over State television. Gorbachev had addressed the United Nations General Assembly in

New York, but I had not paid much attention. Now the Moscow newscaster read a summary of the speech. The Soviet military, Gorbachev had pledged, would be reduced in strength by 500,000 men and 10,000 tanks. The reductions would begin "immediately" and continue over the next two years. The announcer stated that this force reduction would apply to "all ranks and services."

I saw my opportunity. Clearly officers who no longer wished to serve would be allowed to resign.

I went to the sauna to spread the news of this sensational announcement. The men looked up from their benches, some grinning broadly, others wary. A friend of mine, Roman Kravchuk, a dissatisfied senior lieutenant, actually bellowed loudly with pleasure.

"Enough of this shit," he yelled. "This time next year, I'll be running my own electrical shop."

Colonel Prozukhin scowled at the young pilot. But in the sauna, everyone was allowed to speak his mind without direct recrimination. And Roman Kravchuk had clearly voiced the feelings of many of us. Gorbachev's announcement had come like a reprieve to condemned men. The younger lieutenants and captains who had not yet invested their most vital decades in the Air Force obviously wanted out. Glasnost had shown us another life could exist; perestroika, although halfhearted and deeply flawed, had revealed that we could live independent of the rigid Communist economy.

When the whoops and bellows stopped echoing, Colonel Prozukhin got to his feet and adjusted his thick white towel. "Maybe Gorbachev thinks this is a good idea," he said in his best political-lecture voice. "But he'll lose the support of the Army, that's for sure. And one day, if all this glasnost continues, he'll need the Army to defend him from the masses."

As the other young officers toasted their future with brimming beer glasses, I sat alone in the corner, thinking soberly.

Obviously the Air Force would not allow *all* those who wanted to resign to do so. The VVS would lose their rank-and-file pilots in the process. But the force reduction would certainly present the opportunity for those with medical problems to resign.

Amid the steamy laughter and clamor of the *banya*, a plan was forming in my mind. Perhaps a pilot disabled in the course of a high-performance training flight would be granted a medical discharge. That would be my exit, my escape hatch to freedom.

PART
THREE

—11—
Central Aviation Hospital, Moscow
March 21–April 6, 1989

The late morning sun dimmed as the thick, rolled cloud bank of a sudden spring cold front swept across the city. Lieutenant Colonel Frolov's office grew dark, and he switched on his brass desk lamp. I had been talking for over two hours, but had almost completed my story. For the past ten minutes I had been treading a minefield. I had to lie to an experienced and highly skilled psychologist. But if I had risked admitting the truth—that I had faked the mysterious, disabling affliction on that last training flight in February—I would have confessed to a serious criminal offense.

Instead, I had emphasized the corrosive physical effect of the months of stress that had sprung from the conflict of my marriage and the bitter anxiety over my mother's unjust treatment in Samara. I was trying to present Frolov with rational reasons to recommend my medical discharge. But this, too, was tricky ground. By implying I had been pressured into an unsuitable marriage with the daughter of a senior Air Force officer, I was criticizing honored Air Force traditions. By raising the specter of my mother's unjust psychiatric persecution by "the Mafia," a corrupt cabal that had to include both Party and KGB officials, I was involving Frolov in serious matters that went far beyond VVS personnel policy. My hope was he would want to quickly dissociate from this mess, and the easiest way to do so would be to recommend my quiet medical discharge.

When I finally finished speaking, I handed the psychologist a shiny photocopy of the official request for discharge, which I had formally presented Lieutenant Colonel Antonovich the week after my last training flight.

To: Commander, 176th Frontal Aviation Regiment

I hereby request a discharge from the ranks of the VVS due to my physical condition, and to the fact that I am not willing to continue service on the ground.

Signed: Zuyev, Alexander M., Captain

Frolov sighed as he fingered the photocopy. He seemed to be fascinated by my signature, as if he were examining an important piece of criminal evidence.

"Has this request gone forward through proper channels, Captain?"

"Yes, Comrade Lieutenant Colonel," I replied earnestly. Maybe if he thought the process was already well along, he would endorse it.

Again Frolov sighed, drumming his long pale fingers on the copy. "Captain Zuyev," he said softly after a long pause, "your 'physical condition' does not warrant a discharge. It's unfortunate that you submitted such a request."

"But, Comrade Colonel," I tried to reason, "I can no longer fly fighters. The regulations are clear. When a pilot is disabled in the cockpit, he is permanently grounded."

Frolov nodded decisively and began gathering together the documents that made up my thick personnel file. "Exactly. And I concur. Given your somatic reaction to stress, you are no longer suited for active flying duty in a Frontal Aviation unit. As you put it, Alexander Mikhailovich, you are indeed grounded." We stared at each other in the dim office. "Permanently," Frolov added for emphasis. For a moment I thought he was going to help me. Then a cold, sour clot formed below my throat as I realized the full meaning of his words. I was officially unfit to fly, but still medically qualified for ground duty. My emotional state and my bitterness toward the Soviet system were not grounds for a medical discharge.

I caught a glimpse of a document from my file that I had not seen before, the flimsy blue record copy permanently removing me from flight status. It had already been signed by my case physician, Lieutenant Colonel Merkulov. Now Frolov cosigned the document, writing carefully with a gold East German fountain pen.

"I am sorry about this, Alexander Mikhailovich," he said, screwing the cap back on his pen. "But the matter is out of my hands. You yourself set this process in motion."

Frolov did not go so far as to accuse me of faking illness during my last training flight. But he emphasized that my requesting a medical discharge had provoked the permanent grounding order. There could be no appeal of the order, once the hospital's full medical-personnel board met to review it later in the month. Officially I was still healthy enough to serve, but unfit for flight duty.

"Lieutenant Colonel Frolov," I said, "perhaps I haven't made myself clear. I do not wish to serve as a military officer defending a system I can no longer believe in."

This was, indeed, dangerous ground. Frolov quickly stacked my records, closed the pale green pasteboard file records, and tied the ribbon, as if washing his hands of the unpleasant and sensitive matter.

"Captain Zuyev," he said sincerely, "you are obviously under considerable stress. Have you taken the medication I prescribed?"

"Yes," I lied. The bottle was unopened in the drawer of my bedside table upstairs in the ward.

"Good. That should help relieve your discomfort."

He shifted the thick file to the corner of his desk, a sign that our long consultation was over.

"I can*not* serve as a ground officer, married to that girl, Comrade Colonel."

Frolov nodded sympathetically. "I agree. Get a divorce. It is not the end of the world. Obviously you married for the wrong reasons, and she is not the type of woman you need. Your life will be much better when you're free of this marriage."

"Comrade Colonel"—I tried to keep my voice even, one reasonable officer appealing to another—"we know the force reductions are about to begin. I can no longer fly. Why can't I be one of the Air Force officers discharged?"

"You would lose your pension, Captain." Frolov seemed astonished that I would risk the "generosity" of the State by seeking a discharge before my full twenty-five years' service.

"I don't need any pension, Comrade Colonel." Again I tried to sound reasonable. "I'm too young to worry about that. How can a man live on two hundred rubles a month? Besides, there are many new opportunities in the civilian sector."

Now Frolov rose from his desk. "Perhaps, Captain. But I am not authorized to endorse such a discharge. The entire matter of force reduction is under review by the chief of staff of the VVS."

I remained stubbornly rooted in my chair. This was my last chance. The elaborate deception was coming apart, about to fail completely. The physicians had judged me fit for ground duty, and Frolov's recommendation as a psychologist would confirm the diagnosis. I had perhaps ten more days of follow-up tests here at the hospital before the board met, then I would have to return to Tskhakaya. In two months the final divorce process would be finished. Prozukhin would make sure to see me transferred to the dusty abyss of Central Asia. I had gambled, and I had lost.

"I'm no longer a Communist," I blurted out. "I've come to hate atheism. I want to learn more about religion. How can I serve as a Soviet officer?"

Frolov even had an answer for this. He nodded gravely. "Captain, many pilots are religious. You are not alone. You may have doubts about the Party, but you have sworn to serve the Soviet people."

How could I respond? Finally I stood, and Frolov quickly shook my hand, eager to see me go. "Just take your medication, Captain," he said. "Everything will be better soon."

Two days later I learned exactly why Frolov had been unable to help me. Lieutenant General Vasily Semakhin, chief of Air Force personnel, came to the hospital with an entourage of aides to brief all the pilots undergoing treatment on the impact of Gorbachev's well-publicized force reduction policy. Over 350 active-duty and retired pilots—some of them white-haired veterans of the Great Patriotic War—crowded the hospital theater to hear Semakhin.

The chunky, thick-waisted general spoke brusquely, his face set in an overbearing frown that signified his impatient distaste at having to personally explain such a policy to this collection of aviators. Having the ultimate decision on personnel assignments was a gold mine. And Semakhin was known to be a true Moscow general, a man who had made a personal fortune from the *blat* that came his way during the Brezhnev era. Some poorly qualified but well-connected fighter pilot who had received a plum had reportedly contributed to Semakhin's wealth.

Semakhin began his remarks by noting that the press had distorted Gorbachev's United Nations speech. True, the general said, there would definitely be cuts in the ranks of all the services. But this did *not* mean officers would be arbitrarily relieved of their service obligation. Reductions in the Air Force ranks, Semakhin said, "will come first from those who have already completed twenty years' service. If we can't fill our allotment of cuts with these officers, we will next discharge those with medically documented alcohol problems. That will more than cover our quota."

Around me in the theater, pilots whispered. There were a few barely audible groans. Men, like me, who had come to this briefing hoping to be discharged soon, had those hopes abruptly punctured.

Now Semakhin was speaking about unit reduction and reassignments. Frontal Aviation regiments would be cut from forty aircraft to as few as thirty-two, with new MiG-29 and Su-25 fighters replacing older aircraft. Many pilots from MiG-21 regiments would be reassigned to bombers. "I know this goes against fighter pilots' grain," Semakhin stated, almost sneering, "but we're modernizing our forces, not running a popularity contest. Despite glasnost," he added, "the Air Force still reaches its decisions without the benefit of public opinion polls."

Again there were groans. I stared at the heavy-faced general and his silent coterie of colonels in their well-tailored uniforms. Despite Semakhin's scorn for glasnost, it had been foolhardy to reveal the cold truth about Gorbachev's actual intent in his famous policy speech. This force reduction had nothing to do with a shift to a defensive military posture. Gorbachev and his Defense Minister, Marshal Yazov, intended to streamline and modernize the forces. Pilots taken from obsolete aircraft were to be reassigned to bombers. Was that a "defensive" posture?

"This whole matter has been badly handled by the politicians," Semakhin added with unfeigned disgust. "A full eighty percent of the pilots serving in Siberia and Central Asia have already submitted written requests for discharge. This is ludicrous. All your units will soon receive official guidelines. Unless you have twenty years' service or the medics have certified you an alcoholic, don't waste our time applying for a discharge."

Semakhin, a man who had never even flown an L-29, looked at his elaborate pilot's watch and snapped that he would have time for a few questions.

One old veteran of the war stood and unceremoniously demanded to know if the Air Force intended to raise veteran pensions to a reasonable living standard.

Semakhin said the Defense Ministry was trying to "pass legislation" on the matter in the Supreme Soviet. This was hardly a reassuring answer to a brave old man trying to survive on 120 rubles a month.

A major wounded in Afghanistan now rose. "When can we expect an all-volunteer military?"

Semakhin was not taken unprepared. He smiled now, a reasonable leader. The USSR, he said, "simply cannot afford" such a force. "We would have to increase salaries tenfold. This is not realistic."

A colonel rose at the rear of the room. "Does that mean there'll be no increase in pay?"

"A good question, Comrade Colonel," Semakhin crooned, again stressing his reasonable nature. "We're working on a proposal for a thirty-ruble pay raise to come this summer."

The groans were louder now, but Semakhin pretended not to hear. After a moment another decorated senior pilot stood up to address the general. "A thirty-ruble salary increase is an insult."

Again, Semakhin had a ready answer. "We are soldiers, comrades. And a soldier can never be wealthier than a merchant."

"What shit," a stocky major seated nearby said, not even trying to whisper. Semakhin's reputation as a profiteer was well known.

This briefing was unlike any military meeting I had ever attended. Although few of the assembled officers knew each other—and no one could tell who might be an Osobist knocker—men were boldly speaking their minds. Now it was my turn.

"Comrade Lieutenant General," I asked, staring directly into Semakhin's mottled face, "is the decision to reduce our forces by five hundred thousand servicemen a reflection of our grim economic situation or an indication of our nation's peace-loving policies?"

No one groaned, but I did hear chairs shift as officers strained to see who had the audacity to ask such a question.

Semakhin spun on his polished heel to face me, as if squaring off for a fight. "Our reduction of forces, Captain," he said coldly, "was clearly explained in the press by the President of the USSR, the respected Mikhail Sergeyevich Gorbachev."

It was a clever response that shielded Semakhin from the potential criticism of hard-liners in the room.

But I remained standing to ask another question. "I have been grounded from flight duty," I explained, "but still have seven years' service. I have no need of my pension because I want to work in a civilian field. Can you help me be among the five hundred thousand to be discharged?"

Semakhin seemed about to dismiss me brusquely, but then his face softened. It would cost him nothing to humor me. He nodded toward one of his aides, a tall colonel. "Give your name to this officer after the meeting, Captain."

I sat down. There was still a slight chance that the general would personally review my case. Around me in the theater, my colleagues were frowning and speaking quietly. They seemed troubled and confused. All of us were.

Four days passed and I heard nothing from Semakhin's office. When I tried to call the colonel, a typically rude secretary said he was away on an official mission and that I would be contacted "in good time" after I returned to Georgia. I had heard often that phrase on trips to Moscow when I was trying to secure patronage for my application to the Akhtubinsk test pilot school. From that frustrating process, I'd learned that a man's most successful patron was himself. The medical bureaucrats would not complete the official evaluation of my case for at least a week, so I planned to use the time to prepare for the worst case.

I would probably have at least two months of ground duty at

Tskhakaya before Prozukhin managed to have me transferred. That was ample time to prepare my unofficial exit from the Soviet Union. But whatever means of travel I chose would cost money. And here in Moscow there were unusual opportunities for making money. Jana had been in Kiev for several months the previous year and I had actually managed to save most of my salary. I now had almost one thousand rubles. That certainly was not enough to bribe smugglers to guide me over the mountains into Turkey or Iran, but I discovered a way to invest my money profitably.

My Georgian friend Malhaz had asked me to bring back color posters of girls, preferably blond Western girls in skimpy bikinis or lingerie. These tantalizing items had just appeared in Moscow, but were unknown in the southern republics. Georgian men were crazy about girls, especially blondes. Although patients were under orders not to leave the hospital grounds, many of us ignored the restrictions. One afternoon I climbed the low wall and took the *elektrichka* commuter train into Yaroslavski Station. I found exactly the posters I needed in a new private stationer's store in a narrow street off the Arbat. The shopkeeper was a young Estonian in stonewashed jeans with matching jacket. At first he wanted five rubles apiece. But I pointed out that the color separation was blurred on several, and offered to buy a hundred on the spot for two rubles apiece. We settled for two rubles fifty kopecks.

I got through on the phone to Malhaz the next night and described the posters. "Can you see their tits?" A good business-man, he was never one to mince his language.

"Yes, most of them."

"Blondes?"

"Redheads and blondes, four different girls."

"I'll pay you twenty-five rubles each. Buy as many as you can."

The next day I sneaked over the wall through Sokolniki Park and went into the Arbat again to buy another hundred. By investing five hundred rubles, I stood to gain five thousand.

I realized that money for my trip would not be an insurmountable problem. But I began to have second thoughts about using smugglers' trails into Iran or Turkey. Smugglers were close-knit tribesmen who lived desperate, often bloody lives. You paid them in cash, and once paid, there was no longer a reason to keep you alive.

Moscow had excellent libraries and bookstores, so I used the coming days for research. A tourist visa to Hungary or Czechoslovakia was now out of the question, so I would have to find the means to travel alone over the southern mountains frontier of the USSR. What I discovered was encouraging. Since I was an experienced pilot, it made more sense to fly. From aviation club journals and hobby flying magazines, I learned that the Baltic Republics were now manufacturing hot-air balloons. I could order a small balloon with a propane burner and plans for a passenger basket for less than seven thousand rubles. And hang gliders were now available to authorized sports clubs. It would be relatively simple to form a one-man club in distant Georgia and obtain a suitable hang glider.

One hobbyist magazine showed how you could modify the hang glider with a simple aluminum-tube frame and mount a propeller driven by a motorbike engine, transforming it into an ultra-light airplane with a range of over seventy miles. The article stressed that no one should fly these amateur aircraft without first obtaining the necessary permits. But I did not plan to seek permission for my last flight through Soviet airspace. In any event, a hang glider of thin aluminum tubing and a cloth airfoil would be invisible to radar, a real advantage in the dense PVO air-defense sector on the southern frontier.

But I knew none of these plans would bear fruit if I was already under surveillance from the KGB. It was almost impossible to tell whether my conflict with Prozukhin and my feigned illness had provoked the Osobii Otdel counterintelligence officers at Tskhakaya to begin an official investigation. If they had, I would be arrested when I bought a balloon or a hang glider and began to modify it.

I spent several afternoons in central Moscow, playing the foreign agent, ducking in and out of stores and steamy cafeterias, looking for the proverbial thick-necked comrade in the leather jacket. I ate my fill of stale sweet rolls and swilled dozens of cups of tea, watching over my shoulder. I did not seem to be under surveillance.

But to be certain, I decided to go right to the lion's den, or at least to socialize with some KGB friends. I had met a fellow named

Yuri through my KGB friends in Georgia, where Yuri was completing a field-training course. Now he worked at the "new" KGB headquarters near the Outer Ring Highway. He was a specialist in secure satellite communications systems, and, like many in his service, came from a KGB family. His father was a retired colonel who had also served in secret communications, in overseas missions.

I had visited Yuri's family in their comfortable three-bedroom apartment off Rublovskoje Chaussee in the affluent Kuncevo district on other visits to Moscow. I telephoned Yuri's family to announce I was in Moscow, and, as I knew they would, Yuri's father insisted I come for dinner. Next I filled a two-liter bottle from my large canister of Armenian cognac and rode the Metro across the river to visit them. Yuri's mother was a former physics teacher, a gaunt, very cultured person who had been partially paralyzed by a stroke. She and her husband were Communist true believers who had benefited from the system. Their apartment was furnished with handsome possessions Yuri's father had amassed overseas. And twice a week a medical van arrived to take Yuri's mother to the nearby Kuncevo Clinic, which was reserved for Politburo and high-ranking KGB patients.

He was overjoyed to see me. When Yuri came home that evening, the young officer was already a little drunk. That was good. I planned to get him truly drunk this evening. I helped in the kitchen, preparing a nice collection of *zakouski,* small plates of herring, pickles, Hungarian sausage, and aubergine salad.

Yuri's mother sat stiffly at the kitchen table, speaking softly as she directed the three of us. It was an informal, relaxed situation, and I made sure to keep Yuri's tumbler well filled with cognac as we sampled the food and exchanged toasts. This was a crucial moment. If I were under KGB surveillance, my phone call to their apartment would have alarmed the investigators. Yuri's position was one of the most sensitive in State Security.

Yuri and his family seemed sincerely glad to see me. I saw absolutely nothing unusual in their behavior toward me. We were still eating *zakouski* when "Sergei," one of Yuri's colleagues, arrived to join us for dinner. I had skied with him at Terskol and knew he was in training for a clandestine overseas assignment. He would be another coal miner's canary.

We moved to the dining table, and I kept the cognac flowing.

Naturally the conversation turned to the unprecedented rash of street demonstrations in Moscow. In the month I had been in Moscow, unauthorized demonstrators had assembled in the thousands, not only in Pushkin Square, the traditional site for dissident demonstrations, but also at Moscow University, in the red brick pedestrian streets of the Arbat, and on the windy, cobbled expanse of Red Square itself.

Many of these demonstrators demanded independence, or at least self-government for their republics. The Baltic independence movements were the best organized, and demonstrators brazenly unfurled illegal Latvian, Estonian, and Lithuanian flags. Other crowds were more surly, less stable. Armenians and Azerbaijanis sometimes fought each other with fists and the wooden staffs of placards. Although the city Militia and newly formed OMON counterdemonstration troops from the Interior Ministry had intervened brutally on several occasions, the sheer scale of the demonstrations overpowered the resources of the forces assigned to oppress them.

And when the paramilitary troops had intervened, not only Western news organizations recorded the brutality, but camera crews from Vremya and a new State television investigative program, *Vzglyad*, "Glance," also recorded the awful images of the OMON thugs beating peaceful men and women with rubber truncheons.

But the pro-independence demonstrations were not the only tangible image of popular unrest broadcast over State television. Under prodding from reformers like Boris Yeltsin, the former Moscow Party chief whom Gorbachev had deposed, the hardliners in the Politburo had reluctantly agreed to the first free national elections in the history of the Soviet Union. On Sunday, March 26, 1989, hundreds of millions of Soviet citizens would assemble for the *golosovat*, the "vote" that was the most absorbing topic of conversation all across the country. They would elect the new Congress of People's Deputies, an actual parliament that would be theoretically empowered to pass laws independent of the Communist Party. The Congress certainly fell far short of what I understood to be democracy in the West, but it was a major departure from the Party's absolute control of Soviet life.

Now thousands of otherwise docile citizens assembled under placards and banners to hear political candidates openly defy

government dogma, their voices rasping through electric bullhorns, and the people chanting back slogans in return.

I had seen the sullen faces of uniformed Militia and plainclothes
KGB officers assigned to monitor these demonstrations. Clearly
they would have loved orders sending them into the crowd with
their truncheons swinging. But the rusty door of glasnost had
creaked even further open. The angry men from the "Organs"
had to stand there impotently and watch. And it wasn't just
political chanting that assailed them. The Memorial organization
actually organized moving demonstrations in Dzerzhinski Square,
opposite the brown sandstone façade of KGB headquarters, demanding that the State Security archives be opened to reveal the
true fates of hundreds of thousands of "enemies of the people"
who had disappeared into the black maw of the gulag.

All this smacked of *bardak*, "disorder." For seven decades
the only demonstrations on the streets of Moscow, or anywhere
else in the Soviet Union, had been vast *pokazuka* festivals,
carefully choreographed to lavish praise on the Party and its
leaders. Now the people were waking up, a frightening prospect
for people like Sergei, Yuri, and his parents, seated around me at
the dining room table.

When I had first met Yuri's parents in Moscow two years
before, he had simply told them, "Sasha is one of us." They had
no reason to believe I had changed—unless the KGB had alerted
them that I was under investigation for suspicious behavior.

That week construction workers had unearthed an unmarked
mass grave in a pine forest south of Minsk. The trench contained
hundreds of skeletons. Each skull had been shattered by a single,
large-caliber pistol bullet. And the few actual bullets recovered
were found to have been fired from the big Nagant revolvers
carried by Stalin's NKVD execution squads. This secret grave was
just the latest of more than a dozen discovered in that region
alone. Private groups investigating the massacres now estimated
that more than 200,000 Byelorussians had been executed during
the Great Terror of the late 1930s. And Byelorussia was a small
republic. Now Memorial and other unofficial organizations were
demanding a complete government accounting of these atrocities.
Again, opening the secret KGB archives was the principal demand.

"What do you think of all this, Sergei?" Yuri asked. "Do you believe they'll let the television crews into the basements of the Lubyanka?"

Yuri was referring to the Lubyanka prison adjacent to KGB headquarters, where the NKVD archives were said to be kept.

"I hope they do not," Sergei said flatly. "At least not in my lifetime."

"They contain information on actual atrocities?" I asked, looking levelly at Sergei.

He nodded grimly, and seemed to suppress a shudder, as if what had already been discovered and made public was relatively minor compared to the horrible record in those dusty files. "Yes, Sasha," he said softly, "there were terrible events. But the people should never learn the details. It simply will not help them at all."

Yuri and his family seated opposite me nodded in unison. For them, glasnost had already gone too far.

"A nation has the right to know its history," I said, keeping my voice as calm as possible. The four of them stared at me, their eyes going hard. I cleared my throat, and the painful silence spread.

Finally Sergei sighed and spoke. "Sanya," he said, reaching over to touch my arm, "you are a nice fellow. I hope we will end up on the same side of the barricades."

I looked into his eyes. "Do you think it will all come to fighting in the streets?"

Sergei sipped his cognac and smiled now. "Sasha, where do you think perestroika will eventually end?"

I knew from his tone this was a cynical Moscovite's sophisticated riddle. "I don't know."

"*Perestrielka*," he said, "gunfire." The others at the table nodded again. Their faces wore a strange mix of apprehension and mirth.

"It's a fact, Sasha," Sergei added. "You're always reading. Check the dictionary."

In the latest State lexicon, the next entry after the word "*perestrielka*" was, in fact, "*perestroika.*" This was an accident, of course, but for hundreds of thousands of hard-liners, the coincidence was an omen.

Sunday, March 26, I went to the hospital gym to exercise. I had no intention of voting. Officers on my ward had told me the

Air Force had sent unofficial word as to which candidates standing for election in Moscow districts were "acceptable." Certainly Boris Yeltsin, who had supported the campaign to expose the gross excesses of Raisa Gorbachev during her shopping sprees in foreign capitals, was not a favorite of the Air Force. Yeltsin was standing in the north-central Moscow district that included this hospital. If I were going to vote for anyone, it would be him. But, because I was stationed in Georgia, I was not registered to vote in Moscow. Almost all the officers voting were also stationed elsewhere. The whole exercise was a fraud in which I refused to participate. Then my case physician, Lieutenant Colonel Merkulov, found me in the gym.

"Captain Zuyev," he said sternly, "you haven't voted yet. Colonel Golubchikov sent me to find you."

Golubchikov was the director of the internal medicine division, a professional surgeon trying to do the best job he could, which naturally included pleasing his superior officer, Colonel Ivanov. This was not an easy task for a dedicated physician.

Ivanov was known as a harsh taskmaster, a wealthy Communist zealot, as close to its own Mafia boss as this hospital had. His position would have brought him a constant stream of "gifts" and favors. He had many influential friends in the Defense Ministry. They no doubt expected him to deliver a solid block of military votes for the Party's handpicked candidates.

"Comrade Lieutenant Colonel," I told Merkulov, "I do not intend to participate in this election."

Merkulov was hardly a troop commander. He seemed more disappointed than angry. "Then you'll have to report to the colonel to explain."

That meant a shower and changing into a clean uniform. But, at least for the moment, I was still a Soviet Air Force officer, and direct insubordination did not come easily.

Fifteen minutes later I stood before Golubchikov's desk. "What's the problem, Alexander Mikhailovich?" he asked quietly, more weary than angry.

"If I were to vote, Comrade Colonel, I'd do it at my base in Georgia where I knew the candidates."

Sheepishly Golubchikov slid a sample ballot across his polished maple desk. The names of the three "acceptable" candidates had been circled in red ink. We were ordered to vote for notorious Party apparatchiks who were cronies of the Defense Minister, Marshal Yazov. "You know your duty, Captain," the colonel said. "Go to the registry desk in the Lenin Room and cast your ballot. All the other officers in this hospital have already voted."

"For these candidates, Comrade Colonel?" I let the irony ring in my voice. All across the eleven time zones of the Soviet Union on this long Sunday, military officers and employees of institutes and factories under tight Communist control were undoubtedly also being pressured to vote for the candidates approved by the Party. This was the bosses' version of democracy.

"The vote is secret, Captain Zuyev," Golubchikov said, his voice neutral. But his meaning was clear; once I registered, his responsibility ended.

The colonel handed me my registry card and a blank ballot. For a moment I felt like ripping it up. But this hardworking doctor was not my enemy. I took the papers and came to attention. "I serve the Soviet Union."

In the Lenin Room a young captain sat warily at the registration desk, obviously concerned that my minor rebellion might land him in the middle of something unpleasant. He was clearly relieved when I approached the desk, then bent to sign in the one remaining empty space on the page. I was, indeed, the last officer to vote.

I took the ballot into the booth, slid shut the blue curtain, then dropped the ballot, unmarked, into the slot of the varnished box. Now I whispered the ritual phrase of military obedience: "I serve the Soviet Union."

Two days later I saw Colonel Golubchikov on the third-floor corridor. He looked like a boxer who had just lost a fight. That morning *Pravda* had announced the election results. Communist candidates had been defeated in every important district. No important Party man had been elected in Moscow, Leningrad, or Kiev. The Party bosses in the Baltic Republics had been defeated, as had the general commanding the KGB in Estonia and the four-star general commanding all Soviet forces in Germany. Boris Yeltsin had been elected to the Congress of People's Deputies by a massive majority, defeating the Party hack whom the Air Force had found so "acceptable."

"Good morning, Comrade Colonel," I said pleasantly as we passed. "It's a great day for our nation."

Golubchikov stopped, his hands thrust deeply into the side pockets of his starched white medical coat. He seemed about to speak, but then scowled silently and turned on his heel.

For the next eight days I had my final round of X rays, blood tests, and orthopedic examinations. This was an official review of my physical condition required as part of my formal permanent removal from flight status. In principle, I could have petitioned to remain on limited flying duty in low-performance aircraft, as had my friend "Karpich" Karpov, who had suffered the spine injury when his stupid zampolit shot him down with an R-23 missile. Karpich hoped to end his military career flying an old An-2 Anushka biplane, dropping scared cadets at Armavir in parachute training. He could not imagine a life outside the protective blanket of the military. To me that blanket had become a suffocating shroud. I declined my right to appeal.

During those days, shuttling among the laboratories and radiological service, I learned from friendly nurses about a medical scandal of explosive proportions. The previous autumn, there had been five officers from the Republic of the Congo at the hospital undergoing complete physical examinations as part of their jet fighter pilot training in the Soviet Union. At that time, I had also been in the hospital briefly for a physical exam. The African pilots had stayed in a small ward of their own, just beside my six-bed ward. Their Russian was poor, but they seemed friendly enough fellows, and I always made a point of exchanging small talk about the cold Moscow weather and soccer matches with them. The Defense Ministry placed great stock in such "golden friends." Selling both military equipment and training to third world countries was a major source of hard currency for the government.

And these handsome, ambling black fellows certainly had plenty of hard currency. Like many Middle Eastern or African pilots, their selection had more to do with tribal or family connections than natural aptitude. Their main interest in Moscow seemed to be buying luxury goods at a special Voyentorg that accepted only hard currency. After a week, their ward was piled high with cartons of stereo equipment and television sets.

Their other main interest was Russian girls. Although it was strictly against hospital regulations, the five of them dressed in well-tailored civilian suits each night and marched out of the ward, bound for the city center. When they returned late each night, they had obviously been drinking. A Soviet pilot who spoke some French learned that the fellows from the Congo thought highly of Russian girls, but found them "*très cher,*" very expensive.

Then one morning I saw a whole covey of senior doctors in their flapping white medical coats, led by Golubchikov, rushing toward the office of Colonel Ivanov. I had not thought too much about the incident then. But when I returned to the hospital in March, Natasha, a pleasant Urkainian nurse, had told me that three of the Congolese pilots had tested positive for HIV, the virus that caused "SPID," AIDS.

The ominous news had flashed around the hospital within an hour, she said. Not only had those fellows slept with Russian girls, the hospital had used the same hypodermic syringes to draw blood from the Congolese and other patients, including me. Although the Central Aviation Hospital had a West German CAT scan, computerized Japanese laboratory equipment, and the latest imported surgical devices, the Ministry of Defense was unable to obtain disposable syringes. And the nurses told me that lazy and incompetent medical orderlies rarely sterilized the reusable syringes correctly. And, six months earlier, I had sat in the laboratory with these African fellows while blood samples were taken from all of us.

After a sleepless night, I went to see Olga, the friendly technician in charge of the blood chemistry section of the medical laboratory.

"You're not the only one who's scared, Sasha," she told me. Olga had a tiny supply of German plastic disposable syringes. She used one to draw my blood for an unauthorized test for HIV. I paced the corridors for three hours until she brought me the results. From her smile, I knew immediately I was negative. But over a glass of tea in the officers' cafeteria, Olga told me the scandal had caused an uproar in the hospital. The five Congolese pilots had already been sent back to Brazzaville. The hospital staff had been sworn to secrecy.

"By regulation, they should have been tested for SPID the first day they were here," she whispered. "The Congo is right next to Zaire. All those countries are rife with the virus. And they should have been quarantined until they were tested."

"Aren't they trying to trace the women those pilots were with?" I realized the question was absurd; the hospital obviously did not intend to even have Soviet military patients at the hospital tested for possible infection from contaminated hypodermic syringes. It was only my friendship with Olga that gave me the opportunity to put my mind at ease.

Olga shook her head, again whispering. "No. There was no investigation. Senior officers want to pretend the incident never happened."

That night I again had trouble sleeping. But my insomnia was not caused by the sour dread of possible AIDS infection. I sat up in bed. Outside the ward, the dull orange glow of the fire alarm lamp lit the silent corridor. Sleet clicked unpleasantly on the windows. I realized the whole sordid business offered me a last, desperate chance to win my medical discharge through blackmail.

Apparently the hospital was trying to suppress a scandal of major proportions. Some of the patients who could have been infected from those needles included senior pilots. But the hospital probably felt they had too much to lose to ever allow the story to surface. I now had other plans.

April 6 was a drizzly spring day with the birch and maple trees in the park coming into their first full bud. I went to Lieutenant Colonel Merkulov's office and asked for an immediate meeting with Colonel Ivanov. Something in my manner must have jarred Merkulov because he didn't protest this unusual request.

Half an hour later we were in Ivanov's handsome office. The first thing I noticed were the ultimate symbols of status on the corner of his wide desk: four squat telephones. The telephones complemented the deep leather armchairs. Suddenly I remembered visiting the apartment of my young friend Elena's family all those years before in Samara's exclusive Microrayon 4. Then, I had naïvely assumed these accouterments of wealth and power were the reward for hard work. Now I knew better.

Ivanov, unlike the professional physicians on his staff, saw himself as a gruff frontline troop commander. "Is this the officer who refused to vote?" he snarled, hardly looking at me.

"Yes, Comrade Colonel," Merkulov answered. "Captain Zuyev wants to discuss the matter of a medical discharge."

Ivanov glowered, already shaking his head. Again I tried to reasonably explain that I could serve the State better as a civilian, and that I had no need of the small pension due an officer discharged for medical reasons.

Ivanov hardly seemed to listen. Instead, he flipped through the pages of the final review board determination. "You are officially removed from flying duty, Captain," he said, reading from the dossier. "But you are fit for ground duty. I see no reason whatsoever to grant you a medical discharge."

He flipped closed the dossier and reached across his desk for Merkulov to take it back. My chance to end this business reasonably had passed. Ivanov, a good apparatchik, was using all that paper in the dossier to keep his ass clean. I could bellow about this injustice for the next seven years in Kirghiz or Uzbekistan and no one would hear me. It was time to gamble.

"Comrade Colonel," I said slowly, "when was the last time you granted an interview to members of the independent press?"

Ivanov's head rotated slowly, like a startled land tortoise. He fixed me with his sharp eye. "What are you talking about?"

"Do you remember you had pilots from the Congo in the hospital last autumn?"

Again, his large head moved with the languid wariness of a startled reptile. Beside me, Merkulov was almost trembling with fear.

"What's wrong with that, Captain?" Ivanov shot back.

"How many had AIDS?" I neglected any honorific title of address. This was not the time for courtesy.

"That's not your business, Captain."

"Why not?" I let my anger surface now. "When I was here, I used the same toilets as them and probably was injected with the same hypodermic needles."

"We handle medical matters here, Zuyev," the colonel shouted. "All of this is none of your affair."

"It's my business if I've been infected." I tried to reason now. "How can you be sure none of the other pilots were exposed to the virus? Shouldn't we all be tested?"

Now Ivanov sunk deeper into the thick folds of his bemedaled uniform blouse, the tortoise in defense. "Again, Captain, this is not your affair."

I swallowed, and licked my dry lips. "It seems to me that this scandal has been covered up very well. But, you know, Comrade Colonel, with glasnost, it is my duty as a Communist to bring this matter to the attention of the independent press."

Finally Merkulov tried to intervene. He realized my intent. "Zuyev, how can you talk to the colonel like this?"

I did not have time to answer. Ivanov leapt to his feet, a bull, no longer the wary tortoise. He was actually sputtering with rage. "Murkulov," he shouted, "I give you two hours to get this captain out of the hospital. Then we will write a formal report on this outrage to his regiment."

Merkulov had me by the arm, but I hung back. "Comrade Colonel," I tried to reason, "you still have a chance to stop this matter before I go to the press. Otherwise, you are making a big mistake."

Ivanov glared at me, his face a mask of hatred. "Get out!"

I was discharged from the Central Aviation Hospital before noon that day. Normally the bureaucratic process of discharge from a military hospital took several days. But Ivanov's staff was obviously motivated to be unusually efficient.

PART
FOUR

— 12 —
Massacre
April 7–14, 1989

T he Aeroflot flight from Moscow to Sochi on the Black Sea was scheduled to land in midafternoon. As always, the twin-jet Tu-134 airliner was filled to capacity. This flight went on to Yerevan and many of the passengers were Armenians. I noticed one group of young men seated behind me who seemed nervous, almost apprehensive. They were whispering among themselves and at one point called over the Armenian flight attendant for a hushed conference.

Their conspiratorial behavior forced me to consider my own situation. Colonel Ivanov probably had good connections in the KGB and the GRU Chief Directorate for Military Intelligence. My desperate attempt to blackmail him to obtain a medical discharge could well indicate that I was capable of even more desperate action. An officer like me serving in a MiG-29 regiment might be considered a dangerous security risk. So there was a good chance the Osobii Otdel would be waiting at the Sochi airport to put me under surveillance.

Then, on the final approach to Sochi airport, I heard the pilot apply full throttle and begin climbing away in an aborted landing. The flaps came up and the landing gear thumped back into their wells. We crossed the coast and banked left onto a southwest heading over the Black Sea. I checked the angle of the sun and noted the time, 2:27 P.M. Ten minutes later we were still heading out to sea and had obviously cleared Soviet airspace. This had to be a hijacking attempt by those furtive young Armenians behind me.

I tried to relax in my seat. This was the height of irony. Every day for the last three months I had been trying to find a foolproof escape route from the Soviet Union, and now I had apparently been given a free ticket to Turkey.

Then the engine pitch changed again and we banked further left, back toward the Soviet mainland. Soon we were set up on final approach to another airport. When we touched down, I realized at once that we had landed at Sukhumi, 150 miles down the coast. As we taxied to the terminal, the attractive young flight attendant finally deigned to tell us what was happening. "Dear passengers," she said, batting her dark eyes seductively. "We followed our assigned route all the way to Sochi . . . but then we landed here in Sukhumi." She laughed sharply and turned her back on us.

Around me the disgruntled passengers were grumbling loudly. Some were on health-cure holidays to resorts near Sochi. The buses from those resorts were waiting over a hundred miles away. These passengers realized that, once more, Aeroflot had taken their money and not delivered proper service.

As I shuffled out past the cockpit, I asked the copilot why we had aborted at Sochi.

"Sudden fog," he said. "Zero ceiling, zero visibility."

Walking across the sunny tarmac to the terminal, I considered this piece of news. Obviously the aborted landing had indeed been sudden; we were locked up on short final when the pilot climbed away. If the KGB surveillance team was waiting for me up at Sochi, they probably hadn't had time to reassign a new team down here. People thought the KGB was omnipotent, with thousands of agents evenly spread across the country. But I knew from my friends Zaour and Vladimir just how shorthanded they were here in Georgia.

I had not earned a free ride to Turkey. But at least I wasn't being followed yet.

Twenty minutes later the porters shoved my bag off their rusty cart, and I cut through the crowd to the line of Volga and Zhiguli taxis half blocking the crescent drive outside the terminal building. The taxi ride to Tskhakaya normally cost twenty-five rubles per person, but I offered a driver—a mustached young Georgian with prominent gold teeth—seventy-five to take me straight to my base with no side trips to deliver other passengers.

"What kind of car?" I asked.

He grinned, a flash of gold. "A Volga, of course," he replied with typical Georgian bravado.

"I'll be right back." It was a two-hour ride and I had to use the toilet.

In the stuffy terminal toilets, I decided to take off my raincoat and rolled it neatly into my carry-on sports bag.

A shiny Volga was standing with the motor running at the head of the taxi rank when I returned, but the young Georgian with the gold teeth was gone. Momentarily confused, I stood on the curb and looked around for the driver.

Then a stocky older man stepped from the other side of the car and reached for my suitcase. "You're going to Tskhakaya, aren't you?" His words were more of a statement than a question.

"I've already made my deal for seventy rubles," I said, keeping a grip on my suitcase handle. I didn't like the way this fellow had pushed in here. So I decided to see if he'd accept five rubles less.

"Sure, of course," the man replied.

We were about six miles from the airport when the driver turned to face me. "Say," he said without a trace of the typical singsong Georgian accent, "didn't you forget something at the terminal?"

"What?" I was genuinely confused now.

"Your raincoat."

I stared back at the man's eyes in the rearview mirror. A chill pang stabbed beneath my throat. This driver had not been out here when I'd reentered the terminal to use the toilet. How did he know I had been wearing a raincoat? Was it possible that the KGB *had* managed to shift surveillance so quickly? Then I noticed the man's cheap leather jacket. Despite the heat of the afternoon, he had that jacket zipped to his throat.

"I've got it here," I answered, patting my nylon sports bag. My voice sounded shrill. The paranoia had begun.

Carrying my suitcase up the steep stairwell of my apartment building *podyesd*, I met my friend Valery coming down. He had been back from his last tour in Afghanistan for almost two months, but I'd hardly had a chance to talk to him. He was dressed in civilian clothes, carrying an overnight bag slung on his shoulder.

After we had shaken hands heartily and embraced, he looked me over and a warm smile spread across his face. "I hear you're making waves, Sasha."

I smiled back and shrugged, a neutral gesture devoid of information. The last thing I wanted to do was to ensnarl Valery in my escape plans. But his pleasant greeting and unfeigned pleasure at seeing me again provided important evidence that—whatever the Osobists were doing—they had not yet tried to suborn my friends as knockers.

Valery explained he was off to Tbilisi for several days' leave to see his father, a retired Russian factory worker who had lived in Georgia for years.

I had a shock when I unlocked the door of my little apartment. Papers and clothing were scattered on the floor, and the doors hung open on the hardwood armoire I had finally managed to buy the previous autumn. It looked like the Osobists had, after all, paid a visit. Then I realized what had actually happened. While I was in Moscow, Jana had returned from the university in Kiev to collect her possessions. A quick check of the apartment revealed that was not all she collected. The small strongbox where I kept our meager savings was open, empty. She had taken more than her share. But at least she was gone.

That night at the officers' dining room I learned that our regimental Osobii Otdel officer, Major Soloyov, was occupied on other matters than my escapades in Moscow. Captain Rustam Salamov had apparently become a scandalous irritant to the zampolits and Osobists. The issue was still Salamov's wife, Anna, the pretty Hungarian girl he had married while stationed at a MiG-23 regiment in western Hungary. Even though she was legally married to Salamov, she had only been granted a tourist visa. The fact that he had divorced a Russian girl to marry a "foreigner," and had then audaciously brought this alien back to visit an officers' housing compound of a Soviet air base, was viewed by the authorities as a blatant provocation.

They knew, of course, that Salamov intended to provoke them to the point of landing a discharge, at which point he would simply emigrate to Hungary and go into private business with his wife's prosperous family. His tactic seemed to be working. Like me, he was grounded and pressing his superiors hard for a favorable resolution to the whole painful situation. Major Soloyov and his invisible crew of knockers were reportedly working around the clock, keeping Salamov and his suspicious alien wife under constant surveillance.

So much the better for me. I had delicate preparations to make in the coming weeks, and I certainly did not want to have to worry about every fellow I saw on the street wearing a leather jacket.

The next afternoon, Sunday, April 9, I was alone in my kitchen, listening as usual to the news summary on Radio Liberty. But this news bulletin was hardly normal. There were preliminary reports from Tbilisi that "Soviet security forces" had violently dispersed pro-independence demonstrations before dawn that morning. At least six people had been killed and scores more injured. Early eyewitness accounts were confused, the calm Russian-speaking reporter in Munich conceded. But it was clear that "several hundred" Army and MVD Interior Ministry troops, supported by armored vehicles, had converged on Lenin Square and attacked peaceful demonstrators.

I carefully tuned the set when the signal began to fade. Then the familiar buzzing thump of shortwave jamming began. Quickly I snapped on the alligator clip of my wire antenna and managed to boost the signal from the Munich transmitters so that I could hear the announcer clearly, despite the attempts to jam the broadcast.

The commentator was now giving a background report on these latest independent demonstrations in Tbilisi. For the past week, several thousand demonstrators had gathered on the wide boulevards of central Tbilisi, some demanding greater autonomy, others actual independence from the Soviet Union. Senior Georgian Party officials, including First Secretary Dzhumber Patiashvili and the Georgian Minister of the Interior, Shota Gorgodze, had repeatedly declared the demonstrations illegal and ordered that the crowds disperse. The Communist officials' refusal to even discuss the issue of Georgian autonomy from Moscow seemed to incense the demonstrators. That morning at least a thousand more joined the peaceful demonstration, waving pro-independence banners and singing the republican anthem.

Despite the size of the crowds, there had been none of the mass anger and minor violence that had often marked the independence demonstrations in the Baltic Republics. Instead, the leaders of the Georgian movement had responded with a different tactic: The day before, several hundred had declared a hunger strike. Surrounded by supporters, they had gathered beneath the budding shade trees on Rustaveli Prospekt and Lenin Square, fronting the handsome neoclassic building of the Georgian Council of Ministers.

The Radio Liberty commentator noted that the Tbilisi demonstrators had combined the spontaneous passion of the Georgian people with unusual mass coordination. Their banners were printed in Russian, Georgian, and English. A typical placard read: "Down with the decaying Soviet Empire." Many people waved the black, white, and claret flag of the once-independent Georgian Republic.

By Monday morning Radio Liberty's reports were more detailed and alarming. Approximately six thousand demonstrators had been massed along Rustaveli Prospekt and on Lenin Square at four o'clock Sunday morning, still singing their republican anthem and waving banners. The crowd had been swelled by thousands of rugby fans, who had left a match at the big Tbilisi stadium to march to Lenin Square. There were hundreds of children among the demonstrators, some infants in their mothers' arms. It was a warm spring weekend night, and the crowd was in an exuberant, almost joyful mood. Speakers with bullhorns mounted the steps of the government buildings on the square to address the crowds. One, the local patriarch of the Georgian Orthodox Church, warned the demonstrators that the Communists were planning a violent military crackdown. But few people in the crowd seemed alarmed.

They should have taken the warning seriously.

Ten minutes later MVD Interior Ministry troops and Army paratroopers launched an unprovoked attack on the peaceful demonstrators. In the ensuing massacre, Radio Liberty announced, sixteen people had been killed outright, almost three hundred were badly wounded, and thousands were overcome by thick clouds of an unnamed "toxic gas."

The final Radio Liberty bulletin I heard before catching the bus to the base that morning confirmed that three wounded demonstrators had died in Tbilisi hospitals, bringing the total killed to nineteen. The gravely wounded were now estimated at 260, with 4,000 treated for serious gas inhalation. Eyewitness accounts stated that the Army and MVD troops had beaten many demonstrators with heavy clubs and slashed others with sharpened military trench shovels.

There was no mention of the massacre on that morning's all-Union news summary from Moscow.

At breakfast I asked the men in my squadron if they had heard reports of a massacre in Tbilisi. They all shook their heads and shrugged. All except Major Petrukhin. Obviously he was still a devoted listener to Radio Liberty. He looked grave and troubled when I mentioned Tbilisi. But he refused to acknowledge amid the bustle and clatter of the breakfast dishes that he had heard the same shocking reports.

By that night, however, no one could pretend that the massacre had not occurred. The official Moscow news media belatedly reported there had been "unfortunate loss of life" when "violent nationalist demonstrators"' assaulted security forces in central Tbilisi and those forces had responded with "legal actions" to disperse the crowds.

Georgian television, however, revealed a far different sequence of events. Although I couldn't follow the Georgian language commentary, a Georgian pilot in our ready room translated, his face drawn into a tight mask of rage. Among the nineteen victims killed, he said, there were pregnant women and several young boys and girls, whose heads had been crushed or who had been dismembered by the troops wielding sharpened shovels. Others had died of gas poisoning. The hundreds still in the hospital had suffered irreversible lung damage from the dense clouds of the mysterious gas the troops had sprayed into the tightly packed ranks of demonstrators.

Despite the warnings for Soviet officers to avoid confrontations with Georgians in town, I went into Mikha Tskhakaya that night to meet Malhaz. I had my suitcase full of those sexy posters and I needed money, no matter what the mood among the civilians. As I expected, Malhaz was cold toward me, but relaxed a little when I offered my obviously sincere condolences for the shocking massacre.

Then he reached under his counter and handed me a sheaf of

photocopies. These were unofficial press photos of the massacre scene. They needed no translation. The wide sidewalks fronting Rustaveli Prospekt were littered with shoes, discarded placards, women's purses, and overturned strollers and baby carriages. I saw none of the bricks or cobblestones that the Tass bulletin read over Vremya had proclaimed the "rioters" had used to attack the security forces.

By the next day the authorities' attempts to suppress news of the massacre had failed completely. Despite a curfew throughout the republic, throngs of angry Georgians had demonstrated in almost every town and city. The commander of the Transcaucasus Military District, Colonel General Igor Rodionov, appeared on television appealing for calm. The Army, he said, is "in complete control of the situation." Instigators of the unrest had been detained. "The extremists wanted blood and attacked the security forces," the general read awkwardly from a prepared text. All further demonstrations were banned. "Patriotic comrades," Rodionov concluded, "we must put this event behind us and refrain from anti-Socialist nationalism."

He made no mention of the men, women, and children who had been slaughtered. He did not speak of the gas that had been used under the shade trees of Rustaveli Prospekt.

The next morning the first secretary of the Georgian Communist Party, Dzhumber Patiashvili, and his chief subordinates resigned in disgrace. Patiashvili stated the massacre could not be denied. It was, he said, "our mutual grief." Before resigning, he declared ten days of public mourning for the victims.

The Politburo then announced that Patiashvili had been replaced as the republic's Party leader by another Georgian, Givi Gumbaridze. He was the head of the KGB in Georgia.

As after the Chernobyl disaster, Mikhail Gorbachev had initially remained silent. He had been on a State visit to England in the days before the massacre. Either Gorbachev had been unaware that his Defense Minister, Marshal Yazov, had been preparing a major military operation against the peaceful demonstrators of Georgia, or he had used his absence as a plausible means to deny his involvement in the massacre. Whatever the truth, I sat before the television in the pilots' ready room on the night of April 12, watching Mikhail Gorbachev address the nation from Moscow. He offered no sympathy to the families of the dead and wounded. Instead, he spoke harshly, shaking his finger as he warned against "extremism by adventurist elements." Gorbachev's statement had been followed by the first official videotapes from Tbilisi, which showed the streets patrolled by BMP armored troop carriers. The intersections of Tbilisi's stately boulevards were barricaded with more armor, and troops in steel helmets and bulletproof vests searched civilian cars and pedestrians.

Gorbachev's message was clear. Despite glasnost, despite perestroika, anyone questioning the authority of Moscow would be crushed. And the Soviet military was the chosen instrument of repression.

Around me in the dim room, my fellow pilots were glum and silent. I knew better than to speak to them here.

Back at my apartment building, I again encountered Valery, who had just returned from Tbilisi. We went to my kitchen to talk. He immediately described the massacre that his father and others had witnessed that terrible night in central Tbilisi.

After the patriarch's warning, other speakers had taken their bullhorns and urged the crowd to remain calm. "It was late," Valery said, his voice thick with anger. "Many of the women were already walking home, carrying their small children. Then it began."

The streetlights suddenly were cut and the city center went completely dark, Valery related. People heard the throaty rumble of BRT armored cars and the snarl of tracked BMP armored personnel carriers. These armored vehicles converged on the demonstrators from several directions. Rank after rank of paratroopers and MVD troops charged the crowds, which had already been dangerously compressed by the advancing armor.

"They had no place to run," Valery added. "The troops pushed them up against the stairs of the Council of Ministers. It was like driving livestock to a slaughter." The flesh on his left chin was pulsing uncontrollably, a tic I had first noticed two years before when Valery had described some of his worst experiences in Afghanistan.

"The troops separated about three hundred people, Sasha," Valery continued, his voice flat and slow, as if he were tiredly recounting yet another combat operation. "They pushed them directly toward the armed squads at the top of the stairs. Don't you see? They were trying to *simulate* an attack on those guards. It was a provocation planned to trigger the massacre."

He stopped speaking a moment and looked away. Sinews and ropy veins throbbed on his rigid neck. Valery was gripped by a turmoil I had never seen before. "Luckily the fellows from one of the rugby teams managed to break the paratroopers' cordon," he added. "And a hundred people escaped the trap. But the rest of them were chased down in the shrubbery to the right of the building. That's where they were slaughtered with the trench shovels and gas."

"It was poison gas?" I asked, because Valery had experience with these chemical weapons.

"A combination, Sasha," he explained. "One gas we call *cheryomukha* because it smells like cherries. There's about four variants of different strengths. The troops in the square used them all, both in gas grenades and with the MVD's cloud sprayer. The other gas is called phenyl chloride," Valery continued. "In open spaces, it's not lethal. But everyone knows it's deadly if used in a restricted area. The women and children on the ground didn't have a chance. If the gas didn't get them, those bastards with their trenching tools did."

"Who did this, Valery? What troops?" I was prepared to believe that OMON thugs from the Interior Ministry were capable of such slaughter. But it did not seem possible that regular Soviet soldiers had taken part in the massacre.

"There were OMON troops from Perm, Voronezh, and Tbilisi," Valery said, a veteran soldier reciting tactical details from memory. "But at least half the troops were from the Army, Sasha." He looked at me sadly. "From *our* Army."

I shook my head, as much in sad recognition as disbelief.

"This was not a riot, Sasha," Valery said, staring into his cup of cold tea. "It was a coordinated combat operation involving both Defense and Interior Ministry forces. Moscow must have approved it."

At our regimental briefing the next morning, Lieutenant Colonel Antonovich announced that the base had been placed on a high security alert status. Each squadron would organize nine-man foot patrols to guard base buildings, the parking aprons, and the main gate. The regular guards on the aprons would be doubled. Because we were short of soldiers, they would be placed on indefinite four-hour-on, four-hour-off duty and sleep rosters.

We all knew that Georgians in the city of Tskhakaya were simmering with anger and anti-Russian hatred, and that there had been mass protest strikes and spontaneous demonstrations all across Georgia. But now Antonovich explained how dangerous the situation had become. Soviet officers in the bazaar had been caught by mobs and severely beaten. Until further notice, he said, our enlisted soldiers would be restricted to the base.

"And if any of you officers go into town," he said, "I suggest you wear civilian clothes, not uniforms."

The next afternoon Antonovich and other senior officers returned from their regular monthly commanders' conference at Vaziani. A lieutenant colonel zampolit from the 7th Air Army flew back with them to brief us on the situation. Like Antonovich, he stressed that the situation was extremely volatile. "The Army has to be prepared to maintain law and order," he bellowed, his voice echoing in our briefing room. "We must stand ready to stop the extremists before they go any further."

After his stirring patriotic address, Lieutenant Colonel Viktor Dovbnya, our own zampolit, rose to assure us that the "legal actions" of the security forces in Tbilisi had been made necessary by the violent demonstrators. And these same adventurist elements, he added, could rise up here in Tskhakaya. We were to check our personal weapons and conduct careful inventories of the arms and munitions assigned to us, to be certain no guns or ammunition was stolen by extremists.

The message of the two zampolits was just as clear as Gorbachev's televised warning two nights before. If necessary, the Army would crush all those who threatened Moscow's authority in any way.

That evening I again sat alone in my kitchen, hunched over my transistor, listening to Radio Liberty. To emphasize Gorbachev's message to the people, I heard, the Army and MVD had just staged military "maneuvers" in the capitals of the three Baltic Republics, terrifying citizens still in shock at the news of the Tbilisi massacre. Tanks and armored vehicles rumbled through the Baltic cities, a stark warning that, like the Georgians, anyone defying Moscow risked death.

Sitting there in the shadowy kitchen, I could picture other

Soviet tanks crushing demonstrators, in Budapest in 1956, in Prague in 1968, in the streets of Azerbaijan the year before when reportedly scores had died. But they were only Muslims like my friend Boris Bagomedov. Now Soviet European troops had been ordered to kill their own people. And they had obeyed those orders.

The local Party hack in Tbilisi had been purged as a scapegoat, only to be replaced by the head of the KGB. How long would it be before the pilots of the 176th Frontal Aviation Regiment were ordered to bomb and strafe "adventurists" in the streets of nearby cities?

In his national address Gorbachev had warned that nationalist demonstrators in Georgia had delivered a "stab in the back for perestroika." What shit. They had been peacefully exercising their rights as Soviet citizens when their Army attacked them with poison gas and sharpened shovels. And now we had been ordered to prepare for similar action to "defend" Soviet law and order.

I found myself standing, twanging with outrage. "I'll show you bastards perestroika," I shouted in the empty room.

Suddenly everything was clear. All the ass-licking zampolits, the Osobists, the military bosses in Moscow, and the Mafia bosses in cities like Samara—who used illegal psychiatric "treatment" to destroy honest citizens—all this privileged, corrupt gang ultimately depended on the Soviet military for support. As long as the Army blindly obeyed the Party, my country would never be free of the criminal clique, the Mafia, that controlled our lives.

Standing on the hot pavement of Lenin Square in Armavir so many years before, I had sworn an oath to defend the Union of Soviet Socialist Republics, to do my duty with courage and discipline, even in the face of death. Now, in this tiny spartan kitchen, I saw where my true duty lay. My life was no longer balanced on a *tochka opori*, a fulcrum. The balance had tipped. I had made a decision.

I would not leave the Soviet Union like a fleeing criminal on some smugglers' trail through the mountains. I did not want my friends in the regiment scrambled from duty alert to chase me some night hanging from a balloon or slung beneath an ultra-light aircraft. But I would *fly* to freedom. As soon as I could prepare and execute a practical plan, I would seize one of my regiment's

MiG-29s, take off, and loop back on a cannon run to destroy as many of the parked aircraft as possible without killing any of my colleagues. This would be an act of vengeance and a warning; vengeance not just for the victims of the Tbilisi massacre, but for all the other faceless millions crushed in the name of Soviet Communism. And the warning would be read clearly by the criminals who ruled my country: If a skilled and dedicated young professional officer like me had been driven to such desperate action, whom could they trust in the future?

Then, if neither PVO missiles nor fighters from other regiments shot me down, I planned to fly the aircraft to the nearest NATO base in Turkey.

I sat down again and rubbed my hand repeatedly through my hair, an unconscious mannerism I'd had since childhood, whenever concentrating on a difficult problem. Despite the hazard and audacity of my planned escape, I felt calmer than I had in months.

13
Counterattack
April 14–May 20, 1989

I n mid-April I flew to Samara for one last visit at home. Once I
actually hijacked a MiG-29, the chances were slim that I'd ever
see my family again. I contacted my mother and had her obtain
a certificate for emergency treatment. When her telegram arrived
in Tskhakaya, Lieutenant Colonel Antonovich immediately granted
me five days' compassionate leave.

This was another indication that Colonel Ivanov in Moscow
had not found an ally in the military district in Tbilisi or the 283rd
Aviation Division in Tskhakaya to initiate Osobist surveillance
on me. But I couldn't count on my good luck holding much
longer.

Those few days in Samara passed too quickly. Mother was
still weak, but recovering steadily. Through discreet inquiries, she
had discovered that the staff at the psychiatric clinic had spared
her from the worst brutality that had been originally ordered for
her. If the clinic doctors had actually carried out their instructions
and injected her with the full treatment of multiple antipsychotic
drugs, she would have suffered irreversible brain damage, the
fate of so many countless thousands of the "mentally ill" who had
run afoul of corrupt apparatchiks and been committed to Soviet
psychiatric hospitals.

Now she was in numb limbo, her mind still clouded by the
drugs. I certainly did not intend to bring my family into my plan.

They would be subjected to a KGB investigation, whatever the outcome of my escape attempt. So the less they knew, the better. But I did give them sixteen hundred rubles, as much as I could spare from the war chest I had built from the sale of the posters to Malhaz.

Whatever happened, my family were in for a rough time in the months ahead. But one advantage of glasnost was that the KGB would not be able to simply swoop down and haul them off to some camp in the gulag. With a few exceptions, those camps were now empty, ghost settlements inhabited only by the spirits of the millions of innocent victims who had starved and frozen in the shoddy barracks and concrete punishment cells. The State no longer took vengeance on the families of traitors. And I was confident that the American government would help protect my family. With the failure of perestroika, Gorbachev found himself increasingly dependent on the West, especially the Americans. That dependence would be the insurance policy for my family.

But that was all in the future. Now I just wanted to say goodbye. Mother and I walked one afternoon in a neighborhood park. The spring foliage was already well advanced, and the streets and sidewalks had been swept clean of winter sand and cinders.

"I will be leaving the military soon," I told her.

She nodded. I didn't have to explain my reasons. Mother now believed that the system I had so proudly served had been taken over by "Dark Forces" that she had never suspected existed in our Socialist Motherland.

"I'll build a new life . . . *somewhere*," I added.

Her shoulders were stooped and her head still moved slowly. But I saw recognition in her eyes. "That's for the best, Sasha," was all she said.

We passed the large bronze statue of Lenin, the Young Revolutionary, his quaint tailcoat eternally flapping in the riverside breeze of Samara. The handsome government buildings and solid apartments of the affluent *microrayon* seemed monuments to Socialist wisdom and energy. But I knew they were hollow shells.

Mother, however, smiled at the statue in the well-groomed park. "Samara," she said, "is so lovely in the spring."

We sat on a bench in the sunshine. Across the street, a gray line of women, many still wearing drab quilted winter coats, appeared around the corner of the red brick building. There was a State dairy store on the side street, and this long line had spilled over to the park square. We watched them a moment, noting their empty plastic mesh and net *avos'ka* shopping bags.

"Sasha, why do we live so badly?" Mother asked. "What has happened to our country? Why this disaster?"

"It's taken a long time for us to reach this point, Mother," I told her. "Decades, really. And for all those decades our people have been forced to live in fear, enslaved, not just their bodies, as when you were young, but their minds as well. And for all those years the Communists have used us in their bloody experiment. But that experiment has failed. And now people are no longer afraid. Now we are brave enough to look around with our eyes open and talk about what we really see."

A gaudy scarlet propaganda poster, showing a giant Lenin beaming at the production line of the *Buran* space shuttle, occupied half the building façade above the drab line of women. They did not seem impressed. To me, that pitiful scene was the essence of the Soviet Union in its eighth decade. The Communists had squandered so many countless billions on the *pokazuka* of our glorious space program and our massive military establishment. But old babushkas still had to stand on their swollen feet, shuffling for hours to buy a bottle of milk. I glanced around the handsome square, wondering where the bosses' secret storerooms were located. Lenin's paternal gaze seemed to follow mine.

Later that afternoon when Misha returned from school, I sat in the kitchen with him as he laid out his schoolwork, just as I had done so many years before. Although only eight, he was proud of his calligraphy and arithmetic papers. Then he presented his most challenging assignment.

"These are poems to memorize, Sasha," he said, staring seriously at the pages of his textbook. "They're twenty-four lines long and we have to have them perfect."

I hadn't been paying close attention, but now I focused on the poems and felt a sudden flush of anger.

"It's all about Dedushka," Misha continued, "about Vladimir Ulyich Lenin when he was a young man in prison."

I found myself scowling. Not *that* old lie. The myth we taught our children was that the brave young Lenin, imprisoned by the Czar's secret police, had taken his milk ration but refused to drink it, using the precious fluid instead as invisible ink to write revolutionary tracts that galvanized the masses. What shit. Didn't the idiots who still pushed such propaganda realize that people would look fondly to those evil days when there was still milk available, even for prisoners?

I picked up Misha's book. The chapter of poems began with the bold red title "Lenin Lived, Lenin Lives, Lenin Will Live."

I slammed the textbook shut. "Misha," I said loudly to the startled boy, "do *not* learn this crap. Remember this always. Lenin was a liar."

He blinked with confusion. My mother looked up from the sink where she was peeling vegetables. "Sasha," she admonished me, "what are you telling the boy? That is his class assignment. Do you want him to fail in school?"

I clenched my teeth. The afternoon in the park she had asked me to explain the disaster that had overcome our country. Yet here, in her kitchen, her younger son was staring at the ultimate source of that disaster. How could I explain to her that our nation, the Rodina, had not simply been stolen by renegades who had abandoned Lenin's golden dream of a Socialist utopia. Leninism had not been abandoned by those corrupt shadowy men. Lenin *was* the source of all their evil.

When I returned to the Ruslan Air Base, I was ordered to see Lieutenant Colonel Antonovich. The "report" on my conduct that Colonel Ivanov had threatened to send had passed through the district and division, and now lay on the desk of my regimental commander.

Antonovich stared glumly up from the folder on his blotter. When he spoke, his voice was cold, devoid of any friendship. "I should have grounded you last autumn." He tossed the report across the desk, and I had to reach quickly to keep it from falling on the floor. "Is this true, Zuyev?"

I studied Colonel Ivanov's message, which bore a boldly

inscribed subsection: "List of Charges." He had requested formal court-martial proceedings against me, and both higher headquarters here in Georgia had endorsed this request. Antonovich's hands were tied. Reprimands would no longer suffice. He had no choice but to convene an officers' court to try me.

The first charge was preposterous. According to Ivanov, I had "expressed contempt for the democratic election process," by refusing to vote, which was proof of my "political unreliability." At the very least, such an accusation would cause my dismissal from the Party. At this point, I could not have cared less.

The second charge stated that I had "feigned an illness" to obtain a military discharge and pension under fraudulent terms. This was a criminal offense. Ivanov, of course, ignored the fact that I had specifically *not* requested a pension.

The third charge stipulated that I had violated direct orders by repeatedly going into the city of Moscow without permission. This was chronic insubordination, grounds for my demotion to the lowest commissioned rank, lieutenant.

Finally Ivanov officially requested a formal military investigation in this district's jurisdiction, "leading to appropriate punishment."

"Well?" Antonovich said impatiently. "What about it?"

"It's all shit, and nothing more."

Antonovich shook his head. "That may be so, Sasha. But this regiment has to shovel your shit. And there will be an officers' court."

I returned his angry glare. "Like there was for Major Matushkin?"

Antonovich winced but remained silent. We both knew that the persecution of a loyal officer like Matushkin was a scandal, a desperate sacrifice to preserve the shaky authority of a parasite like Colonel Prozukhin.

"Don't you think it was a mistake to have grounded First Class pilots like me and Matushkin with the regiment preparing to go back to Mary?"

I was speaking freely because I certainly had nothing to lose. Besides, I liked and respected Antonovich and wanted him to understand this corrupt system as I did. What kind of military "justice" was it that drove the best pilots from the Air Force?

"I'll worry about this regiment's combat proficiency, Zuyev. You worry about writing a proper explanation to these charges."

Antonovich glanced at a note in my file. "I have assigned Captain Igor Novogilov to prosecute in the officers' court. You will follow his instructions."

Igor was my Armavir classmate and a good friend. Obviously Antonovich knew this and was hoping the matter would not end with criminal punishment.

"Thank you," I said, my tone softer.

"That's all," Antonovich said, taking back the report.

I couldn't let things end here. "Anatoli Ignatich," I said. "We've known each other long enough to trust each other. You should understand what happened in Moscow."

By regulation, Antonovich, who would be the president of the officers' court, should not have listened to my story in this informal setting with no witnesses present. But he was too good an officer and a friend to send me away.

I picked up Ivanov's report again. For the next twenty minutes I refuted his charges point by point. The only area I neglected was the actual circumstances of my "illness" during my final flight on February 13. Being too honest about this would put Antonovich in an awkward position. His face flushed, and he shook his head bitterly when I explained the true facts of the "democratic" process for the election of candidates for the Congress of People's Deputies. When I detailed the hospital's cover-up of the AIDS scandal, Antonovich clenched his fists but remained silent.

"And Ivanov is a wealthy man, Anatoli Ignatich," I finally added. "I am convinced that he abused his influential position. If my accusations triggered an investigation, he'd be ruined. That is why he has to crush me."

Finally Antonovich spoke. "Perhaps. For certain, you were stupid to challenge someone like that."

I shook my head sadly. "So we just have to accept the authority of people *like that*? The corruption has reached the point where the entire government is a criminal gang," I said bitterly. "They'll destroy anyone who challenges them. Before they had the gulag. Now. . ." I fell silent. The terrible events in Tbilisi were still too fresh in our minds to bring to this conversation. "Anatoli Ignatich," I finally asked, one pilot to another, "don't you know the history of our country?"

"I know all this better than you can ever realize," he replied, his voice weary.

I had not expected such a frank answer. "Then don't you realize that all of us wearing this uniform actually do not *defend* our people? We defend that criminal gang *from* the people."

The silence swelled between us. Defending the people of the Rodina was as much a foundation of faith to Antonovich as belief in the Socialism of Lenin was to my mother.

Antonovich returned the report to my file and slammed shut the cover. "Sasha, I know you," he said softly. "One way or another, you'll find a way to leave the Air Force. But if all the young officers like you are gone, who's going to make changes here in the military?"

"I can try my best in civilian life. I can write articles. I can . . ." I stopped. It was not easy to lie to a friend. I had no intention of trying to reform the Soviet military. I did intend to attack it, to strike a blow of vengeance that would be noted around the world.

"And I, Sasha," Antonovich said, "will stay here doing my duty. Conditions *will* improve. Not for me certainly. Maybe not for my children, either. But *their* children will have a better life."

Antonovich was like many talented young senior Air Force officers. He firmly believed reform was possible.

"Anatoli Ignatich," I replied, "my grandparents told my parents the same thing."

He looked away, out his office window at the distant line of sleek gray fighters on the parking aprons.

"Dismissed, Captain," was all he said.

With the regiment so busy preparing for the next big combat test at Mary, scheduling my trial was not a high priority.

Even better, Antonovich assigned me as the regiment's controller of flight operations, the "boss" who supervised the control tower dispatchers, the duty-alert section, and coordinated our flying schedule with other units and the PVO missile batteries in the region. This assignment included rotating, day-on, day-off, as the regimental duty-alert officer, which meant I had an official reason to be on the flight line, day or night, for the indefinite future.

*   *   *

Now that I had said goodbye to my family and knew I had at least a month to prepare, I set about seriously planning my "operation." This task would be much more complicated than anything I had ever done. If the plan succeeded, I would live. If it failed, I would die. That was a strong incentive for success.

As I concentrated on the practical details, the solutions to the problems came slowly, one answer colliding with the next, like the tumblers in a combination lock slowly but inexorably falling into place.

The first question I had to answer was exactly where I planned to fly the hijacked fighter. But answering that relatively simple question actually led to several more complex problems. I had already decided on Turkey because it was one of only three countries—Israel and Chile were the other two—that had not signed international aviation treaties, which guaranteed to return hijackers.

After completing a training exercise the year before, I had kept several tactical aviation charts that included Turkish airspace. Now I studied those charts late at night in my kitchen, my apartment door double-locked. I had marked headings and flying times to several potential NATO targets. Unfortunately the big air base at Incirlik in the south of the Anatolian peninsula was out of range. If I could only land there, I would fall literally into the hands of the American Air Force, without having to depend on Turkish intermediaries.

And I realized that, whatever my destination, I would have to fly low, right down on the deck, below radar detection, where fuel consumption was maximum. And I would have to fly fast, at least until I was well clear of Soviet airspace. If I actually managed to steal a MiG-29, there would be other fighters sent up to intercept and destroy the plane before I crossed the frontier. Flying fast and low would limit my escape radius to three hundred miles. I measured that distance on the chart and looked for suitable airports within the fan-shaped wedge of my flying range.

I immediately spotted the civilian airport at Trabzon, a port 130 miles west of the Soviet border along Turkey's mountainous Black Sea coast. Given the steep coastline, the Trabzon airport was down at sea level and looked long enough to accommodate civilian airliners. At least I hoped it was.

Trabzon became my primary destination.

The next problem was obvious. I had to find a safe course to Trabzon, a route that offered the maximum chance of survival. Flying a direct southwest course from Tskhakaya across the Black Sea would take me over the Soviet naval base at Poti, which was defended by a PVO brigade, armed with low-, medium-, and high-altitude missiles, as well as with radar-controlled antiaircraft artillery. Equally bad, the Soviet naval contingent at Poti was almost exclusively antiaircraft missile frigates and destroyers. On any given day during the coming good spring weather, a number of ships from the flotilla would be at sea on maneuvers, fully armed with Dvina and Neva antiaircraft missiles. Those naval units' specialty was intercepting both low- and high-flying intruders.

But if I chose the wiser course of hugging the mountainous coast and flying through the narrow valleys and hopping ridges when necessary, I would have to pass right over the extensive PVO missile complex at Batumi on the Soviet-Turkish frontier. Using the coastal mountains for terrain masking from both Soviet and Turkish radar, however, was the attractive feature of that route.

So my Plan One would be to fly south from Tskhakaya, right down on the deck, cut a sharp dogleg around our air base at Meria, and climb into the mountains well east of Batumi, still north of the frontier. I would then climb a valley, masked by the ridges, and pop over the summit ridge into Turkey to descend down the opposite valley. That would be risky flying, but the whole escape was a risk. If for some reason that route was not possible, my Plan Two would have to be the direct course over the Black Sea.

My next hurdle was obvious: how to gain access to one of our armed and fueled MiG-29s without being challenged. I needed an armed plane to destroy our parked aircraft.

All the MiG-29s parked on the aprons were fueled and carried a full cannon magazine of 150 shells. But seizing one, even late at night, would be difficult. Since the Tbilisi massacre, the guard patrols had been increased and the normal guard roster on the parking aprons doubled. So merely climbing into one of the parked aircraft at night would arouse suspicion.

And there was another problem. When the maintenance officers put our regiment's MiG-29s "to bed," they always secured the throttles with a thick split-pipe lock that slipped right over the rails and held the throttle knobs in the stop position. Locking the throttles had acquired the status of an important ritual in 1986, when the Osobists had warned us that a Western spy had been ordered to steal a MiG-29 and fly it out of the Soviet Union. But there was no way a spy or one of our pilots could fly an aircraft with that lock in place, and the maintenance officers kept possession of the keys. I certainly could not climb into a cockpit and start cutting away with a hacksaw without being arrested.

There was another possibility. The keys to these locks were kept in the technical maintenance building, a facility I visited regularly, day and night, as part of my newly assigned duty. It might be possible to steal the keys, make impressions of them, and have duplicates made in the bazaar. Copying keys from wax or clay molds was illegal, but this was Georgia.

The fighters on the main aprons, however, did not carry the one-ton belly tank of extra fuel, which might be the deciding factor between success and failure. I would certainly need as much fuel as possible, and that belly tank would increase my range to 430 miles. So why bother with the squadron fighters when there would *always* be four MiG-29s—carrying full belly drop tanks and armed with cannon and missiles—ready for immediate takeoff on the duty-alert apron, nicely isolated at the far western end of the runway?

By strict regulation, the duty-alert planes had to be in perfect mechanical condition, ready for takeoff within five minutes of the first alert. And I knew for a fact that the throttles of the duty-alert planes were never locked. Even the Osobists could not risk having a scramble for the intercept of an actual intruder aborted because some mechanic could not find his key.

At an absolute minimum, I could be airborne in under four minutes after I climbed into the cockpit of an alert plane. I made this calculation carefully because my life obviously depended on its accuracy. It would take fifty seconds to start one engine and begin taxiing toward the end of the runway. I could start the other engine while rolling along the ramp. Call it forty more seconds for the taxi, and twenty more for the engine thrust to stabilize. Round that off to two minutes, then double it to be on the safe side: a minimum of four minutes from the time I climbed over the cockpit sill until I slammed the throttles forward for a full afterburner takeoff.

Now another obvious conclusion fell into place, like more tumblers in the combination lock. I had to think beyond my attack on the regiment's parked aircraft, to my reception in Turkey. Stripped-down models of the MiG-29 had already appeared at Western air shows, so the fighter itself was no longer a mystery to the American Air Force. But the MiG-29's advanced Archer infrared- and Alamo radar-homing missiles represented a coveted prize for the American military. A duty-alert plane became doubly attractive.

More imaginary tumblers clicked. I would not be able to take full advantage of the belly tank fuel, after all. In order to fire the cannon, I had to drop the belly tank. After engine start, the first 220 pounds of fuel came from the main inboard tanks. Then the fuel was drawn from the drop tank. On an afterburner takeoff I would use more than half for taxi and takeoff. Depending on how long I held the tank on my climb, I might burn an additional 200 pounds. So flying a duty-alert plane with a belly tank would present a net gain of about 500 pounds of fuel, no small consideration in an emergency. Of course not attacking the parked planes would allow me to keep the fuel. But this was an act of vengeance, not just an escape.

Of course I could never simply climb into one of the alert plane cockpits, start the engines, and taxi away. Stopping such unauthorized, *nonsanktionaire* takeoffs was the principal responsibility of the alert apron guard. The guard would have to be disarmed and neutralized without alarming the men of the duty section in the alert building. Somehow. Another seemingly impossible challenge.

Ironically, as controller of flight operations, one of my principal duties was preventing such takeoffs. I was well versed in the procedures employed to stop a hijacking. At the first sign of trouble, the twelve-man guard section had orders to draw their AKM assault rifles from the armory in the alert building, then quickly block the runway with trucks. The duty-alert officer would then ask division headquarters to pass the alarm to the PVO units in the region. From experience, I knew the PVO missile batteries needed thirty minutes to warm up their terminal intercept radars and prepare their weapons for launch. Whenever the Ruslan Air Base runway was blocked by snow in the winter, we had to turn regional alert responsibility over to the PVO at Poti and Batumi. Their officers constantly reminded us that we had to give them at least a half hour before they were "up."

The invisible combination lock in my mind clicked once more. As flight ops controller, I was the duty-alert officer every other day. And I certainly would not sound the alarm on myself. So the hijacking would happen on a day when I had the duty—actually late at night on one of these duty days.

There still remained the small problem of neutralizing the men of the duty-alert section. This contingent included the two ready pilots, dressed in their uncomfortable high-altitude pressure suits, three maintenance officers, and the alert guard section of twelve soldiers. The pilots and officers had their own dayroom, mess, and small dormitory. The soldiers had a separate mess and bunk room.

My first actual action in implementing the plan was to carefully measure the distance between the alert building and the section's parking apron. It was almost precisely six hundred feet, as I had already estimated. That afternoon I called regimental headquarters and spoke to Major Khurikov, the operations officer. "I need to verify the combat readiness of alert section guards," I told him. "Don't worry if you see soldiers running around down here."

"Good work, Zuyev," he replied.

Ten minutes later I sounded the alarm and dispatched the guard section to the alert apron. It took exactly fifty-five seconds for them to run from the building to the parked aircraft. But they had not yet drawn their weapons from the armory in the corridor leading to the officers' dayroom. The vault doubled as storage for classified documents, so the steel door was heavily reinforced and secured with a thick padlock. The chief engineer on duty kept the key for that lock chained to his belt. But if the lock was jammed, I realized, the only weapons available to the alert section would be the AKM of the single apron guard and the officers' Makarov pistols.

On the night I took the plane, the alert section would hear the roar as soon as I started the engines. A vigilant officer might arouse the soldiers immediately. It would take them at least thirty seconds to pull on their boots and follow the officer down to the apron to investigate. But there would be some confused delay when they found the armory padlock jammed. Call it about a minute, plus the fifty-five seconds needed to run the six hundred feet to the parked aircraft: two minutes. My margin of safety required four minutes.

I had to find a way to incapacitate both the guard section and the officers, at least to slow them down and give me the four minutes necessary to start engines and take off. That still left the problem of the apron guard. But I was confident I could surprise, disarm, and bind him without his sounding an alarm.

Now I ranked all the problems facing me in order of difficulty.

Both the duty-alert building and the control tower beside it were connected to regimental headquarters by telephone lines. Preventing outgoing calls was not my only problem. I had to be certain no incoming "intruder" alert could arrive to wake up the sleeping section just as I pointed my pistol at the apron guard. So all the lines had to be cut. I could do this easily, especially late at night. I made a note to buy a pair of sturdy wire cutters at the bazaar in town.

The duty-alert officer kept the keys for the fuel and maintenance trucks parked beside the building, which the guards would use to block the runway. Without keys, the vehicles were no threat.

I had to find a way to disable the armory lock that was both foolproof and simple. Then I picture the wide key slot on the heavy padlock. A thin file jammed inside and broken off would do nicely. That was another purchase in the hardware bazaar.

Those problems were simple. But how could I neutralize the duty section officers and guards *and* the duty dispatcher and communicator up in the control tower? I had no intention of killing people. So I had to find a way to drug them, to leave them so groggy that they would take longer than four minutes to respond to the rumble of my engine starting.

I paced around the duty-alert building and the control tower, relentlessly attacking the problem from every angle. I saw no way to overpower and drug the dispatcher and communicator in the tower greenhouse. But they were unarmed. And with their phone line cut, they only had an emergency aircraft radio channel to spread the alarm. The chances were good that alarm would go unanswered. And they certainly had no way to block the runway physically.

So I could forget about the tower and concentrate on the officers and men in the alert building. The most serious threat lay with the twelve-man guard section. But if I did obtain knockout drugs, how would I feed them to the guards? They ate rations from their own mess, usually a disgusting slop of thin kasha or a watery ragout of half-rotten potatoes and fried fish. But they certainly did drink tea, as did all the officers in the alert section. In fact, we felt sorry for the guards and always gave them extra sugar for their tea. The boys drank it constantly.

I entered the side door to the small officers' dining room. The tea and sugar were kept locked in this pantry. If I obtained enough drug to spike the sugar in the large tin canister, I would make sure to deliver two hundred grams or so as a kind gesture to the guard section the night of the hijacking. And of course I would fill the sugar bowl that stood beside the electric samovar in the officers' dayroom. I stood in the narrow pantry, engulfed with the sweet scent of tea leaves and the sharp aroma of pepper. Maybe I had found the vector for my drugs.

Now I had to investigate what type of drug would meet my needs. I studied the pharmacy text I had bought so many years before as a cadet. In the section "Hypnotics and Tranquilizers," I found a long list of possible candidates under the category "Available at State Pharmacies." But I discovered that almost all of the strongest drugs—guaranteed to put a man to sleep—were *not* water soluble. There were, however, two possibilities: a sedative called chlorpromazine and a barbiturate known as clonazepam.

After a fruitless search among the pharmacies in Tskhakaya the next afternoon, however, I learned that neither drug was available, with or without a prescription—or even a suitable *prezant*. Then I remembered the unused bottle of neozepam tranquilizers that Lieutenant Colonel Frolov had prescribed me. The pharmacy manual said that neozepam was often indicated for insomnia. Two of the normal ten-milligram tablets would put a man to sleep for several hours. Back in town the next day, I found that neozepam was available in three of the pharmacies.

Another calculation revealed how much neozepam I would need. There would be ten guards sleeping in the bunk room, one on apron duty, one at the guard desk inside the alert building door, three engineers and maintenance officers, and the two alert pilots. That made a total of sixteen men to drug, seventeen if the desk guard drank drugged tea. If not, I could overpower and bind him before setting out for the apron, provided the other men were deep asleep.

Then I made an unpleasant discovery. Neozepam was available in the appropriate quantities, but it was not water soluble. Again I found myself pacing the walkways and ramps around the alert building, chewing on the problem. If I couldn't get these men to drink tea, I suddenly realized, I could certainly entice them all to eat a tempting sweet. Given the high prices and shortages, it had been a long time since any of us had seen cake or pastry.

That night I crushed a neozepam tablet, wet the tip of my index finger, and gingerly licked the dull white powder. It was almost tasteless.

I searched my kitchen cupboard and found a cache of two kilos of sifted white flour. I knew I could obtain butter, sugar, and eggs at the bazaar. Sweet condensed milk for the frosting would probably be a problem. But I still had enough money left from the poster sale to make all the required purchases to fill my unusual cake recipe. I had to be certain the cake was big enough and adequately laced with drugs to incapacitate at least sixteen men.

For the first time, I made actual written notes. If the Osobists discovered them, all they'd find was a shopping list for a cake. Let the bastards ponder *that*.

Then I performed another mental calculation. Sixteen men times two tablets equalled thirty-two. But I wanted them sound asleep, not just groggy. I certainly did not want to give the PVO any of the half hour they needed to come on-line. That precious thirty minutes was my life insurance. So I decided to lace the cake with six times the minimum neozepam required to put those men to sleep. The pharmacy text made it clear that there was no danger of a lethal overdose, but warned "prolonged torpor" could result from taking too many.

My goal was to purchase eighteen ten-tablet bottles. The next Saturday afternoon I began my shopping. My ploy was simple. Dressed in civilian clothes, I went to the chief pharmacist of each store, explained I was a patient at the nearby sanitarium and that I had "problems sleeping." Then I requested neozepam, making sure to flash my thick roll of new red ten-ruble notes. By the next Tuesday, I had twelve bottles of the drug. After a quick bus trip to Poti, I had the other six bottles.

By Friday, May 12, I had the 180 neozepam tablets and almost all the other ingredients for the cake. I was nearly ready to execute the plan. Now I had to pick my day. It suddenly came to me. May 19, a Friday that week, marked the fortieth day since the Tbilisi massacre. In the Orthodox religion this was a significant anniversary, the day the souls of the dead finally departed their bodies. I planned to give them a suitable ceremony to mark their passage into the next world.

But an unexpected obstacle presented itself. There was no condensed milk to be had in the bazaar. Even Malhaz could not locate any. Finally I managed to borrow six cans of Sgushyonka from my neighbor Natasha, a female warrant officer who was our regimental control tower dispatcher. I did find fresh spring strawberries in the bazaar, however, and spent fifty rubles of my depleted war chest to buy two kilos. Now I had all my ingredients.

If I had any qualms about my actions during that final week, they were quickly banished by Lieutenant Colonel Dovbnya, our regimental zampolit, who kept up a constant harangue about our patriotic duty to "suppress adventurist elements" who might capitalize on the tense situation here in Georgia. His message was clear: The regiment had to be prepared to turn its weapons on our fellow citizens. He made me sick.

One afternoon in the duty-alert dayroom. I found myself alone with Petrukhin. His orders to the military training mission in North Korea had just come through. But he still had three months to serve in Georgia.

"What do you think of Dovbnya's stirring words?" I asked

him, probing. "Are you ready to fly missions against your fellow Soviet citizens?"

Petrukhin shook his head at once. "Of course not."

"What about your next assignment?" I leaned toward him still pressing hard. "Will you attack the South Koreans if ordered to do so?"

He jumped up from his easy chair and threw down the illustrated sporting news he was so fond of reading. "Leave me alone," he muttered. "That's a different matter and you know it."

I had my answer. If ordered to scramble and intercept my hijacked aircraft, Petrukhin would not hesitate to shoot me down.

Next I prepared an escape kit containing a flashlight, compass, extra socks, matches, and two cans of stewed beef. I hid the waterproof sack in the high grass near the airfield perimeter. If I failed in my hijack attempt. I planned to head south into the nearby swamps on foot and make my way to the mountain frontier.

Slipping the bag into the weeds felt strange. It was my first overtly treasonous action. Then I got to my feet and breathed the cool moist air. I felt calm again. It had finally begun.

The next afternoon I brought a French video film to the duty-alert dayroom and presented it with great fanfare. "We can watch it tonight, boys," I told the engineers. "It will be a welcome treat after all the good news on Vremya."

They laughed and clapped.

"There's more where this came from," I said, placing the video beside the television set. "My Georgian friends tell me they've got something pretty spicy."

Again my comrades clapped. The stage was set.

Alone in my apartment the next morning, I removed pictures from my photo albums and began selecting the ones to take with me. This was a harder task than I had imagined. I certainly did not want the pictures I left behind to fall into the hands of the Osobists and be stuck on the bulletin board of some investigator's office. So I planned to burn those I didn't take. But the actual choice was a wrenching experience. Finally I stacked twenty pictures of my family and friends on one side of my kitchen table and swept the others into a paper bag. That night I burned them with my personal papers out on the far corner of the soccer field. When I came back to the apartment, I sat for a long time staring at the pictures I had selected to carry with me. There was my grandmother with her wide, stoic face and kindly eyes; me in a sailor suit on a river excursion; my first day of school with my white collar and my heavy book bag; a picture with my mother the summer I was fourteen, just before I left with the survey brigade. She looked young and untroubled. I looked so innocent, so optimistic. Then there was Kursant Sergeant Zuyev, Alexander M., in his first year at the Armavir Academy. There was Karpich with his big nose and ears, and Firefly after his first solo in the L-29. Finally I could no longer look into my past. I slid the precious mementos of my life into an envelope and sealed it.

Later that night I carefully reviewed my handwritten diagrams and specifications of the MiG-29's missile and fire-control systems, and the multiple pages detailing the latest Soviet air-combat maneuvers. To the Americans, these documents would be my most valuable cargo. I lay them carefully inside my flannel helmet bag.

I definitely intended to reach the safety of American custody as quickly as possible, even though it was impossible to fly directly to the NATO base at Incirlik. For several weeks I had been thinking about the last Soviet fighter pilot to escape, Senior Lieutenant Viktor Ivanovich Belenko. In September 1976, Lieutenant Belenko had flown an advanced PVO MiG-25 interceptor from a base in the Soviet far east to Japan. The official Soviet explanation of his escape flight and defection to America had been that the unfortunate young pilot had become lost in bad weather and had only landed in desperation at the Hakodate Airport in northern Japan when he was completely out of fuel. Belenko had then been "kidnaped" by the Americans, at least according to Soviet authorities.

Viktor Belenko was a graduate of the Armavir Academy. His audacious exploit was a taboo subject among the cadets. But we all suspected his flight had been a well-planned escape, not the unfortunate result of bad weather. Our suspicions were confirmed later when the KGB circulated reports in the Soviet military that they had tracked down and executed the "traitor" Viktor Belenko in America. I doubted that the KGB had actually accomplished this; their propaganda was intended to scare pilots like me from attempting a similar escape flight. But in any event, I knew the Organs of State Security were capable of such behavior. Delivering a MiG-29 to the West would mark me for death, but I didn't intend to become an easy target for KGB assassination squads.

I baked my cake on the morning of Wednesday, May 17. It was magnificent, a full seven pounds and three layers high, frosted in creamy white, and studded with fresh, ripe strawberries. Looking at this beautiful cake, there was no way for anyone to know that the lower right-hand corner was any different from the rest. But the creamy frosting in that corner was free of the crushed neozepam tablets that I had so carefully mixed into the other frosting. Just to be certain, I placed the biggest ripe strawberry on the safe corner. That would be the piece that I cut first and set aside for myself.

Then I opened my kitchen curtains and made a show of washing out several shirts and a pair of trousers. I hung them prominently on the clothesline of my balcony. Any man planning a desperate action would not take the time to wash and hang up laundry. At least I hoped that was the impression I gave to any unseen watchers.

I carried two heavy boxes of my best aeronautical engineering textbooks and expensive international aircraft almanacs to the duty-alert dayroom that afternoon and told the officers they could help themselves.

"I won't need these on ground duty," I explained.

I had signed each of the books: "To my friends and acquaintances with the best of luck for the future."

Even Dovbnya, the shit-eating zampolit, thought this was a magnanimous gesture.

Before leaving the building, I upbraided the sergeant of the guard for the filthy condition of the troops' kitchen, bunk room, and latrine. "I want these areas scrubbed and painted," I ordered. "No damned excuses."

He began to complain that the men were already short of

sleep from the extra patrols and that this duty would exhaust them. This was exactly my intention.

"No damned excuses, Sergeant," I said in my best parade-ground voice.

That afternoon at sunset, I again climbed the green slope of Dzveli Senaki outside of town. I wanted to be alone on this peaceful mountain to gather my thoughts for the day and night ahead. Again, bells sounded in the cool afternoon. Without thinking, I had stopped before the walls of the church. I entered the courtyard. An old babushka with a twig broom smiled from the doorway. I asked if the priest was there.

He came out brushing dust from his cassock, as if he'd been helping the old woman clean the vestry. The priest was an elderly man with soft, intelligent eyes. Like most Georgians these days, he viewed me cautiously.

I had never spoken to a priest before and was clumsy when I asked him for a "blessing."

"Why?" he asked, a practical Georgian beneath his cassock and beard.

"I need it, Father."

He still eyed me warily. "Is it for good or for evil?"

"For good, Father. I'm a Soviet officer," I said quietly. "I am very sorry for what happened in Tbilisi."

The priest solemnly studied my face for any hint of mockery. "We are planning a memorial to mark the fortieth day since the massacre," he told me. "Perhaps you can join us."

I had other plans to mark that grim occasion. But I could not reveal them. "Perhaps, Father."

His eyes softened and he nodded with understanding. Then he raised his right hand with the first two fingers extended and made the sign of the cross near my face. He spoke clearly in Georgian, and I understood the word "Kristos."

Warm calm seemed to flood physically through my body. I was ready.

The weather turned suddenly bad that night. By midnight a rainy gale howled across the base. Then conditions grew worse, with an even lower ceiling and high wind. Antonovich suspended flying for the next day. I called the meteorological office and learned a sudden front had spilled across the Caucasus. We could expect below minimum conditions for the next twelve hours. Flying through the mountain passes in this weather was impossible.

Reluctantly I readjusted my schedule. I would make the attempt at dawn on Saturday, May 20.

Late that night I pulled my kitchen curtain and sat before my tape recorder. It was time for me to explain my decision to my family, my colleagues, and the people of my country. I knew the KGB would search this apartment, and wanted them to know exactly why I had taken this drastic step. Investigators at many different echelons would hear this tape, and I hoped reformers in both the Air Force and the KGB would unofficially spread news of my message. I also wanted to make it clear that I had acted alone.

I clicked on the machine and spoke, addressing my words to "the people of Russia and the country called the Union of Soviet Socialist Republics."

I began by stating that many would wonder why a veteran Soviet fighter pilot, "ready to give his life for his country and the ideals of Marxism-Leninism," had taken this drastic step. Then I suggested they ignore whatever official explanation the authorities gave and to listen to my own version. "I have come to hate Socialism, the system into which I was born and raised." I explained that I had believed too strongly in that system, but that now all I felt for it was "hatred and contempt." But I did feel pity and compassion for all those still suffering under this totalitarian system that had already massacred millions of innocent people and was obviously intent on continuing the slaughter. "Communism has created the greatest prison in the world," I said. And Marxism-Leninism had ruined the country's economy and enslaved hundreds of millions simply to support a criminal clique that wrapped itself in the protection of the Party.

I spoke about the sad state of the Soviet military, in which young recruits and old veterans alike found release only in suicide. I exposed the hypocrisy of Gorbachev's "defensive" force reduction.

Then I detailed what I knew of the Tbilisi massacre and the elaborate efforts in the military to suppress the truth. My flight, I said, had been planned for May 19, forty days after that horrible carnage. I spoke directly to the Organs of State Security, the KGB and the MVD, and to the special units under their command.

"Fellows, what are you defending, the people? If so, why do you herd them like cattle to be slaughtered with gas and shovels?" I asked them if they were prepared to become as cruel as Stalin's butchers.

"Wait before you pull the trigger," I concluded. "Listen to the voices of the demonstrators. Think before you pull the pin from that gas grenade. The consequences you face are more frightening than ever before in our history."

I clicked the switch of the tape recorder. The room fell silent.

Then I started the machine for the last time. "My dear mother," I said, "please forgive me. I have to do this. I have no way out. I love you all."

As I removed the tape and put away the recorder, I again carefully reviewed all the steps I had taken to protect my family from official retribution after my escape. First, I had kept them completely ignorant of my plans. All my mother knew was that I was trying to obtain a discharge from the Air Force. My family had no idea of the drastic action I was about to take. So they would be absolutely convincing during their inevitable questioning by the KGB. There was nothing I could do to prevent this interrogation, but I was confident that it would not be especially harsh. The record of my movements over the last several months was clear; I had spent very little time with my family, so they were obviously not coconspirators.

More to the point, the days of the KGB's ruthless Stalinist methods were over forever. With glasnost, the Organs of State Security could no longer simply dispatch their Black Raven vans in the night to haul innocent people away to the gulag. The independent press, especially the popular investigative magazine *Argumenti i Facti*, which had supported the work of the Memorial organization so effectively, would be certain to publicize any illegal retribution against my family.

And I was also confident that the United States government would intervene on their behalf. Gorbachev desperately needed the support of the West. He simply could not afford to reveal a Stalinist side to his government, especially after the Tbilisi massacre. And, once I was safely in American custody, my first priority would be to appeal for my family's protection, and, if possible, for their emigration to the West. So, as I carefully planned for the most dangerous and difficult military operation of my life, my

family's welfare was one problem I felt certain would be successfully resolved.

I climbed down the narrow steps from the control tower at
2330 hours that Friday night, leaving the duty dispatcher and a
communications sergeant in the greenhouse. The regiment had
just completed a three-hour night flying exercise, the last training
of a hard ten-day stretch, which had been marred by the poor
flying weather that morning. Now the sky had cleared. A quarter-
moon was rising over the snowy ridges to the east. The weather
forecast for the morning called for thin, scattered ground fog, but
no wind or overcast.

I would make my attempt in less than six hours, at dawn on
Saturday, May 20. Appropriately Antonovich had just declared Saturday
a holiday. At this moment he and most of the regiment's pilots
were in the sauna, drinking beer. I hoped they became very sleepy.

I strolled across to the concrete-block duty-alert building.
Officially I had about seven more hours to serve before the
section was relieved at 0700 Saturday.

A lanky Ukrainian sergeant sat at the operations alert desk.
He hardly glanced up when I returned from the control tower.
The first door off the hall was the officers' dormitory. I peered
inside, noting the double row of empty cots. As I had planned,
my colleagues would be in the dayroom.

The door of the armory was made of steel and framed with
heavy girders. Inside I touched the twin racks of AKM assault
rifles and tested the padlock securing them. I opened the safe and
deposited the bundle of secret intelligence folders the duty officer
carried with him to the control tower during training operations.

In the hall I pulled shut the steel armory door and snapped
the heavy padlock. Then I tapped the pocket of my flying
jacket to feel the narrow file I would use later to jam this lock.

The officers' dayroom was brightly lit, cheerful. The television and videocassette deck stood like an altar at the far end of the
room, beyond the pilots' roster blackboard. The two pilots on
duty alert tonight were Major Vladimir Petrukhin and Captain
Vladimir Voldeyev. They sat uncomfortably in easy chairs, dressed
in their tight stratospheric pressure suits. Petrukhin nodded
coolly as I entered the room. Voldeyev was a good fellow, not the
world's greatest fighter pilot, but a steady wingman. Typically he

accepted the drudge work. Tonight he was laboring diligently on the next week's flight schedule.

Petrukhin lounged in his chair, leafing through a sports magazine with colorful pictures. The three maintenance officers were grouped before the television, watching the late edition of Vremya from Moscow. Judging from the clean tea glasses around the electric stainless-steel samovar, they had just come back from helping secure the regiment's aircraft for the weekend. Now they were waiting for the Friday night broadcast of *Vzglyad*, "Glance," the new investigative show that was scheduled to report on the findings of the official investigation of the Tbilisi massacre.

"Zuyev," Dmitri Karpov, the maintenance captain, called, seeing me enter, "where the hell are the videos? You promised something new tonight."

I grinned, held up my empty hands, and shook my head. "Be patient," I answered. "I just got out of the tower."

Following my plan that week, I had bent regulations to rent another new Western movie from Malhaz. The duty section had already been treated to *Sweet Dreams* and a sexy French farce about a bigamist airline pilot. "I'll go fetch the new movie as soon as Colonel Antonovich is in the sauna," I added.

The two officers closest to the television groaned in unison. The news from Moscow had just ended with an announcement that *Vzglyad* had been canceled on the orders of the Central Committee, pending the "completion" of the Tbilisi investigation.

"Shitmouths!" Karpov cursed. "Glasnost, unlike turds, does not seem to float across the Moscow River."

I looked at my watch. "I'll go get us something decent to watch."

"Not too decent," Voldeyev called.

When I came back through the doorway of the duty-alert dayroom carrying the cake, the men cheered. This was a much better treat than a video. I cleared a place on the samovar table and sliced the cake into generous pieces. But I kept my eye on the right-hand corner, where I had placed the largest ripe strawberry. Before I invited the men to help themselves I took the untainted wedge for myself.

Major Sergei Stupnikov came in to check the flight schedule with Lieutenant Voldeyev. I could see the major had drunk a few beers in the sauna. His face was flushed, and his normal hearty laugh was boisterous. He immediately saw the cake.

"Where did *that* come from?" he shouted.

"A very pretty woman made it," I answered. I hoped the men in the section would gobble up my gift before Stupnikov took a piece.

Stupnikov stood near the samovar table, shaking his head in admiration. "This is one beautiful cake," he said. "Some lucky guy must be keeping a woman very happy to get a cake like this. Who is he?"

I forced myself to grin at my friend. "You know him very well," I said.

He roared with laughter, took his copy of the flight schedule, and strode out of the room. A moment later I heard his old GAZ rattle away.

I smacked my lips loudly as I ate my small wedge of cake, then turned to stare out the window at the dark runway. The other officers were grouped around the samovar table, scooping up hunks of cake, laughing and talking. I had put aside twelve pieces for the soldiers in the guardroom. Hopefully they'd be fair and the whole section would eat a piece, including the men about to rotate the apron guard at 0400.

But there were still several pieces on the table. Petrukhin remained in his easy chair, now reading the new issue of *Red Star*.

"Comrade Major," I called formally, "you don't want to miss your cake."

He looked up coolly, then smiled. "No, thank you," he said, "but I really don't care for any."

My throat went tight and I felt my heart begin to thud. Petrukhin was a notoriously light sleeper. Unless he ate some of the cake, he'd be wide awake when I took off. And if I had to engage him in a dogfight, I would lose precious time. I could see my careful plan unraveling.

"These strawberries are fresh, Major," I said. "There's real butter in the frosting."

Petrukhin barely looked up from his newspaper. "Thanks, but no," was all he said.

Vladimir Voldeyev was already on his second piece. He would be no problem in an hour or so. But Petrukhin seemed unmoved by the tempting offer. In desperation, I tried to shame him into taking a piece. "Surely you're not on a diet?"

Petrukhin folded the newspaper and lay it on the knee of his pressure suit. He stared at me for a moment, then smiled sheepishly. "Yes," he said, "as a matter of fact, I am. You other fellows take my share."

Before I could reply, Captain Karpov was smacking down his second piece. I took my tea glass and returned to the window. Petrukhin's refusal to eat was disturbing. I knew he loved sweets. Even on a diet he would have accepted a morsel just for taste. I felt a cold sagging inside. Petrukhin was still a loyal Communist. The Osobists *had* brought him into their confidence. They had been following me for weeks. They had seen me buy the neozepam and interrogated all the pharmacists. They knew every detail of my plan. It was still not too late to abort. I had not yet reached the point of no return.

No, this was just paranoia. I had to keep my wits. If I panicked, I would die.

I carried the cake to the guardroom down the hall. The young sergeant assured me he would save a piece for the man who came off duty at 0400. When I returned to the dayroom, only a few crumbs and frosting smears remained on the cake pan. I refilled my tea glass from the samovar and settled down to watch the late evening documentary. Instead of the truth about Tbilisi, State television was treating the nation to an inspiring account of volunteer oil-field workers struggling against the Siberian winter to produce needed foreign exchange for the Motherland.

This certainly was not an Italian sex farce. The men were tired from a week of alert duty. I hoped they would soon amble down the hall to their dormitory cots.

As I sat watching the documentary, Senior Lieutenant Ivan Gromov, my relief as duty-alert officer, came through the door, carrying his overnight bag. What the hell was he doing here seven hours early? He and Petrukhin seemed to exchange a furtive glance, then Gromov greeted me.

"My roommates brought a bottle of cognac back from the sauna," he said. "I can sleep better over here."

I stared at him, searching for any sign of deception. His face was calm and open. We all considered this duty irksome and restrictive, more suited to bureaucrats than pilots. Was Ivan Gromov part of an Osobist surveillance team? Why had he waited to appear until the last of the cake was eaten?

Then I forced myself to think rationally. Gromov was single. He shared three cramped rooms with six other lieutenants. Compared to his quarters, the alert building was luxurious. Colonel Antonovich had declared a holiday after ten days' intense training. Ivan's young roommates would certainly take advantage of the occasion to continue the sauna party, with cognac now instead of beer. But Ivan couldn't drink the night before taking over the duty section from me. So there was a rational explanation, after all.

But now there would be two officers, Ivan and Petrukhin, who had not eaten any cake. And they both carried pistols.

I hunkered low in my chair and gazed at the comforting images on the television screen. The broadcast from Moscow ended just before 0200. I went outside and strolled around the building. The base was quiet. The thin chunk of moon was high overhead. I could smell diesel fuel and newly plowed fields on the breeze. Away to the north, the snowy wall of the Caucasus shone in the moonlight. It was a perfect night for flying.

When I rounded the corner of the alert building, I saw Petrukhin staring out the window, almost as if he were watching me.

The desk guard had his head down on his folded arms. He was snoring lightly. That was a good sign; the lanky young sergeant must have weighed at least two hundred pounds and had only eaten one piece of cake. The other men were probably already asleep on their cots. Everyone except Petrukhin and Ivan Gromov, of course.

Before returning to the dayroom, I made my final reconnaissance of the dining room. All the section's communication lines connecting the building's three telephones, the public address system, and the old hand-cranked field telephone ran through the dining room in a thick wire bundle. It was there that I planned to cut them, my final preparation before subduing the apron guard. I quietly turned the door handle. To my horror, it was locked. I felt the sweat pop on my forehead. Breaking down the door would wake everyone, no matter how much cake they had eaten. I had planned my every move, but I had never imagined this door would be locked.

Once more, I forced myself to think rationally. The desk guard was required to have keys for all the rooms. I shook him brusquely awake. His face was slack and he couldn't stop blinking. He explained through his yawns that Captain Karpov had asked him to lock the dining room to prevent people stealing cheese from the pantry.

"That's against fire regulations, Sergeant," I snapped, taking the key.

"Yes, Comrade Captain," he said, his eyes already closing.

I unlocked the door and hid my flannel helmet bag under a

table in the far corner. There was another door leading from the dining room to the side of the building. I made sure it was open, in case someone decided to lock the hall door again. Then I knelt at the bundle of communication lines to feel the thickness of each wire. There was nothing here that I couldn't cut quickly.

Back in the alert room, I was amazed to find that everyone was still awake. Voldeyev was bent over his training schedule. The maintenance officers were finishing a hand of cards. Petrukhin studied his damned *Red Star* as if it were a training manual. At this rate they'd still be up when the effects of the tranquilizer wore off.

"I don't know about you sportsmen," I said, nodding to the maintenance officers, "but I'm tired, and I'm going to get some sleep." I stretched slowly and yawned. As I had hoped, the suggestion worked. Voldeyev was yawning now and so were two other officers. I turned on a small desk lamp, then switched off the overhead light. We all made our way to the dormitory.

I curled up with my arm around the pillow and my hand over my eyes. After a few minutes I heard Voldeyev snoring. But Petrukhin rolled back and forth on his cot, trying to find a comfortable position in his tight pressure suit. After a long time I heard his breathing steady into a regular rhythm. In my mind I reviewed all the steps I had taken as if going through a takeoff checklist. My next step was to cut the communication lines from the control tower, steal the vehicle keys, then slip inside the dining room and cut the last wire bundle. Then a final check to make sure the desk guard was still asleep. After that I had to move quickly to overpower the apron guard before regimental headquarters discovered the phones were down.

But it was already almost 0400. I didn't want to be in the middle of tying up the guard on the apron if the relief guard actually woke up and came on duty. Although it was risky, I decided to wait until after the guard had changed. But it was impossible to lie here feigning sleep. I pulled on my boots and quietly left the dormitory.

The desk guard was still snoring. Outside, the night was dead quiet. There was no sign of movement down the runway at the main guardhouse. Down on the alert apron I found the guard pacing slowly around the four aircraft. He stopped when he saw me approach.

"All quiet, Comrade Captain," he said.

"Fine," I muttered, "but I don't want to hear of you sleeping out here. With all these strikes and riots, we've been told to expect trouble."

"Yes, Comrade Captain," the boy replied.

Then I saw a glow from the window of the nearby maintenance building. "What's that light in there?" I demanded.

"Nobody's there, Comrade Captain," the guard answered. "I checked myself."

"Carry on," I told him, striding away to inspect the maintenance building myself. As the boy had reported, the room was empty. I snapped off the light. Leaving the building, I saw the young guard marching along his post on the apron. I certainly hoped the guard sergeant had saved him a piece of cake.

Just to be certain, I made several circuits of the nearby buildings. The only guard I encountered was on the duty-alert apron.

Back in the dormitory, everyone was still sleeping. Ivan Gromov had taken the couch in the alert room. He didn't hear me when I drained the samovar to drink several glasses of strong dark tea. I sat in the easy chair trying to keep my breathing even. It was well past 0400 now, but I hadn't seen the relief guard leave the station.

I went down the hall to the desk and shook the Ukrainian sergeant awake again. He seemed even more groggy now. It was his job, I reminded him coldly, to make sure the guard was changed on time.

"What's the relief guard's name?"

"Chomayev, Corporal," the clerk said, consulting the stenciled roster sheet.

"If I put anybody on report for this," I said, "you'll share the punishment."

The young man's face was confused, unfocused, his voice slurred. It was 0420 when the apron guard was finally changed. I went back outside and circled the building. The guard bunk room was dark again. When I looked back in the alert building, the desk guard was sound asleep, head down on his folded arms, as he had been earlier.

Once more, I circled the area like a stalking cat. Then I entered through the dining room door. With my back turned to the operations desk at the end of the corridor, I hefted the armory padlock and thrust the thin metal file into the key slot. I broke off the file and jiggled the lock, making sure the slot was securely jammed.

Outside, a mist was rising in the still, damp night. The lopsided quarter-moon was low in the western sky. I took the keys from the duty section van and the fuel truck and dropped them through the grate of a storm sewer. The vehicles could no longer be used to block the runway.

Unfortunately the phone lines from the control tower were exposed to view. Twice I approached the end of the tower where the wires looped away from the junction box just above head height. Twice I stopped when I saw someone moving up in the greenhouse.

I paced in the shadows of the nearby maintenance hangar, wiping my sweaty hands on the legs of my flight suit. I could see my plan unraveling. I fought back panic and the urge to bolt, to just scramble under the barbed-wire fence, toss away the incriminating wire cutters, snatch my escape kit from the weeds, and keep running south.

At exactly 0506 I managed to cut the six phone lines from the control tower junction box. I strode away quickly to wait behind the maintenance hangar. If cutting those phone lines had triggered an alarm, the guard van from regimental headquarters would arrive soon. Ten minutes passed. The tower and alert building were silent.

Off to the east, the serrated ridges of the Caucasus steadily gained definition in the first peach glow of dawn. I was still on schedule. But there was no telling how long the neozepam would work.

A terrible sequence of events rolled through my mind like the lantern slides of an illustrated tactical lecture. The division duty clerk tries to phone Natasha in the tower. Dead line. He tries the emergency line. No answer. He sends a runner to the guard captain. They return to check the phone lines and find the cut ends. They then decide to arm the guard section, but discover the jammed lock. An alarm is sounded and the drugged officers stumble awake. Where is Zuyev? Where the hell is he?

But this was only panic. The base was quiet. I marched directly to the side door of the dining room and entered silently. Crouching in the dark corner, I felt each wire with my thumb and finger, then cut it. As I snapped down the cutter blades on the last wire, the thin strand slipped. It took me four stabs to cut it. Then I heard a loud single ding of the telephone bell in the dormitory. Again sweat beaded on my face. Cutting that last line had broken the circuit, triggering the bell's magnet. This was fourth-form physics. Why hadn't I thought of it?

I have to hurry now, I thought, grabbing my helmet bag of papers.

But outside I forced myself to stop and slip into the hedge beside the dormitory window. Just as I had feared, I saw Petrukhin on his feet inside. In the faint light I watched him lift the telephone, then bang down the receiver. Now he was in the doorway to the hall. I didn't want to watch.

As I approached the alert apron, I pulled the Makarov pistol from the left breast pocket of my leather flight jacket, cocked the action but did not set the safety as I normally did. Ahead, the familiar outline of a soldier wearing a black quilted jacket and a floppy southern field hat, an AKM slung on his shoulder, was silhouetted against the flank of the first aircraft. I recognized Corporal Chomayev now, a stocky, broad-shouldered Asian, one of the better soldiers in the guard detachment. He had always been quiet and stoic, but, unlike others, quick to follow orders. Too bad. I did not want to have to hurt Chomayev and hoped I could disarm him quickly. I certainly did not want to fight this tough youngster.

It was dawn. Time to act.

— 14 —

Vengeance
May 20, 1989

I reached across with my left hand to hit the button for the number two engine auto start. Nothing. Just the dry clicking of the igniter.

My eye shot forward to the voltmeter. The battery was at full charge, twenty-four volts. I hit the starter again. Nothing. I turned and craned my neck out of the cockpit, but saw no one near the apron or alert building. Off to the left, I noticed Corporal Chomayev's wide-brimmed field hat lying on the oil-stained concrete apron amid a pile of spent brass shell casings from his AKM. He was either wounded or dead, hidden from sight. Luckily the apron guards had only been issued a single thirty-round magazine. But maybe he wasn't badly wounded, after all. Maybe he was already back at the alert building spreading the alarm. Maybe Natasha was already speaking to Division on the control tower emergency radio channel.

Then my eye caught something blue lying on the apron near Chomayev's hat. My helmet bag full of papers. I had dropped it in the fight. But I could certainly not climb down to retrieve it. If I did not start my engines immediately, I would have to try to escape on the ground.

I engaged the starter a third time. Nothing. Just that bone-dry click.

I knew I was dead. The Osobists *must* have installed a secret new electronic lock on the starting system of the alert planes, just as they had padlocked the throttles of the other fighters after the spy scare last year.

I sagged in the ejection seat. Closing my eyes again, I filled my lungs deeply with the cool morning air. In a minute, two at the most, this fighter would be surrounded by soldiers. Even without their rifles, they could disarm me and drag me to the ground. It would be easy just to sit here with my eyes closed, breathing slowly, waiting for the end. But my years of training would not permit surrender. I remembered the words Lieutenant Tveretin had taught me so many years before on that sun-blasted runway in Azerbaijan. "When a system fails, Zuyev, there's always a reason. A good pilot does not panic."

I opened my eyes and scanned the instrument panel one last time. The battery was fully charged, twenty-four volts. The engine circuit breakers on the PTO electrical panel at my right elbow were set correctly. The throttles were...

The *throttles*. My left hand went instinctively to the two throttle knobs. They were spring-locked in the full stop position at the end of the twin rails. The heel of my hand hit the knobs and I released the stop springs with a quick snap. Like a first-year cadet sweating in the front seat of an L-29, I had made the most obvious mistake imaginable. I had tried to start my engines with the throttles at stop. Now I advanced both throttles to idle and hit the auto start button again. The big number two R-33 turbofan roared to life, shaking the cockpit with the familiar rumble. Amber lights winked out on the caution warning panel. The engine's fuel-flow gauge and tachometer needle sprang alive.

I had no time to waste with a takeoff checklist. Even if Chomayev had not yet reached the alert building, the noise of this engine certainly *had* reached the control tower. The number one engine would start automatically in a few moments, once number two reached twenty-eight percent RPM. I flipped on the remaining switches on the PTO panel and grabbed the stick clumsily with my right hand to trip the ducktail brake release lever.

With my left hand I slid the number two throttle forward to ninety percent, then chopped it back to idle. The plane did not move. I glanced down to make sure my fingers—which were almost numb from the shoulder wound—were properly squeezing the brake release lever. That was not the problem. I leaned out the open cockpit and saw the thick umbilical cable from the starting generator cart anchoring the plane to the apron.

Again I slid the throttle forward, to ninety-three percent, before chopping it back. The engine roared. Still, the airplane did not move. I took the risk of going to full military power. If the cable suddenly popped before I had cut power and braked, the plane could lunge uncontrollably forward and the nosewheel bog down in the "swamp," the soggy grass margin beside the taxi ramp. But I had to accept this hazard.

Then the number one engine roared alive. I slid both throttles up the rail and felt the plane surge ahead. In a desperate two-handed motion, I cut the throttles back, tripped the nosewheel-steering button on the inner throttle knob, and managed to squeeze the brake lever correctly to slow my momentum.

The fighter lurched into a hard right turn and I tapped left rudder with my boot to align the nose on the centerline of the taxi ramp. I was free. In the cockpit mirror I saw the heavy generator cart tumbling end over end, sparking wildly in the 22,500-pound blast of combined thrust.

I was finally moving, but everything felt wrong. The engines seemed so loud because I wore no helmet and the canopy still gaped open. Something hard and sharp jabbed at the base of my spine. It was the rectangular aluminum warning plate connected by elastic lines to the multiple safety pins blocking the arm restraints and igniter system of the K-36D ejection seat. The harness straps and buckles were stiff and jumbled behind my shoulders. Although I could not see the plate, its red warning label, "Remove Before Flight," seemed to mock me. The pain from the unbuckled ejection harness was more than physical. If the fighter lost an engine on afterburner takeoff, or I was shot down before I could properly strap in and remove those safety pins, the system would be useless. I would die.

Away to the right, I saw four men moving near the front door of the duty-alert building. One of them had his arm raised, pointing toward me. He might have held a pistol, but it was too far to distinguish it. It was time to close the canopy. My own pistol jammed between my thighs would no longer be of much use. The Plexiglas dome snapped down smoothly, dampening the throaty roar of the engines. I heard the hiss as the pressure seal closed tightly.

I was taxiing so fast that the plane swayed violently on the rough concrete blocks of the ramp. But I still had to try to align the gyroscopes of my altitude direction indicator (ADI). Without an artificial horizon, fast low-altitude flight would be even more hazardous. As the cockpit wobbled, the aircraft symbol on the ADI ball swung wildly, and the synchronize button flashed its red warning that the gyro platform had not yet aligned. But I certainly was not going to stop here on the taxi ramp and patiently wait for the system to warm up. I stabbed the button with my left thumb to recage the gyros, freezing the ADI aircraft symbol in a drunken thirty-degree left bank, in a slight nose-down pitch. So be it. This was not a training exercise.

But whichever pilot—Petrukhin or Gromov—followed me in the one undamaged alert fighter *would* have to wait for his gyro platform to stabilize. And his ground crew would also take the time to pull all the canvas sheaths and apron covers from his avionics probes and missiles. All that would take at least five minutes. Add a minute for the two undrugged pilots to dash down to the apron, followed by their groggy mechanics. Add another minute for general confusion.

If I took off now, I would have a seven-minute lead on my pursuers. At transonic speed, 630 knots, the direct route across the Black Sea to Turkish airspace would take about ten minutes. Necessity had just intervened to select Plan Two. Whatever Soviet naval contingent was out there waiting for me on this clear spring morning, I would have to face them. Missile frigates were the lesser of many evils. I certainly could not engage a pilot like Petrukhin, or even Gromov, with just my cannon against their Archer and Alamo missiles. Yet I had to accept the aerodynamic drag of my own full set of missiles on the underwing pylons, even though they were useless still wrapped in their canvas ground covers.

The end of Runway 09 was coming up fast. Just before I braked again, I checked the PTO panel to verify that the main weapon circuit breaker was snapped on. Even though I was wounded and the duty-alert section had obviously been alarmed, I still intended to attack the MiG-29s parked behind me on the angled taxi ramp.

I remembered to trip the takeoff flap button on the left console, dumping twenty degrees leading-edge slats and twenty-five-degree flaps. The comforting yellow indicator lights winked on the panel ahead of my left knee. The plane was bouncing now, gathering momentum, even though I had cut the throttles to idle. I was aware that the canvas canopy cover above my head was peeling back in the slipstream like the skin of a rotten fruit.

My eyes shot to the engine gauges on the right side of the panel. Thrust was steady. RPM matched on both engines. And the tail pipe temperatures were in the normal sector. Stable engines. Flaps, slats. That was it. Not much of a takeoff checklist with this drunken ADI, a dead navigation display, and no airspeed indicator. But it would have to do.

I tapped the left rudder and sliced into a hard rocking left turn without braking again, a dangerous maneuver with that full belly tank. The plane actually seemed to bank, swinging here on the end of the runway. I scanned the entire length of the runway, no vehicles blocking the long concrete ribbon. As soon as the nose swung onto the centerline, I released the throttle spring stops and jammed the knobs all the way forward to maximum afterburner.

The sudden thrust kicked me back into the seat, forcing my injured shoulder against the jumbled straps. But that was the best pain I had ever felt. Raw jet fuel was streaming into the twin exhaust streams to ignite in the double-walled chambers of the afterburners. On the master board at the upper right corner of the instrument panel, the twin green symbols Φ lit up, *forsazh*. I had maximum afterburners lit. Nothing on the ground could stop me now.

The fighter bore smoothly down the centerline, gathering speed with every second. Wearing no helmet, I was acutely aware of the burners' thunderous rumble behind me. Instinctively my eye went to the airspeed indicator, and for a moment I was shocked to see the needle stationary. On a thousand takeoffs I had waited patiently for a needle just like this to swing smoothly up to 96 knots. But with the Pitot tubes still covered, the instrument was dead. I had to judge my rotation speed by other means. The grassy margins of the runway spun past in a blur. I had been on the takeoff roll five seconds. Holding the stick in my left hand felt weird. But at least with the throttles locked, I had this hand free.

Then, at the right corner of my panel, I saw the engine inlet indicators switch from the upper louvers of the shark gills to the main inlets. This meant my airspeed had just passed 107 knots. But I held the nose down two seconds longer. I needed adequate airspeed with a full tank and these external weapons.

I must have rotated at more than 150 knots because there was no hint of hesitation. The nose swung up smoothly as if on a hydraulic piston and I was climbing steeply into the hot eye of the rising sun. The instrument panel clock said exactly 0524 hours.

I switched hands clumsily and groped for the gear lever, then retracted flaps and slats. My right hand was becoming so numb on the stick that I was afraid of losing control. I kept the throttles on maximum afterburner and grabbed the stick again with my left hand. I certainly did not want to pitch up too steeply and stall. And my climb angle was much too high. In order to execute a proper strafing run, I had to match the angle of my climb with the desired dive slope of the cannon run, thirty degrees. I pushed the stick gently forward to bring down the nose.

I would have to drop the belly tank in order to fire the cannon. But I hated to waste any of that precious fuel. So I waited as I climbed. My radar altimeter was working, but was only accurate up to 1,500 feet. Without a barometric altimeter, I had to judge my altitude by scanning the terrain for visual cues and taking angular projections on reference points below. The most important of these landmarks was the red-roofed village that lay past the road beyond the air base perimeter.

I did not want to drop my tank with eighteen hundred pounds of jet fuel into that village. As soon as I was certain my momentum would carry the tank beyond those houses into the empty swamp ahead, I groped on the stick for the tank-drop switch. It was protected by a safety cover, which in turn was secured by a wire. I had never dropped one of these expensive tanks before, and my fingers felt unusually clumsy. Then I snapped it open and the airplane reared up wildly, again threatening a stall. Still on afterburner, the sudden loss of the tank's mass was almost disastrous. I thrust the stick forward to "parry the moment," putting all those years of theoretical aerodynamics to practical purpose. Then, with my right hand numb as ice, I cupped the stick and used my left hand to pull the throttles back, first to military power, then down the rails to ninety-four percent.

I snatched back the stick and centered it, slamming the plane violently level. Lieutenant Tveretin would not have approved; this was *not* precision flying. Although I had a feeling he and thousands of other dedicated Soviet pilots *would* applaud my actions secretly. I glanced over each shoulder at the ground below. Six thousand feet altitude. It was time to begin the attack.

I rolled the stick left and banked forty-five degrees, then swung the stick onto my left thigh to continue rolling hard past ninety degrees. The snowy line of mountains tilted. And my windscreen filled with the green valley swinging smoothly past the nose. The sheet-metal roofs of the village tilted toward me, then the highway, and finally the rusty wire fence of the air base perimeter. I centered the stick, then eased it forward to align the nose with the long gray runway.

The base was still in shadow, and wisps of mist hung over the line of parked aircraft on the squadron aprons. I tripped the gun-arm switch on the top of the stick and my head-up display glowed with the pale green funnel of the cannon sight. I selected the *malaiya* "small" target size. A glowing "M" appeared at the left of the HUD. But I immediately saw my dive angle was too shallow to properly sweep the entire line of aircraft. So, like a raw *kursant*, I punched the stick forward to pitch down the nose. For a moment I rose in the seat with negative G, only to slam down hard again. *That* maneuver certainly would displease Lieutenant Tveretin.

But I had the aircraft lined up right in the middle of the sight funnel. The line of gray MiGs swooped into sharp focus. Two long bursts would be necessary to use the full magazine of 150 rounds. I eased the stick right to correct my aim, then squeezed the cannon trigger. Nothing. I verified the PTO panel. The weapons system switch was still on. I had to have a live gun because the HUD sight was illuminated with the proper symbology. I squeezed again. Silence, instead of the harsh rattle of the cannon.

The runway was rising fast now. I was below 1,500 feet. I clenched my teeth. Somehow the bastards in the Osobii Otdel had installed a new inhibitor on the cannon. I had no functioning weapons, no way to defend myself.

Easing the stick back, I leveled at 600 feet, then dropped even lower. The squadron parking aprons swept past in a blur. Ahead I saw men running frantically around the three remaining fighters on the duty-alert apron. The apron floated toward me. The standby magnetic compass swung to 240 degrees. At least I was now on the proper heading for Trabzon. But I had failed in my attempt to avenge the dead of Tbilisi. It was time to leave. Sweeping past the control tower, I rocked my wings back and forth, a farewell to any friends below.

Then I slid the throttles ahead to military power and gingerly eased the stick forward, dropping down to less than 100 feet. The flat orange groves below seemed almost chartreuse in the early morning sunshine. Off to the right, the straight line of the Tskhakaya-Poti highway and rail line cut across the flats of the Rioni valley. I was too low to see the coast ahead. But I knew it was coming up fast. The meandering brown river snapped past and I was beyond any villages. Now I banked the nose south, onto a new heading of 225 magnetic.

Even without the airspeed indicator, I knew my speed had stabilized at .95 Mach, 630 knots, at this extremely low altitude. I had never flown so fast so low. Solid objects on the ground seemed to suddenly liquefy and spray past in a blur of colors as I approached them. But I had to stay down here at least another three minutes. The distant rank of high-tension power lines to the northeast marked Poti East airfield, the site of the PVO missile brigade guarding the Navy base. I knew their improved models of V-75 Dvina missiles were deadly within a kill circle ranging horizontally from three to fifteen miles and vertically right down to 900 feet.

By keeping the fighter at least nine miles from their acquisition radars and at ninety feet altitude, I was probably out of danger. But if the alarm had already been passed to that PVO brigade and they had low-altitude missiles of the modified Romb or Kube class deployed on mobile BRT launch vehicles, I was in trouble. The countermeasure system of this particular fighter was loaded with aluminum-foil chaff bundles, not flares. Chaff was good masking protection from radar-guided missiles, not the infrared-seeking warheads of the mobile launchers.

The horizon ahead shimmered strangely. For a terrible moment I thought that weird glow was a flash of a missile launch. Then I saw it was the reflection of the first direct sun on the marshy Paleostomi Lake southeast of Poti. I rolled further left. There were thousands of terns and migrating thrushes in those marshes. At this speed, a bird strike, even with a tiny sparrow, could shatter the canopy and kill me. But I could not risk climbing higher until I cleared the coast.

I glanced away from the windscreen to verify my remaining fuel. Still 5,500 pounds, enough to make Trabzon, if I didn't have to take violent evasive action. When I looked up, a huge black fence filled the horizon. Instinctively I hauled back on the stick and bounced up to 300 feet. Just in time to clear a double row of drooping high-tension power lines.

I had not realized I was already this far. Those power lines turned south toward Batumi only two miles from the coast itself. Then the entire horizon winked and rippled with the grapey blue of the Black Sea at dawn. The narrow coast road and tan beach sailed by. I was free of the land.

But, stupidly, I hung here too long. The SPO-15 radar-warning receiver display in the right corner of my panel suddenly twinkled like the lights on a tree. I was being swept by the acquisition radar of a missile system. The outer circular row of yellow priority lights blinked in the upper right quadrant, marking first ten degrees, then thirty, then back to ten. That radar beam held me steady for a moment, possibly long enough for launch acquisition. Then three of the nine green bearing lights winked on, indicating that the sweep angle of the beam had narrowed. A moment later the inner row of yellow oblong power lights pulsed. The search and acquisition had narrowed and intensified. That had to be the PVO brigade in Poti.

Without hesitating, I pushed the stick hard forward, steadied it with my numb right fist, and tripped the chaff dispenser switch at the lower center of my instrument panel, flipping to manual control. The chaff dispenser in the boat tail between the two engine exhausts was now popping chaff packets every 1.5 seconds. These packets instantly shredded in the transonic slipstream, bursting into wide clouds of hair-thin aluminum dipoles. Within seconds, I knew the chaff target would swell on the PVO radar screens into a ragged oval, masking my descent toward the waves.

My radar-warning panel went dark. Luckily I had not been wearing earphones so I had not heard the nagging beep of an imminent lock-on.

I was free of that threat, but had to quickly overcome another. Flying at transonic speed so close to the water was much more dangerous than over land. There were no trees or telegraph poles to give definition to the flat, plum-blue surface of the sea. And the distant horizon was masked in evaporation haze. This was like flying into a constricting tunnel of blue glass. I suddenly lost orientation and felt that the plane was sliding inexorably onto its right wing, even though the stick was well centered.

But again I refused to panic. Instead of looking ahead at the flowing sheet of the surface, I rolled my head right and left to stare past the wingtips. The plane was flying straight and level. Off the left wing I saw a darker jumble on the hazy southern horizon. That would be Batumi, the port close to the Soviet-Turkish frontier. The reinforced PVO brigade there had every conceivable air-defense missile and gun in the Soviet arsenal, Dvinas, Nevas, Rombs, and Kubes. But my radar-warning receiver remained dark. Either the Batumi brigade had not yet been alerted, or I was safely below their radar horizon.

I craned my neck to ease the cold cramp spreading from my right shoulder. The adrenaline had flushed through my system and I felt suddenly sick, spongy inside. I clenched my teeth and breathed as deeply as I could. There was still over a hundred miles of this dead flat sea to traverse before the Turkish coast.

Then I was instantly erect in the seat, throbbing with fresh adrenaline. The concentric circles of yellow and green warning lights on my SPO-15 display flashed again, this time from the right rear quadrant. I was being probed by a radar from behind. A quick calculation revealed that the only possible radar back there had to be airborne. Either it was Petrukhin, or the PVO had managed to scramble Su-27s from Gudauta. A scan of my cockpit mirrors showed nothing, just the misty blue morning behind me. Looking back was a waste of time. If they launched on me, it would be from a distance of at least six miles.

Again I juggled the stick in my right hand to trip the chaff dispenser with my left thumb. I had no choice but to slide even lower toward the gentle blue swell. Down here, one false move, one slip with the control stick, would slam me into the sea. But I had to stay this low for several minutes longer, protected by the cloud of chaff from the radar lock-on of an Alamo. I had no choice. At least death would be fast in either case.

The haze had formed a circle now, obliterating the horizon ahead and behind. All I could do was hang on, waiting for the

Turkish mountains to appear ahead. Or for a missile to slam into my tail pipes.

The radar receiver lights flashed briefly once more, then went dark. A minute passed. My chaff supply was exhausted. But the threat did not return.

Now I felt sick and dizzy, a sour metallic taste in my dry mouth. I knew I might pass out at any moment. Better to fight it than surrender. I eased the stick back and let the plane float up to 1,500 feet. At least the radar altimeter was working. At this altitude I would be visible to the radars of any Navy ships out there to the right, especially to the new precision search radars on the Udaloy class destroyers based out of Poti.

But I had to take this risk. Before I passed out or grew even weaker, I had to strap into the ejection seat. I might be too groggy to land this airplane, and I had no intention of dying because I hadn't the strength to strap in properly.

But this proved almost impossible. My right arm was useless now, and I needed my left hand to fly. In a series of jerky motions that sometimes sent the plane lurching hard right or left, I managed to free the twisted straps and buckles behind me. Then I discovered I could grip the stick loosely with my knees and use my left hand to reach behind and pull the safety pins from the arm restraints. Freeing the pin from the seat igniter system was the hardest task of all. Normally the mechanic used two hands to twist and jerk the locking mechanism. I had only one, and the pin was located high and behind my headrest. If I strained to reach it, my knees slipped off the stick and the plane careened violently through the sky. Even at an altitude of 1,500 feet, I was dangerously low at this speed. So I climbed another 600 feet, pushed myself up on my haunches, and somehow fought the pin free.

Time seemed to stop. I was no longer just flying this fighter, I was battling for my life. Then I looked up to find I had clasped the last buckle of the harness in place. I slid the safety pin free of the ejection-seat firing handle between my knees and dropped it on the deck with the others.

I found myself smiling. In those minutes I had fought the ejection harness and the pins, I had passed into Turkish airspace. A brown hump loomed ahead in the mist and slowly gained definition. The coast of Turkey, the mountainous headland of Fener Burnu. I had made a perfect landfall after flying almost one hundred miles right down on the waves. And I was strapped into a fully armed ejection seat.

Whatever happened now, at least I would not die in this airplane.

It was safe to climb even higher. I eased the throttles back to eighty percent and leveled off at 3,000 feet. The tan and green bulk of Turkey rose steeply from the sea, sliced by geometrically flat bands of milk-white mist. Below, a fishing boat cut a widening V-wake through the calm water. This was the most beautiful sight I had ever seen. I stared at those wild brown mountains as they swelled toward me.

Then I remembered what that landfall meant. It was my primary navigation point. Trabzon lay to the left, fifteen miles east of the headland. And the city's airport lay about another mile further east, just past the port. At least according to the detailed VVS navigation chart I had memorized then burnt with my other papers in the soccer field.

I rolled slowly left and scanned the coast. There was a town, but it seemed too small to be the port of Trabzon. Those low stone buildings and the wooden wharf had to be Akcaabat, a little fishing port on my chart. A band of snow-white mist lifted from the coast and I suddenly saw the modern city of Trabzon marching up the bluff from the sea. Trabzon was sliced by steep ravines. The winding streets were rivers of shade trees leading down to the port. I saw large warehouses, a long concrete commercial pier, and an overlapping brown breakwater. There was the tall lighthouse that had been marked on my chart. Behind the city, older houses with orange tile roofs spread into pale green tea groves. I slid the throttles back and eased down the nose.

Where was the airport? The highway leading east of the city seemed to widen into a long gray motorway. No. That highway *was* the airport's single runway. It was right on the edge of the water, perched there like an aircraft carrier. My nose was lined up perfectly. I decided to skip a normal landing circuit and fly a straight-in approach. But I made sure to check the airspace for traffic. There was nothing in sight.

Steadying the stick with my knees, I dumped landing gear, set the slats, then the flaps for landing, and began to verify my panel. But I had no proper instruments, just the radar altimeter and the angle-of-attack gauge, a circular dial just left of the HUD.

That would have to guide me through the approach. I set up at an initial AOA of ten degrees, with the throttles still at eighty percent. With no airspeed indicator, I had to judge this well. I did not want to overshoot the threshold at the edge of the sea because I had no idea how long the runway was. But I did not want to undershoot either.

The plane came whistling down, "steady as a train," as Tveretin used to say. Now I lifted the nose to twelve degrees AOA and used my rudders gently to keep the nose aligned with the long gray runway. The gravelly white beach sailed past. I caught a glimpse of painted lines. I was over the threshold. The main gear touched smoothly, with only a slight squeal. And I was surprised by the gentle bounce of the nosewheel's contact. Instinctively I tripped my tan drag chute and watched the canopy blossom in my mirror.

I sagged in the ejection harness with the sudden deceleration, still surprised to be on the ground so smoothly. If anyone was watching, he had seen a fine display. That was undoubtedly the best landing I had ever flown.

I let the airplane roll past the small terminal and squat control tower. Passing the buildings, I saw no parked aircraft, not even any vehicles. The modern airport looked deserted. I couldn't help but notice how smooth this runway was. If I had any doubt I had left the Soviet Union, this beautiful seamless concrete runway reassured me. I parked at the far right-hand edge of the runway to be clear of any incoming traffic, shut down the engines, popped the canopy, and breathed deeply. The air was cool and clean, with a salty hint of the nearby sea.

Only five hundred yards away, huge double-trailer trucks rumbled along the coastal highway. They were lovely trucks, brightly painted, with shiny cabs and strange orange and yellow letters painted on their tall flanks. I had seen such trucks in Western movies. They were an unmistakable sign of wealth, of commerce, of a world I did not know. Then I noticed the billboards on the other side of the highway. They were also printed with large, bright Roman letters. There were pictures of women in shiny kitchens, a smiling man at the wheel of a car. I wished I could read the words. I was confident they were advertisements, not propaganda slogans.

"I made it," I whispered, then laughed out loud. A warm joy

I had never before experienced rose inside me. Then I remembered I was a Soviet Air Force pilot on my last mission. I went to work to set my cockpit straight, happily tripping circuit breakers and shutting down systems. I stared at the left-hand corner of my panel and felt a sudden stab of cold.

The master weapons sensor panel switch was still in the off/safe position. *That* was why the cannon had not fired.

"*Blyat,*" I swore, hitting the panel with my left fist.

In my muddled condition on the Tskhakaya runway, I had not noticed that switch because the panel had been half-hidden by the accordion-fold anti-glare curtain, meant to shield the HUD from the instrument lights, For years, my fellow pilots and I had written reports complaining about that damned curtain. But the inertia-bound Soviet bureaucracy had not responded. Now those lazy bureaucrats deserved decorations. They had just inadvertently saved twelve MiG-29s from destruction.

I looked at the clock, 0547. I had been on the ground a full seven minutes, but no one had come for me. Maybe Turkey was in a different time zone and it was only just past five in the morning here. I decided to taxi to the terminal. This time, I remembered to set the throttles properly for engine start.

As I swung back down the runway, my shoulder suddenly throbbed with hot pain. All my reserve of adrenaline was burnt. The pain began to swell. I would need a ladder to get out of this cockpit safely. I taxied slowly and swung across the yellow lines of a vehicle parking zone just beside the modern terminal. I shut down my engines and unstrapped the ejection harness to raise in my seat. The terminal still seemed deserted.

Then I saw three faces peering at me through the wide glass doors of the terminal, an old man and two younger fellows. Their eyes were fixed in wide stares. When I waved, the two younger men scurried away into the shadows. But after a while, the old man opened the door and came ahead cautiously to stand near my left wing.

I smiled. Then waved him toward me, trying to gesture that I needed a ladder. He came closer. I saw the white stubble on his cheeks. I realized he was a watchman. This was my first contact with authority in Turkey. I had planned carefully for this moment. I wanted the news of my arrival to reach the Americans as quickly as possible.

"American," I shouted, following my careful plan to this final step. I tapped my chest and called once more in the English words I had painfully memorized from my dictionary. "I am American."

The old man's eyes had been focused on the huge red stars on my twin rudders. Now he smiled.

Epilogue

The convoy of vehicles pulled smoothly to a stop on this narrow country road. Beside us, the fields of ripe wheat moved in the breeze. The morning was still cool, but the summer sun of Anatolia was climbing in the brassy sky. Three miles to the west, Ankara's international airport rumbled with jet traffic. The security officers from the Turkish Ministry of Defense, however, had done well in selecting this rendezvous. There were no houses in sight, no cars, or even farm tractors.

I climbed out of the armored van and stood in the sun, waiting. Muscular young guards in gray suits piled from the other vehicles, brandishing Uzi submachine guns. We were waiting for a similar convoy from the American embassy.

I had been in Turkey almost a month. And those four weeks had been eventful. The first hours in Trabzon, the Turks had treated me with great kindness and professional skill. I had been taken from the airport to a hospital, where my wounds were treated. Luckily the bullet from Chomayev's AKM had caused no permanent damage, entering my upper right biceps, plowing through the muscle to exit from the thick flesh behind my armpit. An X ray revealed the bullet had not touched bone or important

348

ligaments. I was given my own cheerful room and guarded around
the clock by soldiers with automatic rifles. That first afternoon a
Russian-speaking teacher was brought in to serve as translator.
Through him I made my formal request for political asylum and
asked that the Turks contact the Americans.

Within hours the chief of staff of the Turkish Air Force
arrived with a delegation of officers. These officers told me it was
vital that I write the request for asylum in my own hand. But my
right hand was still numb, my arm in a sling. So I clumsily
printed my formal request, using my left hand. The Turkish Air
Force officers were concerned about the safing procedures for my
plane's weapons and ejection seat. It was hard to explain where
the seat's safety pins were because I had hastily dropped them on
the cockpit deck. But after a while, the officers seemed satisfied.
Before they left, they patted me on the back and we all posed for
pictures together. They assured me I would receive asylum.

The next day I heard the rumble of a heavy jet landing at the
nearby airport. My translator explained that a Soviet delegation
had arrived from Tskhakaya to reclaim the MiG-29. Over the next
confused hours, I was able to piece together what had happened.
More bad luck. Although I had no way of knowing, the day I
hijacked the fighter, a high-level Turkish military delegation, led
by their chief of staff, was on an official visit to Moscow, guests of
Defense Minister Marshal Yazov. As soon as the news was flashed
to the Kremlin, Yazov personally extracted a solemn promise from
the Turkish generals that their government would return the
fighter.

The Soviet authorities also pressured the Turks for my extradition back to Georgia. Their demand was based on the claim that
I was a common criminal, not a defector seeking political asylum.
But again, glasnost ironically dominated the situation. In the past
the Defense Ministry would have blatantly stated that I had
murdered the apron guard, making me an obvious candidate for
extradition. But with the new policy of openness, the authorities
had been forced to reveal details about the escape that they would
have hidden in the past. Corporal Chomayev had, in fact, been
interviewed on Soviet television, a broadcast seen in Turkey. He
was obviously not dead. And he gave an accurate account of our
desperate fight on the parking apron. From this interview it was
clear that I had acted in self-defense when I shot him.

His statement, combined with my own wound, bolstered my self-defense appeal against extradition. The Turks asked me to write a complete account of my escape. They assured me that this statement would provide the evidence needed to deny the Soviet government's extradition request, scheduled to be considered at a judicial hearing in a few days. But the Turks also told me there was nothing they could do to prevent the Soviet Air Force from reclaiming the fighter.

When the translator explained all this, I swore bitterly. "Please don't return that fighter," I told the Turkish officers. "It's a weapon and I risked my life to bring it here. If I had known you would send it back, I would have ejected."

Again I used my left hand to write a message, this time a formal request that the Turks refuse to return the fighter.

But I was too late. That afternoon, maintenance officers from my regiment quickly loaded all the missiles aboard the big Il-76. Ironically the pilot who flew the plane back to Tskhakaya was none other than Lieutenant Colonel Shatravka, the staff officer I had defeated in the dogfight on my last official flying day as a Soviet pilot.

But the Turks *were* good to their word about my asylum. They forwarded my request to the American embassy in Ankara. And a week later I was flown to the capital under heavy guard. The Turks had been dealing with the Soviets for seventy years. They knew that the Organs of State Security were perfectly capable of assassinating me here in Turkey.

Before I could be turned over to the Americans, however, there was one last formality to complete. The Soviet ambassador and his haughty KGB *rezidant* were brought to the heavily guarded guesthouse in the suburbs where I was staying. He tried to cajole me into returning to the Rodina, where I would receive medical treatment for both my physical wounds and the psychological stress that had provoked this unfortunate aberration. I knew all about such psychiatric treatment. I told him I was not interested.

Next the ambassador opened his briefcase with a dramatic flourish. "Alexander Mikhailovich," he said, "if you won't consider your own welfare, at least think of your poor mother." He slowly reached into the handsome leather case. "I have a letter from your mother, in which she appeals to you to return to the Motherland. I . . ."

"Don't waste our time with such 'letters,'" I snapped. "They're either forgeries or were forcibly obtained. I know my mother's feelings about my welfare much better than you."

The ambassador glowered, then slammed shut his briefcase. His last ploy had failed.

I was amazed how friendly and helpful the Turks were. For years I had been taught they were ruthless militarists, pawns of imperialists. But their kindness never stopped. The doctors were concerned about possible hidden damage to my skull and neck because of the constant headaches I was suffering. They arranged a CAT scan examination at the most modern hospital I had ever seen. The results were negative.

Then one afternoon as I listened to the Russian language program on the Voice of America, I heard the announcement that the U.S. State Department had just granted me political asylum. I would be delivered to the Americans the next day.

I stood in the warm breeze, watching the ravens sail up the thermal currents above the wheat fields. Even though I had not succeeded in delivering the MiG-29 and its missiles to NATO, my years of experiences with the fighter were certainly valuable.

The American convoy approached along the narrow road from the east, a sedan and two security vans. Unlike their Turkish counterparts, the young American guards wore blue jeans. The ambassador climbed out of his sedan and shook my hand. Then he motioned for me to enter the backseat with him. I had never seen such a luxurious car. An interpreter with a foreign accent leaned over from the front seat to translate.

"I would like you to confirm your request for political asylum in the United States," the ambassador said cheerfully. He seemed like such a young man. In the Soviet bureaucracy no one his age could have advanced so high.

I began to answer, but the ambassador interrupted, telling me to make the request formal by stating my full name.

"I am Alexander Mikhailovich Zuyev," I solemnly recited. "I want to live in the United States of America as a free man. I am asking for political asylum."

The ambassador smiled and shook my hand again. "Alexander

Zuyev, you have been granted political asylum in the United States. Welcome to America."

Northern Virginia, Christmas Day, December 25, 1991, 12:20 P.M.

I stood on the soft carpet of my living room, gazing at the familiar television image of the red brick Kremlin walls. It was night in Moscow but a bright noon on this Christmas Day in Virginia. My little brother, Misha, now a tall, husky boy of ten, stared silently at the television screen.

The night before, Misha had told me what his life had been like in Samara after my escape. The teachers at his school had publicly castigated the "brother of the traitor." They encouraged older boys to beat him daily. He endured all that. Every night he came home from school and washed away the caked blood from his face before my mother saw him. He was determined to accept this suffering stoically. The KGB was pressuring my mother ruthlessly, and Misha did not want to add to her misery.

As I had hoped, the KGB pressure on my family had been more of an annoyance than an actual menace. They had been questioned repeatedly, but not harmed in any way. Glasnost had protected them. And the rapidly changing political conditions in the Soviet Union had permitted them to request official authorization to emigrate without fear of retribution. Their first request for tourist visas to the West had been denied, as I assumed it would be. But then, in 1991, they finally managed to obtain refugee status, and the Soviet government reluctantly granted them exit visas. After several false starts, Mother, Valentin, and Misha had arrived at Kennedy Airport only ten days earlier, the best Christmas present I could imagine.

My mother was cooking in the kitchen. I heard the electronic chime as she boldly investigated the mysteries of the microwave oven.

The red hammer-and-sickle banner of the Soviet Union rippled in the floodlit wind above the Kremlin. The CNN announcer proclaimed the flag of the "former Soviet Union" was about to be lowered for the first time in seventy-four years. It would never rise again. That afternoon in Moscow, Mikhail Sergeyevich Gorbachev had delivered his resignation speech as the last President of the Soviet Union. He had then signed a decree transferring control of the former Soviet military to the Russian president, Boris Yeltsin.

Waiting to watch the Soviet flag drop, I thought of the eventful thirty months that had passed since I had climbed into the ambassador's sedan beside that Turkish wheat field.

Before 1989 had ended, the Berlin Wall had crumbled. Communism began to die all across Eastern Europe. One by one the nations enslaved by the Soviet Empire threw out their Communist bosses and embraced democracy. And, after ten years of bloody struggle, all Soviet forces finally withdrew from Afghanistan.

In the Soviet Union itself, however, Communism would take longer to die.

But as I worked with my new American military colleagues, I was confident that the criminal clique that controlled my former country would one day be defeated. Meanwhile, I helped the American Navy, Marine Corps, and Air Force prepare to defeat Soviet-trained Iraqi pilots flying Soviet-supplied fighters in the Persian Gulf War. One of the F-15C units I worked with destroyed five MiG-29s and over eleven MiG-23s and Sukhoi attack aircraft during Operation Desert Storm. Before I began assisting in the intense training of these American pilots, they had believed many of the comforting myths about obsolete Soviet equipment and tactics. But I had been able to convince them that the MiG-29 Fulcrum, armed with modern missiles and flown by a skilled pilot, represented a dangerous threat. They took my words to heart.

During the five historic days of the failed coup d'état in Moscow that August, I was pleased to learn that other military men had apparently taken my words to heart as well. I was able to broadcast a message on Radio Liberty, appealing directly to the Soviet officers and soldiers in the BMPs and armored cars on the streets of Moscow. I reminded them of the Tbilisi massacre and asked them to consider to whom they owed true loyalty, the Party bosses or the people. Perhaps these words made some difference. In any event, Soviet soldiers refused to obey orders to fire on civilians, or to storm the Russian Parliament to arrest Boris Yeltsin.

And I was also able to influence my former colleagues in another unexpected way. The tape-recorded message I had left behind in my apartment at Tskhakaya had never been seized by the KGB. Instead, pilots from my regiment had found the tape before the Osobists. My friends had apparently passed the tape unofficially among their colleagues. One officer that I knew for certain had heard my message was Lieutenant General of Aviation Yevgeni Ivanovich Shaposhnikov, the deputy chief of staff of the Air Force, who led the official investigation into the hijacking. Shaposhnikov was a real reformer, a patriotic professional officer who knew where his true loyalties lay. After the failed coup, when Yazov and his Communist protégés in the Defense Ministry were disgraced, General Shaposhnikov became the new Defense Minister.

"Sasha," my brother, Misha, said, tugging my sleeve. "Look."

The red hammer-and-sickle banner was sliding down the flagpole above the Kremlin ramparts. Mother came from the kitchen. Valentin stood up beside the Christmas tree. We watched in silence. Then the blue, red, and white banner of the Russian Republic rose in the Moscow wind.

"Is it really over?" Mother asked. "Has it ended?"

"Yes," I answered, stretching my arms around my family. "It has finally ended." I stared at the ancient flag of Russia. Where would all this really end? I spoke again. "It is over. But there is still so far to go."

Glossary

Afghansti: A Soviet military veteran of the Afghanistan war.

afterburner: A thrust augmentation system for jet engines, which sprays fuel to be ignited in the exhaust pipe.

air brake: A movable flap to induce drag and decelerate an aircraft.

AK– 47: *Avtomat-Kalashnikova*: A Soviet 7.62 mm assault rifle designed by Kalashnikov.

Akhtubinsk: One of the key Soviet air-test centers, located in the southern Russian Republic.

AKM: A modernized version of the AK– 47 assault rifle.

Alamo missile: The Soviet R–27 radar-controlled Air-to-Air missile.

An–12: A four-engine Antonov military transport, similar to the U.S. C–130.

An–2 (Anushka): A slow, sturdy, single-engine Soviet biplane transport, often used to drop paratroops.

angle of attack (AOA): The angular distance of an aircraft's lifting surfaces (wings, etc.) above the horizontal.

apparat: Soviet government bureaucracy.

apparatohik: Soviet government bureaucrat.

Archer missile: The Soviet R–73 infrared-homing Air-to-air missile.

avos'ka: A string or plastic shopping bag; the ubiquitous symbol of the failed Soviet economy.

AWACS: U.S. Airborne Warning and Control System aircraft, which directs modern air battles.

babushka: Russian, grandmother.

banda: Russian, criminal gang.

Black Raven: The black van used by Stalin's secret police to transport people under arrest.

blat: Russian, "clout" or influence.

BMP: A Soviet-designed, tracked armored personnel carrier.

CAP: U.S. military acronym, Combat Air Patrol.

chaff: Radar-blocking system employing clouds of thin aluminum strips, ejected in packets from a military aircraft.

Crocodile (MiG-23): Soviet pilots' slang for the MiG–23 fighter.

dacha: Russian, "cottage," size depends on status.

DShK: A Soviet-designed 12.7mm machine gun, often used in air defense.

Dushman: Russian, "bandit," a derogatory term for the anti-Soviet Afghan resistance.

Frontal Aviation Regiments: The fighter and fighter-bomber units of the Soviet Air Force.

full military power: Maximum throttle setting short of afterburner, equal to 100 percent of normal engine power.

G-force: The acceleration forces acting on an aircraft; "G" can be expressed as positive or negative, with 1 G being the aircraft's normal resting weight.

G–indicator: An instrument to measure the acceleration forces on an aircraft.

G–suit: A protective garment worn by military pilots, which employs inflatable bladders to constrict the body and reduce blood flow away from the brain during high-performance maneuvers.

GAZ: The generic term for many Soviet-design military vehicles, ranging from "jeeps" to heavy trucks.

GCI: Ground Control Intercept: the air traffic control of military aircraft by ground-based radar operators.

gorka: Russian, climb (aerial maneuver).

Gosplan: The Soviet Central Planning Ministry.

GSh–301: The 30 mm automatic cannon on the MiG-29 Fulcrum.

Guards: An honorific title applied to certain Soviet military units, which have earned that distinction in battle.

GULag: Soviet acronym, Central Administration for Corrective Labor Camps; made infamous by Russian writer Alexander Solzhenitsyn, who coined the term, "gulag archipelago."

HMS: Soviet Helmet Mounted Sight.

HUD: Head Up Display: an optical cockpit display, which projects crucial data on a transparent screen, which does not restrict the pilot's view forward.

Il–2: The Ilyushin "Shturmovik" fighter-bomber of World War II fame.

Il–76: An Ilyushin Design Bureau four-engine military jet transport similar to the U.S. C–141.

ILS: Instrument Landing System.

IRST: Infrared Search and Track (targeting system).

K-36D: A modern Soviet-design fighter aircraft ejection seat.

Kalashnikov: The designer of the AK–47.

KGB: Soviet Committee for State Security, the secret police.

kolkhoz: Russian, collective farm.

kollectiv: Russian, the Communist and "worker" members of any Soviet organization.

Kolyma: An infamous Soviet mining labor camp in the Far East of Siberia.

Komsomol: The Soviet Young Communist Party Organization.

krug: Russian, a horizontal, circular aerial maneuver.

kursant: Russian, a military cadet.

L-29: A Czech-design single-engine jet trainer.

LA-17: A rocket-powered aerial target drone.

laser range finder: A measuring device using laser light to calculate distance.

Lenin Reem: A part of a Soviet military barracks reserved for troops' reading and propaganda.

look-down, shoot-down radar: A pulse-Doppler fighter radar system that can track low-flying enemy targets normally masked by the ground below.

Mach: The speed of sound at any given atmospheric altitude and temperture.

Makarov: Designer of the standard Soviet semi-automatic 9mm handgun; the gun itself.

malchi-malchi; "Hush-hush"; often applied to nuclear weapons procedures in the Soviet military.

Mi–8: A Mikoyan Design Bureau troop-carrying helicopter; forerunner of the Mi–24 troop carrier assault gunship.

microrayon: Russian, a State-planned housing project, often in isolated suburban areas.

MiG: Soviet acronym for Mikoyan and Gureyvich Design Bureau, the most successful Soviet military aircraft builder, known in later years simply as the "Mikoyan Design Bureau."

MiG–21FM; The two-seat trainer version of the Mikoyan Design Bureau MiG–21.

MiG–23UB: The two-seat trainer version of the Mikoyan Design Bureau MiG-23.

MiG–29: The Mikoyan OKB's first "fourth generation" fighter, equal in performance to U.S. F–16 and F/A–18 aircraft; NATO designation, Fulcrum.

MVD: Soviet acronym, Ministry of the Interior.

nakal: Russian, standby.

NKVD: Soviet acronym, People's Commissariat of Internal Affairs, the predecessor of the KGB, Stalin's main "organ" of terror and repression.

NO–193: The pulse-Doppler radar on the MiG–29.

nomenklatura: The official elite of Soviet society, whose positions were listed on secret registries.

oblast: Soviet designation for local district, corresponding to American county.

OKB: Soviet acronym for military design bureau, often named for the chief designer.

ogon: Russian, firing (a weapon).

OMON: Soviet acronym for Interior Ministry special troops, the infamous Black Berets.

Osobii Otdel: "Special Department," the KGB counterespionage division assigned to all units of the Soviet military.

Osobist: A member of the Osobii Otdel.

P–39: The Bell Air Cobra fighter of World War II; under Lend Lease it was the Soviet *Kobra*.

Partkom: Soviet acronym, Party Committee, of any civil or military organization.

Pilot tube: A pressure-sensitive instrument to measure an aircraft's airspeed.

Po–2: A Soviet World War II biplane night bomber.

podyezd: Russian, staircase (the entrance of an apartment building wing).

poligon: Soviet acronym, a weapons testing range.

ponyal: Russian, "Roger," message acknowledged.

pusk: Russian, "Launch."

prezant: Russian slang, a small bribe.

pulse-Doppler radar: Radar that identifies and tracks moving targets; its ability to "lock" onto an enemy aircraft can be "broken" by maneuvers that cancel the relative differential speeds between the aircraft involved.

PVO: Soviet Air Defense Forces.

RC–135: U.S. military version of the Boeing 707, which has many aerial tanker and electronic intelligence variants.

RD–33: The standard turbofan engine of the MiG–29.

RDF: Radio Direction Finding instruments, variations of the standard "radio compass."

Redeye: A U.S. infrared-homing antiaircraft missile.

RN–40: A tactical Soviet nuclear bomb.

Rodina: Russian, "Motherland."

RPM: Revolutions Per Minute, usually engine speed.

rubege: Russian, range (distance to target).

Ruslan: Soviet military designation for the Tskhakaya Air Base in Georgia.

shlem: Russian, helmet.

Shturmovik: Russian, "fighter-bomber."

Spetsnaz: Russian acronym, "special purpose troops."

split-S: An air-combat maneuver involving a steep descent and reverse of direction, partially inverted.

SPO–15: A Soviet military aircraft radar-warning receiver.

SRZO: A Soviet "Information Friend or Foe" instrument.

stall-limiter: An automatic mechanical system actuated when a fighter surpasses a maximum angle-of-attack and loses aerodynamic lift and "stalls." The stall-limiter thrusts the control stick forward to reduce AOA.

Su–25: A Sukhoi Design Bureau attack jet similar to the U.S. A–10.

Su–27: A Sukhoi Design Bureau multipurpose military jet aircraft. The Su–27 has higher performance than the MiG–29, but is also larger and heavier.

supersonic: Air speeds above Mach 1.0.

tochka opori: Russian, "fulcrum."

trans-sonic: Air speeds approaching Mach 1.0.

valuta: Russian, hard currency.

Voyentorg: Soviet acronym, Military Exchange Store.

vozdukh: Russian, air or aerial.

VVS: Soviet acronym, Air Force.

wingroot: The point at which an aircraft's wing joins the fuselage; wingroots are often extended in high-performance fighters to produce lift at high AOAs.

Yak–28: A Yakovlev Design Bureau Air Defense fighter.

ZAGS: Soviet acronym, State Wedding Palace.

zampolit: Soviet acronym, Political Officer.

Zil: Soviet automobile manufacturer most associated with luxury limousines.

ZU–23: Soviet design 23mm antiaircraft cannon.

zveno: Russian, "link," a four-aircraft military formation.